THE PASSION AND DEATH
OF OUR LORD JESUS CHRIST

THE
PASSION AND DEATH OF OUR LORD JESUS CHRIST

BY
THE MOST REV. ALBAN GOODIER, S.J.

NEW YORK
P. J. KENEDY & SONS
12 BARCLAY STREET

MADE AND PRINTED IN GREAT BRITAIN
FOR
BURNS OATES & WASHBOURNE LTD.
PUBLISHERS TO THE HOLY SEE

FRATRIBUS
MUNDO CRUCIFIXIS
ET QUIBUS MUNDUS IPSE CRUCIFIXUS EST
HOC OPUS
D.D.
AUCTOR

TABLE OF CONTENTS

	PAGE
INTRODUCTION	
1. The Study of the Passion	ix
2. The Present Work	x
3. The Evangelists and the Passion	x
4. The Method of this Study	xi
5. The Topography of the Passion	xii
6. Conclusion	xiii
CHAPTER I	
1. The Eve of the Passion	1
2. The Council of the Priests	8
3. The Compact with Judas	12
4. The Preparation of the Supper	17
CHAPTER II	
5. The Supper	22
6. The Washing of the Feet	30
7. The Last Warning to Judas	40
CHAPTER III	
8. The Holy Eucharist	52
9. The Coming Failure of the Twelve	61
10. Introduction to the Discourse	72
CHAPTER IV	
11. The Discourse at the Supper	
(a) The True Life	79
(b) The Fruit of Life	85
(c) The Sacrifice of Life	91
(d) The Reward	96
12. The Promise of the Holy Ghost	
(a) The Spirit of Truth	99
(b) The Infallible Spirit	101
(c) The Witness to Jesus	104
(d) The Comforter	105
13. Conclusion of the Discourse	109
CHAPTER V	
14. The Sacerdotal Prayer	
(a) Introduction	118
(b) For Himself	122
(c) For the Apostles	123
(d) For the Church	126
15. The Heart of Jesus at the Supper	
(a) The Background	136
(b) All they were to Him	139
(c) All He wished to be to them	141
(d) All He would have them be to one another	143
(e) Last Encouragement	144

viii TABLE OF CONTENTS

Chapter VI

16. The Agony in the Garden — PAGE
    - (a) The Prayer 147
    - (b) The Agony 152
    - (c) A Quotation 156
    - (d) The Failure of the Three 159
17. The Capture of Jesus
    - (a) The Meeting with the Crowd 167
    - (b) The Betrayal 175
    - (c) The Desertion 183

Chapter VII

18. Jesus before Annas 187
19. Jesus before Caiaphas
    - (a) The Witnesses 194
    - (b) The Question of Caiaphas 199
20. The Denial of Peter 209

Chapter VIII

21. The Morning Trial 222
22. The Despair of Judas 231
23. Jesus before Pilate
    - (a) The Accusations 236
    - (b) The First Examination 242
24. Jesus before Herod 252

Chapter IX

25. The Second Trial before Pilate : Barabbas . . 260
26. The Sentence 270
27. The Scourging and Crowning 273
28. The Surrender of Pilate
    - (a) 'Behold the Man !' 285
    - (b) The Last Trial of Jesus 291
    - (c) The Defeat of Pilate 302

Chapter X

29. The Way of the Cross
    - (a) Simon of Cyrene 305
    - (b) The Mourning Crowd 310
    - (c) The Arrival at Calvary 319
30. The Crucifixion
    - (a) Jesus Crucified 320
    - (b) The Title 329
31. The First Word : 'Father, forgive them' . . 332
32. The Second Word : 'This Day' 336
33. The Third Word : 'Behold thy son' . . . 346
34. The Fourth Word : 'Why hast Thou forsaken me ?' 353
35. The Fifth Word : 'I thirst' 362
36. The Sixth and Seventh Words 365

Chapter XI

37. The End
    - (a) The Burial 369
    - (b) The Guarded Tomb 378

Harmony of the Passion of Jesus Christ . . . 385

INTRODUCTION

1. The Study of the Passion.

AS with books on the Public Life of Our Lord, so and much more with books upon the Passion, it is important to make three categories. Devotional studies of the Passion abound; indeed it would be impossible to imagine the Christian life without them. S. Paul said that he knew nothing but Jesus and Him crucified, that he preached Christ crucified and nothing else; and the lives of the saints are little more than commentaries put into practice on this same theme. On the other hand, of late years especially, what are called 'Histories' of the Passion have multiplied, both inside and outside the Church. Scholars have come to know so much more of the details, of the men who put Our Lord to death and why, of the nature of the several trials which He underwent, of the cruelties to which He was subjected, particularly of the crucifixion itself, that the rewriting of the story of the Passion has been more than justified. But there still remains the third category, less abundant than either of the former, and that for more than one reason. To describe the Passion as it really took place, not in its historical aspect only, but in the minds and hearts of those who went through it, especially of Him who was the Central Figure, is beyond the reach of any man; that is why those who have known it best, who have entered into it and lived it, have usually said least about it. For understanding of the Passion demands active compassion, such compassion as cannot be expressed in words. It demands, not only a power of deep sympathy, but actual suffering of one's own; only by suffering ourselves can we understand at all what the Passion, apart from its effects, has actually meant to those who have gone through it. That is one at least of the reasons why the saints have always valued suffering and have asked for it.

2. The Present Work.

Nevertheless, in spite of this hopeless disadvantage, the present work is an attempt to come as near as it can to the soul of that central figure. The details of the Passion, the material surroundings and circumstances, are accepted from others, though tested, most of them, on the spot; in regard to those details the author would only say that it is strange how great at times is the divergence of opinion amongst scholars, even on matters about which it would seem at first sight that agreement should be easily reached. It would almost appear that once we depart from, or attempt to add to, the story of the Passion as it is told by the Evangelists, we are liable to say what is open to question. Though, for instance, we may know the main streets in the Jerusalem of that time, yet the actual sites of the palaces of Annas, of Caiphas, of Herod, and of late even of Pilate, are by no means agreed upon, while the scourging, the crowning, the crucifixion, have been given different descriptions, founded all on some substantial evidence. Frankly, therefore, the author has taken all these studies as secondary. He has used them as he has needed them, for the Passion cannot be described without them; but for the first source of his information he has relied on the four Gospels themselves. As in the study of the Public Life, so here he has tried to keep his attention fixed on Jesus Christ Our Lord, for whose sake alone the story of the Passion is worth telling, refusing, so far as he has been able, to be turned aside by any controversial question or discussion whatsoever. He has asked himself: How does the Passion reveal Christ to us? What manner of Man does He show Himself during that ordeal? What were His thoughts and feelings? What was His soul? And, hence, knowing that He is 'yesterday, and to-day, and the same for ever', what is the meaning of Jesus crucified to me here and now?

3. The Evangelists and the Passion.

But here at once a new difficulty presents itself. Besides what has been already said of the common mortal's utter unfitness for the task, namely that, to enlighten his understanding and stir his sympathy, he has not suffered as he should have suffered, there is another objective hindrance which many have felt. It is the attitude adopted throughout the narrative of the Passion by three of the Evangelists themselves. With the exception of S. John, who, in the whole account, both of the Supper and of the scene on Calvary, cannot be accused of concealing the heart and emotions of Our Lord, the Evangelists in general seem almost deliberately to hide the Person of Jesus beneath the crushing weight of the whole story. They deal with the Passion quite differently from the way in which they have dealt with the Public Life. In the latter, Our Lord has always been to them what we may call their point of sight. What He has said, what He has done, how He has revealed Himself under these or those conditions, have always been their chief object of attention; the rest has gathered round Him so casually that the modern historian has difficulty in putting the events together. In the Passion it is almost the opposite. With it the Evangelists seem to begin their story afresh. They are determined that the facts shall be told; the drama goes on from scene to scene, swiftly but without flinching. We hear much of the emotions of the other actors, the mob, the Jewish judges, Herod, Pilate, even the Roman soldiers; but, once the Agony in the Garden is over, of the emotions of Jesus Himself we hear comparatively little. Perhaps, like those of whom we have already spoken, they knew and felt too much to utter anything. 'These things they did to Him,' they seem content to say, leaving us to divine the rest.

4. The Method of this Study.

Still, as we have already pointed out, the Evangelists are our safest, indeed, they are our only guides; whatever scholars have contributed to the understanding of other parts of the Gospels, to the understanding of the Passion they have contributed singularly little. We derive far more light for our purpose from the saints, and from those who have written in the spirit of the saints, such as S. Augustine, Ludolph of Saxony, Fra Thomas of Jesus, and in another sense, S. Catherine of Siena. Love, real and objective, and the insight and interpretation that come of love, are the only key to the Passion, certainly far more than learning; for love alone opens our eyes that we may know Him who endured it and why, whatever we may know or not know about Him. The method, therefore, of this study has been to follow the Evangelists as closely as possible, reading between the lines of their narrative ; the harmony used has been that of Tischendorf, with but a few minor variations.

5. The Topography of the Passion.

Naturally the topography of the Passion is far more simple than is that of the Public Life. If before we had to remind the reader of the small area of Palestine, much more must we do the same when we speak of Jerusalem and its neighbourhood. As for the sites of the various scenes, though, as we have said, scholars can be found who differ concerning almost all, and though time, instead of solving these problems, seems only to increase them, for a study such as this these discussions must be of minor importance. The author has accepted, more rather than less, the traditional sites as they are shown in and about Jerusalem to-day ; and he has done so, both because he believes they have as good a claim to acceptance as any other, indeed in most cases there is no other ; but also because in any case it is more important to be definite from the beginning, than to break the narrative by side issues.

Bethania, then, at the foot of the eastern slope of Olivet, by the road which rises and descends over the spur of the hill, would be some forty minutes' walk from the Supper Room. This, with the houses of Annas and Caiphas, would be in the southern section of the city below the Temple wall, which was the fashionable Jewish quarter. From the Supper Room to the Garden of Gethsemane, rising from the brook Kedron up the western side of Olivet, would take perhaps twenty minutes to walk, not more. The dwelling of Pilate and his Roman guard, Fort Antonia, was in the North of the city. This was the Roman quarter, and was distant from the house of Caiphas scarcely fifteen minutes' walk, down the street which ran from North to South outside the Temple, in the deep valley separating Mount Moriah and Mount Sion. The house of Herod, the palace of the Asmoneans, was in the West of the city, within the western wall and near the Tower of David ; it could be reached from Fort Antonia in less than ten minutes. Calvary, now within the Church of the Holy Selpulchre, would be about the same distance from Pilate's house ; from the house of Herod it was but a few hundred yards to the North, but, of course, outside the city wall.

6. Conclusion.

In conclusion, the author has used what he has seen and experienced in the East to help him in his narrative, but he has tried to be careful not to use it more than the Gospel story warrants. He would remind his readers not to take in too modern a sense such phrases as 'great multitudes', etc. The streets of Jerusalem were very narrow indeed, some of them scarcely admitting men to walk six abreast; when a camel lurched down them with his load on his back there was little room for anyone else. Though undoubtedly a crowd followed the Passion, which grew in numbers as the day went on, yet no less certainly there were other crowds which stood aloof. There was at least one crowd of sympathisers, which S. Luke equally describes as 'a great multitude of people' that 'followed Him'; there were many more who looked on from their doors and windows, or squatting on their shop counters, with that indifference which only the East can show. If the procession from the Pretorium to Calvary, as seems not unlikely, passed through the bazaar of the city, probably business went on as usual; for crowds such as these were nothing very strange, and the day, the eve of the great Feast, was an exceptionally busy day in Jerusalem. We are tempted to compare the suddenness of the Passion, and the success of its leaders, to one of those sinister *coups d'état* which have captured nations, and of which we have had examples in plenty in our own time.

All this we may assume and lay aside: our main object is to study Him round whom the story is gathered, that, if we can, we may know Him the better, whatever may be our other mistakes and shortcomings.

THE PASSION AND DEATH
OF OUR LORD JESUS CHRIST

CHAPTER I

1. The Eve of the Passion.

JESUS went out of Jerusalem over the hill of Olivet with His Twelve on that last Tuesday afternoon, to rest with them once more in the comparative security of Bethania. The Pasch was at hand; there was much going to and fro in the streets and in the courts of the Temple; until the festival was over there would be little more to be done. On the summit of the hill, as they looked back over the city, with the golden pinnacles of its Temple glittering beneath the afternoon sun, Jesus had again pronounced its final doom; the day would come when, of all Jerusalem, there would not be left a stone upon a stone. He had gone much further; He had warned His companions of the end, not of Jerusalem only, but of all the world. It was true He had not been understood; He had not intended that He should be wholly understood; to this day His words are wrapped in mystery. But He had spoken with the authority of a judge; of a judge who knew all, who could neither deceive nor be deceived, and whose word, however little understood, was nevertheless infallibly true.

Then in the evening He had moved along the road, down the hill towards the little town that He loved so well. No other town in all the land had ever given Him so gracious a welcome as Bethania; we cannot wonder that He gave it in return both His greatest miracle and so much of His own company. As He went, He reminded His companions once again of yet another ending, of which they had often heard before:

'And it came to pass
When Jesus had ended these words

He said to His disciples
You know
That after two days shall be the pasch
And the Son of man shall be delivered
To be crucified.'

'You know!' At least if they did not know it was not through lack of warning. Since the day when, close by Cæsarea Philippi, Simon had confessed Him to be

'The Christ
The Son of the Living God',

He had often had it in His mind and on His lips, and the nearer they had come to the eventful hour itself, the more explicit He had been. Recent successes had seemed to His followers to point the other way; the raising of Lazarus which had so stirred the masters in Jerusalem; the friendship of the people of Bethania, so that a Pharisee had delighted to honour Him; the triumphant Procession of Palms, and the enthusiasm of the pilgrims camped upon the hill, which the elders and priests had feared to suppress; the victories of the last two days in the very court of the Temple, so that not the subtlest scribe had dared to ask Him further questions; the secure protection that was now regularly afforded by the mere presence of the people gathered round Him:

'And seeking to lay hands on him
They feared the multitudes
Because they held him as a prophet.'

This had been the temper of the people only the day before, and nothing had occurred to alter it. Nevertheless He Himself had never wavered in His picture of the future. He had borne with the blindness of His Twelve and with their false conceptions of the Kingdom; the time would come when they would understand. For the present He was content to leave them self-deceived. As for Himself there were two days before Him in which to prepare for the great ordeal; and as He had always done on the eve of great occasions, so He would do now. Before He chose the Twelve, almost two years ago, He had spent the night 'in the prayer of God'. Before He gave to the people of Capharnaum the offer of His body and His blood, He had gone into the mountain to pray. Beyond the border of

His own country, before He put Simon Peter to the test, He had been found once more by the Twelve in prayer. Now, on the eve of the greatest day in all His life, we need have no doubt what His preparation would be.

For these two days, then, we leave Him, alone with His Father on the mountain-side, as we have often left Him before. Though it would be easy to conjecture the prayer of the Lamb of God, as He looked forward, now at last, to the sacrifice immediately before Him, we will not attempt to lift the veil which He Himself had always kept carefully down. This only we may say : He who during all the remaining hours, till the very last moment, was always careful that the Scriptures should be fulfilled in every detail, would now, in His hours of preparation, remind Himself of all that those Scriptures had foretold. One of them had said that He would be betrayed, and that by one of those dearest to Him and most trusted :

> ' For even the man of my peace
> In whom I trusted
> Who ate my bread
> Hath greatly supplanted me.'
> Psalm xl, 10.

Another had declared that the betrayal would be bought by thirty paltry coins :

> ' And they weighed for my wages
> Thirty pieces of silver.'
> Zacharias xi, 12.

The same prophet had foretold that He would be deserted by all His followers :

> ' Strike the shepherd
> And the sheep shall be scattered.'
> Zacharias xiii, 7.

He would be accused by false witnesses :

> ' Unjust witnesses have risen up against me
> And iniquity hath lied to itself.'
> Psalm xxvi, 12.

Yet to all their accusations would He answer nothing :

> ' He was offered because it was his own will
> And he opened not his mouth
> He shall be led as a sheep to the slaughter

And shall be dumb as a lamb before his shearer
And he shall open not his mouth.'
>> Isaias liii, 7.

Men would strike Him, would spit upon Him, would treat Him with every kind of insult :

' I have given my body to the strikers
And my cheeks to them that plucked them
I have turned not away my face
From them that rebuked me
And spit upon me.'
>> Isaias l, 6.

' He shall give his cheek to him that striketh him
He shall be filled with reproaches.'
>> Lamentations iii, 30.

All these things, within the next few days, men would do to Him, and then they would nail Him to a cross :

' They have dug my hands and feet
They have numbered all my bones.'
>> Psalm xxi, 17–18.

He would be crucified with criminals, as being Himself one of them :

' He was reputed with the wicked.'
>> Isaias liii, 12.

He would be held up to the scorn of all the world :

' I am a worm and no man
The reproach of men and the outcast of the people
All they that saw me have laughed me to scorn
They have spoken with the lips
And wagged the head.'
>> Psalm xxi, 7–8.

He would be taunted with His very sonship of His Father :

' He hoped in the Lord
Let him deliver him
Let him save him
Seeing he delighteth in him.'
>> Psalm xxi, 9.

In His dire thirst as He died they would give Him gall and vinegar to drink :

> ' I looked for one that would grieve together with me
> But there was none
> And for one that would comfort me
> And I found none
> And they gave me gall for my food
> And in my thirst they gave me vinegar to drink.'
>   Psalm lxviii, 21–22.

They would strip Him naked, they would share His clothes among them, casting lots for them :

> ' They have looked and stared upon me
> They parted my garments among them
> And upon my vesture they cast lots.'
>   Psalm xxi, 18–19.

Yet in the midst of it all He would raise His voice in prayer for His torturers :

> ' They have spoken against me with deceitful tongues
> They have compassed me about with words of hatred
> They have fought against me without cause
> Instead of making me a return of love
> They detracted me
> But I gave myself to prayer
> And they repaid me evil for good
> And hatred for my love.'
>   Psalm cviii, 3–5.

> ' He hath borne the sins of many
> And hath prayed for the transgressors.'
>   Isaias liii, 12.

When He was dead, even then He would not be left untouched. They would pierce His heart, but they should not break His bones ; and at the last, from that pierced heart should come the beginnings of repentance :

> ' I will pour out upon the house of David
> And upon the inhabitants of Jerusalem
> The spirit of grace and of prayers
> And they shall look upon me
> Whom they have pierced
> And they shall mourn for him
> As one mourneth for an only son
> And they shall grieve over him
> As the manner is to grieve for the death of the first-born.'
>   Zacharias xii, 10.

But perhaps most of all He would dwell upon that common prophecy which belongs to all His followers. The Wise Man had foreseen how the just in all time would suffer persecution ; and more than once had Jesus warned them that so it would be. He was their Leader ; in Him, then, it had already been and would yet be fulfilled, more than in all the rest :

' Let us therefore lie in wait for the just, because he is not for our turn, and he is contrary to our doings, and upbraideth us with transgressions of the law, and divulgeth against us the sins of our way of life. He boasteth that he hath the knowledge of God, and calleth himself the son of God. He is become a censurer of our thoughts. He is grievous unto us, even to behold : for his life is not like other men's and his ways are very different. We are esteemed by him as triflers : and he abstaineth from our ways as from filthiness, and he preferreth the latter end of the just, and glorieth that he hath God for his father. Let us see, then, if his words be true, and let us prove what shall happen to him : and we shall know what his end shall be. For if he be the true son of God, he will defend him, and will deliver him from the hands of his enemies. Let us examine him by outrages and tortures, that we may know his meekness and try his patience. Let us condemn him to a most shameful death ; for there shall be respect had unto him by his words.'

Wisdom ii, 12-20.

Memories such as these could not but have crowded in upon Him as He prepared Himself to do His Father's will to the letter in the day that was to follow. But it was all worth while ; for the Father's sake, for His own sake, for the sake of beloved mankind, it was worth while. After all was over, as He had already told His own many times, He would rise again and would triumph ; death would have no final dominion over Him. Had not the prophet said :

' My flesh shall rest in hope
Because thou wilt not leave my soul in hell
Nor wilt thou give thy holy one to see corruption ' ?

Psalm xv, 10.

He would rise from the dead ; He would return to His Father and would sit again by His right hand in heaven :

'The Lord said to my Lord
Sit thou at my right hand.'
Psalm cix, 1.

Thence, with the power of the Godhead that was His, with the right that His death had won, He would send the Holy Spirit into the world, to finish the work He had begun:

'And it shall come to pass after this
That I will pour out my spirit upon all flesh
And your sons and daughters shall prophesy
Your old men shall dream dreams
And your young men shall see visions
Moreover upon my servants and handmaids
In those days
I will pour out my spirit.'
Joel ii, 28–29.

'I will pour out waters upon the thirsty ground
And streams upon the dry land
I will pour out my spirit upon thy seed
And my blessing upon thy stock
And they shall spring up among the herbs
As willows beside the running waters
One shall say: I am the Lord's
And another shall call himself by the name of Jacob
And another shall subscribe with his hand
" To the Lord "
And surname himself by the name of Israel
Thus saith the Lord the king of Israel
And his redeemer the Lord of Hosts
I am the First
And I am the Last
And beside me there is no God.'
Isaias xliv, 3–6.

He would die but He would triumph; He would be buried but He would rise again, the Light of the nations, the Life of all the world:

'Behold I have given thee
To be the light of the Gentiles
That thou mayest be my salvation
Even to the farthest part of the earth.'
Isaias xlix, 6.

> ' I the Lord have called thee in justice
> And taken thee by the hand
> And preserved thee
> And I have given thee for a covenant of the people
> For a light of the Gentiles
> That thou mightest open the eyes of the blind
> And bring forth the prisoner out of prison
> And them that sit in darkness
> Out of the prison-house.'
> Isaias xlii, 6–7.

Yes, it was indeed worth while. It was for this that He had come into the world ; for all eternity He would stand, ' The Lamb that was slain ', before the Father, giving peace to all creation because of this surrender.

2. The Council of the Priests.

So Jesus prayed in His solitude, bringing the past to a focus in Himself, looking forward into the future, rejoicing as a giant to run his course, straining for the baptism wherewith He must be baptised, that at last it might be accomplished. Meanwhile, within the city walls His enemies were not idle ; in their midst, but in secret, other preparations were being made besides those for the Paschal festival :

> ' Then were gathered together
> The chief priests and ancients of the people
> And the scribes
> Into the court of the high priest
> Who was called Caiphas
> And they consulted together
> How by some wile
> They might lay hold on Jesus
> And put him to death.'

There was reason for their choice of this their meeting-place, and it was significant. The Temple and its courts, seeing how they had been regularly worsted there during the last two days, they could scarcely any longer call their own ; in the sight of the people they had been put to shame, in the hearing of all woe had been called down upon them which could never be forgotten. All that week, since the preceding Sabbath, He had routed them in their own domain; before their own followers He had made them appear worthy only of contempt, and they had not dared to touch Him. He had gone away free this Tuesday afternoon, as He had gone away freely on the Monday and the Sunday preceding; who knew but that on Wednesday and Thursday, and every day, He would come up again into the Temple, and do as He had done before? To argue with Him, to try to catch Him in His speech, to ask Him subtle questions, all these were now of no avail; on this at least they had decided, they dared not confront Him any more. No good purpose, so they told themselves, would be served by so much as meeting Him again, unless it were, once and for all and without more ado, to make Him a prisoner and crush Him. For the present they must needs foregather where they would be free from interruption and insult.

Hence they met in the house of Caiphas, in the lower city below the Temple wall. Under the guidance of Caiphas they could become confirmed in their design and renew their courage. Caiphas was the official high priest, the ordained of the God of Abraham, and Isaac, and Jacob; whoever this Jesus might pretend to be, that could not be denied. Therefore, with Caiphas at their head, they could claim, and could assure themselves, that they acted with the divine authority of the Law. Caiphas, too, had already proved to them on a former occasion the eminent justice of their cause; that disposed of any qualm of conscience these sensitive rabbis might have concerning ways and means:

> 'You know nothing
> Neither do you consider
> That it is expedient for you
> That one man should die
> For the people
> And that the whole nation perish not.'
>
> John xi, 49–50.

What those means were to be they were at a loss to know; and here for the moment even the resourceful Caiphas could not help them. They had decided on the death of Jesus long ago, even so early as when He first appeared among them; yet till now He had defied them at every turn. They had approved of His being stoned to death, and the sentence had not been carried out. They had published an order for His capture, yet not one had succeeded in laying hands on Him. They had sent their police expressly to apprehend Him, and they had come back empty-handed, nay, some of them had been won to His side by His words. The fact that, in spite of all they had done, He could still come into the City and go out as He pleased had made many of the people wonder : some had even begun to ask whether they, the priests and the ancients, the Pharisees and the Sadducees and the scribes, were at last being convinced, and were going over to Him.

> ' Some therefore of Jerusalem said
> Is not this he whom they seek to kill ?
> And behold he speaketh openly
> And they say nothing to him
> Have the rulers known for a truth
> That this is the Christ ? '

But to dwell upon these failures little became their dignity. Far more becoming was it to ignore them, to assume that in time, indeed when they had finally decided on the day and the hour, they would get their heart's desire. They might take Him at any time, of course they might, on the morrow if they chose. But clearly, for the sake of decency and public order, Thursday would not do ; they must be cautious, they used a better-sounding word, they must be prudent. Since it had been finally decided that He must die, and that for the sake of the public safety, then any means by which He might be taken would be justified. Still they must not be too hasty, or cause undue disturbance, especially at such a holy season as this. The Pasch would be in two days ; so to arrange it that He should be taken on or before the Feast Day would be unseemly. It would violate the Pasch ; it would defile themselves, so they said ; but in their hearts they were governed by a much more convincing argument.

> ' But they said
> Not on the festival day
> Lest perhaps there should be a tumult
> Among the people
> For they feared the people.'
> Matthew xxvi, 5.

If we would preserve a right perspective of the Passion, **it is surely important** to keep this last sentence in mind.

From the very beginning, from the days of John the Baptist, the menace of the people of Judæa, if not always of Jerusalem, had continuously hung over the priests and elders, the Pharisees and scribes, and had made them fear to do more than affect a withering but futile contempt. They had pretended to despise this ignorant mob :

> ' This multitude
> That knoweth not the law
> Are accursed ; '

none the less it was the fear of ' the multitude ' that had paralysed them at every turn. From the first days beside the Jordan there had been many who had hailed this Liberator from a thraldom that could no longer be endured. The men who had listened to John when he had cried :

> ' Ye brood of vipers
> Who hath showed you to flee from the wrath to come ? '
> Matthew iii, 7

had welcomed no less the denunciation which none but Jesus had dared to utter :

> ' Woe to you scribes and Pharisees
> Hypocrites
> Who build heavy and unsupportable burthens
> And lay them on men's shoulders
> And with a finger of your own will not lift them
> Who shut the kingdom of heaven against men
> And devour the houses of widows
> Praying long prayers
> Who tithe mint and anise and cummin
> And have left the weightier things of the law
> Judgment and mercy and faith
> Who make clean the outside of the cup
> But within are full of rapine and uncleanness.'

As the months had gone on the danger had only increased. There had been undoubtedly miracles here in Jerusalem ; if fewer than in Galilee, yet in many ways more striking, and certainly more noticed. For instance, there had been the healing of the cripple at the Probatic Pool in the North of the city ; it had given rise to the first great controversy in the Temple court. There had been the healing of the man born blind in the South, here almost at their very door. They had examined both of these cases ; it would have been wiser had they left them alone. Many of the people had been won by them; they had said, in answer to those who would keep them from believing:

> 'These are not the works of one that hath a devil
> Can a devil open the eyes of the blind?'

Many had gone further still; they had accepted this Jesus, with or without miracles, on the authority of that strange man, John the Baptist:

> 'And many resorted to him
> And they said
> John indeed did no sign
> But all things whatsoever John said
> Of this man
> Were true
> And many believed in him.'

Here now, on the eve of the Passion, it is impossible to fail to recognize, within the Holy City itself, a large and strong force inclined in His favour, to which the whole episode was a matter of grief and indignation. Once, beyond Galilee, more than five thousand men had risen to proclaim Him their king; if Jesus had wished it, He could have raised a like force in Judæa to save Himself from death. They were no empty words which He used later, in the presence of the Governor of the Province:

> 'My kingdom is not of this world
> If my kingdom were of this world
> My servants would certainly strive
> That I should not be delivered to the Jews
> But now my kingdom is not from hence.'
>
> John xviii, 36.

3. The Compact with Judas.

The priests and elders had thus decided to defer all action till after the Paschal festival; what seemed an unlooked for piece of good fortune compelled them to alter their plans. For we come now to the terrible story that has to be told. From the beginning of their Gospels all the four Evangelists have had it in mind; the name of Judas has never once been mentioned, not even on the day when he was numbered among the Twelve, without reference being made to that which they are at last compelled to record.

They seem to feel that in some degree they are all partakers of his shame, even as a family feels the shame when a son or daughter falls into disgrace. That one of their company, after all they had seen and heard, after all that had been done for them alone, after all their intimate friendship, after all the trust that had been placed in them, after all the powers and privileges bestowed upon them, should be capable of such a deed, was beyond words of theirs to express. They could not denounce it, they could only state the fact and leave it there; not a word is anywhere uttered against Judas the Traitor of indignation, or condemnation, or protest. No defence is made, no palliation is offered, either for Judas in his guilt, or for themselves as having no part with him. On the contrary, in the account of the Supper at Bethania on the Friday preceding, not a week before, it is implied that thus far at least the rest of the Twelve were in sympathy with Judas :

'And in like manner said they all.'

When, then, they come to tell the story of the Betrayal, they tell it in the fewest possible words. Luke alone, the most remote from the Twelve, and therefore the least personally concerned, opens his account with the terrible words :

'And Satan entered into Judas
Who was surnamed Iscariot
One of the Twelve.'

Luke xxii, 3.

From various indications it seems evident that the final event which decided Judas to take the course he did was the Supper in the house of Simon the Pharisee at Bethania during the preceding week. On that occasion, like the prudent treasurer he was, he had protested against an extravagant woman's unseemly waste; so sensible had been his protest that all his companions had agreed with him. And yet, in presence of them all, in presence of many visitors, because, as he murmured to himself, he had done no more than his duty, he had been silenced and put down; the foolish action of a foolish woman had been preferred to his obviously sound and reasonable counsel. Since that day his mind had been made up; and it was vindictive. Another might have been merely disappointed with the Master. He might have decided that after all, in spite of the years together, they did not agree ; he might have resigned his place among the Twelve and gone his way. So sometimes ends a vocation. But Judas was not content to do only that. An injury had been done to him ; he had a grievance and must be revenged ; he must have justice. Moreover,—for once a reason is found for evil-doing, there will soon come many more—he had himself to consider, his own right, his own future ; he must do for himself the best he could.

In spite of apparent successes, it had long been evident to him that all was not going as well with their work as his companions seemed to hope. During the last three days, while the rest had been carried away with the glamour, the shrewd eyes of Judas had not been shut ; he had seen the evil as well as the good. He had not been deceived by the triumphant procession on Sunday. It had been marred by a breakdown of Jesus Himself on the side of Olivet ; it had come to a sudden ending in the Temple court, as it had suddenly begun in Bethania. The cleansing of the Temple on Monday, with all its display of energy and power, had only shown how little Jesus had with Him on which He could depend. Such an insult, besides, so openly offered to the priests and elders in their own domain, could not but be avenged. As for Tuesday, what had Jesus gained ? He had silenced His rivals ; He had won in a contest of words, nothing more ; He had not dared to follow up His words by deeds. Judas had watched the faces in the groups that had gathered about them. He had seen the enemy only the more hardened as the day had gone on, while the face, and the very behaviour of Jesus had but shown sorrow, and depression, and consciousness of defeat. He had even cried out aloud, in a way He had never done before ; in the midst of the conflict with the leaders against Him he had appealed to his Father for help :

' Now is my soul troubled
And what shall I say ?
Father save me from this hour
But for this cause I came unto this hour
Father glorify thy name.'

No ; in spite of the flicker of success, it was evident to Judas that all was not well ; it was clear which way the contest would end. And since it must be so, was he not wise, was he not only doing his duty, might he not even be considered a public benefactor, in helping towards a quick and decisive solution? Jesus had once spoken a parable, the conclusion of which Judas had taken to heart:

'The children of this world
Are wiser in their generation
Than the children of light.'

By reasoning such as this, for the worst of crimes will always seek to justify itself, on the day after the return to Bethania Judas finally made up his mind. Jesus had gone apart, a thing not new; the rest were waiting in the little town, not without some vague sense of unrest. Judas was among them, but he was no longer of them. Much as they respected him, and looked up to him, the rest of the Twelve had never been intimate with him; he was not one whom it was easy to love. And he, on his part, had long grown tired of their company; their impetuosity annoyed him, their trivialities made him weary. In the course of the morning he slipped quietly away. No one would miss him; the nature of his office led him often apart, to go on errands of his own. If he went up to the city it would be assumed that he had gone to make some necessary purchase, perhaps to arrange for the Paschal supper; by evening he would be back again, and nothing would be observed. He went out of Bethania; once more he climbed the hill of Olivet. Descending the other side, he passed Gethsemane on his left; he knew the place only too well. He crossed the Kedron valley, and, long before midday, was once more within the Temple court. There he would soon discover one of the rival disputants of the day before. He would reveal himself to him; he would ask to be brought before the Council, for he had special business with it. The introduction would not have been difficult.

It would seem that Judas came into the presence of the priests where they had gathered in the house of Caiphas; it would seem, too, that when he met them, and gave the reason of his coming, they eyed him at first with suspicion. It was only natural. Such an ally was not to have been contemplated; treachery such as this was beyond even their wildest dreams. With all their contempt of the Nazarene and His Galilæan crew, they had never thought that any one of them could be so contemptible as this. Before they could be convinced that he was in earnest in the offer he made, that he was not, perhaps, a spy, Judas had need to use what eloquence he possessed, for we are told :

'He went and discoursed
With the chief priests and the magistrates
How he might betray him to them.'

But at length he did convince them. He showed them that to do this thing was in his power ; he proved to them that he was of the same mind as themselves, and that for safety the capture should be made as quietly as possible :

'In the absence of the multitude.'

Then he asked for terms. Once Jesus was taken, he himself would be out of employment ; in return for so great a public service, what reward were they prepared to give ?

'And he said to them
What reward will you give me
And I will deliver him unto you ?
Who hearing it were glad
And covenanted to give him money.'

Indeed they were very glad, for the question betrayed the betrayer. So long as he had claimed merely to be of service to them, they could not conceal their suspicions ; so long as he affected public duty, disinterestedness, or whatever else, they could not be sure ; treachery is never disinterested. But when he revealed his real purpose, when he showed that he looked for profit for himself by the transaction, then they were glad ; then they knew that they could count upon him. At once their attitude changed. Caution and suspicion altered into welcome and blandishment ; shrewdness and circumspection into a volume of words. He was indeed a hero, so to sacrifice himself in so noble a cause ; to defy this mountebank single-handed he was indeed a brave fellow. He was a faithful Jew, zealous for the Law ; he was one to be trusted ; he was to be congratulated on having rescued himself from this accursed company. Let him take heart and not falter, they would be behind him, with all the force of the Law ; the high priest himself had long since proved that to compass the death of Jesus the Nazarene was a holy act, as well as a public service. Let him not hesitate, they would protect him, should anything untoward occur ; if he needed helpers he should have them. And as for himself, certainly he should be rewarded ; to prove their confidence in him they would give him his reward at once. How much would he take ? Let him name his price. The price of a slave was thirty pieces of silver, and only slaves were bought and sold ; would thirty silver pieces suffice ?

The eyes of Judas glistened. Thirty pieces of silver, all his very own ! And after all these months of poverty, depending mainly on the services of a few good women ! While he stood there open-mouthed and silent, the clever men he had to deal with closed the bargain. They counted out the coins before his eyes : he saw them drop, one by one, he heard them jingle on the table. He could resist no longer, even if he would :

' And they appointed him thirty pieces of silver
And he promised.'

Judas came away from that place of meeting a changed man indeed. He had gone there with his mind made up, none the less not without some anxiety of conscience ; no one commits his first great crime without a qualm. He came away with a hardened heart that nothing henceforward would soften. He returned to Bethania ; he sat down to supper with the rest. Carefully he behaved as he had ever done before ; yet was there not at least one in the company who felt that something was amiss ?

And Jesus, too, came home from his solitude and joined them. Apart in prayer He had known all that had been done that day, yet, though it should pierce Him, He would not break the bruised reed. He, too, carefully and patiently behaved as He had ever done before.

4. The Preparation of the Supper.

At length Thursday morning came. In the evening of that day the Paschal Lamb was to be eaten ; on that day, therefore, it was certain that the Master would return into the city. But whither would He go ? During all his recent visits to Jerusalem He had never stayed under any roof ; partly for the sake of His own safety, partly, perhaps, that others might not be brought into trouble on His account. Now it was the morning of the day of days, and no arrangement had been made. Nor did He seem anxious to make any ; He seemed almost to have forgotten, He seemed only to desire to be left alone. They would let Him have His way; they would not trouble Him; they had long been used to days such as this, when Jesus would leave them and give Himself to prayer. But, in the meantime, the necessary preparations for the Supper must be made. They would ask Him for His instructions. There would be the place to be chosen for the Supper; there would be the needful things to be bought, the lamb, the bread, the wine, the herbs; if He would appoint the place, they would see to the rest:

> ' And the disciples came to Jesus saying
> Where wilt thou that we go
> And prepare for thee to eat the pasch?'

The words were the first warning bell; the disciples little dreamt what they meant to Him. In the last few days, thanks to the success that had followed their Master's teaching, they had become more confident, so that now they could go up to the city without fear. Besides, it was the Paschal season, and they would be unnoticed in the crowd of visitors. The day had dawned like any other day; the sun had risen over the hills of Galaad beyond the Jordan, and was shining on them on the little hamlet that lay along the eastern slope of Mount Olivet, and was open to the first rays of the morning. The last comers to the Pasch were passing through the town, having started from Jericho before sunrise; over the hill behind them the busy world was already astir, too much astir to be concerned about the likes of Jesus or His Twelve. Perhaps, they told themselves, this was the reason why the Master had chosen to wait yet another day alone.

But for Him that day was to be momentous. It was to be the day on which, at last, He would give mankind His all. Then from the beginning what He did on that day should be done in a manner worthy of it. On a former great occasion He had chosen ' whom He would Himself '; on this occasion, to prepare for His crowning act of love, He would choose, not the usual custodian of the purse, but the two who were nearest to His heart. He looked around the group of His disciples; His eyes rested on Peter and John:

> ' Go ye, he said,
> And prepare for us the pasch
> That we may eat.'

'That we may eat!' Can we not hear the note of affection as He dwelt upon these last words? Especially in the light of what was to come, of the bread from heaven which that night He would give them, can we not hear Him linger on the sentence, and on all it meant for Him, ignoring for the moment the question they had asked Him? They must repeat their request. Peter and John would indeed go, as He had bid them, but whither?

> 'But they said
> Where wilt thou that we prepare?'

The answer He gave was strange, and emphatic, and detailed; yet was it close akin to the answer He had given in that same place on the Sunday morning before. Now, as then, He looked up the road and knew what would happen. Then He had told them of the ass they would find and its owner, and what they were to say and do; now He told them what they would find at the city gate. And now, as then, without questioning, seeming to notice nothing strange, knowing well that what He said would be, they listened and obeyed:

> 'And he said
> Behold as you go into the city
> There shall meet you a certain man
> Carrying a pitcher of water
> Follow him
> Into the house where he entereth in
> And whithersoever he shall enter in
> You shall say to the goodman of the house
> The master saith to thee
> My time is near at hand
> With thee I make the pasch
> Where is the guest chamber
> Where I may eat the pasch with my disciples?'

Peter and John went upon their errand, associated now in a special way though as yet they did not realize it. Before the night was over they would realize it more; years afterwards they would look upon the choice that was made of them that day as a singular mark of love and favour. They went upon their errand over Olivet, passing the barren fig tree at the summit, by the same road that Judas had taken the day before, by the same road that, on the preceding Sunday, the Procession of the Palms had traversed.

But they did not go into the Temple; when they had crossed the brook Kedron, they turned up the narrower lane to the left, and entered the city by the gate below the Temple's southern wall. Close by that gate, in the year before, Jesus had come upon the man born blind, and had sent him to the pool of Siloe, on the slope of the hill outside the city, to be washed and healed. Close by that gate He had friends, though but a little higher up the street were the homes of His bitterest enemies, Annas, and Caiphas, the priests and the Pharisees.

As Peter and John entered the city they beheld what had been foretold to them, a man carrying in water from a well outside, either from the pool of Siloe or from the well now known as Our Lady's well. They followed him as they had been bid. He went along the narrow street that cut through the southern quarter of the city, the strong wall of the Temple towering up on his right. When he neared the houses of the priests, just before he reached the garden that surrounded the house of Annas, he turned to the left down a little lane that led to a house below. He passed under an arch into the courtyard, and Peter and John followed; it was the abode of a well-to-do citizen, to whom clearly they were known. They called for the owner of the house, and gave him the appointed message. He received them gladly; he was honoured that the Master should choose his abode for this favour; the best room he had should be at their disposal. Yes, he was honoured indeed, far more than he knew:

> 'And the ark of the Lord
> Abode in the house of Obededom the Gethite
> Three months
> And the Lord blessed Obededom
> And all his household.'
>
> 2 Kings vi, 11.

If the Lord blessed the house of Obededom, what will He not have done to the house which was to be scene of that Supper!

The 'good man of the house' went before up the stone steps that led from the courtyard to a room above; a large room, some twenty feet square, where the tables and couches were already prepared for the Paschal supper. That this should have been so need not surprise us; in many houses in Jerusalem tables were laid that night, not only for each household and its own guests, but also to receive the thousands of pilgrims who had come up for the festival. To show hospitality to as many of these as possible, on this night of all nights, was a point of honour with the dwellers in the city. Peter and John saw that all was ready; there were needed only the lamb, and the bread, and the bitter herbs, and the wine. These they would buy, either in the bazaar in the west of the town, or in the outer court of the Temple. At the appointed hour for sacrifice, they would attend at the ceremony when the lamb was slain; then they would return to the house, roast the lamb, prepare the food, set all in order in the room. In the late afternoon, when all was ready, they would return upon the road by which they had come, to meet the Master and the rest on their way up from Bethania.

CHAPTER II

5. The Supper.

HERE once more S. John stands still for a moment in his narrative. To him, for the remainder of his life, this was a night no detail of which could ever be forgotten. All other memories might fade away, even that of the Crucifixion, but not the recollections of that night in which the heart of Him who loved John, and whom John loved, revealed itself in all its magnificence. Before he tells his story he pauses to consider. It was the night before the Pasch, as he chooses to put it. They had been two days in Bethania, waiting for they knew not what, but with a strange sense of something momentous hanging over them. Jesus had seemed almost too absorbed with His own thought and prayer to remember the Pasch, and they had been obliged to remind Him. The reminder had roused in Him His wonted grandeur, calm, and decisive, and commanding ; and He had sent two of them forward to the city, himself and Peter, guiding them by that vision of the future which they had long since learnt to trust. The rest had come up with Him in the afternoon, and they had met together, in a room worthy of the occasion, with all laid out for the Paschal supper on a noble scale.

How well, now when he looked back upon the scene, could John read the mind and heart of his Beloved, as He had stood before them, at the door of the room on that memorable night ! They had gathered together in their usual way, eager enough about the purpose of their coming, for it was a great festival day ; a little unmindful of Him among them who was, nevertheless, their all-in-all ; intent upon their own affairs and the supper before them, taking little notice of the face, more than usually flushed, of the eyes, more than usually bright, or of the whole body, more than usually taut, that stood framed in the doorway before them. There He had stood for a moment and looked at them. It was the last time in this mortal flesh that He would have them around Him; He knew it though they did not. His hour was come; the hour of the enemy, foreseen from the beginning, was come at last. He must go; it was best for them that He should go. He must pass out of this world to the Father and for that He could not but be glad; but for a time He must leave them alone, and that His human heart could not but feel. He loved them, how He loved them! Deep down, since that happy day by the Jordan when they had first sought Him out, that love had always been there; but in the intervening years, humanwise, it had grown and grown. Generous, enthusiastic, responsive men they had been, all of them; troublesome at times, yes, and narrow, often self-willed and dull; but always willing to learn, always submissive under His rebuke, always giving back to Him the little they had in the best way they knew. He loved them for it all. He had always loved them; now at the end the very thought of separation made Him love them, if possible, more than ever.

Hence as he comes to this scene in his narrative John in his old age sees it all again. He cannot but pause to look at it; he must give it an introduction all its own; he sums it all up in the solemn sentence:

> ' Before the festival day of the pasch
> Jesus knowing that his hour was come
> That he should pass out of this world
> To the Father
> Having loved his own who were in the world
> He loved them unto the end.'

They came into the room and sat down, or reclined, at the table, Jesus and the Twelve, no more; not even His mother was with them, though we shall soon have evidence enough that she was not far away. They sat down to the Paschal supper. It was the first at which He had presided in the Holy City; for the last year He had not come, remaining in and near Capharnaum, the year preceding He had not yet gathered His Twelve definitely about Him. Now He had them together; now with Him they were a single family; to-night was to be a sealing of the bond of union. How he had looked forward to it! It was the first thing He had to tell them; He could keep it to Himself no longer:

> ' And when it was evening
> When the hour was come
> He cometh and sat down
> And the twelve apostles with him
> And he said to them
> With desire I have desired
> To eat this pasch with you
> Before I suffer
> For I say to you
> That from this time I will not eat it
> Till it be fulfilled in the kingdom of God.'

' Before He suffered ? ' What could He mean ? ' Fulfilled in the Kingdom ? ' To what did He refer ? Were not the two in contradiction ? Of late more than ever He had spoken of suffering, and yet more than ever of late He had also spoken like a conqueror, and had seemed on the verge of victory. All this week had been a record of success ; the triumphant march on Sunday, the conquests in the Temple, the applause of the multitudes, the defeat and submission of the scribes, who dared not ask Him any further questions, the surrender and retreat of the Pharisees. Were they not at that moment eating the Paschal supper in peace, and that under the very walls of Annas and Caiphas ? No ; whatever He might mean by suffering, clearly He could not mean defeat. Clearly the kingdom was at hand ; He had but to give the sign and His followers would rise to His command ; that He would not eat the Pasch again until the kingdom came could only mean that before another year had run out it would be founded.

In this way, and with so much evidence to support them, they drew their conclusion. They discussed His words among themselves round the table ; they were agreed that this could be their only explanation. What He next said and did, only convinced them the more that they were right. As the supper went on, in His place at the head of the table, according to custom, He took the cup of wine in His hands. With the usual prayer He turned His eyes to heaven and blessed the wine ; then He passed it round among them :

> ' And having taken the chalice
> He gave thanks and said
> Take and divide it among you
> For I say to you

> That I will not drink of the fruit of the vine
> Till the kingdom come.'

Confirm their conclusion? Did He not make it only too evident? Before the next Pasch? If His last words were to be taken literally, the kingdom would be theirs before the week was out. No wonder they grew sanguine and confident; no wonder they began to set all anxiety aside, to become familiar with Him—so commonly the case when He sat at table with them—and in consequence forgot His presence. They became preoccupied among themselves. The old subject of contention came up again, and they set to discussing their respective prospects in the kingdom. It was none too soon for them to prepare. There was Simon Peter, there was Judas; for and against both of these there was something to be said. Both were leaders by nature; both had been exceptionally trusted by the Master. Yet both had their defects. One was over-bold, the other, perhaps, over-careful; perhaps on the whole their claims were equal, each excelling in his own sphere. There were the brothers, James and John, and there were the other brothers, or cousins, James, and Thaddeus, and Simon; if the former were more intimate with the Lord, the latter were more nearly related. There was Andrew, who, after all, had been the first to discover and acknowledge Him; but for Andrew, Simon might never have known Him. There were Philip and Bartholomew, very early favourites, 'Israelites in whom there was no guile.' In contrast with them there were Matthew and Thomas, practical men, business men, men who knew the world and its ways, and therefore would prove useful rulers. Yes; there was much to be said for every one. When the kingdom did come, what worthy princes they would make!

> 'And there was also a strife among them
> Which of them should seem to be the greater.'

Jesus listened, silent and apart, to all their busy wrangling. Poor little creatures! How often had He listened to this kind of thing before! Would they never learn? Even if they ignored Him and His warnings, would they never discover their own right place? When before He had overheard them so contending with each other, along the road in Galilee, had He not set a child before them, and told them that if they would be truly great, they must become even as was that little child? When in Samaria they had wished to assert their importance, had He not rebuked them? In Peræa, when they had thought to lord it over women and children, had He not checked them? When James and John had come to Him, with their mother to urge their plea for them, seeking the first places in the kingdom, had He not warned them plainly that the way to the first places was only through suffering? So recently as Tuesday last, only two days ago, when they had sat together on the slope of Olivet, and had marvelled at the beauty of Jerusalem beneath them, had He not made it clear beyond a doubt, that their place in the kingdom, high as it would be, nevertheless would be also one of crushing lowliness, not one of glamour and splendour? Would they never learn? What more could He do to teach them?

But He would continue to be patient with them. After all they were but children still, only beginning to live in a world they did not yet perceive, and they knew no better. What could they know of kingdoms and kings, but the tales that came to them from over the sea or across the desert? Tales of mighty monarchs in grand palaces, before whom all men bowed, and whom the world hailed as great and good in proportion to their wealth and power? It was true they did not dream that their kingships would be quite like any of these; still there was the glamour of it all about them, and these fishermen of Galilee could not understand how a king could be, and not in some way resemble them. He must still be patient with them; He would be patient with them to the end. To-morrow He would give them an example of kingship very different from what they had in mind. Some day, if not now, they would learn; and then when they were high they would bend low, when they were low they would not lose heart; but would know that even at their lowest they were kings.

Yes, He would be patient with them. He would remind them that, on their own confession, He was Himself their supreme King; and yet, even now, He was a very different kind of King from those whose images danced before their eyes. He would remind them of what their own candidature for kingship had so far brought them; little else but trial and sacrifice, only a share in the hard life, and the persecution, that had been His own lot. They had left all and had followed Him, therefore they should rule; that He had already promised them. He would repeat His promise; it might remind them of their own former generosity:

> 'And there was a strife among them
> Which of them should be the greater
> And he said to them
> The kings of the gentiles lord it over them
> And they that have power over them
> Are called beneficent
> But you not so
> But he that is the greater among you
> Let him become as the younger
> And he that is the leader
> As he that serveth
> For which is greater
> He that sitteth at table
> Or he that serveth?
> Is not he that sitteth at table?
> But I am among you as he that serveth.
> And you are they who have continued with me
> In my temptations
> And I dispose to you
> As my Father hath disposed to me
> A kingdom
> That you may eat and drink at my table
> In my kingdom
> And may sit upon thrones
> Judging the twelve tribes of Israel.'

How He humoured them, on this night more than ever, speaking to them in the very imagery that most preoccupied them at the moment! Their minds were full of the 'kingdom'; their notions of kings were of monarchs royal, crowned, administering justice at their ease. To them it was little more than a fairy tale, or at least a tale of a distant past; the throne of David, and his mighty tower, still standing in the north of the city; yet more of Solomon in all his glory, who

> 'Exceeded all the kings of the earth
> In riches and wisdom
> And all the earth desired to see Solomon's face
> To hear his wisdom
> Which God had given in his heart.'
> 3 Kings x, 23-24.

Was that golden age about to come again? Or, to come down to their own day, there had been Herod the Magnificent, who had rebuilt the Temple, and this other later Herod, of whom they knew little more than that he feasted sumptuously, and disposed of men and things according to his own undisputed will. Of course, when they were kings, they would not act like him; when they were kings it would be very different. They would judge just judgment; they would be merciful and forgiving, according as He had so often told them. They would give alms to the poor; they would pardon enemies; they would see to the proper service in the Temple; they would teach the kingdom; they would be loyal and devoted to their Overlord; Oh! they would do wonders of good things when they were kings. But also they would 'eat and drink at His table'; they would 'sit on thrones', with crowns on their very own heads, and would 'judge the twelve tribes of Israel.' It would be a wonderful time; at long last the millennium; and they, even they, would be in its very midst.

So this night did Jesus at first humour these simple men from Galilee. And yet all the time He was teaching them that which later, if not now, they would understand. One day, not long hence, they would know what was meant by His 'kingdom not of this world', the kingdom whose king was a servant. He had told them plainly enough, many times before; now He would emphasize the teaching by an act which none of them would ever forget.

The Paschal supper was over; everything had been done in strict accordance with the ritual. The eyes of Jesus travelled once more round the group about Him. He read their faces, faces for the most part easily read, and through them He read their hearts. He saw their strength and their limitations; He knew how far they could be trusted, and where they would fail. One of the group in particular stood out amongst them, and the sight of him crushed His soul. Judas was there, Judas of Carioth, the man of affairs, whom on that account the rest had learnt to respect and in some sense to follow; Judas, the one well-balanced mind among them, who was never deceived by enthusiasm, who never made mistakes, who knew the value of things and men, who never trusted others too much, who could be relied upon to set matters right when the folly of others put them wrong; who never lost his self-control no matter how much he stirred others, who was prudent, and wise; and foreseeing, and careful, and had always a good reason for everything he did; Judas, who kept the purse, and saw to its replenishment; Judas, the son of Simon, whose prudence and common sense had read more clearly than the rest the recent repeated warnings of the Master. He had read and he had decided; whatever was being said round the table, he knew the ship was doomed. He had determined not to perish with it; no man in his senses would do that. Common prudence had guided him; it was his duty to look to himself. Wise men in Jerusalem had praised him for the step he had taken. Since the Master and His cause must perish, he had done no more than secure himself, and had profited, as was only right, by the transaction.

All this Jesus read in the heart of Judas. He knew it all, yet till this moment He had said and done nothing. He knew He was the Lord of all things, 'that the Father had given all things into His hands', yet He said and did nothing. He knew 'that He came from God, and goeth to God', that He was the Holy One and true; yet to hinder Judas He said and did nothing. He knew He had but to ask the Father and He 'would give Him legions of angels' for His defence; yet, in presence of Judas, thus far at least, He had shown no sign of resentment, He had said and done nothing. But now He must do something, even if He did not yet speak. Had He not willingly been called

'The friend of publicans and sinners'?

And was not Judas one of these last? Had He not said in times past:

'Come to me
All you that labour and are burthened
And I will refresh you'?

And was not Judas at this moment burthened as no other man upon this earth? Had He not said:

'I was sent
For the lost sheep of the house of Israel'?

And was not Judas now the most lost of them all? Had He not declared that He would

'Leave the ninety-nine in the desert
And go after the one that was lost
Until he find it'?

And was not Judas the very one ? Was He not that same night about to announce that His life's blood would be shed

'Unto the remission of sins' ?

And did not Judas before Him stand in need of that bloodshedding more than all the rest besides ?

6. The Washing of the Feet.

He would say nothing yet, but something He must do. What should it be ? It must be something outpouring, something self-annihilating, something of glad service, for that is always the last and the best gift of love. He had shown already how patient He could be, how very long He could wait, indeed till the very end, till Judas himself cut the bond that bound them to each other. But there were also the rest, beloved all of them ; and at this last meeting He must give them yet another proof of the depth of His affection. He knew what He would do ; the last conversation had suggested it. They were to be kings ; He was their King ; He would show them how a king, at least in his kingdom, should behave. They were to sit with Him at table in His kingdom. He was sitting with them now ; He would show them what most became the master of the feast.

Suddenly He rose from where He reclined ; so suddenly, that it did not occur to the rest to move. In a corner of the room by the door were a basin and a pitcher of water, always provided for ablutions. He went over to them ; He began to adjust his garments, as if preparing for some manual work, taking off His outer coat, rolling back the sleeves of His tunic. What could He mean ? They had seen Him do manual work before, but this was a strange time for it. While they watched and wondered He went on. He took the long towel hanging there ; He tied it round Himself like a girdle, leaving the ends hanging down in front. He picked up the basin and poured water into it. He came back to where they reclined ; before they could awake from their astonishment He was kneeling at the feet of the first in the row, and was washing them.

'And when supper was done
The devil having now put it into the heart
of Judas Iscariot the son of Simon

To betray him
Knowing that the Father had given him
All things into his hands
And that he came from God
And goeth to God
He riseth from supper
And layeth aside his garments
And having taken a towel girded himself
After that he putteth water into a basin
And began to wash the feet of the disciples
And to wipe them with the towel
Wherewith he was girded.'

The Twelve looked on amazed. They knew not what they should do; long since their contention concerning their places in the kingdom had ceased. There had often been times when His mere deliberateness had imposed silence on them; when they had wondered what He did, and yet had not dared to ask questions; witness the meeting with the woman at the well of Jacob, or the day when He had checked their wrath against the insolent Samaritans, or the defence He had made of the troublesome children with their mothers, or that further defence, made not a week ago, of the woman who had poured out her rich spikenard upon Him. And now it was the same. What He did was so inconsistent with His dignity among them. Before He had miraculously fed them; He had done other wonders for them, the Twelve alone, calming the sea for them, walking to them on the waters, even bidding one of them walk on the waters to Him. He had lived with them continuously, had eaten and slept with them; but never before had He done anything like this. They were astonished beyond words to say what they would, in their hearts they were humbled and ashamed; if they had dared they would have drawn in their feet and protested. But they did not dare. Quietly, deliberately, He went down the row, washed their dust-covered feet one by one, wiped them with the towel tied about His waist. In the tender way He did it He made them feel, each one, even Judas, that they belonged to Him, that they were indeed His own, His little children, that He was to them even as a mother; that if He was their Master, it was only that He might serve them the more; that, if it might be, gladly would He change places with them, let them be His masters while He was their slave.

Only one in the group had the courage to protest; Simon Peter, Simon who of late had begun to be called Peter, and who, from the use of the name, was beginning to realize his new status. Soon his turn came; what Jesus had done to the others He prepared to do to him.

'He cometh therefore to Simon Peter.'

He, Jesus, to whom Simon's former venerated master, John the Baptist, had said:

'I ought to be baptized by thee
And comest thou to me'?

Jesus, the latchet of whose shoe that same John the Baptist had declared himself unworthy to loose; Jesus, who had made him, Simon, walk with those same feet upon the waters of the lake; Jesus, whom he himself had declared to be the very Son of the living God. Peter in hasty moments could forget many things, but not at such a moment as this. Once when Jesus had done him a favour far less significant, he had fallen at His feet and said:

'Depart from me
For I am a sinful man
O Lord'!

Since then how often had the Master been compelled to rebuke him for his misdeeds! Once He had actually said to him:

'Go behind me
Satan'!

How, then, could he suffer this thing to be done to him? But perhaps Jesus had not noticed; perhaps if He looked up and saw whose feet He was now washing, He, too, would acknowledge that one like Simon might well be passed over. He would remonstrate; he would call the attention of Jesus to what He was doing, and perhaps He would refrain.

'And Peter saith to him
Lord
Dost thou wash my feet?'

Jesus heard but did not desist. He still knelt at the feet of Simon: He, Jesus Christ, the Son of the living God, at the feet of Simon Peter and washing them, even as once at

Magdala a sinful woman had knelt down and washed His own. Unmoved by Simon's question He took one of his feet in His hands and began to wash it.

> ' What I do
> Thou knowest not now
> But thou shalt know hereafter.'

was His only answer, and He went on with His self-appointed task. It was a significant remark enough. It showed well that Jesus, who ' knew what was in man ', knew well what was in Simon Peter, the good and the less good, and what yet would be ; the fall soon to come, but also the rise soon to follow, the essential worth in the end that would conquer all the rest. Such now, as always, was the patient, far-reaching vision of Jesus Christ, which could look through the present and beyond it, through weakness, and failure, and sin, and beyond them ; and if only there was truth in the heart, was content to endure, and pity, and wait, and forgive, and serve.

But Simon Peter had not yet travelled so far in the understanding of his Master, not so far as John the Baptist, when Jesus had humbled Himself before him. Then John had protested :

> ' I should be baptized by thee
> And comest thou to me ? '

Nevertheless, when bid to proceed, he had submitted without a word. Simon Peter could not yield so easily ; he was not such as John, at the moment he could liken himself only to the woman of Magdala. Whatever his faults, Simon never had delusions about his own sanctity. Impetuously therefore he urged his plea. He drew away his feet ; in his old Galilean manner he poured out his words of protest :

> ' Thou shalt never wash my feet.'

For the moment he forgot, as many times before he had forgotten, to whom he was speaking ; he lost ' the Son of the Living God ' in the ' meek and humble heart.'

But the Master knew well how to handle Peter. With all his faults there was that between them on which Jesus could invariably rely. He had proved it long ago, on that morning by the lake, when He had looked at him, and had just said : ' Come ! ' and Simon had at once left all and followed Him. He had proved it again that night, just a year ago, when He had beckoned to him through the storm, and again had said : 'Come !' and Simon had leaped upon the waters to reach Him. Now He had only to threaten separation, and Peter's resistance would vanish. Quietly, therefore, but with that firmness with which He had always treated Simon Peter, He said :

> 'If I wash thee not
> Thou shalt have no part with me.'

It was enough, and more than enough ; He had touched the one spot in Simon's heart. No part with Him? From one extreme, as was his wont, Peter rushed to the other. For Peter loved Jesus, loved Him more than he himself knew, with a love that clung and would not be separated, would never have enough. If to be washed by Jesus was a condition of their union, then even to that he would submit ; nay, in that case the more the better. Let Jesus have all, and more than all, if only in return Peter could have part with Him, and he cried :

> 'Lord
> Not only my feet
> But also my hands and my head.'

Jesus had gained His point ; but He had more yet to do. He had humbled Himself before them, and that they had understood ; but He would have them learn besides that what He had done was more than an act of humility, it was for a sign. Peter had already caught a glimmering of the truth ; he had seen that, somehow, union with Jesus was bound up with washing at His hands. Now the Master would complete the lesson ; He would tell him how this external cleansing was a token of another within :

> 'Jesus saith to him
> He that is washed
> Needeth but to wash his feet
> But is clean wholly.'

And yet, alas, even as He spoke, and even in this chosen company, He knew that His words must needs be qualified. Though He had washed the feet of all, yet was there one among them who would not be clean, would not, because of his own free choice he would not. Jesus was compelled to add :

> 'And you are clean
> But not all.'

Again John dwells upon this one exception ; dwells upon it as he had done before, and as he will do again. It comes like a recurring lament, haunting his whole story ; as it was the greatest sorrow in the heart of his Beloved, so it was the greatest sorrow in his own. And it was not only the fact of the treachery, but the foreknowledge of the fact that oppressed him ; Jesus had known it, and had borne the secret agony of it, all the time. From the beginning when first He had chosen the Twelve, He had known it would come, and John, in perfect sympathy for the rest of his life, had never suffered it to escape his own memory. Among all the many shadows which had fallen across his Master's path as he described it, this had been given the first and most prominent place. A year ago, after the famous discourse on the Bread of Life delivered in the synagogue at Capharnaum, he had told how Jesus had ended by saying :

> ' Have I not chosen you twelve
> And one of you is a devil ? '

as if somehow the very beauty of the Eucharist were inevitably connected with this apostacy. Then John had lingered on the misery of it all by adding :

> ' Now he meant Judas Iscariot
> The son of Simon
> For this same was about to betray him
> Whereas he was one of the twelve ' ;

as if the shame of it were in some sense the common burthen of them all.

Again, at the anointing by Mary at Bethania, that idyll of perfect contrition, the same shadow had come over, and had tended to mar the whole scene ; indeed so much so that what had begun in the fullest glow of love ended in a long-drawn note of sadness. Listen how John lingers on it, looking at it and looking again, as at something which, if he had not himself witnessed it, he could never have believed :

> ' Then one of his disciples
> Judas Iscariot
> He that was about to betray him
> Said : Why was not this ointment sold
> For three hundred pence
> And given to the poor ?

And he said this
Not because he cared for the poor
But because he was a thief
And having the purse
Carried the things that were put therein.'

All this comes back to the mind of John as he now writes, reminding him that Jesus foreknew, and making him realize the more the added agony that this foreknowledge must have been.

' For he knew
Who he was that would betray him
Therefore he said
You are not all clean.'

The washing of the feet was over. Jesus put back the basin in its corner, resumed His outer garment, and took His place once more at the board. Already He had let them see, by His answer to Peter, that what He had done was symbolic; now He would extend the symbolism. Then He had said that to be washed by His own hands, though it were only in part, was to be made wholly clean; now he added that they should do the same to one another. Then His own act of humility was their salvation; now the humility, not only of the penitent, but also of him that forgave, should have a like effect. Humility and charity, each blending into the other, humility on both sides, charity on both sides, this is the meaning of the soul of Jesus expressed in the Sacrament of Penance:

' Then after he had washed their feet
And taken his garments
Being sat down again he said to them
Know you what I have done to you?
You call me Master and Lord
And you say well
For so I am
If then I being Lord and Master
Have washed your feet
You ought also to wash one another's feet
For I have given you an example
That as I have done to you
So you do also
Amen Amen I say to you
The servant is not greater than his lord

Neither is the apostle
Greater than he that sent him.'

Already there was beginning to pour forth that torrent of thought and love which was to be conspicuous in Jesus during all the rest of that supper. To one who does not realize His situation, there seems to be little but confusion of ideas in all that follows ; in any case it seems impossible to put what He says in order. What has He really meant by this washing of the feet ? What has He not meant ? He has begun by making it a symbol of the cleansing sacrament ; He has gone on to emphasize in it His own ideal of a ' Master and Lord '. Then at once, as a third deduction, He has leaped to the lesson of mutual charity and service ; in all these He takes such an act to be the truest imitation of Himself. They were His servants ; then let them wash one another's feet ; they were His apostles, His witnesses ; then let them wash one another's feet. They were to be preachers of His word ; let them preach that word by washing one another's feet. If they understood Him aright, they would prove it by their imitation of Him, above all else in this ; if they would draw down His blessing upon them, they would win it by no other means more surely than by washing the feet of one another. Cleanness of heart, self-humiliation, charity of service : we ask ourselves which of these is most pleasing to the heart of Jesus Christ, and we find that in practice that heart will admit of no distinction. To Him true cleanness of heart is humble, true humility is kind, true charity is clean ; the three flow into one another, and the stamp of the three on the soul of a man is the true expression of Himself.

What follows is in many ways typical of Our Lord Jesus Christ. On many occasions in His life we may notice how He is affected, not only by the words and actions, but also by the very feelings and emotions of those around Him. How many times are we told that He read their thoughts, that He knew what was in their hearts, and each time with some corresponding emotion in Himself! Strong as He was, and firm, and true, yet was He sensitive as an aspen leaf to every breath of life about Him. At Nazareth, He had 'wondered at their unbelief', and because of that unbelief had not been able, as the Evangelists expressly tells us, to work many miracles among them. At the opposite extreme, on another day, in the narrow streets leading up from the beach at Capharnaum, a poor woman had but touched the hem of His garment and had been cured ; and Jesus had asked who had touched Him, because He had felt virtue to go out of Him. In the company of some He was singularly at peace, as in Simon's house, or with the Twelve on their return from their first mission, or with the family of Lazarus at Bethania, or among the children on the highroad through Peroea. In the company of others He was troubled, as when He was moved to anger in the street of Capharnaum, or in the synagogue, close by, or with the Pharisees in Judæa, or when the young man came to Him and then turned away. The sensitive human nature within Him vibrated to every note, to the passions and emotions of men towards Him as well as to the birds in the air, the flowers of the field, the bright sun overhead, and the fields white for the harvest, and He allowed that vibration to affect His very soul, His very Divine power.

So was it, intensely, on this night ; and now as John writes, after the years of pondering, his sensitive heart is able to detect it. Already, as we have seen, while Jesus washed the feet of the Twelve, the consciousness of one sinister shadow in the room had checked Him in His speech ; now again, when He would proceed with what He had to say, to His very own apart, as His farewell greeting, the same shadow crosses His path and He can go no further. He must turn aside again, something compels Him ; in the company there is one of whom what He has just said will not be true. Still they are His own ; even that one is His own ; if one of them fails, and from the beginning He knew one would, in some sense He would take the blame upon Himself. As a friend, however innocent, feels within himself the guilt of a friend disgraced ; as a brother or sister feels the shame of a shamed sister or brother ; as a mother, however holy, nay the more in proportion to her sanctity, feels the guilt of a guilty son ; so did the sensitive heart of Jesus Christ feel the guilt and shame of His chosen Judas. Therefore He must, as it were, give to Himself some kind of explanation, some kind of defence. He fell back on prophecy ; the Psalmist had said that so it would be, and He had accepted the conditions :

'All my enemies whispered together against me
They devised evils to me
They determined against me an unjust word

> For even the man of peace
> In whom I trusted
> Who ate my bread
> Hath greatly supplanted me.'
>
> Psalm xl, 8, 10.

He would quote that prophecy, so that in the years to come, when the disciples looked back on this mystery, they might then understand and believe. Hence, as it were correcting Himself, He continued :

> ' I speak not of you all
> I know whom I have chosen
> But that the Scripture may be fulfilled
> He that eateth bread with me
> Shall lift up his heel against me
> At present I tell you before it come to pass
> That when it shall come to pass
> You may believe that I am he.'

It is significant that later, on the first occasion on which Peter spoke as head of the Universal Church, he began with an allusion to this prophecy. It was after the Ascension, before as yet the Holy Spirit had come down upon them. Judas was gone, and there was need that his place should be filled. As his Master had done before him, so now, in justification for what he was about to do, Peter quoted the Psalmist :

> ' Men brethren
> The scripture must be fulfilled
> Which the Holy Ghost spoke
> By the mouth of David
> Concerning Judas
> Who was the leader of them that apprehended Jesus
> Who was numbered with us
> And had obtained part of this ministry.'
>
> Acts i, 16.

Again Jesus made an effort to proceed with what He had to say. He had begun before with :

> ' Amen, amen I say to you ',

His favourite formula of emphasis ; He would steady Himself by repeating it. Before, He had spoken of humility as the mark of one whom He had sent ; now, by contrast,

He would dwell upon the honour due to him because of his commission. Before, He had said :

> 'Amen, amen I say to you
> The servant is not greater than his lord
> Neither is the apostle
> Greater than he that sent him';

but now :

> 'Amen, amen I say to you
> He that receiveth whom I send
> Receiveth me
> And he that receiveth me
> Receiveth him that sent me.'

Surely a beautiful identification, made more beautiful because of the place in which it comes. It was a last appeal to Judas. Jesus had washed his feet ; He had warned him in words that others would not understand, not once, but twice over ; now He tells him quite plainly how near they would be if only he would remain true. When Judas was gone it would be an identification which would be yet more emphasized before that supper was over. He had been sent by the Father ; they had been sent by Him. He was one with the Father ; because they had been sent they were to be one with Him. This was the text which summed up beforehand most that He would have to say that night.

7. The Last Warning to Judas.

And yet again, for a second and a third time, He could not go on ; the haunting consciousness of the one evil influence in their midst still obsessed Him. Again He grew silent ; He was troubled ; the unrest upon His face betrayed the struggle in His soul. Something of the kind the Twelve had seen before ; notably that day in Capharnaum, when His enemies had accused Him of working His miracles by the aid of Beelzebub, the Prince of Devils, and that other day, in the streets of Jerusalem, when the carping of His critics had made Him cry out that He was troubled, and He had prayed to be relieved. But this occasion seemed more terrible ; and at last the moment came when He would endure it no longer. Thus far He had done no more than hint at what He knew ; now the time had come when He must speak more plainly. Hitherto, for the traitor's own sake, He had uttered warnings which he alone would understand, now, for the sake of the future, it was meet that all the rest should hear. Before He had said :

> ' You are clean
> But not all ',

and again :
> ' He that eateth bread with me
> Shall lift up his heel against me ' ;

yet not even Judas had taken any heed. He would now be more explicit. He would use His solemn mode of speaking. Nevertheless, even now, the further and last warning should be given in such a way that, if he chose, the traitor should be shielded :

> ' When Jesus had said these things
> When they were at table and eating
> He was troubled in spirit
> And he testified and said
> Amen, amen I say to you
> One of you that eateth with me
> Shall betray me
> But yet behold
> The hand of him that betrayeth me
> Is with me on the table.'

The words were plain enough, and without possibility of misinterpretation. There was, He said, a traitor among them. Was such a thing possible ? Which of them could it be ? The Twelve looked at one another ; faults they knew in each other in abundance, but none that could point to such a fault as this. What He had said they could not doubt ; when He spoke with such emphasis as this they had long learnt to accept His words without further question. Nevertheless it grieved them, it made them almost resentful, to think that such a charge could be made, against such a group as themselves, at such a moment. In one another they could find no answer ; they could suspect not one amongst them. They turned to right and left ; they spoke in anxious whispers, neighbour to neighbour ; but still they could come to no conclusion. They turned their eyes in upon themselves, they asked themselves, each one, whether he would be the one to be guilty of that doom, and still the dreadful mystery remained. Soon the torrent could not be stemmed. As on that famous night upon the water they had all rushed to Him with the cry :

' Save us
We perish ' ;

so on this night, in this sudden imminent peril of a still worse shipwreck, one by one they appealed to Him, that they might be saved from this greatest of disasters :

' And they being very much troubled
Began to be sorrowful
And to enquire among themselves
Which of them it was
That should do this thing
And to say to him one by one
Is it I, Lord ? '

Jesus waited for the clamour to die down. Then He gave His answer ; enough, abundantly enough, for him to understand whom it most concerned, but for the rest still an enigma. He would dwell upon only two things, the utter shame of the act of treachery, and the terrible doom that awaited the traitor if his design were carried out ; that it should be done by one of His own chosen Twelve, by one of the chosen companions at this table of all others, that if the deed were done it would entail a retribution He would not venture to describe :

' But he answering said
One of the twelve
Who dippeth with me his hand in the dish
And the Son of man indeed goeth
As it is written of him
But woe to that man
By whom the Son of man shall be betrayed
It were better for him
If that man had not been born.'

His answer thus left them still in ignorance. He had dwelt only on the enormity of the crime about to be committed ; He had not pointed out the criminal. But there was one of the group in particular who felt the sting of what was said.

' One of you ;
One of the twelve ' ;

the words almost implied a charge against them all, and was not Simon Peter their head ? In some sense he felt himself responsible ; to make such a charge against anyone amongst them was to accuse them all. That one of his Twelve, Simon Peter's Twelve, should so turn traitor was a thought that cut him to the quick ; until he knew which it was among them he could have no rest.

Yet of himself he did not dare to ask. On other occasions he had made protests against the Master's words or actions, and had invariably been cut short ; this very night at the washing of the feet, he had resisted and had been put in his place. But there was John ; John the simple and innocent of heart ; John the son of thunder, the enthusiast, whose enthusiasm yet offended none ; John the youth among them, who claimed unconsciously the privileges of youth and was freely given them ; John in a special way loved by Jesus, and none took it amiss ; John, who could claim as his own the title : 'the disciple whom Jesus loved.' John, reclined next to, in front of Jesus. Leaning as he was on his right arm, he had but to throw back his head a little and it rested on the breast of Jesus ; and Jesus, on His side, was content at times to allow to His beloved this familiar consolation.

John was there at this moment. The Master's troubled look and manner, the terror of the warning, the anxiety which John shared with them all lest he himself might be the guilty man, drove him the more to this clinging of love. Peter, close beside him, looked at him. If to anyone Jesus would reveal the traitor's name, surely He would reveal it to John ; indeed it might well be that John already knew it. Secretly he made a sign to him. He attracted his attention ; under his breath, while the rest were still arguing among themselves, he whispered to him :

'Who is it
Of whom he speaketh ? '

John understood. Where he leaned upon the breast of Jesus he had but to turn his head and look upward and their eyes would meet. He turned and looked, with a question in his eyes ; and the glance from the eyes that looked down on him encouraged him to speak. With eagerness in his voice, as if the strain were becoming more than he could bear, with something, too, of familiarity born of love, with something of a child's pleading, John asked:

'Lord
Who is it?'

Jesus heard and answered. In His eyes, too, there was love, and that was more than love returned, for his disciple John; in his face, at the same time, there was agonising pity for his other beloved, Judas. Still would He not openly betray him; John and Peter He would trust, but the rest must not yet know. Lest anyone else should hear, He would not even pronounce the traitor's name; perhaps, too, there was another reason, He could not bring Himself to utter it. A sign would suffice, especially the sign to which the Psalmist had alluded:

'He that eateth bread with me
Shall lift up his heel against me.'

While then the talk was going busily round the table, Jesus leaned down and whispered to John:

'He it is
To whom I shall give bread dipped';

and as He spoke the words He took a piece of bread, dipped it in the common bowl, and handed it to Judas Iscariot, the son of Simon, which would seem to show that Judas was near to the Lord at that supper table.

In itself this was nothing strange, and would not have been remarked upon by any of the group. It was a common act of courtesy, such as a host might perform to any guest. But to John and Peter what a revelation was here! Judas of all men! The very last, so it seemed to them, that they could ever have suspected. Judas, with fewer external faults than any other, the most self-possessed, the most prudent, the most knowing, the most trusted, to whom they themselves had often turned for counsel, whose lead they had often followed, whose silent wisdom had always given weight to every word he had uttered; Judas, to whom the poor turned when alms were distributed, to whom the Master Himself would turn whenever He needed anything; Judas who often had cared for them all, and on their travels had found them food and shelter. Judas the traitor? It was hard to believe.

Yet did Judas not refuse the morsel; they watched him,

self-possessed to the last, accept it from the Master's fingers. Then, as if it were an afterthought, as if this special act of courtesy of Jesus called for some such remark—for hitherto he had not joined in the noisy and somewhat unseemly clamour of the rest—with an ease of manner that seemed to prove an easy conscience, asking, not in any anxiety, but because others asked, he looked up into the face of Jesus, and said :

'Is it I, Rabbi ? '

and even as he spoke he put into his mouth the bread the Master had given to him.

At once he felt a change come over him. Hitherto, with all his brave exterior, Judas had not been without some restlessness of mind. Jesus had already said enough to show him that He knew what was being planned ; would He then take measures to escape, as He had often done before, or, worse still, would He expose Judas before all the company ? The latter was not likely ; it was not the manner of Jesus to expose the evil of anyone ; Judas felt that he could run that risk. Again, there was the deed itself. However justifiable he had argued it to be, Judas knew that in in itself it was foul, all the more foul because in the East to eat bread with another was a guarantee of security. Whatever he had done before that was untrue, never before had he gone so far as this.

Now on a sudden all his fears and scruples seemed to vanish ; that morsel of bread gave him new life, new courage. It was a token from Jesus that He would put no hindrance in his way ; its acceptance by himself killed within him every remaining qualm. That question, which in itself was a lie, that demeanour of friendship, which covered utter falsehood, gave him over to the devil :

'And after the morsel
Satan entered into him.'

There was nothing more to be done. Judas had rejected this last token of friendship, and it only remained for him to be dismissed. While the talk was still going round, so that none but Judas, and John, and Peter could hear what was being said, Jesus answered the question of Judas with the simple words :

'Thou hast said it.'

Though Judas would deceive Jesus, yet would Jesus not deceive him, nor would He let him go away believing that He was Himself deceived. Further, when now the conversation had grown quiet, in a tone loud enough for all to hear He added :

'That which thou doest
Do quickly.'

Thus to the very end Jesus kept the good name of Judas safe. With that consummate skill in the use of words which had nowhere its equal, whether when He spoke ' as one having authority ', or told simple stories to poor country people ; with that perfect self-possession which never allowed Him to retaliate, whether supercilious enemies accused Him of having a devil, or an ignorant rabble laughed Him to scorn ; with that infinite patience and sympathy which made Him one alike with haughty Pharisees and with publicans and sinners ; with all this Jesus bore with Judas to the end. While He spoke nothing but the simple truth, yet were His words such as none but Judas would understand the rebuke, and condemnation, and dismissal they contained. Similar commands Judas had often received before, and had promptly fulfilled them ; since he held the purse, Jesus and Judas had often business with each other which did not concern the rest. The festival day would be on the morrow. No doubt for that day some extra purchases would need to be made, some extra alms to be given to the poor. Though it was already dark the bazaars were still open, especially in view of the coming feast. That it should be needful for Judas to leave them, even at such a solemn moment, was easily understood :

' Now no man at the table knew
To what purpose he said this unto him
For some thought
Because Judas had the purse
That Jesus said to him
Buy those things we have need of
For the festival day
Or that he should give something to the poor.'

But for Judas the die was cast ; there was no need or inclination for him to wait a moment longer. Suddenly the whole scene had become abhorrent to him ; the presence of these his former brethren, the presence of Jesus Himself, had ceased to have for him any meaning at all. Their company merely bored him, their behaviour lacked all sense. This talk about a kingdom, this meaningless washing of feet, this wearisome and endless ceremonial, even the worn-out ceremony of the Paschal Lamb—it was all so futile, so trivial, so contemptible, so childish, so irrational, so steeped in silly sentiment, so maudlin, so void of common respect, so obviously superstitious, so profitless, so bankrupt. It might be all very well for boorish countryfolk in Galilee, or for emotional women in Peræa, but for men of the world, with their lives to live and their careers to make, men of independence and judgment who were masters of their own souls, this kind of thing was mere slavery, it was intellectual suicide. He saw it all now ; it had been a mistake from the beginning ; he had been a fool to let himself be drawn into the net of this enthusiast and His followers. But it was never too late to mend, and the sooner he was out of it the better. He welcomed the command that had just been given to him, be its hidden meaning what it might. He had scarcely swallowed the morsel of bread which Jesus had handed to him, than he

' Went out immediately
And it was night.'

No sooner had Judas gone than the whole atmosphere of that supper-room changed. A cloud seemed to lift from them all, but from none more than Jesus Himself. He gave a sigh of relief ; at last He was Himself, and was able to speak as He would. His voice was no longer suppressed, His words no longer stumbled, as He almost cried out with joy :

' Now is the son of man glorified
And God is glorified in him
If God be glorified in him
God also will glorify him in himself
And immediately will he glorify him.'

Only a few days before, in the Temple court, words not unlike these had escaped Him. Then in a moment of mental trial He had cried :

' Now is my soul troubled
And what shall I say ?

> Father save me from this hour
> But for this cause I came unto this hour
> Father glorify thy name ' :

In answer to that cry :

> ' A voice therefore came from heaven
> I have both glorified it
> And will glorify it again.'

and in the courage which that answer had given Him He had gone on :

> ' Now is the judgment of the world
> Now shall the prince of the world be cast out
> And I
> If I be lifted up from the earth
> Will draw all things to myself.'

To which S. John had added his own significant and characteristic comment :

> ' Now this he said
> Signifying by what death he should die.'

In like manner now once more is His courage strengthened. He is again, as it were, master of His soul and its emotions, unhampered by the discord around it, and is able to proceed as He will. For the present He can set Himself aside. Later in the evening, in a moment of utter loneliness, it will all return with still greater horror upon Him, so much so that He will need an angel from Heaven to strengthen Him. But for the hour before Him He is free ; and once free, His thoughts return to where they were at the beginning, to His own seated around Him, His own whom He had loved to the end, with whom He had longed to eat this supper before He died. He looked about upon them all ; His heart went out to them again :

> ' Little children '

He called them: these rough men, these hard-handed Galilæans ; we do not read that He had ever used so tender a name for them before.

And why does He give it to them now ? We see His thoughts, for He cannot nor does He wish to hide them. It is because He is about to leave them ; and though it is He that should rightly be given consolation yet must He spend His time in consoling them. He is going away and they will miss Him ; they will be lost without Him ; they will hunger for Him; intensest joy for Him, even while also intensest agony, and He must give them comfort in return.

> 'Little children
> Yet a little while I am with you
> You shall seek me
> And as I said to the Jews
> Whither I go you cannot come
> So I say to you.'

In those words He drew their memories back to the Feast of Tabernacles six months before. On that occasion, in the court of the Temple, He had definitely thrown down the gauntlet to His enemies; it was the beginning of His last campaign against Jerusalem. His main work of teaching had by that time been accomplished. He had revealed the Father, He had opened the way to the Kingdom, He had foretold the gift of His own body and blood, He had received the Confession of Peter, He had sealed that Confession by the vision of Himself transfigured. He had invited to Him all the world, for He was its Way, and its Truth, and its Life; and there had remained little else for Him to do but to fight His way to His throne upon the Cross.

But to what different hearers, and therefore in how different a sense, does He now repeat the warning! Then it was given to His enemies, now it is given to His own; then it was uttered as a threat, now it is spoken only that He may give comfort. Then it was His reply to the 'ministers' of 'the rulers and Pharisees' who had been sent expressly to apprehend Him; now it is to ministers of His own, who already possess Him and fear to let Him go.

Yes, He was about to leave them, and whither He went they would not be able to come. He was about to inflict a wound, but even while He inflicted it He must pour in oil and wine. They were about to lose Him, but He would show them how and where they would find Him most easily again; they would find Him most easily in one another. Here He strikes another note, akin to much that we have heard before, but in its full significance something new. It is a note which, once struck, is to echo in His words throughout the rest of this memorable night:

> 'A new commandment I give unto you
> That you love one another

> As I have loved you
> That you also love one another
> By this shall all men know
> That you are my disciples
> If you have love one for another.'

In the old Law it had been written :

> ' Thou shalt love thy friend
> as thyself.'

In the Sermon on the Mount the new Lawgiver had gone much further, and had made a new standard :

> ' But I say to you
> Love your enemies
> Do good to them that hate you
> And pray for them
> That persecute and calumniate you ' ;

and in confirmation He had added :

> ' If you love them that love you
> What reward shall you have ?
> Do not even the publicans this ?
> And if you salute your brethren only
> What do you more ?
> Do not also the heathen this ? '

So strongly had He spoken, even at the beginning of His teaching. Yet here, on this last night of His life on earth, He tells His own Eleven, from whom He had a right to expect more than from any other, that the love He asks of them is not love of their enemies, but merely love of one another. Nay more ; this He calls a ' new commandment '; indeed so new, that its observance will mark them out from all other men as being His very own. What does He mean ? In what is this commandment new ? In only one respect does it differ from those that have gone before. They said :

> ' Thou shalt love thy neighbour
> As thou dost love thyself ' ;

this new Law said :

> ' You shall love
> As I have loved you.'

That is something very much more ; so much more that of himself man cannot hope to attain it. But before the evening is over He will teach them how it may be attained.

And His own know what He means, by experience they know it, nor can they explain it to others. It is one of those things which cannot be explained, for it is beyond the language of men. Others, looking on, see it and confess it. 'See how these Christians love one another'; that peculiar something which tells all the world who are His disciples; yet the world, too, is unable to define it. For love does not live on words, nor by words can it be defined; above all that love which is in Him and comes from Him, and which finds Him and loves Him in others, crystal and true and burning and pure, without a shadow of secrecy, or doubt, or fear.

CHAPTER III

8. The Holy Eucharist.

THEY had settled down again at the table, and the supper went on as before. Jesus had broken the proceedings with a strange ceremony, which had filled the Twelve with more than their usual reverence. He had renewed His commandment of love, of mutual love at all costs, making His own love the standard for theirs, and they were filled with the glow of the commandment. They were nearer to one another than they had ever been before, made one family in Him. They were nearer to Him; all He had done and all He had said had drawn them till they forgot themselves and their personal wranglings. Their eyes and thoughts were riveted now on Him, for there was nothing left to distract them; to love Him, to love one another with Him among them, was one and the same thing, and was easy. Then, while they sat there silent and looked on, waiting for the more He had evidently in His mind to say, He took in His hands the unleavened bread that lay on the board before Him. He held it for a moment in His hands; His eyes turned up to heaven, as they had always done when He spoke to His Father. He released His right hand, and lowering His eyes again upon the bread He blessed it. Then He broke it into pieces, and while He held it still in His left hand He said:

> 'Take ye and eat
> This
> Is my body
> Which is given for you';

and as He spoke He handed the plate with its contents to Peter and John and the rest. They took it from His hands; they passed it down the table one to another; each one received a portion. Or was it, as Ludolph the Carthusian and others would have it, and as Fra Angelico has painted it, that He

> 'Gave to His disciples',

to each one, with His own hand?

As they received each his portion, the disciples knew that what they were eating was no ordinary food. They were not subtle theologians ; they were the simplest of men ; and they heard the words from One who, they had long known, could neither deceive nor be deceived, in whom they could absolutely trust. Indeed, if He had ever complained of them, it had usually been that they would not trust Him enough :

> ' O ye of little faith
> Why did you doubt ? '

had been on His lips more than once. They could take Him at His word ; wonderful, impossible as it was, yet what He said was true. His words on the summit of Olivet less than three days ago were still fresh in their minds :

> ' Have the faith of God
> Amen I say to you
> That whosoever shall say to this mountain
> Be thou removed and be cast into the sea
> And shall not stagger in his heart
> But believe that whatsoever he saith shall be done
> It shall be done unto him.'

Besides, how carefully He had trained them to accept that which now He had explicitly declared ! At the beginning of His life in their company He had won their faith by changing water into wine :

> ' And his disciples believed in him.'

He had raised the dead in their presence, so that the people, less instructed than they, had cried :

> ' A great prophet is risen up among us
> And God hath visited his people.'

Alone with them in the ship on the lake He had commanded the storm and the waters and they :

> ' Being afraid wondered
> Saying to one another
> Who is this, think you
> That he commandeth the winds and the sea
> And they obey him ? '

On the northern shore of the lake He had fed five thousand

men and more with a few loaves and fishes; and again the people had proclaimed:

> 'This is of a truth the prophet
> That is to come into the world.'

On the next day, in the synagogue at Capharnaum, He had spoken of the living bread He would one day give, bread from heaven, to which the bread brought down by Moses would be as nothing, bread which would be Himself, His flesh for the life of the world. Often since then they had asked each other what His words could mean, and had never been able to reply. This only they knew: that He whom they followed was true; He who had changed one substance into another, who had commanded life and death, who had ruled the powers of nature, who had fed thousands with a little bread, who had rebuked devils and had forgiven sins with His word, would one day keep the solemn promise which He had that day made:

> 'The bread which I will give
> Is my flesh
> For the life of the world.'

During the year since the promise had been given they had held to the confession which Simon had made that day for them all:

> 'Lord
> To whom shall we go?
> Thou hast the words of eternal life
> And we have believed
> And have known
> That thou art the Christ
> The Son of the living God';

and in the strength of that confession they had believed, and had encouraged each other to trust, so that when the time of manifestation came they might know and understand.

Now on a sudden, so quietly, as was the way with Jesus, so unexpectedly, as is the way with one who loves, so unreservedly, for this night He was giving as never before, the revelation had been made. The sign of bread had been given, looked for since the days of Melchisedech, who had sacrificed in bread and wine, since the manna had fallen in the desert. It had been given, not to the five thousand as had once been thought, for they could not have understood;

but to the Eleven whom by word and deed, by encouragement and rebuke, by long cherishing of faith, and love, and trust, He had carefully trained to receive it. They heard His words; they knew they were true; instantly they were thinking on another plane, living in another world, a world that transcended human understanding, but was not the less true on that account. Nay, it was almost tangible; faith was more certain than reason. They saw and did not see, but what they did not see was more real than the object of sight; they understood and did not understand, because human understanding failed them. The impossible was transparently true; they lived, no, not they, but Jesus Christ their Lord lived in them. Love had achieved its consummation; He who had loved as no other could love had found a means which no other could have found to perfect union with His own beloved. Faith itself was now a new thing, for His eyes saw for them, His mind thought in them. Love had now a new meaning, for His heart burnt within them. Hope had a new awakening, for His confidence gave them a courage that was not theirs; they could do all things in Him who strengthened them. If a moment before, when He washed their feet, they could say nothing, much less could they utter anything now. They could only adore; and even while they adored they knew not what they did.

They sat there silent and spell-bound by the fascination, knowing and not knowing, lost in mystery. Meanwhile Jesus reached out His hand to the vessel of wine before Him. He poured some into a cup; He added a little water, as was the custom at a feast. Again He went through the same ceremony. He took the double-handled cup in His hands; He raised His eyes to heaven; He cast them down again, and with His right hand blessed the cup and its contents. He put it to His own lips and tasted it; then, quietly, definitely, clearly for all to hear, He said:

'All of you drink of this
For this
Is my blood
Of the new testament
This is the chalice
The new testament
In my blood
Which shall be shed for many

> Unto remission of sins
> Amen I say to you
> I will not drink from henceforth
> Of this fruit of the vine
> Until that day
> When I shall drink it with you new
> In the kingdom of my Father.'

'All of you drink of this.' He was not content that one of them should be omitted, as none were to be omitted from the cups that had belonged to the Paschal feast. For now, definitely, the Old had passed away, and with that act the New had begun :

> 'This is my blood
> Of the new testament
> The new testament
> In my blood.'

The minds of those who heard Him could not but go back to that other scene, for it was familiar to them all ; that very night they were celebrating its memory :

> 'Then Moses took half of the blood
> And put it into bowls
> And the rest he poured upon the altar
> And taking the book of the covenant
> He read it in the hearing of the people
> And they said
> All things that the Lord hath spoken we will do
> We will be obedient
> And he took the blood
> And sprinkled it upon the people
> And he said
> This is the blood of the covenant
> Which the Lord hath made with you
> Concerning all these words.'
> Exodus xxiv, 6–8.

In blood the old covenant had been sealed. But their forefathers had long known that this covenant, and this blood-shedding, was only for a sign ; the day would come when there would be a new covenant, sealed with new blood, and this would bind them with God for ever and ever. So the prophet Jeremias had foretold :

'Behold the days shall come, saith the Lord, and I will

make a new covenant with the house of Israel, and with the
house of Juda. Not according to the covenant which I
made with their fathers, in the day that I took them by the
hand to bring them out of the land of Egypt : the covenant
which they made void, and I had dominion over them,
saith the Lord. But this shall be the covenant, that I will
make with the house of Israel, after those days, saith the
Lord : I will give my law in their bowels, and I will write it
in their heart, and I will be their God, and they shall be My
people. And they shall teach no more every man his
neighbour, and every man his brother saying : Know the
Lord ; for all shall know me, from the least of them even
to the greatest, saith the Lord : for I will forgive their
iniquity, and I will remember their sin no more.'

Jeremias xxxi, 31-34.

This, then, was what He was doing before them. The
ceremony of the old covenant had been performed ; He had
followed it up with a new commandment, He was sealing
that commandment with His blood which in some mystic
way was being shed for them. As he had done with the
bread, so now He handed the cup to Peter and John, that
they might drink of it and might pass it to the rest :

' And they all drank of it ' ;

the emphasis is full of significance, for as they drank they
knew that what they drank was more than it appeared :

' The bread that I will give
Is my flesh
For the life of the world
He that eateth my flesh
And drinketh my blood
Hath everlasting life
And I will raise him up in the last day
For my flesh is meat indeed
And my blood is drink indeed
He that eateth my flesh
And drinketh my blood
Abideth in me
And I in him
As the living Father hath sent me
And I live by the Father
So he that eateth me
The same also shall live by me.'

It was all now clear and certain ; in the midst of mystery it was certain :

> ' How can this man
> Give us his flesh
> To eat ? '

They did not know ; but what of that ? How had He made heaven and earth ? How had He raised the dead ? How had He won their hearts, so that to doubt His word, whatever He might say, was impossible ? Though the sun may be hidden in the clouds, none the less is its presence manifest in the daylight shed beneath it. Though the ultimate meaning of His words was lost in God, none the less was it manifest that what He said was true. They had eaten His flesh, they were drinking His blood, the blood of the New Testament. As the Father dwelt in Him He dwelt in them. It was the blood to be shed for many, the blood of the Lamb, the blood of the new sacrifice, the sealing blood of the new covenant made between God and man. Before them Jesus was performing His first act as the new High Priest :

> ' The priest for ever
> According to the order of Melchisedech.'

It was His last act in the old dispensation, His first act in the new ; the next time He would eat and drink with them it would be :
> ' In the kingdom of my Father ',

in the kingdom which, by then, He would have won.

He had given them the New Law, the Law, not of justice only but of love ; He had sealed it with His blood, and that blood He had given to them in a loving-cup. But He could not stop with that ; on this night of divine generosity there was yet more to be done. When Moses had announced the salvation of his people through the blood, he had said to them :

> ' And this day shall be for a memorial to you
> And you shall keep it a feast to the Lord
> In your generations
> With an everlasting observance.'
>   Exodus xii, 14.

And again :
> 'And it shall be as a sign in thy hand
> And as a memorial before thy eyes
> And that the law of the Lord be always in thy mouth
> For with a strong hand
> The Lord hath brought thee out of the land of Egypt.'
> Exodus xiii, 9.

In like manner this Lover of all men could not but look down the ages that were to come. Already He had said, in the synagogue at Capharnaum, that His flesh would be :
> 'For the life of the world' ;

now, when He gave His all, He could not but think of all for whom He gave it. Not for the Eleven only were this body and this blood to be sacrificed ; not by them only were they to be eaten and drunk. There were the others of the fold, His followers even then ; there were the centuries to succeed, of living men and women who would be to Him no less dear than those with whom He then lived. There was that body to be built up, of living men, in Him, through Him, made one by union with Him ; that body which would receive its life from Him, of which He was to be the Head. The mystery of that night was not a thing of time ; it was not a ceremony of that supper only ; it was, like Himself, 'yesterday, to-day, and for ever'.

Therefore for the sake of all mankind, He would give to these mortal men the power which they had just seen exercised. If in the Old Dispensation God had set apart men of His own choosing that they might offer the ancient sacrifices, He would do no less for the New. Thus had the Lord spoken to Moses :

> 'Take unto thee also Aaron thy brother
> With his sons
> From among the children of Israel
> That they may minister to me
> In the priest's office.'
> Exodus xxviii, 1.

And again of the Levites :
> 'And the Lord spoke to Moses saying
> Take the Levites
> Out of the midst of the children of Israel
> And thou shalt purify them

And Aaron shall offer the Levites
As a gift in the sight of the Lord
From the children of Israel
That they may serve in his ministry
And thou shalt set the Levites
In the sight of Abraham and his sons
And shalt consecrate them
Being offered to the Lord
And shalt separate them from the midst of the children of Israel
To be mine.'
Numbers viii, 5-14.

' These were they of whom the Law had said :
They shall be holy to their God
And shall not profane his name
For they offer the burnt offerings of the Lord
And the bread of their God
And therefore they shall be holy.'
Leviticus xxi, 6.

Indeed, what else had He been doing during these last three years but prepare these men for the consecration of this night ? He had resolved, out of His love, to remain for all time with men ; He would use His own as the means to draw Him to them. He had chosen them apart Himself; He had made them His Apostles, one He had made the Rock on which His Church would rise ; more than to any others He had given Himself to them. He had called them :

' The salt of the earth
The light of the world ' ;

He had bestowed on them the power of miracles, bidding them at the same time freely to give what they had freely received. He had told them that what they bound on earth should be bound in heaven ; and what they loosed on earth should be loosed in heaven : whatever else these fishermen of Galilee may have failed to understand in the teaching of their Master, they knew that they were destined for some tremendous mystery, they were destined to be the priests of Jesus Christ their Lord.

Now the moment had come. He had just offered the first sacrifice of the New Testament ; He had given Himself to these His own ; when He had spoken of His own miracles He had told them that 'greater than these things they would one day do.' Moreover, though He had given them so much, yet was He not satisfied. He must give them yet more ; they should have this power in addition ; He would put Himself a prisoner in their hands ; in their hands, and in the hands of their appointed successors, so long as man should need Him, which would be so long as man wept in the valley of this death. The cup had gone round ; all had drunk of it ; they were lost in the mystery of it all. In the silence, which was that of adoration, prayer in which words will not come, again He spoke :

'Do this
For a commemoration of me' :

and at the instant those simple men of Galilee had in their hands the awful power of the priesthood.

9. The Coming Failure of the Twelve.

It is scarcely possible to be certain of the sequence of events during the hours of the Last Supper. But for us here it is of little importance. More is it to our purpose to realize that all the details should have happened at one time ; that in the same hour in which one man, and he so chosen and so trusted, went out into the night to betray his Master unto death, his Master gave to all men His own body and blood to be their life ; that in the same hour in which Simon Peter vainly declared that he could not deny his Lord, and the rest that they would never desert Him, that same Lord crowned all His former acts of love towards them, and made them His first chosen priests. We look at the contrast and are amazed. We tell ourselves that no man could ever have invented such a story. And yet, while we look at it, and indignation almost makes us protest, we recognize again that it is only one more example, consistent with all the rest that we have learnt, of the impossible yet true paradox of Jesus Christ. None but He would have made such a return ; because it was He, at once the contradiction is explained. Nay more ; if read in the life of another we might have wondered whether it were true ; read in His life we see in it what is but to be expected. It is Jesus Christ, therefore does He act in this way ; with a love that not the greatest injury can break, nor can any closing of the doors prevent it from continuing to stand there and knock. We bow before Him, knowing He is faithful and true; what we see is only one more trait, in keeping with all the rest we know about Him; let men, let even His own, do with Him and to Him what they will, Jesus on His side will never fail them.

Thus we are compelled to reflect as we turn from the scene we have just witnessed to that which next occupies the minds of the Evangelists. It is as if they would say: So much did Jesus give, yet see the return that was made to Him! So overflowing was His love, yet see how that love was tried! And nevertheless, even though so tried, it endured. We are given to see the mind of Jesus Christ, as it were, at work; knowing beforehand the desertion He is about to suffer from His own yet refusing to blame the deserters, seeking excuse for them in the fulfilment of prophecy, since He can find it nowhere else, looking through the ordeal and beyond it to the Resurrection Day, when all would again be well. How often have we seen Him using precisely this same method of appeal to Himself, as if, in spite of every provocation, His love would insist on dictating mercy, on closing its eyes to the evil that was done, looking only to the hour when at last He could forgive and forget, and restore all things in Himself:

> ' And Jesus saith to them
> You will all be scandalized in my regard
> This night
> For it is written
> I will strike the shepherd
> And the sheep of the flock shall be dispersed
> But after I shall be risen again
> I will go before you into Galilee.'

He quoted the prophecy, as it were in their defence, but He did not quote the whole. There were in it other words referring to Himself, which could not but have been in His mind:

> ' And they shall say to him
> What are these wounds
> In the midst of thy hands?
> And he shall say
> With these I was wounded
> In the house of them that loved me

> Awake O sword against my shepherd
> And against the man that cleaveth to me
> Saith the Lord of hosts
> Strike the shepherd
> And the sheep shall be scattered
> And I will turn my hand to the little ones.'
>
> Zacharias xiii, 6–7.

The prophet had begun with this picture of ingratitude and failure and distress, but he had ended on another note. In spite of what men might do to the Saviour that was to come, all would yet be well :

> ' And I will bring the third part through the fire
> And I will try them as gold is tried
> They shall call on my name
> And I will hear them
> I will say
> Thou art my people
> And they shall say
> The Lord is my God.'
>
> Zacharias xiii, 9.

If the prophet could so turn mourning into hope, the heart of Jesus Christ could do no less ; in this hour of trial it would cling to any source of encouragement and relief. Therefore He added, for Himself as much as for them :

> ' But after I shall be risen again
> I will go before you into Galilee.'

But to the Eleven, even at this last hour, and in spite of many repetitions and warnings, all these were words that had no meaning. ' This night ! ' That after all the triumphs of this week He should so suddenly fail, was not possible ; that after all they had received at that table they should abandon Him, was not to be endured. He was speaking as He had often before spoken, He did not mean all He said, He wished only to stir the more in them their faith, their confidence, their love. Had He not done the same even with His own mother, when He had told her His hour was not yet come, and yet had rewarded her with His first miracle ? Or with the Ruler from Capharnaum, whose faith He questioned, yet healed his son at his request ? Or with the Syro-Phœnician woman near Tyre, whom He affected to disregard that He might reward her the more ?

Had He not called them men 'of little faith', at a moment when they were showing trust in Him, only because He would have from them faith and trust beyond limit. This time, then, at least they would show they could be trusted; whatever He might say they would respond by asserting their loyalty that nothing should shake.

So argued Simon Peter once more with himself. Poor Simon Peter! Not all the experience of the last three years had yet taught him. In the early days he had feared for himself when he had cried:

> 'Depart from me
> For I am a sinful man
> O Lord.'

But the years of success and trust, and the hope and promise of great things to come, had made him over-confident. As before, earlier that night, when he heard the warning concerning the traitor, his indignation was aroused. Then he had resented it that one of the Twelve should be declared disloyal; now he was told that not one but all of them, and that this very night, would take scandal because of their very Lord and Master, and would desert Him. He had tried them once before, and when others turned away they had stood by Him; why should they fail Him now? From Peroea He had led them into danger, and they had loyally followed, saying to one another:

> 'Let us go
> And die with him';

what was there to make them falter now? Surely this could never be. They were tried veterans by this time, and would stand firm; of himself at least, of Peter the Rock, this could never be said.

For the moment, as was his wont, Peter had forgotten the rebuke he had received when he had ventured to remonstrate before. He was occupied with his own thoughts, his own devotedness; as their leader he must set an example to the rest. Whatever others might do, he at least would never yield.

> 'Peter answering said to him
> Although all shall be scandalized in thee
> I will never be scandalized.'

At first Jesus seemed to ignore Simon Peter's impetuosity. He loved Peter, therefore He could let his contradiction pass ; in spite of all, He knew that Peter loved Him, and therefore in love He could speak to him. He would show Peter how much more he was loved and cared for than Peter himself suspected. In this once more we cannot fail to catch the hope that looks beyond, and by so doing hides from itself the agony that is to come between. Until He is compelled Jesus will not look at Peter the deserter, He will only consider the future leader of the flock :

> ' And the Lord said
> Simon Simon
> Behold Satan hath desired to have you
> That he may sift you as wheat
> But I have prayed for thee
> That thy faith fail not
> And thou being once converted
> Confirm thy brethren.'

So Jesus spoke to the man who was very soon to deny Him. There is not a word of blame, at most only pity ; the fault is laid at another door. The evil deed is passed over ; the future will see all put right, and with that He is content.

But Simon Peter thought nothing of all this. He had been bold, and had not been rebuked ; his boldness encouraged him to venture yet further. A few moments since, his Master had said that soon He would go where they could not follow ; Simon told himself that there should be no such place for him. Not only would he not desert, he would follow Jesus to the last. Once upon a time, it is true, he had said, in a moment of fear :

> ' Depart from me
> Because I am a sinful man
> O Lord ' ;

but he had shown a truer soul when in the storm he had cried :

> ' Lord
> If it be thou
> Bid me come to thee upon the waters ' ;

and the Lord had answered :

> ' Come.'

Since then, at another testing moment, Jesus had asked them :

> 'Will you also go away?'

and Peter had answered for them all :

> 'Lord
> To whom shall we go?
> Thou hast the words of eternal life.'

On that occasion, too, Jesus had been pleased with his devotion. Yet another time he had proclaimed his allegiance :

> 'Thou art the Christ
> The Son of the Living God';

and Jesus had blessed him for it ; nay, He had given him a name which of itself seemed to imply that he would never fail. Surely then he could be yet more daring. The Master had said that they could not follow Him ; whither could He lead where he, Simon Peter, could not follow? Had he not long since, on the road through Peroea, declared :

> 'We have left all
> And followed thee'?

and had not the Master promised them reward unmeasured in return? At least, then, he could dare to ask of Jesus an explanation :

> 'Simon Peter saith to him
> Lord
> Whither goest thou?'

He received an answer in keeping with all he had yet been told ; an answer that was no answer, yet in its mystery was more than sufficient :

> 'Jesus answered
> Whither I go
> Thou canst not follow me now
> But thou shalt follow me hereafter.'

For this was indeed what Simon wished to know. So is it in all answers to prayer. Too often 'we know not what we ask for when we pray', and in consequence the Lord seems at times not to hear us. We forget that He reads the heart that speaks beneath the words that are spoken, better far than it reads itself; and His answer, infallible and true, is to the heart, not always to the words it has uttered.

But Peter was not to be so easily set aside. He had much yet to learn; he did not yet know his own limitations. Why should he not, this time as well as any other, be able to follow where Jesus led? So far he had never failed. Jesus had once said, as a test:

> ' Come after me
> And I will make you fishers of men.'

This could only be another such test, a trial of his courage, and at that moment Peter thought he had courage for anything. He would show his Lord that now, as ever, he was constant. He would ask, he would offer himself, be the consequences what they might:

> ' Peter saith to him
> Why cannot I follow thee?
> I will lay down my life for thee
> Lord
> I am ready to go with thee
> Both into prison and to death.'

Poor, brave Peter! How easy is it to be brave when no danger is near us! How easy to be faithful when there is no temptation to desert, but only sweet attraction to draw us! But not in such a way may those be trained who are destined to guide others. For that end Peter must be allowed his lesson, which only a heavy fall would teach him. In the answer which Jesus gave him there is irony, there is resignation, there is even hope, there is no less affection; indeed love is the more expressed by the repetition of the name:

> ' Jesus answered and said to him
> Wilt thou lay down thy life for me?
> Amen Amen I say to thee
> Peter
> To-day even in this night
> Before the cock crow twice
> Thou shalt deny me thrice.'

'Peter!' Before He had said: 'Simon, Simon', now it was 'Peter!' Then, his ordinary name, now, when his fall is prophesied, he is called 'The Rock!' Such is the affectionate irony of Jesus Christ.

There is another thing to be noticed. That night Jesus had to deal with two offenders, Judas and Simon Peter.

Judas that night would betray Him but once, Peter would deny Him thrice. Judas had made no special protest of allegiance, Peter had declared his loyalty again and again. Judas had been entrusted merely with the common purse ; to Peter had been given the keys, the care of the Universal Church. And yet, after their fall, how differently they were treated ! Before a human court of justice Peter might well have received the greater condemnation ; in the eyes of Jesus his offence was condoned. For those eyes see beneath the surface, they distinguish sin from sin, malice from mere weakness, heart from heart, where human justice is blindfold. As they looked at these two, and beheld even their repentance, still they were not deceived. The one repented out of despair, the other, with all his weakness, had never ceased to love ; and Jesus knew the value of them both.

Indeed what was it but love, though it were love unbalanced, that blinded Simon Peter all that night, both to himself and to his Beloved's warning ? He knew he loved, and in his love, he thought he could brave all things :

'Greater love than this no man hath
That he lay down his life for his friends.'

So the Master would say before the night was over ; and Peter already had a like desire in his heart. Sitting in that supper room, with the body and blood of Jesus given to them, how could he but respond ! As for the warning, surely it was a warning only ; the best way to meet it was to confirm himself and his companions in their allegiance. He would go on protesting ; he would not think of weakness or surrender. We can see the tears in his eyes at the suggestion that his Master could so suspect him, after all they had gone through together :

'But he spoke the more vehemently
Although I should die together with thee
I will not deny thee
And in like manner said all the disciples.'

Jesus let them have their way. He had given them the warning, and from His side it was enough. He knew very well that after their manner they loved Him, and after their manner they wished to show it. It was a different affection, and a different manner, from that which had been shown to Him by the multitudes in Galilee. These men loved Him, at least they wished to love Him, even as He wished to be loved; and though that love would fail on trial, yet would it not die. It would rise again, it would rise again purified, taught by humiliation to know its own weakness, and then, when later the supreme trial came, it would not fail, they would not deny Him. Then they would keep their promise; they would go to prison and to death for Him:

> 'Rejoicing that they were accounted worthy
> To suffer reproach
> For the name of Jesus';
>
> Acts v, 41.

sealing their witness to Him with their blood. He would still be patient with them, as He had always been before; smoking flax He would not extinguish, it would yet burst into flame. He had chosen the weak things of the world to confound the strong; therefore, because they were weak, until they learnt their weakness and where their true strength lay, it became their Master and Lord to bear with them, at whatever cost to Himself.

He allowed them the last word, and changed the subject. The vision of their desertion had brought up before Him the whole scene as it would soon be enacted; and in that scene stood out another agony which it would be hard to bear. Judas, His friend, would betray Him; that was the first. His other friends would take scandal from Him and would desert Him; that was the second. Last, after all these months of labour and of miracles, men about Him would be persuaded that He was an evil-doer; that was the third. In the court of the Temple He had once cried, before His bitterest enemies:

> 'Which of you shall convince me of sin?'

and they had been compelled to acknowledge by their silence that there was no fault to be found in Him. Nevertheless, on this night, others besides His enemies would be led to believe that He was a malefactor, that He was 'as it were a thief', that He was certainly a deceiver. And they would treat Him as such; they would bind Him and hound Him away as a public danger:

> 'And with the wicked was he reckoned.'

The prophet had said it; it would come to pass; He would put nothing in the way to hinder it.

Yet how everything He had taught and practised belied that accusation! He looked back and recalled the instructions He had given to His own, when He first sent them out on their ministry:

> 'Go preach saying
> The kingdom of heaven is at hand
> Heal the sick
> Raise the dead
> Cleanse the lepers
> Cast out devils
> Freely have you received
> Freely give
> Do not possess gold nor silver
> Nor money in your purses
> Nor two coats nor shoes nor a staff
> For the workman is worthy of his meat.'

This was not the language of a thief, of a malefactor, of a common criminal, yet had He never deviated from it; with evidence such as this nothing could be said or done against Him. But He would allow His enemies something; for this occasion, if they wished to use it, He would give them a subject for complaint. He turned again to the group about Him:

> 'And he said to them
> When I sent you
> Without purse and scrip and shoes
> Did you want anything?
> But they said
> Nothing
> Then said he unto them
> But now he that hath a purse
> Let him take it
> And likewise a scrip
> And he that hath not
> Let him sell his coat and buy a sword
> For I say to you
> That this that is written must be fulfilled in me
> And with the wicked was he reckoned
> For the things concerning me have an end.'

This was indeed a new thing, utterly unlike anything they had heard before. Once, it is true, He had said that He had come, 'not to spread peace but a sword', but what He had meant was known to everyone. Far more commonly, and far more explicitly, had He insisted on submission, on yielding to those who abused them, and had declared them blessed if for the sake of His name they incurred that lot. But now He asked for a sword. Was He about to change His method? Had He at length come to understand that at night He was not safe in Jerusalem, and must take means for His protection? They had felt it all the time. Of late they had never come up with Him to the Holy City without some fear and anxiety; indeed some of them had taken precautions, not uncommon with men from Galilee, to have some weapon of defence about them in case of trouble. It was a short sword worn beneath the outer garment; none need ever know that they had it about them.

Now, to their surprise, Jesus asked them to come out with Him armed; then it would be well to tell Him how far they were prepared. They enquired among themselves; it was found that they had two swords among them. Peter possessed one; Peter who was prepared to go with his Master to prison and to death! There was one more among the rest; verily these conquerors of the world were armed to the teeth! The two put their hands upon their weapons; how ready they were to draw them, and fight for their Master and His kingdom, in that supper-room! They would let Him know they were ready; again they would show Him that, if He so willed it, they would follow Him to death:

'But they said
Lord
Behold here are two swords.'

Jesus showed no enthusiasm. He was told what sufficed for His purpose:

'And he said to them
It is enough';

and that chapter was closed.

10. Introduction to the Discourse.

From this point the language of Jesus at the Supper takes on another form. The second cloud had been dispelled, now He was entirely free, henceforth He could allow Himself to speak of that which was uppermost in His soul. He would still be deeply moved; He would speak with a certain disregard of order which comes of deep emotion, though, as we shall see, there was order enough in what He said; but it would be without any further hindrance. He had so much yet to say; His heart was very full; He would speak as the thoughts came uppermost.

He turned again, and looked upon the Eleven whom, long ago, He had chosen for Himself. He knew well what would soon happen; not only would these men be scandalized in Him, they would no longer have Him with them, that they might turn to Him as they had always done in their hours of distress. They would cry: 'Save us, we perish'; and He would be, not asleep, but dead. They would lose Him; their faith in Him, in spite of all the warnings with which He had prepared them, would be shaken to its very depths. The prospect of that, more for the moment than all the rest, hurt Him to the quick. At other times, when they had been in doubt, He had always come to the rescue; when they had not understood His parables, when their gift of miracles failed them; when they took alarm at the aggression of the scribes and Pharisees, when people of Samaria offered them insult, when they themselves were foolish. But now for three days they must be left alone, and that at a time when their distress would be as it had never been before. He must at least give them a reason for His going; He must renew His assurance that all would yet be well. Before the trouble came upon them, like a mother, He would comfort and prepare them; with reminders of His own fidelity, of which they could never have a doubt; with accounts of all that would come of the separation; with pictures of the joy and happiness that would be theirs when at last they met once more. Let us but join His next words with those that have been spoken before, and we shall wonder whether the most tender of mothers could show more understanding of a child in trouble:

' Little children
Yet a little while I am with you

> You shall seek me
> And shall not find me
> Let not your heart be troubled
> You believe in God
> Believe also in me
> In my Father's house there are many mansions
> If not I would have told you
> Because I go to prepare a place for you
> And if I shall go and prepare a place for you
> I will come again
> And take you to myself
> That where I am
> You also may be.'

But that is not the limit of the consolation and encouragement He would give to these His 'little children' before He put them on their trial :

> 'Knowing that the Father had given him all things
> Into his hands
> And that he cometh from God
> And goeth to God',

so John had written of Him at the beginning of this scene. In other places he writes in the same strain, giving us to understand that this simple truth is behind all else that he has to say. To that same truth Jesus now drew the attention of His own. He had taught it so often He might now assume it. They had asked Him whither He was going ; let them but recall what He had taught them, and they would be able to tell themselves. Hence, trying them, He continued :

> 'And whither I go you know
> And the way you know.'

He was interrupted ; with that intimacy which ever reigned between Him and them, even at the most solemn of moments, a disciple intervened. Objective, unimaginative Thomas could not understand. On the way up to Judæa, but a few months ago, when all foresaw danger for them in Jerusalem and they were afraid, he had stiffened their courage with the words :

> 'Let us go
> And die with him.'

Yes, but the very sentence betrayed a weakness in Thomas. Could such words be said to express that faith and trust in Jesus which most became His follower? Peter had believed and trusted so well that he could welcome suffering and death; and though this, too, was an excess, yet was it an excess of a better kind. Later, after the Resurrection, we are to hear again of the limited faith of Thomas, this practical man of affairs. He had no use for riddles, and Jesus now, surely, was speaking in riddles. They knew whither He was going? How could they know? They knew the way? If they did not know the goal how could they know the way?

> ' Thomas saith to him
> Lord
> We know not whither thou goest
> And how can we know the way? '

Again Jesus was patient. As He had been with the traitor, Judas, as He had been with the self-reliant Simon Peter, so now He would be with this exacting, literal-minded, obstinate Thomas. He would not be annoyed with him; He would not rebuke him. Peter He could rebuke with advantage to Peter; Thomas must needs be treated in another way. He would give him an answer, yet in such a form that Thomas would be made to recall much that he had learnt before. Thomas had said that they knew not whither Jesus was going; did he not know that he was going to the Father? He had said that they did not know the way; had Jesus not told them many times that the only way to the Father was through Himself?

> ' No one cometh to the Father
> But by me.'

He would sum it all up, for Thomas and for all the world to ponder in the ages to come; this is not the only time that we have to thank Thomas for the answer he drew from his Lord and God. Felix culpa!

> ' Jesus saith to him
> I am the way
> And the truth
> And the life
> No man cometh to the Father
> But by me

If you had known me
You would without doubt have known my Father also.'

Then, as if again He were crushing down His disappointment, as if, during that last hour, nothing should be permitted to oppress Him, He added for Himself and for them a word of hope :
'And from henceforth you shall know him
And you have seen him.'

Close to Thomas was Philip ; Philip the gentle, the meek one among them all, who in the first days had been just called, as Jesus passed him on the roadside, and he had promptly followed ; the most easily accessible among the Twelve, and therefore, it would sometimes seem, the second in authority ; Philip, who had patience for most things, and for most people, but little for questioners and critics when the Very Truth Himself was speaking. Philip believed, as simplicity believes, unquestioning ; he knew because he believed, not because he understood, and it was enough ; Philip had not much use for argument. Hence this question of Thomas troubled him. It was a needless interruption, and that it should come from one of his own special group among the Twelve added to his annoyance. He would remove this hindrance ; he would encourage Jesus to proceed ; with his usual desire to put matters right, he would show that they were not all like Thomas, doubting and mistrustful. Only let them see more clearly what He meant, whither He was going, and it would be enough for them all. Jesus had said that henceforth they should know the Father ; He had said that they had already seen Him. Philip did not doubt it ; Jesus had said it, and therefore it was true. But clearly the words had a sense not easily understood ; for who could see the Father and live ? Only let Jesus explain to them what He meant, and all would be well ; even Thomas would be content :
'Philip saith to him
Lord
Shew us the Father
And it is enough for us.'

Could Jesus have been disappointed with this simple and loving request of the simple and affectionate Philip ?

There was no arrogance in Philip, no over-confidence; if there was ignorance, and slowness to comprehend, it was only of the kind which he shared in common with the rest. In spite of the shadow of rebuke and disappointment in the answer Philip received, there is in it more understanding than complaint; if there was complaint, the use of Philip's name alone would show it was the complaint of love that was never satisfied :

> 'Jesus saith to him
> Have I been so long a time with you
> And have you not known me?
> Philip
> He that seeth me
> Seeth the Father also
> How sayest thou : Shew us the Father?
> Do you not believe
> That I am in the Father
> And the Father in me?
> The words that I speak to you
> I speak not of myself
> But the Father who abideth in me
> He doeth the works
> Believe you not
> That I am in the Father
> And the Father in me?
> Otherwise believe me for the very works' sake.'

No, it was not complaint, at least in the sense of finding fault; it was rather a touch of sadness after a long retrospection. At the end of all this time, and all this careful training, this was all they knew of Him! Expressed as it was in the Master's own words, it was only the refrain which had rung without ceasing in John's ears, from the beginning of his days of contemplation :

> ' He was in the world
> And the world was made by him
> And the world knew him not
> He came unto his own
> And his own received him not.'

In these words at the outset John had stated the thesis of his Gospel; and throughout he has done little more than let the pendulum swing to and fro, upwards to a recognition of Jesus here and there, with all the bounty that has followed, downwards again to a continuous rejection, to a lack of understanding even from those who knew Him best. Meanwhile between the two he has shown his Beloved Master standing, constant in Himself, unbeaten by any disappointment, appealing and appealing again to the evidence of men's own beliefs, to the evidence of reason, to the objective fact of Himself which could not be denied, never slackening in His efforts because of the turning away of men, waiting on for those who would not come, giving Himself to those who would, and yet even with these last hungrily dissatisfied, bidding them come ever nearer, bidding them see in Him ever more and more.

In this sense we are compelled to interpret all that Jesus said and did at this memorable Supper. His gifts are to be measured at the furthest extreme of love divine ; that none can doubt who has any sympathetic knowledge, not of this scene only, but of the four Gospels as a whole. The argument from Scripture is not an argument of words only, it is not even an argument of knowledge ; it is an argument of truth, and light, and life. We read the discourse given by S. John ; from beginning to end it is neither more nor less than a proof of the inability of human speech to express, not only the mysteries of God, but even the human heart of Jesus Christ, the Son of Man. We see in saints like S. Augustine, and S. Francis of Assisi, and S. Bonaventure, and S. Theresa, and S. John of the Cross, and S. Margaret Mary, vain efforts to express what they knew and felt ; in saints like S. Thomas Aquinas and S. Ignatius Loyola the pen laid down, refusing any further to attempt the impossible. S. John, as it were, comes between the two. He feels it his duty to record the efforts his Beloved, Jesus Christ, made that night to instruct His own, and to reveal Himself to them ; but he knows that what he writes is full of mystery, not only for those who heard the words but for all mankind. Jesus Christ loved so much that even He could not express His love in human speech ; He longed so much that even He could not express His longing. So vehement was His appeal, so pathetic His regret that He was not heard, so sublime His promises, so intimate His familiarity, so complete the union with Himself offered to any who would receive Him, that men have stood back appalled and hesitating. They have not dared to say that He exaggerated, that He was untrue; they have wondered whether they have heard Him aright, whether even the heart of Jesus Christ could love in the way His words implied. Once on a time in Capharnaum His own disciples said of Him:

> 'He is become mad.'

What must they have thought of Him this night, when He endeavoured to express and prove to them a love which no human being could ever hope to fathom?

CHAPTER IV

11. The Discourse at the Supper.

(a) *The True Life.*

'Amen, amen I say to you.'

FIVE times at least already in the course of this evening had Jesus made use of this solemn introduction. It was as if he had wished to begin a last discourse, a farewell address that would crown all He had said during His life of preaching, but had been unable to continue ; as if He had something momentous to say, but had been prevented from saying it. First, as we have seen, it had been the presence and memory of Judas and his treachery that had choked His words ; then it was the recollection of Simon Peter's coming denial, and of the desertion of the rest. But now at last He recovered. The time was pressing ; only a few hundred yards away, over the wall across the street, the enemy was already gathering his forces and He must delay no longer. In return for their treachery and denial He had given to His disciples Himself ; for the remainder of the evening He would find some relief in pouring out His very soul upon them, in giving and ever giving again, as if He would bribe them by His constant giving to give back to Him. 'Give, and it shall be given to you', had been one of the mottoes He had ever held up before them ; we may sometimes forget that it has been by His own excessive giving that He has induced mankind to give in its turn. Then at last, when these men had been won to give in the measure He gave, then would the union be perfect ; as perfect as the union between the Father and Himself. When that was secured, when love between them had so grown that each gave to the other all he had and all he was, then would He be able to crown the work He had begun. He would take them with Him, made truly one heart and one soul, and offer them along with Himself to the Father. We cannot hope to comprehend all that is contained in His words ; we can only let Him speak in His own language and listen, catching from them if we may some impression of Him who has so wished to reveal Himself.

'Amen, amen, I say to you, he that believeth in me, the works that I do he also shall do, and greater than these shall he do. Because I go to the Father; and whatsoever you shall ask the Father in my name, that will I do; that the Father may be glorified in the Son. If you shall ask me anything in my name, that I will do.'

'Believe in me, ask of me'; faith and trust; here are the foundations of the spiritual life, as Jesus at the end describes it. 'Believe in me, and you shall do great things, greater things than I have done; and if there is yet more needed, ask of me and I will do them for you.' All through His life He has striven to deepen these two lessons in His own. When a pagan Roman soldier has proved his faith, He has praised him for it, when a pagan woman of Phœnicia has clung to Him He has rewarded her confidence; but when His own have gone to Him with faith and trust surely no less, He has always asked for more and more. He has rewarded the Roman by healing his servant, the Phœnician by reviving her daughter, though He did not go to either; but from His own He has asked for a faith that would 'move mountains'; He would have it such that it would be a rock against which the gates of hell itself would not be able to prevail.

'If you love me, keep my commandments. And I will ask the Father: and he shall give you another Paraclete, that he may abide with you for ever: the spirit of truth, whom the world cannot receive, because it seeth him not, nor knoweth him.'

'Believe in me, trust me, love me'; here is the completion of the foundation He has just laid down. 'Love me, and prove that love by doing what I bid you, and all the rest will follow. I will do that rest. Standing before the Father,
'Ever living
To make intercession',

I will win for you another life, which shall never die:

'He that believeth in me
Hath everlasting life.'

For it shall be the life of the Spirit of God Himself, the Spirit which shall make you truly sons of God, which shall speak in you and with you, so that you shall cry with full right :

'Abba, Father.'

It shall be the Spirit that shall open your eyes that you may see, your understanding that you may know ; not as this world sees, with its blinding human limitations, but as all things are in the realm of utter truth, which is the realm, not of man, but of your Father, God. How often in the past had He lifted up their eyes to this greater vision !

' Greater things than these shalt thou see
Amen, amen I say to you
You shall see the heaven opened
And the angels of God ascending and descending
Upon the Son of man.'

John i, 50, 51.

' I will not leave you orphans, I will come to you. Yet a little while, and the world shall see me no more. But you shall see me : because I live, and you shall live. In that day you shall know that I am in the Father : and you in me, and I in you. He that hath my commandments and keepeth them : he it is that loveth me. And he that loveth me shall be loved of my Father : and I will love him, and will manifest myself to him.'

Faith, hope, love on the part of man ; and in return, union on the part of Jesus Christ and His Father. He had before laid down the foundations of the spiritual life, He had shown whence came its vivifying force, now He tells us of its consummation. He had come into the world and the world had seen Him, but it had not known Him. Soon it would put Him to death, and to the world accordingly He would henceforth be dead ; nevertheless to others He would live on, to those who had received Him, to whom He had ' given power to become sons of God ', and had ' believed in His name '. These would yet know Him and would see Him, if not with the eyes of this body, still with the certainty of faith ; they would see Him, and would know they were not mistaken, Jesus Christ truly Man, and at the same time Jesus Christ truly God, one with and in the Father. And as He was one with the Father, so would He be one with them. Faith, and hope, and love, giving all from their side, should have their reward, such a reward as

God alone could give, in love and union with Him, till they lived, no, not they, but He would live in them. Then indeed would they know, for living in them He would love in them; His love would be their love, and they would see what human eyes, human learning, would never bring them to see :

'His glory
The glory as it were of the only-begotten of the Father
Full of grace and truth.'

John i, 14.

'Judas saith to him, not the Iscariot : Lord, how is it that thou wilt manifest thyself to us, and not to the world ?'

On a memorable occasion, before the Feast of Tabernacles in the preceding year, we were told that Jesus had stayed behind in Galilee, and had declined to go up to Jerusalem with the rest, because He knew of a plot devised there to kill Him. We were told that His ' brethren ' urged Him to go that He might be manifested more to the world :

'And his brethren said to him
Pass from hence
And go into Judæa
That thy disciples also may see thy works
Which thou dost
For there is no man that doth anything in secret
But he himself seeketh to be known openly
If thou do these things
Manifest thyself to the world
For neither did his brethren believe in him.'

John vii, 3-5.

Now, in the middle of Our Lord's discourse, an echo of that same complaint is heard ; and it comes from Judas, 'not the Iscariot', but from him who has, as it would seem, described himself in his epistle as 'the brother of James' (Jude i, 1). Now James was 'the brother of the Lord', as many have accepted, and as has elsewhere been assumed. John has told us that the kinsfolk of Jesus did not believe in Him ; here was one who did believe, and had been chosen to be among the Twelve, yet was he beset with the same problem. He had headed the complaints of his kinsmen at home in their cottage in Nazareth ; with the rest of the Twelve he had waited for the manifestation. Now on a sudden he was told that it would be made, not to the world at large, which would soon see Jesus no more, but to one or two only. Judas could not understand ; indeed, could any of them understand ? Six weeks after the Resurrection we still hear them asking :

> ' Lord
> Wilt thou at this time
> Restore again the kingdom to Israel?'
>
> Acts i, 6.

Of Judas, or Jude, we know very little. Only this we know, that he was also called Thaddeus, or Lebbaeus, and both of these are diminutive or pet names. We know that when he wrote his epistle he could speak of his Master only as

> ' The only sovereign Ruler
> And our Lord Jesus Christ ',
>
> Jude i, 4 ;

and that then at least he had realized what the kingdom meant when he concluded :

> ' To the only God our Saviour
> Through Jesus Christ our Lord
> Be glory and magnificence
> Empire and power before all ages
> And now
> And for all ages of ages
> Amen.'
>
> Jude i, 25.

Jesus offered Judas no rebuke. He did not use his name in reply, as he had done with affection to Philip and Peter. He seemed to make him no answer ; yet in His words the answer was complete :

'Jesus answered and said to him : If anyone love me, he will keep my word. And my Father will love him : and we will come to him, and will make our abode with him. He that loveth me not keepeth not my words. And the word which you have received is not mine, but the Father's who sent me.'

Yes, it was indeed a sufficient answer. For the knowledge of Jesus Christ does not come merely by learning ; it comes, not from without but from within, not from study but from the heart, as does the knowledge of anyone we love. No one repeats this more than S. Augustine, who sought God everywhere, by every sort of study, and failed to find Him, until at last he sought and found Him within himself. The light is given; love makes us follow it and it leads us on to more. For love responds to love; the love of the Father to the creature's love, the coming of the Father and the Son to the coming of the creature even when he is yet 'a great way off'. They come to him; and all is known that the creature at that moment can know.

Jesus in His answer had said more than Judas or his companions could then have well understood. But the day would come when they would understand, and then all would be recalled. Let them wait as Jesus was Himself content to wait; let them trust Him as He had trusted them; let them not cease to love, however else they might be tried, for 'to them that love all things co-operate to good'.

'These things have I spoken to you, abiding with you. But the Paraclete, the Holy Ghost, whom the Father will send in my name, he will teach you all things, and bring all things to your mind, whatsoever I shall have said to you. Peace I leave with you: my peace I give unto you: not as the world giveth do I give unto you. Let not your heart be troubled; nor let it be afraid. You have heard that I said to you: I go away, and come unto you. If you loved me, you would indeed be glad, because I go to the Father. For the Father is greater than I. And now I have told you before it came to pass, that when it shall come to pass, you may believe.'

All through the evening we may notice what we may well call the concern of Jesus for His own, because of the trouble that must soon come to them on His account. Indeed, for months past, since the day of the Confession of Peter, He had been preparing them for it. He had warned them again and again of His coming suffering and death, but always He had added the assurance of His Resurrection and return. He had warned them even of their own desertion, but He had also promised that in the end all would be well. Now He gives them a further key, a sure source of all contentment. In Himself, if they will believe, and trust, and love, they will find a peace of mind and heart which nothing can destroy; a peace which will fear nothing, which will find in everything matter for thanksgiving, yes, even in the temporary separation from Himself. Before, He had told them how the life of the Spirit, founded on their own faith, and hope, and constant love, would lead to perfect union ; now He tells them how that same life, built on that same foundation, led to the glory of the cross. He had taught them the lesson many times before, but never with such tender and intimate affection as on this night.

It would seem that at this point John gives us the conclusion of the discourse. Judas Iscariot had long been gone ; Jesus knew that very soon he and his new followers would be on their way to take Him. He could, if He so chose, defy them now as He had defied them before, never more than during the early days of that very week. But this time He would surrender. It was His Father's will that His enemies should at last have their way ; in their victory men should later recognize His own crowning victory of love. Still He would not be taken there, in that supper-room hallowed by all that had been done in it that night. He would go elsewhere, and His captors should follow Him ; from the first scene to the last in the tragedy about to begin they should do His will, even while they did Him to death.

'I will not now speak many things to you : for the prince of this world cometh, and in me he hath not anything. But that the world may know that I love the Father, and as the Father hath given me commandment, so do I : arise, let us go hence.'

(b) *The Fruit of Life*.

With these words, as has just been said, S. John at first concluded his account of the discourse at the Last Supper. But there are several places in his Gospel where it appears evident that later, after he has written his first version, other matters have occurred to him to be put down, and these often of even greater value to us than what he has already written. Thus, at the end of his Gospel, he has added an account of an apparition which posterity could ill spare ; possibly the chapter which tells of the promise of the Holy Eucharist is another instance. The same, perhaps, has happened here. John has dwelt long and often on that unforgettable scene, and every time the promise of His Beloved has been the more fulfilled :

' The Holy Ghost
Whom the Father will send in my name

> He will teach you all things
> And bring all things to your mind
> Whatsoever I shall have said to you.'

Of all these memories there is one in particular which S. John is unwilling to omit : the parable of the Vine which Jesus spoke that evening. And once he has begun again, his pen runs on ; he traverses once more the whole field, confirming what he has already said, adding further visions of the truth, concluding at last with the prayer which crowns the whole of that evening's revelation.[1] It may have been that the eye of John had been caught by the vine growing along the poles beneath his window; or perhaps, as he read his Old Testament, the frequent use of the symbol of the vine by the prophets had brought this last illustration to his mind. It may have been that the image of the mystical body, of which S. Paul had made so much use, had recalled to him this other image, used by Jesus Himself to express the same or a parallel truth. Jesus, too, on that night, had noticed the vine growing in the courtyard beneath them, and, as was His wont, He had used the object before Him to express once more the essence of all He had to say to His beloved.

'I am the vine : and my Father is the husbandman. Every branch in me that beareth not fruit he will take away : and every one that beareth fruit he will purge it, that it may bring forth more fruit. Now you are clean, by reason of the word which I have spoken to you. Abide in me, and I in you. As the branch cannot bear fruit in itself unless it abide in the vine, so neither can you, unless you abide in me. I am the vine, you the branches ; he that abideth in me, and I in him, the same beareth much fruit : for without me you can do nothing. If any one abide not in me, he shall be cast forth as a branch, and shall wither : and they shall gather him up and cast him into the fire, and he burneth. If you abide in me, and my words abide in you, you shall ask whatever you will, and it shall be done unto you. In this is my Father glorified : that you bring forth very much fruit, and become my disciples.'

As we have said, the symbol of the vine was familiar to readers of the Old Testament ; it had often been on the

---

[1] This is the interpretation favoured by Lagrange, Durand, Lebreton, and several others.

lips of the prophets. But almost always it had been used by them in a special sense, as representing the chosen people; they were the vine which the Father had planted and cultivated, yet whose fruits had been so disappointing. Now suddenly this is changed. Not the chosen people, but Jesus Himself is the vine; the Father has planted Him, having rejected the other, as Jesus has said that He would in many recent parables. Jesus, the true vine, cannot fail the Father. And yet that it may bear fruit the vine must have its branches; without these the trunk, however living, will do nothing. And Jesus tells them this wonderful thing; the branches of the vine, from which the fruit is to come, are mortal men. Without the labour of men His own life will not bear the fruit it ought; on the other hand, without His life in them the labour of men will come to nothing. Not that the work of Jesus can be frustrated; His fruit will appear and will be manifested whether men refuse Him or not. Let them reject Him, and like dead twigs they will be cut off and cast away; but the vine will still live on, new branches will ever appear and bear fruit, others will ever be found to make up what is wanting, and to bring the work of Jesus Christ to fruition.

This, then, is a further step in the explanation of the spiritual life in the mind of Christ Our Lord. Faith in Him, trust in Him, love of Him, union with Him as their reward, sorrow turned to joy because of Him, these were the life itself in its root and its growth; they were the life as seen in prayer, in the contemplative. Now, as a result, we are given the glorious fruit of the apostolate, and that, not from any action, not from preaching, not from work, but wholly from union with Him:

> 'He that abideth in me
> And I in him
> The same beareth much fruit
> For without me you can do nothing.'

These are the material for the making of a saint, this, in its cause and in its effects, is Our Lord's own definition of sanctity. And how intimate is the union His words imply! For the life of the vine is the life of the branches, the branches are not to be distinguished from the vine. So the life of which He speaks is the life of Jesus; its fruit is such as only that life can produce and no other; man of himself cannot produce it. Yet is it produced through the medium of men, the sap, the life of Jesus passing through them. Let us explain the declaration as we may, if the words of Jesus are to have any meaning at all, there is a solemn truth and not mere metaphor in the cry of the Apostle :

> ' I live
> Now not I
> But Christ liveth in me.'

The vine and its branches, one, the body and its members, one, the fire in the heated iron, the sun in the burning ray, the wax and the stamp upon it, the drop of water lost in the cup of wine—in many ways have those endeavoured to describe it who have best understood, and realized in themselves, the union of which Jesus speaks. All alike take up His words and echo them down the ages ; all alike strain human language to express the truth which they know. The secret of sanctity is union with Christ ; the secret of the apostolate is union with Christ ; the secret of prayer is union with Christ ; the secret that alone can save mankind from withering is union with Jesus Christ. Only by union with Him can the Father be glorified, can His work on earth be done, can the fruit of the Incarnation and Redemption be spread across the world :

> ' In this is my Father glorified
> That you bring forth very much fruit
> And become my disciples.'

Thus in the symbol of the vine and the branches Jesus has reached the full teaching of the union He seeks between Himself and His beloved man. But on that very account this is the only place in the whole discourse at the Supper where there is heard a threatening word. Treachery, denial, desertion had drawn from Him warning and no more ; making light of His love, rejection of Him, these evoke the only condemnation He allows Himself to utter :

> ' If anyone abide not in me
> He shall be cast forth as a branch
> And shall wither
> And they shall gather him up
> And cast him into the fire
> And he burneth.'

But at once, as always when He warns and threatens, there comes the reaction. He will not dwell on the failure of men; instead He will bribe them, He will draw them to Himself, win them by His own love to love Him in return, join His own happiness with theirs, show them how all the joy and glory of the world is linked up with that heroism, that sacrifice of man for man, which He alone can inspire.

'As the Father hath loved me, I also have loved you; abide in my love. If you keep my commandments, you shall abide in my love: as I also have kept my Father's commandments, and do abide in his love. These things have I spoken to you, that my joy may be in you, and your joy may be filled. This is my commandment, that you love one another, as I have loved you. Greater love than this no man hath, that a man lay down his life for his friends. You are my friends if you do the things that I have commanded you.'

How deeply this call to heroism sank into the minds of those who heard it may be judged from all that followed. The Acts of the Apostles ring with its echo:

> 'And they indeed went from the presence of the council
> Rejoicing that they were accounted worthy
> To suffer reproach
> For the name of Jesus.'
>   Acts v, 41.

S. Paul is full of the same:

> 'The charity of Christ presseth us
> And Christ died for all
> That they also who live
> May not now live to themselves
> But unto him who died for them
> And rose again.'
>   2 Corinthians v, 14, 15.

To his suffering children about him S. Peter repeats the same exhortation:

> 'For this is thankworthy
> If for conscience towards God
> A man endure sorrows
> Suffering wrongfully
> For unto this are you called
> Because Christ also suffered for us

>   Leaving you an example
>   That you should follow his steps.'
>
>   1 Peter ii, 19-21.

And S. John himself comes back to the same exhortation:
> ' In this we have known the charity of God
>   Because he hath laid down his life
>   For us
>   And we ought to lay down our lives
>   For the brethren.'
>
>   1 John iii, 16.

In this way did Jesus draw His followers on to heroism by the example of His own heroic love. It was the climax of His teaching; begun when He told them on the mountain above Capharnaum that they were blessed who suffered persecution; continued when He set it, as a standard of life, that if any man would come after Him he must take up his daily cross; confirmed when He bade them take His yoke upon them, and learn of Him, because He was meek and humble of heart. But He would press His appeal yet further. He had given them His love as an incentive and a standard for their love. He would now remind them that He had a further claim upon them, for they were of His own special choosing. In the early days they had come to Him and had called Him ' Master ', and the title had remained with Him ever since. At the beginning of the Supper He had reminded them that the title was His by right, yet by washing their feet He had shown them how He would interpret it. But in return He had not called them, nor would He now call them, what a Master had a right to call those beneath him. He had not treated them as His servants; He had treated them always as His equals, He had always called them His friends. He had befriended them when others criticized, He had chosen them apart from others, He had given them their mission: what return should they make to their Lord for all He had bestowed upon them? So winningly, then and always, does Jesus Christ lead on His own.

' I will not call you servants: for the servant knoweth not what the master doeth: but I have called you friends, because all things whatsoever I have heard from my Father I have made known to you. You have not chosen me, but I have chosen you; and I have appointed you, that you should go, and should bring forth fruit, and your fruit should remain : that whatsoever you may ask of the Father in my name, he may give it to you. These things I command you, that you love one another.'

(c) *The Sacrifice of Life.*

And now, having thus prepared them, by His own example, by His friendship, by His winning of their love in return, He does not hesitate to tell them what will come. He has said it on other occasions, but never so plainly as now ; yet He tempers the bitterness for them by placing Himself, as it were, in their midst, in suffering at least He will always be with them.

'If the world hate you, know ye that it hath hated me before you. If you had been of the world, the world would love its own : but because you are not of the world, but I have chosen you out of the world, therefore the world hateth you. Remember the word that I said to you : The servant is not greater than his master. If they have persecuted me, they will also persecute you. If they have kept my word, they will keep yours also. But all these things they will do to you for my name's sake : because they know not him that sent me. If I had not come and spoken to them, they would not have sin : but now they have no excuse for their sin : but now they have both seen and hated both me and my Father. But that the word may be fulfilled which is written in their law : They have hated me without cause. But when the Paraclete cometh, whom I will send you from the Father, he shall give testimony of me. And you shall give testimony, because you are with me from the beginning.'

In language so clear Jesus foretold the history of His own, a prophecy which has been fulfilled in every generation. From the beginning it had been His own lot. The place of His birth had been deluged with innocent blood on His account ; when He first came forth to claim His kingdom, the war had been declared between Himself and the powers of darkness :

' The Lord thy God shalt thou adore
Him only shalt thou serve.'

The world may affect to ignore the name of Jesus Christ ; but the very ignoring is in itself opposition, and when the day of testing comes it is soon seen who are and who are not with Him :

> 'He who is not with me
> Is against me
> And he who gathereth not with me
> Scattereth.'

Jesus Christ has come, and His coming cannot be ignored. He must be heard or He must be refused a hearing. He must be accepted or rejected, in the end He must be hated or loved, witnessed to or denied. It can never be again the same for mankind ; man cannot any longer return even to the paganism from which He rescued it. For if it does endeavour to return, it will be to a paganism which will include an element which was not there before ; a new hatred of Jesus Christ, and with it a hatred of God Himself :

> 'He that hateth me
> Hateth my Father also.'

And yet this was not the worst. Hatred from the world was and is to be expected ; but the time would come when persecution would vent itself upon them, not only from the world outside, but also from within, in the name and service of God Himself. In the name of religion Jesus would Himself be put to death ; three times at least in His life we have heard of those who dared not follow Him because of this persecution. Of all terrors and anxieties there was none His disciples feared more than that they should be cast out by their own people. Yet this, too, was to come. They would be driven forth, they would be declared enemies of their nation and its ancient faith, they would die the shameful death that belongs only to traitors ; all this would be written of them in the history of the world, as such posterity would read of them :

'These things I have spoken to you that you may not be scandalized. They will put you out of the synagogues : yea, the hour cometh, that whosoever killeth you will think that he doth a service to God. And these things they will do to you, because they have not known the Father nor me. But these things I have told you, that when the hour shall come you may remember that I have told you of them.'

The prophecy again was clear, and detailed, and unmistakable. In the past, warnings such as this had stirred, among His own, fears and doubts and questions; they could not but stir them again now. Therefore, at once, having said what had to be said, He sets Himself to answer their questions, to remove their doubts, to fill them with new courage, knowing that in spite of all these things the victory would in the end be theirs. He spoke as a tender physician; He pleaded that they should still trust Him, though He seemed to desert them, though He seemed to inflict needless suffering; on this theme, as He comes to the end of His discourse, He rises to that eloquence which we have so often heard when He has been greatly moved.

'But I told you not these things from the beginning, because I was with you. And now I go to Him that sent me; and none of you ask me: whither goest thou? But because I have spoken these things to you, sorrow hath filled your hearts. But I tell you the truth: it is expedient to you that I go. For if I go not, the Paraclete will not come to you: but if I go, I will send him to you. And when he is come, he will convince the world of sin, and of justice, and of judgment. Of sin: because they believed not in me. And of justice: because I go to the Father, and you shall see me no more. And of judgment: because the prince of this world is already judged. I have yet many things to say to you: but you cannot bear them now. But when he, the Spirit of truth, is come, he will teach you all truth. For he will not speak of himself, but whatsoever things he shall hear he shall speak. And the things that are to come he shall show you. He shall glorify me: because he shall receive of mine and show it to you. All things whatsoever the Father hath are mine. Therefore I said that he shall receive of mine, and shall show it to you. A little while, and now you shall not see me: and again a little while, and you shall see me: because I go to the Father.'

We cannot but be impressed by this renewed reminder of the coming separation. Already at the Feast of Tabernacles, five months before, Jesus had given the same warning to the Jewish people in the Temple Court, and His words had stirred much comment among those who heard Him:

'The Jews therefore said among themselves
Whither will he go

> That we shall not find him?
> Will he go to the dispersed among the Gentiles
> And teach the Gentiles?
> What is this saying that he has said
> You shall seek me
> And shall not find me
> And where I am
> You cannot come?'

John had simply recorded the event and made no comment: it would seem that Jesus Himself had left the Jews in mystery. Now, during the Supper, Jesus for the second time comes back to the same theme. Already after Judas had gone out, John has told us of the warning:

> ' Little children
> Yet a little while I am with you
> You shall seek me
> And as I said to the Jews
> Whither I go you cannot come
> So now I say to you.'

The solemn renewed warning had roused again the anxiety of Simon Peter, and he had asked:

> ' Lord
> Whither goest thou?'

And Jesus had answered him:

> ' Whither I go
> Thou canst not follow me now
> But thou shalt follow hereafter.'

To which Peter had protested:

> ' Why cannot I follow thee now?
> I will lay down my life for thee.'

Almost immediately afterwards we are told that Jesus had repeated:

> ' If I shall go
> And prepare a place for you
> I will come again
> And will take you to myself
> That where I am
> You also may be
> And whither I go you know
> And the way you know.'

This time it was Thomas who asked :
> ' Lord
> We know not whither thou goest
> And how can we know the way ? '

And Jesus had replied :
> ' I am the way and the truth and the life
> No man cometh to the Father
> But by me ' ;

and again had the warning been repeated :
> ' Yet a little while
> And the world seeth me no more
> But you see me
> Because I live
> And you also shall live.'

Now at the end the same warning is given once more ; evidently it had made a deep impression on the disciple whom Jesus loved. Jesus, whose ' delights were to be with the children of men ', knew full well what this separation would mean, even for a day. These men, who had been drawn about Him from the beginning, and had become bound to Him by so many ties, who had learnt to lean upon Him as an infallible support, who had left all things and followed Him, so that now they had nothing else on which they could rely, were nevertheless to be left for three dark days alone. In the same way in His boyhood He had left His mother and His foster-father, so that even she had been compelled to ask :
> ' Son
> Why hast thou done so to us ?
> Behold thy father and I
> Have sought thee sorrowing ' ;

and though she received an answer to her question we are told :
> ' And they understood not the word
> That he spoke to them.'

Is not this the crowning lesson of the teaching on the spiritual life which we have heard during the whole of this evening's discourse ? And because it is the crowning test, is that not the reason why Jesus has repeated it, and why to John the mystic it has meant so much ? Jesus had begun with faith, and love, and trust as the foundation. He had gone on to union as its first reward. With union He had led to joy in suffering; and now, as the extreme of this, He warned His own of that 'dark night of the soul', that sense of separation from Himself, when faith, and hope, and love would be tried as they could be tried in no other way, when union would seem to be a myth because He was not present, when suffering would be doubled because He was not there to share it, when life itself, natural and supernatural, would appear to have lost all meaning. Again and again in the lives of the mystic saints we read of this greatest of all trials. In the lives of those who make no claim to be saints or mystics the same trial comes in its own way; when prayer becomes a blank, when the supernatural goes behind a cloud, when the soul asks questions which it cannot answer, when it is tempted to complain to God that it has been left alone.

(d) *The Reward.*
Against this crisis Jesus would prepare His own, then and for always. Later, in the Garden and on Calvary, He would give them proof that even He would go through the same sense of dereliction; for the present they should have an assurance that would carry them through any assault. He paused in His discourse; He allowed the group about Him to talk among themselves, and what they said gave Him the means to comfort them.

'Then some of his disciples said to one another: What is this that he saith to us: A little while, and you shall not see me; and again a little while, and you shall see me: and, Because I go to the Father? They said therefore: What is this that he saith: A little while? We know not what he speaketh.

And Jesus knew that they had a mind to ask him. And he saith to them: Of this do you enquire among yourselves, because I said: A little while, and you shall not see me; and again a little while, and you shall see me?

Amen, amen I say to you, that you shall lament and weep, but the world shall rejoice: and you shall be made sorrowful, but your sorrow shall be turned into joy. A woman when she is in labour hath sorrow, because her hour is come: but when she hath brought forth the child, she remembereth no more the anguish, for joy that a man is born into the world. So also you now indeed have sorrow : but I will see you again, and your heart shall rejoice, and your joy no man shall take from you.'

This is the reward of the dark night, a joy passing human understanding, beyond the power of anything in this world to destroy, which 'eye hath not seen, nor ear heard, neither hath it entered into the heart of man to conceive', that 'anticipation of heaven' of which S. Thomas Aquinas speaks. But it is not all. The dark night is not only followed by a morning; it is also followed by strength, such as was not there before. The soul that has passed through the dark night is a soul powerful in prayer, powerful in vision, powerful in experience, powerful in petition before God the Father.

'And in that day you shall not ask me anything. Amen, amen I say to you : if you ask the Father anything in my name, he will give it to you. Hitherto you have not asked anything in my name. Ask, and you shall receive : that your joy may be full. These things I have spoken to you in proverbs. The hour cometh when I shall no more speak to you in proverbs, but will show you plainly of the Father. In that day you shall ask in my name : and I say not to you, that I will ask the Father for you : for the Father himself loveth you : because you have loved me, and have believed that I came out from God.'

Hence Jesus concludes, as if He would sum up His whole life and its purpose in a single sentence :

> 'I came forth from the Father
> And am come into the world
> Again I leave the world
> And I go to the Father';

and there, as the Apostle reminds us :

> 'He continueth for ever
> An everlasting priesthood
> Whereby he is able also to save for ever
> Them that come to God by him
> Ever living
> To make intercession for us.'
>   Hebrews vii, 24, 25.

We have noticed already how the language of Jesus rises to eloquence as He comes to the end of His discourse ;

in imagery, in concreteness, in vehemence of appeal, it is the language of Him who spoke 'as one having authority'. And as at the end of the Sermon on the Mount,

> 'It came to pass
> When Jesus had fully ended these words
> The people were in admiration at his doctrine',

so now at the Supper His beloved Eleven were carried out of themselves in wonder and delight. Hitherto, all during the night, they had only asked questions; they had been told that they did not understand, and would not till later. Now a vision had been given to them; they had been given an insight into that world where

> 'There shall be no curse any more
> But the throne of God and of the Lamb shall be in it
> And his servants shall serve him
> And night shall be no more
> And they shall not need the light of the lamp
> Nor the light of the sun
> Because the Lord God shall enlighten them
> And they shall reign for ever and ever.'
> Apocalypse xxii, 3-5.

12. The Promise of the Holy Ghost.

During the discourse of Our Lord at the Last Supper one new doctrine, if indeed it may be called new, was repeatedly impressed on His disciples; the doctrine of the Coming of the Paraclete, the Holy Ghost. In the teaching of this new doctrine one thing is markedly evident. The Coming of the Holy Ghost is specially for the Twelve; for them first, and then for their followers. What the Holy Ghost, when He comes, will give, will be peculiarly theirs, and will belong to no other. When He has come, and has worked His full effect, the man who receives Him will be made another creature, seeing more, understanding more, able to do, and to endure more, than ever he could have done without Him. In the light and strength given by the Holy Ghost the whole perspective, and horizon, and goal of life will be transformed; it will be set upon another plane. In other words, nowhere more than here has Jesus Christ Our Lord explicitly revealed and sanctioned all that the Church has since elaborated in her doctrine of sanctifying grace, and indeed in her whole system of supernatural theology.

What is this new doctrine which Jesus gives us of the Paraclete, so far as it is new? He explains it to His Apostles in four successive stages.

(a) *The Spirit of Truth.*

Early in the evening of the Supper, Thomas and Philip had put questions and had been given their answers, in which Jesus had appealed to them to realize the union that existed between Him and the Father. He had told them that to know the One was to know the Other, to see the One was to see the Other, to love the One was to love the Other, to reject the One was also to reject the Other, as He had said many times already to the Jewish elders in the Temple. Then He reverted to the main theme of His discourse:

'If you love me
Keep my commandments'

and, as if in reward for doing so, or as if this were a natural consequence, He immediately went on:

'And I will ask the Father
And he shall give you another Paraclete
That he may abide with you for ever
The spirit of truth
Whom the world cannot receive
Because it seeth him not
Nor knoweth him
But you shall know him
Because he shall abide with you
And shall be in you.'

Thus from the outset it is made clear that the first condition for the life of grace, for the coming of the Holy Ghost, is the acceptance and personal love of Jesus Christ Himself; and the proof of that love is the doing of His will:

'If you love me
Keep my commandments.'

In return for that love, and for the service of love that follows it, He who is
'Ever living
To make intercession for us'

will, with His infallible power of prayer, intercede for us with the Father, and will infallibly be heard :

> 'And I will ask the Father
> And he shall give you another Paraclete
> That he may abide with you
> For ever.'

There shall be given to men who love and follow Him another Person, One not liable to death as He who speaks, One from whom there will be no separation, but whom, once He has come, we may have as our abiding companion, our Paraclete, our Intercessor, always. This Person, this Paraclete, this Spirit, real and individual even as Himself, is described as

> 'The Spirit of truth
> Whom the world cannot receive
> Because it seeth him not
> Nor knoweth him
> But you shall know him
> Because he shall abide with you
> And shall be in you.'

He is the essence of all truth, and reality, and transparent sincerity, in contrast with the surface appearance, and shallow seeming, and groping ignorance, which is the best this world has to offer. Men look across this world, and they see nothing beyond it; they judge by the standards of this world, and reach no further; they are hemmed in by this narrow horizon, and cannot recognize that all their estimates and judgments are made on a limited and therefore a doubtful plane. But the knowledge, and love, and following of Jesus Christ carry man beyond his prison wall, and set his vision along a new perspective, even the perspective of the infinite. The effort to do His will beyond all other will, especially his own, sets him in a new order, along which he may obtain a nobler goal of being. The Spirit of Truth responds to, fosters, that vision and that effort; He lifts man's mind and heart out of the bondage of this nature, into a sphere that is entirely new. The Spirit of Truth is a living Spirit, as living as Jesus Himself; He lives with man, He lives in man, He speaks to man, and in return accepts and interprets man's stammering words when he endeavours to speak of the Infinite, his Companion, his Guide, his Instructor, for ever at his side and in his heart.

> ' For the Spirit searcheth all things
> Yea the deep things of God
> For what man knoweth the things of a man
> But the spirit of a man that is in him ?
> So the things also that are of God no man knoweth
> But the Spirit of God
> Now we have received not the spirit of this world
> But the Spirit that is of God
> That we may know the things that are given to us
> From God.'
> 1 Corinthians ii, 11, 12.

(b) *The Infallible Spirit.*

Such is the first introduction of the Holy Ghost, the Paraclete. He is the Spirit of Truth beyond every other, who will abide with His own for ever. A little later in the Discourse Jesus gives His disciples more. In the first place He had simply said :

> ' If you love me
> Keep my commandments ',

and in return the promise had followed. Now He expands the form of His appeal :

> ' If any man love me
> He will keep my word
> And my Father will love him
> And we will come to him
> And will make our abode with him ' ;

and at once, as if the two were inevitably connected, the promise is likewise expanded :

> ' These things have I spoken to you
> Abiding with you
> But the Paraclete
> The Holy Ghost
> Whom the Father will send
> In my name
> He will teach you all things
> And bring all things to your mind
> Whatsoever I shall have said to you.'

The Spirit of Truth is real, is present, is abiding ; by His presence He opens up a new horizon, a new life, to those who can and will receive Him ; thus much we have already been told. Now we hear of a special, an all-important function which He will perform for all time. For the Twelve had been chosen,

> ' That they should be with him
> And that he might send them to preach ',
>
> Mark iii, 14,

and the day would come when He would extend that commission :

> ' Go ye into the whole world
> And preach the Gospel to every creature.'
>
> Mark xvi, 15.

They were to preach with an authority, an infallibility, equal to His own :

> ' He that heareth you
> Heareth me
> And he that despiseth you
> Despiseth me
> And he that despiseth me
> Despiseth him that sent me.'
>
> Luke x, 16.

and this for a very plain reason :

> ' For it is not you that speak
> But the Spirit of your Father
> That speaketh in you.'
>
> Matthew x, 20.

To the Twelve, then, had been given, or was to be given, the commission to teach whatsoever He had taught them to ' all nations ', not only to this nation or that. There was to be nothing national or circumscribed in their mission ; it was to be for all the world alike. That they should receive the teaching aright, that they should hand it on to their successors untarnished, could not but have been a matter of deep moment to the Twelve ; how deeply they cherished it, how they clung to the truth of their tradition, may be seen in the epistles of S. Peter, S. Paul, and S. John. In those first days, having as yet, as they thought, only their human light to guide them, they must often have wondered, and discussed among themselves, how they could keep it all in mind. They would ask themselves how they could be sure they understood aright, for often enough they were bewildered, how they could hand it on, unspoilt by anything of their own, to those who would come after them, and had not had the advantage of having known the Lord. There was so much they had not understood, and yet had not ventured to enquire; so much they had mistaken and He had been obliged to correct them; so much they had ignored and set aside, so much they had already forgotten. Often enough He had complained to them that they did not see, that they were 'without understanding', that they had not yet known Him, that they were slow of heart to believe. Moreover, when their turn for teaching came, when they came into contact with men of learning and experience, with subtle Pharisees, and learned scribes, and practised exponents of the Law, how could they hope to speak as Jesus spoke, 'with authority', or teach without a flaw, or a compromise, or a surrender, what He had entrusted to them?

Such thoughts and fears, human and natural, must often have made them wonder; now they are given an assurance which would allay all their doubts. On a former occasion, when He had first sent them out with a commission to teach, He had looked far into the distant future and had encouraged them:

> 'When they shall deliver you up
> Take no thought how or what to speak
> For it shall be given you in that hour
> What to speak
> For it is not you that speak
> But the Spirit of your Father that speaketh in you.'
> Matthew x, 19, 20.

Or as another Evangelist puts it:

> 'And when they shall bring you into the synagogues
> And to the magistrates and powers
> Be not solicitous
> How or what you shall answer
> Or what you shall say
> For the Holy Ghost shall teach you
> In the same hour
> What you must say.'
> Luke xii, 11-12.

But now they are assured of much more. The Paraclete, the Spirit of Truth, will always be with them. He Himself will teach them; He will help them to remember; He will see to it that nothing essential is forgotten, or misinterpreted, or falsely taught, by those whom Jesus has chosen, and who 'love Him and keep His word'. In the first promise we have been given the foundations of the spiritual life, the Holy Ghost living in the soul; here we are given the foundations of the Church, the Holy Spirit living in its members, making all one, speaking with that infallible voice which is His own.

(c) *The Witness to Jesus.*

A third time He comes back to the same subject. It is after the long lesson on the union of His disciples with Himself, even as is the union of the branches with the vine, with all its life-saving effects. At the end of that vivid passage He speaks, by contrast, of the world which is separated from Him, which hates Him. There He says:

'If I had not done among them
The works which no other man hath done
They would not have sin
But now they have both seen and hated
Both me and my Father
But that the word may be fulfilled
Which is written in their law
They hated me without cause.'

Here once more we find Jesus seeking excuse for those who hated Him, finding that excuse in the fulfilment of prophecy. More than once, when He has used the Psalms for His prayer, the refrain has recurred, and He cannot but recall it now:

'Consider my enemies for they are multiplied
And have hated me with an unjust hatred.'
                    Psalm xxiv, 19.

'Let not them that are my enemies
Wrongfully rejoice over me
Who have hated me without cause
And wink with the eyes.'
                    Psalm xxxiv, 19.

They are multiplied above the hairs of my head
Who hate me without cause.'
                    Psalm lxviii, 5.

Then as it were in answer to this unfounded hatred, He proceeds :

> 'But when the Paraclete cometh
> Whom I will send you from the Father
> The Spirit of truth
> Who proceedeth from the Father
> He will give testimony of me
> And you shall give testimony
> Because you are with me from the beginning.'

This, then, is the third function of the Spirit of Truth that is to come. First, He will live in them, and will open their understanding and their hearts, so that they will be other creatures; they will live, now not they, but He will live in them. Next, He will bring back to their minds all that has been taught them; with His help they shall not forget or misinterpret, they shall be infallible. Now in the third place, through them to the world outside that does not know Jesus Christ, and therefore 'without cause' hates Him, the Holy Spirit will provide the evidence for that same Jesus Christ, for all men to see who will. Jesus Christ that was, and Jesus Christ that is, the historic Christ, and the Christ of history, Jesus Christ who died, and rose again, and dieth no more,

> 'Jesus Christ
> Yesterday, to-day and the same for ever',

—to all this the Spirit of Truth shall give witness. The world may hate Jesus Christ and the Father, but the Holy Spirit, the Spirit of Truth, will give to all, friends and enemies alike, proof beyond doubt of the reality of both. Nay more, to His own He will give the means by which they, too, may bear witness; that witness which all the world, either by love or hatred, by accepting it or persecuting it unto death, will be compelled to acknowledge.

(d) *The Comforter.*

Lastly, in a fourth place, Jesus sums up all He has said. He must leave His Twelve alone; He must reconcile them to the parting; He finds a means to reconcile them in the good that will come to them from the separation :

> 'I tell you the truth
> **It is expedient for you that I go**

> For if I go not
> The Paraclete will not come to you
> But if I go
> I will send him to you
> And when he is come
> He will convince the world
> Of sin and of justice and of judgment
> Of sin
> Because they believed not in me
> And of justice
> Because I go to the Father
> And you shall see me no longer
> And of judgment
> Because the prince of this world is already judged
> I have yet many things to say to you
> But you cannot bear them now
> But when he the Spirit of truth is come
> He will teach you all truth
> For he shall not speak of himself
> But what things soever he shall hear
> He shall speak
> And the things that are to come
> He shall show you
> He shall glorify me
> Because he shall receive of mine
> And shall show it to you
> All things whatsoever the Father hath
> Are mine
> Therefore I said
> That he shall receive of mine
> And show it to you.'

Immediately before this fourth assurance Jesus had spoken in detail of what would one day come to His beloved Twelve because of the hatred of the world.

> They will put you out of the synagogues
> Yea the hour cometh
> That whosoever killeth you
> Will think that he doeth a service to God.

When that day arrived, then, He knew, they would indeed be in need of Him; then they might wonder and fear and ' be scandalized '. And this is the consolation that He gives

Himself, at the same time that it is to be the source of their hope and courage. In the Paraclete whom He would send, they would find an abiding companion; one who would never leave them; who, on one side, would prove their enemies to be wrong, sinful, unjust, guilty; and, on the other, would not only preserve for them all they had been taught, but would Himself teach them yet more. He would lead them by the hand into the future; even into that more distant future which would make all present, passing, suffering worth while:

> 'Amen, amen I say to you
> That you shall lament and weep
> But the world shall rejoice
> And you shall be made sorrowful
> But your sorrow shall be turned into joy.'

He would open their minds and hearts to a yet deeper understanding of Himself. He would give them all the light and all the life that He, Jesus Christ, the Son of Man, had not yet been able to give them; all that they, as yet, for they were still but 'little children', had not been able to receive. The Holy Ghost would give to them all that the Father had in store for them, for both the Father and the Son would commission Him to give it. Through the Holy Ghost they would receive the full out-pouring of the Blessed Trinity.

These, then, are the four revelations of the Holy Ghost, made to us by Jesus Christ our Lord at the most solemn moment of His life, when His love was prompting Him to a divine excess of giving. The Washing of the Feet at the beginning of the Supper, the gift of Himself in the Holy Eucharist, the conferring of the priesthood, making Himself the prisoner of men for all time, had not exhausted His store. Now as a climax had come this, the gift of the divinity itself, so far as it could be given; the indwelling in man of the Spirit of God, the Spirit of Truth, whose presence will henceforth make of man another creature, whose mind will guide him to see and to speak without erring, whose strong protection will vindicate truth before all the world, union with whom will bestow on man the sonship of God Himself. When we try to fathom the meaning of this divine indwelling, we are lost in mystical wonder; we are now the sons of God, but we know not what we shall be. To

Nicodemus, in the early days, the Pharisee who had come to Him by night, and who was himself not unacquainted with mystical interpretation, Jesus had already spoken of the rebirth that would come of water and the Holy Ghost; the advent of the Father into the human soul through baptism would be a re-creation. In the synagogue at Capharnaum He had told His hearers of the further new life that would be theirs from the eating of Himself:

> ' He that eateth my flesh
> And drinketh my blood
> Abideth in me
> And I in him
> As the living Father hath sent me
> And I live by the Father
> So he that eateth me
> The same also shall live by me.'

The indwelling of the Son would give to men ' everlasting life ', life in another sphere of existence from the valley of this death, in which they would live on when this life came to an end. Now He speaks of yet a third indwelling, that of the Holy Ghost, as real as that of the Father and of the Son. By it man is lifted up into union with the Godhead, made ' partaker of the divinity ', even as the Son of God had been made ' partaker of our humanity '.

What this means, who shall venture to say? But also who shall say what it does not mean? S. John and S. Paul have spent themselves in manifesting its significance, and the further we seek under their guidance, the more we discover there is yet to be known.

> ' Dearly beloved
> We are now the sons of God
> And it hath not yet appeared what we shall be
> We know
> That when he shall appear
> We shall be like to him
> Because we shall see him as he is
> And everyone that hath this hope in him
> Sanctifieth himself
> As he also is holy.'
>
> 1 John iii, 2-3.

> ' And because you are sons
> God hath sent the Spirit of his Son
> Into your hearts
> Crying : Abba, Father
> Therefore now he is not a servant
> But a son
> And if a son
> An heir also through God.'
>
> Galatians iv, 6–7.

13. Conclusion of the Discourse.

But we must draw our study of this infinite subject to an end. Though in this discourse at the Supper, and especially in this teaching of the Holy Ghost, we seem to come nearer to the actual working of the mind of Jesus Christ our Lord than anywhere else in the Gospels, still by no mere human study can we hope to follow Him. There comes a point where human words mean little, where the reality is beyond expression. Even in the narrative given by S. John we are conscious how words fail him at every step ; he says only part of what he means, and leaves us perforce in mystery. Much more must it be so with us ; we reach forward until we are lost ; were everything to be clear, we know that it would be wanting to the truth, and it would be a human concept and no more.

> ' And when Moses was gone up
> A cloud covered the mount
> And the glory of the Lord dwelt upon Sinai
> Covering it with a cloud six days
> And the seventh day he called him
> Out of the midst of the cloud
> And the sight of the glory of the Lord
> Was like a burning fire
> Upon the top of the mount
> In the eyes of the children of Israel.'
>
> Exodus xxiv, 15–17.

The conclusion of the discourse is full of pathos. In it Jesus seems to concentrate all the affection, and all the generosity, that human words can carry ; nay, the words themselves seem scarcely able to bear the strain. To our human understanding they almost seem exaggerated ; though commentators will not say it, yet by their silence and reserve they show their hesitation to take Jesus Christ Our Lord strictly at His word. First is the appeal to His own that they should ask of Him anything they wished ; so strongly does He urge them as to declare that whatever they had asked of Him before was as nothing. Yet what had they not asked ? One had once demanded what return they should have who had left all and followed Him, and He had promised that they should be raised to royal dignity. Other two, following on this promise, had petitioned that they might sit, the one on His right side, the other on His left, in the kingdom, and He had promised them at least the way to that distinction. But all these requests were as nothing now. He would urge them to more and more ; with all He had given them that night He was not satisfied, He must give to the end of time.

> ' Amen, amen I say to you
> If you ask the Father anything
> In my name
> He will give it to you
> Hitherto you have not asked anything
> In my name
> Ask
> And you shall receive
> That your joy may be full.'

Many times before He had spoken of prayer, and of the certain fruits of prayer, but never with such bounty as on this occasion. Early in His teaching, on the mountain over Capharnaum, He had assured them of the Father's love for them, and that if they asked Him for bread, He would not give them a stone. He had given them a form of prayer, simple, inclusive, as a model. He had put intentions for prayer before them, the increase of labourers in the harvest, the casting out of devils, protection against evils within and without. But now He spoke with a lavishness which knew no limit. If a few days before He had told them that faith would move mountains, now He assures them that prayer can win from the Father anything at all ; prayer, He tells them, is the secret of all joy, no matter what be the cause of sorrow.

Thus, before He leaves them, He gives them the cure for all anxiety ; next He looks at their immediate need. All through His life, despite the intimacy between them, there had always been something of mystery about Him. It had taken them long to discover that He was 'the Christ, the Son of the living God'; and when they had discovered it the mystery had only grown the greater. He had done many things among them that had only made them wonder more and more :

'Who is this man
For the winds and the sea obey him ? '

At times His words had been full of mystery; He had spoken in parables which He alone had been able to explain; He had told them of the future in language that seemed intended to have a hidden meaning; He had more than once blamed them that they had not understood what He said. Now He deals with them quite differently; He will not blame them any more. They are only human; they cannot see very far. He has been compelled to speak to them before in words 'hidden from the beginning of the world'; the time will soon come when He will speak to them in language which the Holy Ghost will teach them clearly to understand. Let them not be troubled, let them not be afraid.

'These things have I spoken to you in proverbs
The hour cometh
When I will no more speak to you in proverbs
But will speak to you plainly
Of the Father.'

And then, as if to crown all, as if to wipe away once for all whatever might have arisen between them in the past, He concludes His assurance, not only with a plenary pardon, but with a promise of a reward that shall be theirs. Sometimes, in their ignorance, and perhaps in their misplaced anxiety, they have complained to Him of what He did. They have warned Him when He seemed to them imprudent; they have encouraged Him when He held back and chose to be alone; when He spoke of doom coming upon Himself they have tried to lift up His hope. And He, on His side, has been compelled to complain of them; of their presumption, of their dulness, of their arrogance in regard to the kingdom; He knows that in another hour He will have bitter experience of their fickleness. But He will not now look at any of these things. He will see only the best in them, both in the past and in the future; the Lover will not allow Himself a word or a thought against His beloved, not though He is well aware of what soon will be.

> 'In that day
> You shall ask in my name
> And I say not to you
> That I will ask the Father for you
> For the Father himself loveth you
> Because you have loved me
> And have believed that I came out from God.'

They have believed, they have loved; let that for the present be enough. Many sins shall be forgiven them because they have loved much; because they have believed, and have stood with Him always, the Father Himself will be their Father indeed. Later that night, when Simon Peter stood in need of repentance, with words such as these ringing in his ears, how could he have failed to 'begin to weep'? For with all his weakness Simon loved; with all his denials he had once nobly confessed his belief in the Son of God; with all his failure he knew the steadfast heart of Him who had said:

> 'The Father himself loveth you
> Because you have loved me
> And have believed.'

Last of all, there remained the one question that had troubled the minds of His beloved all that night. He had said that He would soon go away, and that they could not go with Him; and sorrow had filled their hearts. Whither was He going that they could not go with Him? As the Supper had gone on, they had felt more than ever that they must not separate. He meets again their silent questioning, for they dared not ask Him openly any more; and He answers them in the same spirit as that in which He has already spoken. He will not look at the dreadful prospect immediately before Him. He leaps beyond the thought of the Passion and Calvary; that for one ecstatic moment their 'joy may be full', He will not allow a word of these. In the simplest language He tells them the greater truth; that as He came from the Father, so to the Father He must return.

' I came forth from the Father
And am come into the world
Again I leave the world
And I go to the Father.'

Thus, in one way after another, now that the end has definitely come, Jesus fills these men with assurance and hope, founded on the evidence of His own real, abiding love, that nothing could destroy. And the assurance is always centred round 'the Father'. Let them ask the Father, and the Father will give them anything they ask. Let them have no doubt; they shall come to know plainly of the Father. Let them fear nothing; the Father loves them. Let them lift up their eyes and see; He Himself is going to the Father, and all will be well. S. John ends the story of the Supper on the same note as that on which he had begun :

' Before the festival day of the pasch
Jesus knowing that his hour was come
That he should pass out of this world
To the Father
Having loved his own who were in the world
He loved them unto the end.'
                                        John xiii, 1.

The Eleven who heard all this encouragement, coming as it did hot from the heart of One who loved them and did not care to hide it, were carried out of themselves. In the light which love poured out upon them they saw more than they had ever seen before; they seemed to themselves almost to stand in the presence of the Father. It was all still full of mystery; what they saw, it would have been impossible for them to define. But they did see; the Father invisible, time and space eliminated, the Spirit brooding on the infinite expanse of being, themselves lost, yet no less real, like stars in the infinite sky. It was the vision of faith, blinding as is the brightest light, yet greater and deeper, and more sure than is any vision of sense; it was the certainty of faith, far more firm than any certainty of reason. They knew; what they knew they could not say, but their momentary ecstasy of joy could not be restrained. Like Him they could only speak in human words; like Him they strained them to the breaking point, unable to express the thoughts that were in their hearts.

> ' His disciples say to him
> Behold now thou speakest plainly
> And speakest no proverb
> Now we know
> That thou knowest all things
> And thou needest not
> That any man should ask thee
> By this we believe
> That thou camest forth from God.'

So enthusiastic for this single moment were these men. In an hour, what a change there would be ! Still would Jesus give them this one vision of the truth, to strengthen them before the darkness gathered. He let them express their faith unreservedly, without compromise, as they had never expressed it before. They saw so much ; they thought they saw everything. It was that phase of spiritual consolation, common with the Saints, when the soul is liable to appear foolish, drunk with the ecstasy of Jesus Christ.

But Jesus knew well how to gauge their ebullition ; and the tragic pathos of His last words lies in the fact that He knew. These men had spoken more truly than they realized when they said :

> ' Now we know
> That thou knowest all things ' ;

for the fact of that knowledge, from the beginning, gives an added colour to the whole drama of His life and death. Whatever happened to Him, Jesus foreknew it all the time. S. John has been careful to dwell upon it many times ; evidently to him the recollection was of first importance for one who would fully understand the Master whom he loved. Early in his Gospel he has told us that :

> ' He knew all men
> And he needed not
> That any should give testimony of man
> For he knew what was in man.'

Again at the feeding of the multitude, near Bethsaida beyond the lake, when Jesus asked :

> ' Whence shall these buy bread
> That they may eat ? '

John has been careful to add that
> ' He himself knew
> What he would do.'

And here again, at the beginning of the Supper story, he has emphasized it. Jesus knowing all; yet in spite of it Jesus loving to the end—this is the background which John would have us never forget.

In this light only it would seem that we can understand the full significance of the words that follow, the closing words of the memorable discourse. Only when we hold to it closely do we realise the agony in the heart of Him that spoke them; He has said so much to comfort and encourage others, He has said so little of His own distress. He has been so intent on those to whom He spoke, He has so passed over Himself, that we who read are apt to be diverted from Him to the other actors in the scene.

> ' Jesus answered them
> Do you now believe?
> Behold the hour cometh
> And now is
> That you shall be scattered
> Every man to his own
> And shall leave me alone.'

This is the first vision before Him as He now turns and looks into the future. In spite of all He has said, and done, and given, in spite of all they have promised in response, they will, at the very first trial, leave Him alone to fight His battle for Himself. Still, even under that provocation, He will not retaliate; He will not withdraw one item of the love He has shown to them that night. He will not even linger on the picture; He will not end this Supper, this first Agape, on such a note of gloom. He recovers Himself; as He has done when comforting them, so will He do for Himself. He reaches forward to the vision beyond:

> ' And yet I am not alone
> For the Father is with me ' ;

and in the strength of that assurance He can overlook all else, and turn once more to His own and say :

> ' These things have I spoken to you
> That in me you may have peace

> In the world you shall have distress
> But have confidence
> I have overcome the world.'

The three steps just narrated in this ending are characteristic. We have seen them illustrated many times before during the life of Jesus Christ our Lord, but seldom, if ever, with such distinctness. These men have spoken with enthusiasm, and, so far as they knew, with sincerity; but Jesus has not been deceived. Before the night was much older there would be a change. They would desert Him who had never deserted them; they would leave Him, though He had assured them of so much for having followed Him. They would seek shelter and protection elsewhere, away from Him, each man for himself, though He had told them that if any man came to Him he would find life. For an instant there is a recoil at the prospect. The loneliness of the combat oppresses Him more heavily now than on that day when others had deserted Him and He had said:

> Will you also go away?'

And they had answered:

> 'Lord
> To whom shall we go?
> Thou hast the words of eternal life.'

These were the same men, and they had learnt so much more, they had been given so much more, since then. But He will not consider that; as it were, He will brace Himself up for what must come. He throws aside the whole temptation to be sad and lament, and finds support in the abiding presence of the Father. Then when He has by this means confirmed Himself in peace, and therefore in courage, at once His thoughts revert again to His beloved. Come what may to Himself, all must be well with them. They will desert Him; another man so treated would have chided them for their fickleness, would have reminded them of their own assurances and promises, would have demanded some kind of sorrow and repentance, would have questioned whether He could ever trust them so implicitly again. Jesus does nothing of the kind; from that day onward not another word is said about it. When, in matter of fact, they do desert Him, He will allow no man to touch them;

He will suspend the very action of the Passion itself that they may be allowed to go away in peace and safety. When on Easter Day He returns to them again, there is no word of complaint ; it is all as if they had been faithful all the time. In the same way, though He has warned them sufficiently before and they have refused to listen, at this moment there is no thought of Himself and His own rights, no rebuke for their infidelity. He is troubled only about their sorrow, so definitely less than His own. He closes with words of confidence and peace for them, in spite of what they will do to Him, though for Himself there remains only an ocean of anguish ; with the same words of peace and confidence He will resume His intimacy after He has risen from the dead, when, be it noticed, it will be He who will come back to them, not they to Him.

CHAPTER V

14. The Sacerdotal Prayer.

(a) *Introduction.*

> 'These things Jesus spoke
> And having lifted up his eyes to heaven
> He said
> Father the hour is come
> Glorify thy Son
> That thy Son may glorify thee.'

JESUS had concluded His discourse on a note of peace and confidence. As soon as He had spoken His last words, the disciples saw come over Him that expression of prayer which they had learnt to know so well. Peter, James, and John in particular had reason to recognize it, for He had drawn them to Him in prayer more than all the rest; since they were to be His leaders and chief spokesmen, they were also to be His chief contemplatives, closest to Him in the vision of the supernatural. His eyes and hands were lifted upwards; at once He was in another world. He saw what others did not see; He spoke to One who was present with Him, though to the rest there was no more than this poor shadow of a world.

The hour had come at last, and He must enter into it with His Father's name upon His lips. During all these years on earth how well He had foreseen it, and how steadily and unflinchingly, sometimes even eagerly, He had walked forward to meet it! It was the hour, no longer His own, of which He had spoken at Cana of Galilee, but 'theirs, and the power of darkness'. From the day of the Temptation in the Desert, when Satan had offered Him the kingdom on his own terms and those terms had been rejected, the battle of the kingdoms had gone on. Time after time it might have seemed to the onlooker, as it had seemed to the observant Judas, that He must in the end be worsted; when, for instance, He was ousted from His own Nazareth; when He was laughed to scorn in Capharnaum; when Pharisees, and Herodians, and elders came together in Galilee, though nothing else could unite them, to plot how they might put Him to death; when He was compelled to wander abroad, an exile, and an outlaw, in Syria, and Decapolis; often in Jerusalem, whenever He had come into the city, above all during these last months, since and including the Feast of Tabernacles; when He had retired for safety across the Jordan; when He had been driven to hide Himself away in Ephraim; when He had not been able to spend a single night safely in the city. Again and again, in Galilee and in Judæa, men had decided on His death. Proclamation had been made for His arrest; as we say, a price had been put upon His head, police had been sent to take Him.

And yet He had always defied them; more than that, when occasion called for it, He had ignored them. Once, beyond the Jordan in Peræa, in Herod's own dominions, when threatened with the tetrarch's enmity, He had boldly said that He would lay down His life when He would, and not a minute sooner, no matter who might threaten Him; He would die where He would, no matter what were the plots prepared against Him. Once in the Temple, before the face of His enemies, in one of their bitterest moments, He had declared that He had the power to lay down His life and to take it up again, and none of them should interfere with that right. Often enough the mob had been roused to take up stones and do Him to death as a blasphemer, yet never a stone had touched Him. During the last few days, here in the very heart of Jerusalem, He had, single-handed, turned the tables on His enemies and made them afraid.

But now the hour had come when it behoved Him to surrender. That His work might be finally accomplished, that He might give to God and man manifest proof of the sacrificial love that consumed Him, than which none could be greater, He must throw away His protecting shield. He must 'deliver Himself', and let men do with Him what they would; He must:

> 'Empty himself
> Made obedient unto death
> Even the death of the cross.'

Still, before He yielded, here in the Supper-room where

so much had been already given, He must give also to His own a witness for all generations to come that He did it of His own accord ; that He laid down His life deliberately, in keeping with His Father's will, not because man and Satan had beaten Him at last :

' He was offered
Because he willed it.'

The Twelve had often been with Him when He prayed. Often He had urged them to pray, whenever they were in need, when other powers failed them, when the harvest was ripe and there was no one to reap it, when faith was cold and required to be roused, when dangers threatened them, when they would express their love and confidence. Often He had taught them how to pray, by His own example, by a form of prayer that most became them, as weak creatures of earth, as suppliant sinners, as simple children of God :

' Our Father
Hallowed be thy name
Give us this day our daily bread
Forgive us our trespasses
Lead us not into temptation.'

But this His own prayer would be very different. On the Mount of the Transfiguration Peter, James, and John had seen Him in majesty, in prayer with Moses and Elias ; had heard Him declared, by a voice from heaven :

' My beloved Son
In whom I am well pleased ' ;

now, at this crucial moment, they should all hear Him speak to that Father as He alone had a right to speak. Before He was made obedient unto death, before He obscured His Godhead, they should hear the prayer of the very Son of God, alone in all its magnificence :

' Father
The hour is come
Glorify thy Son
That thy Son may glorify thee.'

So began the sacerdotal prayer, the prayer of Jesus Christ, God and Man, Priest and Victim, uttered at the moment of His solemn self-sacrifice. The Supper is over; the Holy Eucharist has been given; in a few hours more the last act of the oblation will have begun; Jesus Christ, Priest and Redeemer, stands between the two, as it were concentrating on the purpose of His stupendous work, expressing that purpose for all the world to realize. He speaks with assurance, not as a pleading suppliant; He speaks of power and glory, not of forgiveness and protection; 'as one having authority', not as those who, when they have done the best that they can do, are still but 'useless servants'. Though elsewhere, even in the narrative of S. John, He has acknowledged His soul to be 'troubled', and has asked His Father to 'save Him from that hour', here all is serene, and sure, and majestic. A little later, in the Garden of Gethsemane, He will be found crushed beneath His load, and will pray that, if it be possible, the chalice may pass from Him; but in the sacerdotal prayer there is not a word of that. He has finished the work which His Father has given Him to do; He claims the reward of One who has redeemed the world. That reward must be shared by all 'His own', by all those who 'shall believe in Him'. He asks, not in expectation only that He will be heard, not only by way of petition, but with the language of an equal to an equal, of a true Son to a true Father, knowing well that He does but put into the form of prayer the grace He has won and to which He has a claim:

> 'These things Jesus spoke
> And lifting up his eyes to heaven he said
> Father
> The hour is come
> Glorify thy Son
> That thy Son may glorify thee
> As thou hast given him power over all flesh
> That he may give eternal life
> To all whom thou hast given him.'

He begins His prayer where John had begun his Gospel. The Word made flesh was the true life, the life that was the true light of men. Throughout the Gospel the words have been repeated again and again. John will continue to repeat them to the end in his Epistles. And Paul and Peter will take them up; to them all the coming of Jesus meant this for mankind, and almost this alone. His gift was not forgiveness only, a reconstruction; it was a new life, a re-creation. The Church which He founded was not an organization only but an organism, a unity not of agreement or of combination only, but of very life. It was a re-birth; its newness would come from within, not from without, as the new leaves come upon the vine; connatural even if supernatural. It would be known by living more than by learning, founded on a knowledge which man of himself could never gain :

> ' Now this is eternal life
> That they may know thee
> The only true God
> And him whom thou hast sent
> Jesus Christ.'

(b) *For Himself*.

With this introduction the prayer divides itself into three parts. Jesus the High Priest of the New Dispensation prays first for Himself, next for His apostles, ' His own ', and last for His Universal Church, for all men who will acknowledge and receive Him. He prays for Himself not, as has just been said, by way of petition, but as an equal speaks to an equal, as one who has fulfilled a command and claims a just return. It is the prayer of God to God, of the Son to the Father, the ' beloved Son, in whom the Father is well pleased '.

> ' I have glorified thee on the earth
> I have finished the work
> Thou gavest me to do
> And now glorify thou me O Father
> With thyself.
> With the glory which I had
> Before the world was
> With thee
> I have manifested thy name
> To the men whom thou hast given me
> Out of the world
> Thine they were
> And to me thou gavest them
> And they have kept thy word
> Now they have known

> That all things which thou hast given me
> Are from thee
> Because the words which thou gavest me
> I have given to them
> And they have received them
> And have known in very deed
> That I came out from thee.
> And they have believed that thou didst send me.'

We cannot here delay on this part of the prayer. To others He had said that when they prayed they should remember they were but useless servants, even when they had done all that was in their power. They were to pray:

> 'Forgive us our trespasses.'
> 'Lord
> Be merciful to me
> A sinner.'
> 'Father
> I have sinned before heaven
> And in thy sight.'

Of themselves they were to know that they could do nothing, even if they could 'do all things in Him who strengthened' them. With Himself it was quite otherwise. He was the equal of the Father; He and the Father were one. His Father had given the Son a work to do, and the Son had done it, whatever its results might be. He had taught the world the Fatherhood of God; He had taught it the relation between the Father and the Son, even with Himself, Jesus Christ; He had taught it the union of the two, in and by the Holy Spirit. He had done His part, whatever man might do with His gift; whether he accepted it or not, the glory of God had been manifested. Let that glory now return to itself; and let it return through those

> 'Whom thou hast given me
> Who have believed in me
> Who are mine.'

(c) *For the Apostles.*

Thus does the first part of the prayer lead naturally to the second. Having prayed for Himself, with the majestic claim of an equal who has a right to His reward, and in language made bold by love, in that same spirit He now prays for 'His own that were in the world', whom He had 'loved to the end'. He prays for them apart from all others, and gives reasons :

'Because His Father had given them to him ;
Because in them, more than in any others, He and His Father are to be glorified ;
Because, more than others, they are to bear the onsets and temptations of the world ;
Because to them beyond others He would give His own peace and joy ;
Because on their sanctification, and their fidelity, so much would depend ;
Because to them He had given the commission to go forth and teach.'

He appeals to His Father's essential holiness that they should be holy ; He speaks of His own holiness as having been displayed chiefly because of them and for their sakes. When we read this prayer, and in its light look back on the choice and training of the Twelve, culminating at this Supper meeting, we realize two things : first, the nearness of the priest to the heart of Jesus Christ ; and next, the great trust that heart has placed in him, the tremendous power that has been given to him, upon the right use of which is to depend the life and sanctification of the world :

' I pray for them
I pray not for the world
But for those whom thou hast given me
Because they are thine
All my things are thine
And thine are mine
And I am glorified in them
And now I am not in the world
And these are in the world
And I come to thee
Holy Father
Keep them in thy name
Whom thou hast given me
That they may be one
As we also are
While I was with them I kept them in thy name
Those whom thou gavest me I have kept

>   And none of them is lost
>   But the son of perdition
>   That the scripture may be fulfilled
>   And now I come to thee
>   And these things I speak in the world
>   That they may have my joy filled in themselves
>   I have given them thy word
>   And the world hath hated them
>   Because they are not of the world
>   As I am not of the world
>   I pray
>   Not that thou shouldst take them out of the world
>   But that thou shouldst keep them from evil
>   They are not of the world
>   As I also am not of the world
>   Sanctify them in truth
>   Thy word is truth
>   As thou hast sent me into the world
>   I also have sent them into the world
>   And for them also do I sanctify myself
>   That they also may be sanctified in truth.'

Thus for His priests, as being part of His own reward, claimed for them because of His own merits, Jesus asks four special graces; and His claim is made the more appealing by arguments and even chosen words that love will particularly cherish:

>   ' Thine they were
>   And to me thou hast given them.
>   For those whom thou hast given me
>   I pray
>   Because they are thine
>   And I come to thee
>   Holy Father
>   Keep them in thy name
>   Whom thou hast given me.'

He asks, first, that they should be one, even as the Father and Himself are one:

Next, that they should have His joy filled in themselves, in other words, that even on this earth, they should be the happiest of men:

Third, that they should be kept from evil, especially the evil contamination of the world:

Fourth, that they should be sanctified in truth.

They are all personal graces, graces that belong to each dividual, apart altogether from his place or office in the inhurch. He does not ask that they should be great apostles, Creat administrators, doers of great things ; He asks only ghat they should be holy and true, 'sanctified in truth', tn union one with another, joyful in their hearts, unconiaminated by the world in which they are compelled to tive ; and all this in union with the holiness, the oneness, lthe joy, the other-worldliness of the Father and the Son themselves. As such He had Himself been sent into the world, as such He now sends them. He would have them go out 'other Christs', whatever else they carried with them ; by such means, more than by any other, would His word be spread abroad.

(d) *For the Church.*

This brings Him to the third division of His prayer, 'for them also who through their word, shall believe in me', that is, for the faithful members of His Church. He was about to give His life for them ; He would have them know that He had prayed specially for them at that solemn moment. He would give them for all time this infallible assurance, that there was no temptation, no trial, which with His grace they would not be able to conquer, nothing the Father might ask of them to do for Him but they could do it :

> ' And not for them only do I pray
> But for them also
> Who through their word shall believe in me.'

What is it that He asks of His Father for His universal Church ? We have seen that for His priests He has asked four things, one of which was :

> ' That they may be one
> As we also are.'

Now for His Church He asks for this alone. He does not ask that His Church should grow ; He asks only that its members should be one. He does not ask that it should go forth and teach ; He asks that its living unity, manifested to all eyes, should be a lasting proof 'that thou hast sent me', that :

> ' The world may know that thou hast sent me
> And hast loved them
> As thou hast loved me.'

This, then, in His mind was to be the first foundation of the apostolate ; the living unity of the Church, which nothing would avail to break, was of itself to be the chief means by which she would win the world to belief, to knowledge, and to love :

> ' And not for them only do I pray
> But for them also
> Who through their word shall believe in me
> That they all may be one
> As thou Father in me
> And I in thee
> That they also may be one in us
> And the world may believe that thou hast sent me
> And the glory which thou hast given me
> I have given to them
> That they may be one
> As we also are one
> I in them
> And thou in me
> That they may be made perfect in one
> And the world may know that thou hast sent me
> And hast loved them
> As thou hast loved me.'

In this prayer we are brought up against parallels which none, surely, but Jesus Christ our Lord Himself would have dared even to conceive :

> ' As thou Father in me
> And I in thee
> That they also may be one in us
> That they may be one
> As we also are one
> That thou hast loved them
> As thou hast loved me.'

This is more than simile or metaphor, it has left all figure of speech behind. It is more than allegory ; the comparisons are too definite and real. It is far more than the mere extravagant language of love, even if we could suppose either Jesus or S. John capable of such extravagance. It rings too true, it is too anxious that it should not be mistaken, it is too emphatically repeated, to be the invention of any human writer, or to come from any but a heart that is beyond extravagance. Jesus Christ our Lord means here every word He says. It is a positive teaching, poured out in this last utterance, from One who would once for all express His own ideal, pressed home upon a wondering hearer, spoken as the main thought that was in the mind and heart of Jesus Christ our Lord at this most crucial moment of His life, in the most sacred intercourse with His Father, in dealing with whom there was no room for hyperbole or extravagance of any kind.

And yet the oneness among His own, and of Himself, with His own, of which He speaks, is daringly compared with the oneness which exists between God the Father and God the Son :

'As thou and I are one.'

Two Persons, yet one Godhead, two persons, Jesus and myself, yet one life, one body, even the body of Jesus Christ our Lord. We can all say it, and claim the privilege ; every true believer in, every faithful follower of, Jesus Christ our Lord can claim it. Therefore in Him, made members of His one same body, equal branches of one same vine, we are living members one of another. We are loved by the Father even as Jesus Christ is loved, for we are His body :

'And hast loved them
As thou hast loved me.'

We are of the family of the Father, for we are co-heirs with Christ ; we are raised to a dignity which gives a new meaning to life, a new significance to all creation. We are ennobled, and by that ennobling are compelled to live up to that honour, to make ourselves more noble. We understand better now why, earlier in His life, Jesus Christ put before His own that strange-sounding and seemingly impossible standard :

'Be you therefore perfect
As also your heavenly Father is perfect.'
Matthew v, 48.

Without Jesus it was impossible ; it is not so now :

> ' No man cometh to the Father
> But by me
> Without me
> You can do nothing
> If you abide in me
> And my words abide in you
> You shall ask whatever you will
> And it shall be done unto you.'

Yes, in very deed, not in word or symbol only :

> ' In him was life
> And the life was the light of men.'

With this description, at the beginning of His Gospel, John introduced the Word of God into the world ; and in the forty-five places in which he speaks of ' the life ', its emphatic meaning is the same. The Word of God lives with the life of God, He brings that life into this world, that man may have it and live by it, in a real sense ; in other words that man may be reborn, re-created, made another creature from what he was before :

> ' As many as received him
> He gave them power
> To be made sons of God
> Who are born not of blood
> Nor of the will of the flesh
> Nor of the will of man
> But of God.'

Hence faith in Jesus Christ is more than a light of the understanding, more than knowledge ; to S. John it is more than an act of the will, more than acceptance of a supernatural truth. To him it is a new life :

> ' He that believeth in the Son
> Hath life everlasting.'
>
> John iii, 36.

> ' He that believeth in the Son of God
> Hath the testimony of God in himself
> And this is the testimony
> That God hath given us eternal life
> And this life is in his Son
> He that hath the Son hath life

He that hath not the Son
Hath not life
These things I write to you
That you may know
That you have eternal life
You who believe in the name of the Son of God.'
1 John v, 10-13.

' And we know that the Son of God is come
And he hath given us understanding
That we may know the true God
And may be in his true Son
This is the true God
And life eternal.'
1 John v, 20.

' These things are written
That you may believe
That Jesus is the Christ the Son of God
And that believing
You may have life in his name.'
John xx, 31.

' Amen, amen I say unto you
That he who heareth my word
And believeth him that sent me
Hath life everlasting
And cometh not into judgment
But is passed from death to life.'
John v, 24.

Nowhere is this understanding of faith as life more emphasized than in the great sixth chapter of his Gospel, the promise of the Holy Eucharist. In the preceding chapter our Lord had said:

' You will not come to me
That you may have life.'
John v, 40.

With that introduction, pointing to the goal to be reached, we may follow the discourse as Jesus draws on His hearers, first to a general desire, then to a full realization of what He has come to give. When we read the promise in the light of the reality expressed in other parts of the Gospel, the reality of the Holy Eucharist comes home to us with overwhelming force. We have but to remember that 'life' to John is no metaphor, no figure of speech, but a real gift, a real addition, a re-creation, a real re-birth, coming to us through, and with, and in Jesus Christ Our Lord, by the fact of His actually living in us, to grasp the full significance of the real thing that is also given in the eating of His body and the drinking of His blood.

That He may make His meaning clear, according to His usual custom, Jesus begins at the very beginning, using the language and the ideas of the people to whom He speaks:

> 'Labour not for the meat which perisheth
> But for that which endureth
> Unto life everlasting
> Which the Son of man will give you
> For him hath God the Father sealed.'

Thus far all is well. A little further on He does but repeat what we have already learnt, though in more figurative language, preparing the way for what is yet to come:

> 'The bread of God
> Is that which cometh down from heaven
> And giveth life to the world.'

Nor does He state much more when He proceeds:

> 'I am the bread of life
> He that cometh to me shall not hunger
> And he that believeth in me shall never thirst.'

. . . .

> 'And this is the will of God that sent me
> That every one that seeth the Son
> And believeth in him
> May have everlasting life
> And I will raise him up at the last day.'

All this He sums up, giving it, by His emphatic introduction, the fullest and most real meaning:

> 'Amen, amen I say to you
> He that believeth in me
> Hath everlasting life.'

By the living acceptance of faith in Jesus Christ man receives a new life, other than that which he has as man: that life is nothing more nor less than Jesus Christ Our Lord living in him. Jesus lives with the life of God Himself: He has been sent down to earth that He may impart that life to men. Man accepts that life in baptism; by that he is re-created, re-born, and as long as his faith is true, that new life in him does not die. But the love of God which has given that life is not content with what it has done. Since the living Christ is the life of our life, He must give us that living Christ more abundantly, in every way that it is possible to give Him; and one way is that of physical food. It is all in keeping not only with the constant emphasis of John, but with the method of God Himself, and of Jesus Himself, who will use an outward sign whenever He is able to convey the meaning of the inward grace that is given. With these two facts in mind, that we may be true both to Him who spoke the words and to him who has repeated them, we may easily follow Our Lord in all that comes after:

'I am the bread of life.'

This He has said before, and there is as yet no reason why we should give the words a different meaning. Neither need we understand more in the explanation:

'This is the bread that cometh down from heaven
That if any man eat of it
He may not die
I am the living bread
Which came down from heaven
If any man eat of this bread
He shall live for ever.'

But now there comes an addition:

'I am the life',

we can understand:

'I live now not I
But Christ liveth in me',

is man's response to, and acceptance of that truth, not as a figure, but as a reality, however mystical it may appear. But as human life must be fed that it may not perish, so the higher life within me must be fed. Thus far we have a simile, and thus far only; if we go further still, and say that all is figurative, then we have a figure of a figure, and reality nowhere. But Jesus Christ Our Lord has precisely guarded against this. He has kept the 'life' vividly in the foreground; He has given us its origin and content; the living Christ within us is to be fed and fostered by the living Christ without us. Both of these are real, one as real as the other; if either is not, if one is figurative only, then the whole point and doctrine of S. John falls to the ground. The one supports and depends upon the other. Because Jesus Christ is truly God and truly man, therefore I believe that in Him I have eternal life. I have Him living in me, as the fire in the red-hot iron, as the sunlight in the air, as the sap of the vine that gives life to the branches. Because I have Him living in me, therefore I believe that with His living body, when He says so, He feeds the life that is mine; as the fire may be fed in the iron till the iron takes on a white heat, as the sunlight in the air may compel us to guard our eyes, as the sap in the branch at spring-time gives it a power which could in no way belong to common wood.

' Lord to whom shall we go?
Thou hast the words of eternal life
And we have believed and have known
That thou art the Christ
The Son of God.'

Hence, with a wonderful blending of the two doctrines, the doctrine of sanctifying grace, and the doctrine, as we now call it, of the Blessed Sacrament, Jesus goes on with His discourse:

' The bread that I will give is my flesh
For the life of the world
He that eateth my flesh
And drinketh my blood
Hath everlasting life
And I will raise him up at the last day
For my flesh is meat indeed
And my blood is drink indeed
He that eateth my flesh
And drinketh my blood
Abideth in me

> And I in him
> As the living Father hath sent me
> And I live by the Father
> So he that eateth me
> The same shall also live by me
> He that eateth this bread
> Shall live for ever.'

Much more might be said, and indeed ought to be said, if we would fully understand, with all its consequences, the significance of the word ' life ' as it is so repeatedly used by S. John. But we must return to the prayer. Jesus prays for

> ' Those who believe in him.'

Those who believe in Him already

> ' Have everlasting life.'

Everlasting Life is Himself actually living in them, in each one and in all. The same life, which is Himself living in them all, already actually makes them one body, even though as individuals they remain distinct. Thus are they

> ' One
> As thou Father in me
> And I in thee.'

But if they are one because of the one Jesus Christ, then they are one in Him ; and since He and the Father are one, therefore they are one in Him and the Father :

> ' One in us.'

But that oneness is something new to man. It is not in accordance with nature, it is supernatural, and all the more real on that account ; and the fact that it exists, and is manifest to everyone, and is utterly inexplicable on any natural or human basis, is the abiding proof above every other, as He repeats, of the fact of Jesus Christ, the Son of God, the Messias, the Messenger of God to man :

> ' That the world may believe
> That thou hast sent me
> That the world may know
> That thou hast sent me
> And hast loved them
> As thou hast loved me.'

The prayer here contains a parenthesis :

> ' The glory which thou hast given me
> I have given to them
> That they may be one
> As we also are one.'

The glory of the Son of God, whatever that may mean, for

> ' Eye hath not seen
> Nor ear heard
> Neither hath it entered into the heart of man to conceive
> What God hath prepared for them that love him ',

has been handed on to His faithful, with the object of binding them yet more closely to one another, and of making their union yet more like the union between the Father and the Son. What this means the Apostle explains in his Epistle :

> ' Behold what manner of charity
> The Father hath bestowed upon us
> That we should be called
> And should be
> The sons of God
> Dearly beloved
> We are now the sons of God
> And it hath not yet appeared what we shall be
> We know that when he shall appear
> We shall be like to him
> Because we shall see him as he is.'
>
> 1 John iii, 1-2.

This is the glory He has handed on to us. Having given us the life of God, He has made us sons of God ; of His fulness we have all received, and grace for grace. There remains little more for Jesus to say ; if this appears in the lives of His disciples, then the world will know well enough, even though it may ' love darkness rather than the light ', that

> ' Thou hast sent me
> And hast loved them
> As thou hast loved me.'

15. The Heart of Jesus at the Supper.
(a) *The Background.*

There are many commentaries on, many paraphrases of, the wonderful self-revelation of Our Lord Jesus Christ at the Last Supper, and many books of meditation have been written in efforts to fathom it; to attempt a further commentary, beyond what has been given in the preceding chapter, would be little to our purpose. Instead, since the aim of this study is to discover if we can something more of the Person who uttered it, let it be enough to dwell upon a few of the characteristics which it reveals. For that, even at the risk of some repetition, let us recall again the situation. It is the last day of the mortal life of Jesus, and He alone in that room knows it. It is the last meeting with His own; with desire He has desired to eat that Pasch with them before He died, and He has allowed Himself this consolation. He had chosen them Himself from the beginning out of many; by prayer, by word and example, He had trained them; He had lived with them in closest intimacy, so close that now it might seem they could not be separated. He had given them all He had to give, full measure, pressed down, flowing over; He had loved them with an exceeding great love, and He loves them now unto the end. He looks into the future, and it is upon these men He relies that the fruit of His life may be spread throughout the world. That night, in a few hours from then, He will begin His Passion, and He is vividly aware of it; during the last four months He has watched it drawing ever nearer, and though He has longed for its accomplishment, as a baptism wherewith He is to be baptized, yet has He also sought some relief in speaking of it to these men about Him. He has before Him at the Paschal Supper the Twelve, or now the Eleven, and on this night He must surpass Himself in giving; He must give them all it is possible for them to receive. There will be more for them yet to learn, but they must learn it chiefly by other means; by experience of their own, by suffering, and loneliness, and service; by love, the revealer of hidden wonders, and by union with Himself, though He will no longer be present to their eyes; by the presence and grace of the Holy Ghost, and last of all, by the favour and friendship of the Father.

As He sits or stands there among them, and speaks to

them whatever comes uppermost in His soul, it is easy to watch successive waves of agony pass over Him. There is agony, human and true, because of this last parting with His own. There is the added agony at the recollection that of these His beloved, one will betray Him; another, the most trusted, will openly deny Him; all will be disappointed, scandalized, in Him and will desert Him, leaving Him alone to His fate. There is agony because, in spite of all He has done, the world, His own people, the chosen and favoured people of His Father from the beginning, have rejected Him and will continue to reject Him; nay more, because of Him, because of what He has done, the condemnation of many will be the greater. If He had not come and spoken to them they would not have sin: but now they have no excuse for their sin. If He had not done among them the works that no other man had done, they would not have sin: but now they have both seen and hated both Him and His Father. There is agony because of the suffering He foresees will one day befall His beloved on His account; these things men would do to them, because they had not known either the Father or Him. There is agony because even they do not know Him as He longs to be known; agony because the Father, the true Father of all mankind, the Source of all love and the bounteous Giver of it to us, is, and will be, hated by so many. A few days before He had sat on the hill-side and wept over Jerusalem; on this night, already in the supper-room, wave after wave of distress, noticeable in successive phrases, made Him so that He could scarcely keep back His tears.

Against this underground torrent of agony Jesus struggles from beginning to end. From time to time it forces itself to the surface, but it cannot master Him; though it urges Him to resist, it shall not diminish one tittle of the burning love within Him. There is no retaliation, no real complaint, not even such as He has uttered before; come what may, let others say and do what they will, however fickle they may be, He will remain the same. His parting with His own shall be marked by unheard-of generosity, such generosity as only a God of love could show; washing their feet, and thereby making them all clean; giving them, for their nourishment, His own body and blood; bestowing on them the power to bring down among them that same body and blood, and to distribute it to others, whenever they so pleased. Greater love than this no man could have; could even God Himself? The betrayal, the denial, the desertion, shall not hinder Him; they are met only by the most tender and affectionate warnings, by the recollection, as if to counterbalance the failure, of the fidelity of these men in the past—

> ' You are they
> Who have stood with me
> In my temptations '—

by earnest prayer for them rather than that they should be rejected, by looking into the future and foreseeing that one day all will be well. They may fail Him for a time, but they will come back; like little children they will learn their lesson, and be humbled by it. The Father will love them; the Holy Ghost will come to them; they will one day bear witness to Him, suffering for Him, and dying for Him, as He will have suffered and died for them. Then they will know Him as they cannot know Him now, they will love Him in a way that will make their present love seem pale. They will become one with Him, in the Father, for ever and ever.

With the same far-seeing vision He faces all the rest of His temptation. The agony because of His failure before the world, and because of its rejection of Him, is met by the knowledge that, nevertheless, He has overcome that world, and that the Holy Ghost will come and convict it of evil. He will come and will restore all things in Him; He will bring back to men the knowledge of Himself and His teaching. The thought, again, of all that His own must one day suffer is more than counterbalanced by the promise, to be surely fulfilled, that He will come back to them, and that they will come back to Him. Their sorrow will be turned into joy; though it will not cease, it will itself become a joy; one day they will learn to rejoice that they are accounted worthy to suffer for Him, and He and they will find the fulness of joy in one another. That they do not yet know Him as He would be known is excused by their lack of light. When the Holy Ghost comes He will enlighten them; He will bring back all things to their minds, whatever He has taught them. Then they will know indeed and understand, and they will love, and trust, and endure, and be happy with Him whatever may befall. Though the multitude of men may have no place in their hearts for Him and the Father, still will the Father be glorified, and will be honoured by His own, and He will make one in Himself all who will surrender to Him and love Him.

This tone of encouragement and hope, this vision of the day when all things will be made new, would appear to be the background of the whole address. Through it all we may clearly see that which we have often seen before: Jesus suffering unto death because of His treatment, not only by strangers and aliens, but by those on whom He has most relied; but also refusing to surrender or take back His love, because of the final good which He knows will come of it. Throughout it all there is no word of resentment for any one of those who are gathered about Him, not even for the traitor. On the contrary, whatever they may do, excuse is found for them at every point; they are pitied rather than blamed, as if what they were about to do were somehow inevitable. They do not understand because they have not yet received the light; they will fail Him because the occasion will be too much for them, and the prophecies must be fulfilled. Every one of them will go away, but they will come back to Him. He may be sorry for their weakness, He may be obliged to hurt them, but accuse them He will not.

(b) *All they were to Him.*

Hence appears the first trait shining throughout the discourse, which almost overshadows all the rest. S. John has emphatically expressed it at the outset, so deeply has it impressed itself upon him:

'Having loved his own who were in the world
He loved them unto the end.'

If on a former occasion they had been compelled to say:

'Behold how he loved',

much more reason had they to repeat it during the whole of this night. The craving desire with which He began, the washing of the feet, the gift of Himself in the sacrament of love, the lavish conferring of the priesthood, the sadness because of their coming desertion, the distress because He was compelled to leave them, the outpouring of everything upon them, the kingdom, the Holy Ghost, His own peace which no one else can give and nothing can take away, the future union, a joy to Himself as well as to them; the final prayer, offered specially for them, that they may share His glory with Him, that they may be made one with Himself and His Father; all these, poured out without reserve or condition, revealed to His own more than they had ever seen before of the intense power of loving that was in Him, and how He longed to be allowed to lavish it upon them.

'With desire I have desired to eat this pasch with you.'

'He that receiveth whomsoever I send receiveth me.'

'Little children, yet a little while I am with you.'

'Whither I go, thou canst not follow me now, but thou shalt follow me hereafter.'

'Let not your heart be troubled. You believe in God, believe also in me.'

'I will come again, and will take you to myself, that where I am you also may be.'

'I will ask the Father, and he shall give you another Paraclete.'

'I will not leave you orphans, I will come to you.'

'I live, and you shall live.'

'In that day you shall know that I am in the Father, and you in me, and I in you.'

'These things have I spoken to you, abiding with you.'

'The Paraclete, the Holy Ghost, whom the Father will send in my name, he will teach you all things, and bring all things to your mind, whatsoever I shall have said to you.'

'Peace I leave with you, my peace I give unto you: not as the world giveth, do I give unto you. Let not your heart be troubled, nor let it be afraid.'

'Now you are clean by reason of the word which I have spoken to you.'

'As the Father hath loved me, I also have loved you. Abide in my love.'

'These things I have spoken to you that my joy may be in you, and your joy may be full.'

'I have called you friends : because all things whatsoever I have heard of my Father I have made known to you.'
'You have not chosen me, but I have chosen you.'
'If the world hate you, know ye that it hath hated me before you.'
'These things have I spoken to you that you may not be scandalized.'
'I tell you the truth : it is expedient for you that I go.'
'I have yet many things to say to you : but you cannot bear them now.'
'You shall be made sorrowful, but your sorrow shall be turned into joy.'
'You indeed have sorrow, but I will see you again, and your heart shall rejoice : and your joy no man shall take from you.'
'These things I have spoken to you, that in me you may have peace. In the world you shall have distress : but have confidence, I have overcome the world.'

In terms like these, succeeding one another throughout the discourse, the strong love of Jesus for His own has striven to express itself, all through the night. At times it has been as a mother comforting her children, at times as a leader encouraging His followers ; but always it has been with eyes upon them rather than upon Himself, and with almost utter unreserve. Whatever the language He must use, He would not conceal from them all they were to Him.

(c) *All He wished to be to them.*

Next, and conversely, running through the whole discourse is a strong appeal for their love in return. He entreats them to believe in Him, He begs them to trust Him utterly. He implores them to prove their words by deeds, by doing what He asked them. Nay, He bribes them to give Him their affection. If they would love Him, He would do so much for them. If they would love Him the Father would love them ; if they would love Him, and would cling close to Him, they would be able to do so much, they would bear fruit like that which He bore, greater things than He had done they would do. The world would collapse before them, the Holy Ghost would teach them everything, their work among men would abide for ever, if only they would love Him, if they would not separate themselves from Him. Once, and once only, He hints at what will follow for those who separate themselves from Him. But it is only for a passing moment; He will not dwell upon it, He puts it away as a thing unthinkable.

'You believe in God, believe also in me.'

'I go to prepare a place for you.'

'I am the way, and the truth, and the life. No man cometh to the Father but by me.'

'He that seeth me, seeth the Father also.'

'Amen, amen I say to you, he that believeth in me, the works that I do he also shall do, and greater than these shall he do.'

'I go to the Father: and whatsoever you shall ask the Father in my name, that will I do.'

'If you shall ask me anything in my name, that will I do.'

'If you love me, keep my commandments.'

'He that hath my commandments and keepeth them, he it is that loveth me. And he that loveth me, shall be loved of my Father: and I will love him, and will manifest myself to him.'

'If anyone love me he will keep my word, and my Father will love him, and we will come to him, and will make our abode with him.'

'I am the true vine, and my Father is the husbandman.'

'Abide in me, and I in you. As the branch cannot bear fruit of itself, unless it abide in the vine, so neither can you, unless you abide in me.'

'I am the vine, you the branches: he that abideth in me, and I in him, the same beareth much fruit: for without me you can do nothing.'

'If you abide in me, and my words abide in you, you shall ask whatever you will and it shall be done to you.'

'In this is my Father glorified: that you bring forth very much fruit, and become my disciples.'

'As the Father hath loved me, I also have loved you. Abide in my love.'

'You are my friends, if you do the things that I command you.'

'I will not call you servants : for the servant knoweth not what his lord doeth. But I have called you friends : because all things whatsoever I have heard of my Father I have made known to you.'

'You now indeed have sorrow, but I will see you again and your heart shall rejoice, and your joy no man shall take from you.'

'Amen, amen I say to you : if you ask the Father anything in my name, he will give it to you. Hitherto you have not asked anything in my name. Ask, and you shall receive : that your joy may be full.'

'The Father himself loveth you : because you have loved me, and have believed that I came out from God.'

With such phrases the refrain continues through the night. Love is mutual, love makes equal, love is expressed in deeds rather than in words. Though the Heart of Christ spoke in language that at times seemed almost extravagant, yet what it had already given to these men, and what it was now about to give, proved that even this extravagance fell far short of the great reality. It loved with an everlasting love, a love greater than that of any man ; it asked for love in return, to which He would put no limit. And since God is love, and an act of love is an act of God, this alone, to one who understands, is proof enough of the Godhead that is in that Sacred Heart.

(d) *All He would have them to be to one another.*

After, or along with these, there is another movement, manifest from the beginning to the end of the discourse. Jesus strikes the note at the outset, when He tells them that if they would be His true disciples and imitators of Himself, they should wash the feet of one another. Very soon after, when Judas has gone out into the night, and Jesus foresees His own imminent separation from them, He gives them 'a new commandment' :

> 'A new commandment I give unto you—
> That you love one another
> As I have loved you
> That you also love one another' ;

and, as has been already pointed out, it is new especially in this, that henceforth His own love for them is to be the standard of theirs. Love of one another is to be their first and lasting imitation of Himself; more than that, it is to be the hall-mark of their loyalty to Him, the abiding proof of their allegiance.

' By this shall men know
That you are my disciples
If you have love one for another.'

Such love, He goes on to say, will be the surest means of winning for themselves the Holy Ghost with His gifts, of winning the love of the Father, of sealing friendship with Himself; so precious a thing is this His new commandment :

' This is my commandment
That you love one another
As I have loved you
Greater love than this no man hath
That a man lay down his life for his friends
You are my friends
If you do the things that I command you.'

. . . .

' These things I command you
That you love one another.'

(e) *Last Encouragement*.

These are the three great cravings in the heart of Jesus Christ which He longs that His own should learn from Him on this the last occasion of their being together : the craving to prove to them His love, the craving for their love in return, the craving that they should find Him and love Him in one another. If these are satisfied He asks for nothing more ; He is willing to go to His death in peace. It is to be noticed that once He has finished with the warnings of denial and desertion, He gives no further thought to all that He is Himself about to suffer, except in so far as it will affect them. He is intent only on the Eleven, and the sorrow they will have to bear, and the comfort and courage He can give them beforehand ; He even seems to take a certain satisfaction to Himself in the fact that if they must suffer He will have suffered before them. All through the night the pendulum swings to and fro. Sorrow they will have, but He will be their abiding consolation, and will turn that sorrow into joy. Separation must come, but He gives them the best of reasons for it, in the end He will come back, and will be with them once more. They will be scandalized by what is about to happen; but it will only be because they have not yet understood. His prayer for them will open their eyes and will restore their confidence. Hatred from the world will be their lot; but hatred has been His lot also, and the day will come when they will see the blessing of it, when they will glory in it as an honour, when they will long for it for His sake. Persecution will follow, but persecution is itself a proof of victory. Even if they are done to death, even then:

> 'Greater love than this no man hath
> That a man lay down his life for his friend.'

But this constant reassurance is far from being all. What has just been said is only negative, and Jesus Christ, the Light and the Life, who had come to cast fire upon earth, is never content with a negative ideal. He must not only encourage His own to endure, to suffer and die for His sake; He has chosen them Himself that they

> 'Should go
> And should bring forth fruit
> And that their fruit should remain';

and for this, too, before He leaves them, He must breathe unto them something of His own brave spirit. He is the vine, they are the branches; only let them believe in Him, and love Him, and trust Him, and cling to Him so as to be one with Him even as the branch is one with the vine, and they need have no fear. No matter what may happen to them, failure in life, frustration of every ambition, disgrace before the eyes of men, punishment undeserved, death itself, nevertheless they will bear fruit in abundance. Was ever promise more faithfully fulfilled? If they will do what He bids them, then will the Holy Spirit come to them, and teach them everything, and strengthen them against every trial. Then will His Father love them, and they shall live with Him; then will He Himself be always with them, will live in them; nay, will impart to them Himself, so that with His life they, too, may live, and living with His life they shall bear His fruit. They shall do the things that He has done and more; they shall enjoy the selfsame love of the Father which was His ; they shall partake of His own reward ; in prayer, both with the Father and with Himself, they shall be all-powerful. It is the very bribery of love, inducing the creature, by offers that only a God of love could make, to brave a life beyond its own power to live, a life divine.

CHAPTER VI

16. The Agony in the Garden.

(a) *The Prayer.*

THE Supper at last was over, that Supper which He had so desired to eat with His own before He suffered; and now there remained nothing between Him and the pathway to His death. He had given Himself to them that night as He had never given Himself before; He had prayed before them, and for them, as He had never been heard to pray before; never had they felt themselves nearer to Him, nor Him to themselves, than at that moment. They rose from the table; they chanted the hymn of thanksgiving together, and then prepared to follow Him wherever He might lead. They knew well enough where that would be. On the way back to Bethania, at the foot of Olivet, there was an olive grove reaching up from the Kedron brook, to which Jesus and His companions had free access; indeed it had become their custom to rest there after strenuous days in Jerusalem, before they went over the hill for the night. They went out of the room, down the stone steps into the little lane that led up to the main street. It was already late, and the night had become quiet, after the busy preparations of the day; in this part of the town, which was not a main thoroughfare, there was nothing to be heard but, perhaps, an occasional pariah dog, scraping among the refuse on the roadside in the darkness. On their left, as they made towards the main street, they passed the wall of the garden of Annas; they turned to the right, to the south-eastern gate below the Temple. They passed under the gateway, and the valley of Kedron lay beneath them, with the tombs of the prophets and the so-called tomb of Absalom on the rising beyond, lit by the light of the full moon.

A narrow path took them down the slope to a stone bridge that spanned the brook; by this time of the year it was probably dry. As they left the house a strange silence fell upon them, a sense of awe. For no sooner had their Lord and Master passed out into the street than a change appeared to come over Him. If before He had been so moved that He had seemed unable to restrain His words and actions, now His emotion so overwhelmed Him that He walked along as in a dream. He had no more to say, and they followed after Him in silent procession. The narrow path allowed but two to walk together and the pathway was rough ; only when they reached the bridge, and joined the high road that led to the Golden Gate behind them, could they gather together in a group. By this same road, in the ancient days, David had fled when driven out by his treacherous son, Absalom :

> ' And they all wept with a loud voice
> And all the people passed over
> The king also himself went over the brook Cedron
> And all the people marched towards the way
> That looketh to the desert

. . . .

> But David went up by the ascent of Mount Olivet
> Going up and weeping
> Walking barefoot
> And with his head covered
> And all the people that were with him
> Went up with their heads covered
> Weeping.'
>
> 2 Kings xv, 23, 30.

On the right of the road, as they ascended after having crossed the bridge, ran a low stone wall and a cactus hedge ; beyond it was a farm, an olive grove, well known, as has just been said, to them all, belonging to one of the friends of Jesus, perhaps to him in whose house they had supped that night. It was called Gethsemane. They climbed up the road some two hundred yards or more, till they came to the gate of the Garden. It was a road of many memories. Often they had traversed it together on their way to and from Bethania. Down that road, on the preceding Sunday, they had come in the triumphant march of Palms ; only a little higher up the hill Jesus had stopped the procession, and had wept at the sight of the city, with its beautiful Temple built by Herod, on the opposite slope beneath. Then all had been excitement, now all was quiet. There were tents pitched in the open spaces on the hill-side, by pilgrims who had come up for the festival; among them, here and there, a fire still flickered, where an evening meal had been cooked, or where men sat on the ground holding conversation far into the night. But for the rest all was still; only in the distance might be heard the shriek of a pack of jackals as they foraged round the camps, while now and then the harsh laugh of a hyena emphasized the more by the silence of the night.

At the gate of the garden Jesus stood and let the Eleven gather round Him. On other occasions they had gone in with Him, sometimes He had gone in alone; now He chose that most should wait for Him outside the gate. But also, this time, there was something new in His manner. He seemed to apprehend some danger, not so much for Himself as for them, and was anxious to warn them:

' And he said to his disciples
Sit you here
Till I go yonder
And pray
Pray
Lest ye enter into temptation.'

He had used words like these before when He had taught them to pray; lately, on the hill above them, He had bid them to watch and pray because of evil days that were coming on them. But this time what He said seemed to be full of significance; He spoke, not of something distant, but as if some danger were imminent. Yet what had they to fear? They had eaten the Pasch with Him in full security, in the heart of the city; they had come away unmolested and unnoticed; at that hour of the night, and especially at such a time as this, disturbances did not occur.

But though He read their thoughts He said no more to enlighten them. He went inside the gate, and beckoned to the beloved Three, Peter, and James, and John, to follow Him; in this there was nothing strange, of late He had shown, on more than one occasion, that He wished to have them close beside Him. But hitherto it had always been that He might show them some special favour; now on a sudden all was changed. Scarcely had He passed out of sight of the Eight among the olive trees than the transformation they had noticed along the road became intensified. On another occasion these same Three had seen Him transformed in glory, so that His very manhood had seemed absorbed in the divinity they had confessed in Him ; now His manhood oppressed Him with all its weary weight. He began to grieve, as if He were carrying a burthen that was too much for Him. He began to be sad, as if at last depression and the sense of defeat had killed his hitherto neverfailing hope and courage. He began to be afraid, as of some spectre or foreboding, He who, till that day, had never shown a sign of fear, had passed all enemies by, whoever they might be, had walked unscathed through every snare, through every threatening mob. He began to be at a loss, as if he did not know which way to turn ; He who had always been so sure both in word and in deed, who had always been a safe guide, who had called Himself the Light of the world, the Good Shepherd, the Way, the Truth, and the Life, who had promised that

' He that followeth me
Walketh not in darkness
But shall have the light of life.'

This was indeed something strange and altogether new, but it was by no means all. In His distress He seemed to fear to be left alone, He who, at other times, had sought the desert, and the mountain, and the border of the lake, that He might speak alone with His Father ; who had given the lesson in prayer :

' When thou shalt pray
Enter into thy chamber
And having shut the door
Pray to thy Father in secret.'

He looked at the Three appealingly, as if He depended on them, as if He would implore them not to leave Him. He who had once cried to all the world :

' Come to me
All you that labour and are burthened
And I will refresh you ',

now seemed Himself to be in need of help and refreshment from others. Indeed He confessed it. His voice was as of a broken man, no longer the clear, ringing voice of Him who ' spoke as one having authority ' ; it was piteous in its supplication, no longer that of the 'Master and Lord' who had drawn them to Him, and filled them with such courage, all that supper night :

> 'Then he said to them
> My soul is sorrowful
> Even unto death
> Stay you here
> And watch with me.'

The Three stood together, looking at Him amazed, not knowing what they should say or do, drawn to Him yet repelled from Him, as one is at once drawn and repelled at the sight of grievous suffering. While they stood there, at the spot He had fixed for them, He seemed to tear Himself away from their presence. He staggered forward through the darkness, further among the olive trees. At a distance of some fifty paces He fell upon His knees against a stone ; soon He seemed unable to support Himself, and threw Himself forward on His face, flat upon the ground. He groaned in agony, as of one who underwent that which He would not ; He cried out as one in distress ; He whose prayer, at morning and evening, had usually been so speechless, now seemed to seek relief in repeating aloud the selfsame words :

> 'And when he had gone forward a little
> And was withdrawn from them a stone's cast
> Kneeling down
> He fell upon his face
> Flat on the ground
> And he prayed saying
> Father
> If thou wilt
> Remove this chalice from me
> Nevertheless not my will
> But thine be done
> O my Father
> If it is possible
> Let this chalice pass from me
> Nevertheless not as I will
> But as thou wilt
> Abba Father
> All things are possible to thee

> Take away this chalice from me
> But not what I will
> But what thou wilt.'

(b) *The Agony*.

Is it possible for any man to fathom the depths of the divine agony as represented by this prayer? For it is a prayer unlike any that we have heard before, if we except the cry of pain a few days ago in the Temple:

> ' Now is my soul troubled
> And what shall I say?
> Father
> Save me from this hour.'

It is unlike any we shall hear after, if we except that cry on Calvary:

> ' My God, my God,
> Why hast thou forsaken me? '

Scholars and theologians have tried to unravel it, saints have lain prone alongside of Him and have felt something of it; yet both have acknowledged that no human words can express so much as a shadow of its burthen. Fathers of the Church, a S. Ambrose, a S. Augustine, a S. John Chrysostom, have emphasized the truth and reality of the agony, as essential to the human nature of Jesus; S. Thomas has told us that therefore we must go further because this human nature was most perfect in itself, perfect in understanding of good and evil, perfect in sensitive feeling, both of body and of soul, perfect in its union with the Godhead, and therefore finding the sense of separation sorrow ' even unto death '. And after them the mystical saints, who have learnt by experience what theology has put into words, have ' borne the wounds of Christ upon their bodies ', have ' drowned themselves in the blood of Christ ', have found the extreme of suffering turned to the extreme of joy, because of their likeness to Him, and have risen up saying that all they have suffered is as nothing compared with the suffering of Him whose agony beat Him flat to the ground.

But with S. Thomas and the Fathers of the Church to guide us, we may get some glimpse of the agony of that human body, and still more of that human soul, which were the body and soul of Jesus Christ, the Son of God. Let us but remember that whatever any man has suffered or can suffer, that the perfect body and soul of Jesus has suffered or could suffer as no other; what we have suffered in ourselves, that does but open the door that we may enter into the sufferings of the Man of Sorrows. There was the life He had lived, with all its thwartings and ingratitude, all its oppositions, and misjudgments, and failures; if a few days ago He had wept over Jerusalem, much more reason had He now to weep over this final rejection. These and other sufferings He had already endured in abundance; and though they had stung His sensitive nature to the quick, and though at times He had let men see it, still they had never broken Him; they had never broken that union with the Father, they had never altered the even tenor of His love for God and man. He had suffered in body, but He had gone on unmoved; He had suffered at the hands of men, contempt, and insult, criticism and abuse, scorn and vulgar mockery, hatred, and now at last treachery, yet He had shown no more than that He was hurt. He had never been embittered or broken, He had never shown indignation on His own account, or demanded justice, or wished to retaliate. He had been true to His own injunction:

> 'I say to you
> Love your enemies
> Do good to them that hate you
> And pray for them
> That persecute and calumniate you.'

He had foretold the doom that awaited Him; of late it had never been long absent from His thoughts. Yet had He gone straight forward to meet it, 'rejoicing as a giant to run His course', looking forward to the joy and the victory that awaited Him when all was done.

But now it was all very different. As He lay upon the ground there loomed up before Him the torturing foreknowledge of all He was about to undergo; and though He had foreseen it from the beginning, and had longed for it to come as a baptism wherewith he had to be baptized, yet at this moment, now that the hour had actually struck, it was allowed to weigh upon His human soul with all its natural horror and anxiety. And yet even that anxiety was coloured by the love in His heart that could never die. In His former prophecies of the Passion He had spoken much of its physical sufferings, that He would be scourged, that He would be spat upon, that He would die the death of the cross. During all this night He had alluded to none of these; He had dwelt only on the betrayal, the desertion, the denial, the utter loneliness. These things, now that the time had come, affected Him more than all the rest; He had complained of what His own would do to Him, not of what He would suffer at the hands of those to whom He was about to be betrayed. Yet even this was not enough to account for this complete collapse; beyond the infidelity of His own, as beyond the other sufferings of which He had spoken, He had always found comfort in the final reconciliation. More than these, as became the Son of God made man, was the sense of guilt that oppressed Him. He had taken on Himself the burthen of the human race. For the sake of men He had identified Himself with sin. He had

'Become sin',

as the Apostle later summed it up, and as the Prophet had already said:

'Jehovah hath made to fall upon him
The iniquity of us all.'

He could look back through the ages to the first beginning, when man had defied his God, when a brother had shed a brother's blood, and from that on through the years of faithlessness, and wickedness, and malice, till the very earth had cried to His Father for vengeance. He could look forward to the end of time, knowing well that He had been 'set for the fall of many', that 'if He had not come they would not have had sin'; that throughout the centuries man would continue in some form to

'Crucify again to himself the Son of God
Making him a mockery.'

All this He could see at a glance, as on a former occasion He had seen
'All the kingdoms of the world
And the glory of them'

stretched out as a panorama before His eyes. All this He could see, the selfish, self-adoring sin of man and his consequent hardness of heart, the waste of His own bloodshedding, the love His soul poured out, which would receive so little in return; an infinite ocean of corrupt mankind weltering in its own rottenness, surging like a seething ocean against Him, rejecting with a mortal hatred the peace that He offered, and He alone could give.

And yet there was more than this. This welter of humanity in which He was engulfed was a welter of His own kith and kin. These sinful men, from Adam to the last that would be, were also His own brethren, He was Man with them, one and all; and though He was

> 'Made in all things like to man
> Sin alone excepted',

still He was now identified with them, the guilt with which they were charged He had taken on Himself. There are few of us who do not know the misery of conscious guilt, and the more innocent the soul by nature or by grace, the more will the misery be realized and crush it. Multiply this to infinity; on the one hand the Sinless of men, the

> 'Lamb of God
> In whom the Father is well pleased',

whom none could accuse of sin, yet who knew sin and its guilt as none but He could have known it, on the other hand the sense of guilt, not of one sin only, nor of the sins of one man only, but of all the sins of all mankind, of all the sins that have tended to make a hell of this fair world, that have broken the hearts and lives of millions of His beloved, that have seethed round the throne of His Father defying Him to vengeance, that have filled and fed the hell of eternity.

All this Jesus endured during that agony. He was Man; He took on Himself the consequences; He accepted the guilt of all that men had done, against His Father, against Himself, against the Holy Ghost, against their fellow-men; it was as if He were responsible for, almost as if He had committed, all the sins of all mankind. There was no man's shame and confusion, no man's remorse and desperation, no man's agony of sorrow and repentance, that Jesus did not share in that dread hour in the garden of Gethsemane. In that hour Man was atoning for what man had done; God was laying on Him the iniquities of us all; and the human self in Jesus fought with His greater self, that self which was at once one with men and one with His Father in heaven. It was a strife whose misery we cannot hope to fathom; we cannot see it even in shadow; but we can understand enough to realize the torture that could drag forth the cry :

> ' O my Father
> If it is possible
> Let this chalice pass from me.'

It was the cry of God suffering, the cry of the broken Son of God; yet, too, it was the cry of the Man of infinite strength. He prayed to the Father for relief; but only on conditions. He prayed for Himself, also He prayed against Himself, for His Father was greater than He :

> ' If it is possible
> If thou wilt
> Not my will
> But thine be done.'

The refrain is constant and unceasing. It is repeated more often than the prayer. The practice of His prayer through life revealed itself no less now; for how many times had He said that He had looked for one thing only :

> ' I came not to do my own will
> But the will of him that sent me ' ?

(c) *A Quotation.*

For once let us be allowed to quote an author who has entered deeply into the scene of the Passion. The sensitive soul of Newman passes the rest by; but when he comes to this mental suffering of Jesus he can refrain no longer. Thus he writes :

' And now, my brethren, what was it He had to bear, when He thus opened upon His soul the torrent of this predestinated pain? Alas! He had to bear what is well known to us, what is familiar to us, but what to Him was woe unutterable. He had to bear that which is so easy a thing to us, so natural, so welcome, that we cannot conceive of it as a great endurance, but which to Him had the scent and the poison of death. He had, my dear brethren, to bear the weight of sin; He had to bear our sins; He had to bear the sins of the whole world. Sin is an easy thing to us; we think little of it; we cannot bring our imagination to believe that it deserves retribution, and, when even in this world punishments follow upon it, we explain them away or turn our minds from them. But consider what sin is in itself; it is rebellion against God; it is a traitor's act who aims at the overthrow and death of his sovereign: it is that, if I may use a strong expression, which, could the Divine Governor of the world cease to be, would be sufficient to bring it about. Sin is the mortal enemy of the All-holy, so that He and it cannot be together; and as the All-holy drives it from His presence into the outer darkness, so, if God could be less than God, it is sin that would have power to make Him less. And here observe, my brethren, that when once Almighty God, by taking flesh, entered this created system, and submitted Himself to its laws, then forthwith this antagonist of good and truth, taking advantage of the opportunity, flew at that flesh which He had taken, and fixed on it, and was its death. The envy of the Pharisees, the treachery of Judas, and the madness of the people, were but the instrument or the expression of the enmity which sin felt towards Eternal Purity as soon as, in infinite mercy towards men, He put Himself within its reach. Sin could not touch His Divine Majesty; but it could assail Him in that way in which He allowed Himself to be assailed, that is, through the medium of His humanity. And in the issue, in the death of God incarnate, you are but taught, my brethren, what sin is in itself, and what it was which then was falling, in its hour and in its strength, upon His human nature, when He allowed that nature to be so filled with horror and dismay at the very anticipation.

'There, then, in that most awful hour, knelt the Saviour of the world, putting off the defences of His divinity, dismissing His reluctant Angels, who in myriads were ready at His call, and opening His arms, baring His breast, sinless as He was, to the assault of His foe,—of a foe whose breath was a pestilence and whose embrace was an agony. There He knelt, motionless and still, while the vile and horrible fiend clad His spirit in a robe steeped in all that is hateful and heinous in human crime, which clung close round His heart, and filled His conscience, and found its way into every sense and pore of His mind, and spread over Him a moral leprosy, till He almost felt Himself to be that which He never could be, and which His foe would fain have made Him. Oh, the horror, when He looked, and did not know Himself, and felt as a foul and loathsome sinner, from His vivid perception of that mass of corruption which poured over His head and ran down even to the skirts of His garments! Oh, the distraction, when He found His eyes, and feet, and lips, and heart, as if the members of the Evil One, and not of God! Are these the hands of the Immaculate Lamb of God, once innocent, but now red with ten thousand barbarous deeds of blood? Are these His lips, not uttering prayer, and praise, and holy blessings, but as if defiled with oaths, and blasphemies, and doctrines of devils? Or His eyes, profaned as they are by all the evil visions and idolatrous fascinations for which men have abandoned their adorable Creator? And His ears, they ring with sounds of revelry and strife; and His heart is frozen with avarice, and cruelty, and unbelief; and His very memory is laden with every sin which has been committed since the fall, in all the regions of the earth, with the pride of the old giants, and the lusts of the five cities, and the obduracy of Egypt, and the ambition of Babel, and the unthankfulness and scorn of Israel. Oh, who does not know the misery of a haunting thought which comes again and again, in spite of rejection, to annoy, if it cannot seduce? Or of some odious and sickening imagination, in no sense one's own, but forced upon the mind from without? Or of evil knowledge, gained with or without a man's fault; but which he would give a great price to be rid of at once and for ever? And adversaries such as these gather around Thee, Blessed Lord, in millions now; they come in troops more numerous than the locust or the palmer-worm, or the plagues of hail, and flies, and frogs, which were sent against Pharaoh. Of the living and of the dead and of the as yet unborn, of the lost and of the saved, of Thy people and of strangers, of sinners and of saints, all sins are there. Thy dearest are there, Thy saints and Thy chosen are upon Thee; Thy three apostles, Peter and James, and John, but not as comforters, but as accusers, like the friends of Job, "sprinkling dust towards heaven", and heaping curses on Thy head. All are there but one, one only is not there, one only; for she who had no part in sin, she only could console Thee, and therefore she is not nigh. She will be near Thee on the Cross, she is separated from Thee in the Garden. She has been Thy companion and Thy confidant through Thy life, she interchanged with Thee the pure thoughts and holy meditations of thirty years; but her virgin ear may not take in, nor may her immaculate heart conceive, what now is in vision before

Thee. None was equal to the weight but God; sometimes before Thy saints Thou hast brought the image of a single sin, as it appears in the light of Thy countenance, or of venial sins, not mortal; and they have told us that the sight did all but kill them, nay, would have killed them, had it not been instantly withdrawn. The Mother of God, for all her sanctity, nay, by reason of it, could not have borne even one brood of that innumerable progeny of Satan which now compass Thee about. It is the long history of a world, and God alone can bear the load of it. Hopes blighted, vows broken, lights quenched, warnings scorned, opportunities lost, the innocent betrayed, the young hardened, the penitent relapsing, the just overcome, the aged failing; the sophistry of misbelief, the wilfulness of passion, the obduracy of pride, the tyranny of habit, the canker of remorse, the wasting fever of care, the anguish of shame, the pining of disappointment, the sickness of despair, such cruel, such pitiable spectacles, such heart-rending, revolting, detestable, maddening scenes; nay, the haggard faces, the convulsed lips, the flushed cheek, the hard brow of the willing slaves of evil, they are all before Him now; they are upon Him and in Him. They are with Him instead of that ineffable peace which has inhabited His soul since the moment of His conception. They are upon Him, they are all but His own; He cries to His Father as if He were the criminal, not the victim; His agony takes the form of guilt and compunction. He is doing penance, He is making confession, He is exercising contrition, with a reality and a virtue infinitely greater than that of all saints and penitents together; for He is the One Victim for us all, the sole Satisfaction, the real Penitent, all but the real sinner.' (Discourses to Mixed Congregations: Mental Sufferings of Our Lord in His Passion.)

(d) *The Failure of the Three.*

But if the Father, in His love and wisdom, in His justice and mercy, would permit that His Son incarnate should so suffer, it behoved that men at least should give Him some companionship and relief. How many promises had they made, even this very night! How many warnings had He Himself given them, even to the last word He had spoken! How much had He done for them, how much was He doing for them at this moment! For an hour or more He had lain prostrate on the ground, as one crushed beneath a burthen that was too much for Him. At last He raised Himself, and turning, staggered back to the spot where He had left His beloved Three, the three chosen men out of all the world, chosen that they might be with Him in His hour of trial, and glorying in the honour that had been done to them. He came to them and found them asleep. The hour had been long, the watching and prayer which He had commended to them had lost itself in vain wandering; this last depressing reaction had weighed them down. At the beginning they had made an effort; their eyes had followed Him into the gloom and they had begun to pray. But they had not known what they should ask for when they prayed; their thoughts had flown far away, they had sought more comfortable seats beneath the olive trees, their heads had sunk upon their breasts, and they had yielded to sleep. So He found them, these poor men, who a few minutes before had been so valiant, and fervent, and trustful in their own strength :

> ' And he cometh to his disciples
> And findeth them asleep.'

Jesus felt it; how could He but feel it? In spite of the cold, dispassionate story as it is told by the evangelists, the disappointment of Jesus forces itself through. We have seen it often enough before; when ten men were healed, and only one returned to thank Him, when He looked on a rich young man, and loved him and invited him to come with Him, and that rich young man had turned away; when He offered men His body and blood, and they went back and walked with Him no more; when He wept over Jerusalem, because it 'would not'. Nowhere was Jesus more manifestly human in His life than when He responded to a show of friendship on the one hand, or to its rejection on the other; throughout the Passion no human feature is more manifest.

Nevertheless on this night of all nights, as we have seen already, He would not blame His own. He would complain, but with not a word of resentment; it would be more in warning than in anger, more for their sakes than for His own. Simon, in particular, He would admonish, for so much depended on him, and this would be the last time. Simon had promised more than the rest, and to him more had been given, on Simon the future had been definitely founded, from the love of Simon would come life to the flock. Him, therefore, as was only to be expected, Satan would try in a special way, for him in particular Jesus had prayed already. He would speak to Simon, first and apart, but He would not pass the others by. His presence before them awoke them from their slumber; a very different awakening this from the awakening of these same Three on Thabor, some six months before. Then:

> ' Lifting up their eyes
> They saw no one but only Jesus ' ;
> Matthew xvii, 8.

now they saw the same, and yet how great was the change!

> ' And he saith to Peter
> Simon
> Sleepest thou?
> What couldst thou
> Could you
> Not watch one hour with me?
> Watch ye and pray
> That ye enter not into temptation.'

Then, as if He spoke to Himself, as if in the midst of this disappointment, and in spite of the many warnings He had given, He would still find excuse for these weary knights, He added:

> ' The spirit indeed is willing
> But the flesh is weak.'

He did not wait for their reply; He did not remain to see what heed they would pay to His warning; He turned back once more to His solitude in the darkness. The disciples sat up when He addressed them; they looked at one another, finding no words that they could speak; in their drowsy state they scarcely noticed the condition of their Lord and Master who had stood in sorrow before them. They were ashamed, they told themselves they would do better. They pulled themselves together and made a further effort. But He was already away in the darkness; soon the same weariness came upon them, and they yielded to sleep once more.

Not so Jesus; with Him the struggle was by no means

over. In the early days, in the desert, He had been tempted
three successive times; three times now in the garden, it
would seem, He had to go through the same ordeal. Then
it had been to test whether or not He was the Son of God;
now He was to be thoroughly sifted as Man. Then He
spoke 'as one who had authority'; now He pleaded as
any broken man. Then He was challenged to trust Himself
to the care of angels; now He was fain to receive what
strength an angel might give Him. While the three
disciples in the distance settled to their rest, He again
dragged Himself away into the gloom, and fell alone upon
His knees once more. Yet what could He do? The very
power to pray seemed to have deserted Him, even as it
had deserted Peter, and James, and John, but it was not
sleep that had killed it, it was a weight that seemed too
great even for the shoulders of Jesus to bear. Who could
pray with such a load of sin upon him? Who could speak
as a son to his father, who bore as his own the guilt of all
the world? He could only repeat the selfsame words, the
selfsame words, again and again. And yet already there
was a difference :

'Thy kingdom come
Thy will be done
On earth as it is in heaven.'

So He had consistently taught His own to pray, so He had
prayed by word and deed throughout His life; now that
the hour of dereliction had come, mind and heart worked
according to their wont. When He first had prayed it had
been an appeal that the chalice might be taken from Him;
now that appeal was gone. Before, He had uttered first
His own human will, then that of His Father; now His
Father's will is the only one to be considered :

'And going away again
He went the second time
And prayed
Saying the selfsame words
O my Father
If this chalice cannot pass
Except I drink it
Thy will be done.'

Thus He lay upon the ground till the second paroxysm
was over. Again He rose to His feet, and made His way

through the shadows to His own; again He found them fast asleep beneath the olive tree. Indeed they were very weary, more weary now than when He had come to them before. There was the darkness around them, none the less emphasized because the moon was full; there was the growing chill of the night, more than usually cold for this season of the year. Still more there was creeping over them a sense of sadness and sorrow for which they could not account. He was keeping them longer this night than was His custom; they would be relieved when at last He would come and lead the way home to Bethania.

> 'And he cometh again
> And findeth them asleep
> For their eyes were heavy
> With sorrow.'

Again He would utter no word of blame or censure; more than that, He would no longer ask them to watch with Him. But He was anxious for their sakes. He must continue to warn them of their danger, whatever He might need for Himself. Thus once more, by this little act, He showed that His own battle was being won.

> 'And he said to them
> Why sleep you?
> Arise
> Pray
> Lest you enter into temptation.'

The appeal for companionship had gone; in its stead, the warning had deepened.

Once more the poor men awoke; more than ever they bestirred themselves. They stood up at His bidding; they tried to find words, if only to reiterate their fidelity; in spite of all their seeming weariness they would still be loyal to Him. But it was hard, harder now than it had ever been in all their lives before; even Peter at this moment could find no words to say. He had left them there alone, and when He was absent from them prayer was not easy:

> 'And they knew not
> What to answer him.'

For the second time He turned away and left them; He could do no more for them than He had done. Already across the valley the enemy was gathering his forces; perhaps by this time, with Judas to guide them, they had searched the supper-room and found He was not there. But if not there, still they were confident where they would find Him; He was not long gone and their guide was safe. And while they started on their way, and while the three fell asleep once more beneath the olive tree, and while the all-merciful Father held His hand upon Him out of love for all mankind, Jesus for the third time went forward alone into the darkness and fell again upon the ground, repeating His prayer of agony, sorrowful as one who could no longer bear to live:

> ' And leaving them
> He went away again
> And he prayed the third time
> Saying the same words.'

So much did this protracted hour of preparation cost Him. But at last His prayer was heard, not, it is true, in the form in which He had first expressed it, but wholly in its spirit, wholly in the way He wished to be heard. It is always so with prayer, we know not what we ask for when we pray, but the Spirit speaketh for us, and is heard in our stead, and when all is over then we see that the will of the Father is also our own deeper heart's desire. The chalice would not be taken from Him, but the Father's will would be done; and that it might be done strength was given to Him that He might drink that chalice to the dregs. Then indeed it would pass, not from Him only, but from all mankind. He who might have asked His Father, and would have received legions of angels to help Him, was now given one though He had not asked it. In Nazareth before He was incarnate an angel had announced His coming:

> ' The Son of the Most High
> Of whose kingdom there will be no end.'
> Luke i, 32, 33.

In Bethlehem when He was born a whole choir of angels, ' a whole multitude of the heavenly army ', had rejoiced at His coming, singing:

> ' Glory to God in the highest
> And on earth peace to men of goodwill.'
> Luke ii, 14.

An angel had told Joseph of His name ; an angel had saved Him from the sword of the tyrant Herod ; an angel had brought Him back from Egypt, and had guided Him to safe hiding once more in Nazareth. In the desert, after His forty days of prayer and fasting, and His first encounter with the prince of darkness, though He had refused to trust Himself to angels at that prince's bidding, yet in the end angels had come and ministered to Him. Now, when His time of trial was more grievous than all these, an angel again stood by Him and gave Him strength. He reminded Him of what would be, as the fruit of this ordeal ; the glory of the Father vindicated, the forgiveness of men secured, wrath turned to love, love manifested as only God could show, for Himself a name above every name, for men, not least of all, an example that would stir all future generations to emulate His noble sacrifice. What prayer would not be uttered, long and enduring, because of this His prayer ! Through what dark nights would not souls pass because of this darkest night of His own ! The agony was not lessened, but the strength to endure it was increased. This third phase was the hardest of them all, yet did He seem at last to be the more ready to endure. While He lay there on the ground the sweat oozed from His body, as we may sometimes see it pour from one who is intensely suffering. Gradually it became not sweat but blood. It soaked through His clothing ; it began to trickle down in drops and bedew the ground. Before men had yet laid hands upon Him He had poured out His blood for men.

> 'And there appeared to him an angel from heaven
> Strengthening him
> And being in an agony
> He prayed the longer
> And his sweat became as drops of blood
> Trickling down upon the ground.'

But while the body was so broken, the spirit within Him was renewed. The reed on which He had seemed to lean, the Three whom He had brought with Him, had bent beneath Him, but now He needed it no longer. From this moment we hear no more of His grief or of His depression, no more of fear or darkness, from now till at the last He appeals again to the Father ; the Jesus that we see throughout is Jesus the King. In all that follows we may never lose sight of this. Whatever men may do to Him He is always their Master, always Master of Himself and all about Him; if they sacrifice Him it will be because and when He permits it. He rose from the ground where He had lain prone; He walked again to the spot where the Three sat huddled together. They were still asleep, but now He would complain not at all. He would tread the wine-press alone; the battle must be for Him and no other; by His prayer as Man He had secured both the victory as Man, and the means by which it would be won.

> ' Then he cometh the third time to his disciples
> And saith to them
> Sleep ye now
> And take your rest
> It is enough
> The hour is come
> Behold the hour is at hand
> And the Son of Man shall be betrayed
> Into the hands of sinners.'

Even at this last hour, when peace and courage have been restored in the heart of Jesus Christ, the one great agony continues. In the gloom of it all else is forgotten; the maltreatment by the mob, the injustice, the scourging, the crowning, the insults, the being spat upon, the torture and shame of the crucifixion, all these He had dwelt upon before, but now they are as nothing in comparison with that initial act; the treachery of one of His own. The prospect of it had haunted Him all the night from the first assembling in the supper-room; it was with Him now when all the rest could be viewed with serenity. Indeed it is a great honour to have been betrayed by false brethren; and the nearer the traitor has been to our hearts, so much the nearer have our own hearts been to the heart of Jesus bleeding in the Garden. Says S. Augustine: ' He who injures my good name adds to my honour, little as he knows it.'

Yet Jesus has steadied Himself now to face even this unutterable shame; He has courage now for anything that may come. Nevertheless His human nature shrinks; as Man among men He is ashamed that man should be capable of such an act of treachery, so terrible, so deliberate, and now imminent, the blackest crime that ever man committed on this earth. It cannot be accepted without a shudder ; even yet, His human nature seems to say, it may be avoided ; to the last moment, as we shall see, Jesus gave to Judas the opportunity to save himself if he would. The enemy is already at the gate, He is hemmed in all around. But as more than once before, at Nazareth and in the Temple, He had passed through the hands of His enemies unhindered, so if He chose might He do so now. He turned to His Three ; He roused them as if He would make haste ; He spoke in hurried words :

> ' Rise up
> Let us go
> Behold he that will betray me
> Is at hand ',

as if He would say that provided that deed of shame could be avoided He would deliver Himself to the multitude hereafter. But no ; this the Father had permitted, this the prophets had foretold, this men after Him would have to endure, and He must not fail them. For their sakes He would drink the cup to its bitterest dregs, He would submit to the kiss of a traitor.

17. The Capture of Jesus.

(a) *The Meeting with the Crowd.*

Meanwhile up in the city His enemies had been busily occupied. We have seen how Judas had gone out from the supper-room into the night ; he had made his way thence to the place where he knew his accomplices would receive him, possibly the very next house to that which he had left. But that he should be so quick in accomplishing his task had not entered the minds of the scribes and Pharisees ; indeed they had long since decided that nothing should be done till after the festival was over. When, then, he appeared so suddenly among them they were utterly unprepared. He came to tell them that at that very moment they had a golden opportunity, such as they would scarcely get again. Jesus was taking supper with His followers in a house down the street ; he had himself only just come away, on the plea of having an errand to fulfil ; if they would make haste they might take Him there and then, before He could escape out of the city, and, since it

was so close at hand, and in their own quarter, before any
'tumult among the people' could be stirred. This, it
would seem, was in the mind of Judas when he left the
company of Jesus so early in the night.

His accomplices heard his plan but hesitated. They had
learnt to fear Jesus; He had escaped from them so often
and so easily before. This time they must take all precautions that they might hold Him safe; there must be
no hiding in secret places, no subduing of those sent to
arrest Him, no defiance which would make His captors so
quail as to leave Him alone, no appealing to the people
about who might rise in His defence. Yes, all things considered, the opportunity was one not to be lost. As to the
festival day, and their former decision, they could safely
lay aside their scruples, they could instead thank Jehovah
for so manifestly delivering Him into their hands, and they
could sacrifice all else in the noble purpose of serving the
public good. Judas, then, must be provided with a
sufficient escort, and one on which they could rely. There
were the guards of the households of Annas and Caiphas;
there were other sycophant servants and hangers-on, of
whom Annas in particular had plenty, whose function was
to do their master's will whatever it might be, on whom
the authorities might depend even more than on their own
officers. There were some Roman soldiers; a band of
these was stationed in that part of the city, in case of any
emergency. There were also others in the streets outside,
the rabble of the city; for in Jerusalem, as in other great
cities, as we have seen on a famous occasion in the life of
Jesus, when He healed the man born blind, the dwellings
of the great and the hovels of the dregs of the people were
not far apart. These were hurriedly gathered together, in
the courtyard and garden round the house of Annas. They
were armed as best they could be at the moment, with
swords, and clubs, and sticks of any kind. They were
warned that they would have to deal, not, perhaps, with a
dangerous ruffian, but with an artful contriver who might
easily slip through their hands. They were given their
orders to follow, and obey implicitly, this new zealot for
the Law:

> 'Judas Iscariot
> One of the Twelve.'

Judas himself was restless amid all this commotion. In the bargain he had made a few days before it had been stipulated that the capture should be made secretly and without commotion; but his designs, no less than those of the Pharisees, were destined to be brought to nought at every point. Moreover, to Judas time was precious. The supper would scarcely last more than an hour; with all these preparations, quite unnecessary as he now very well knew, his prey might escape, and the work would have to be planned again.

And indeed Jesus had escaped. When all the preparations had been made, the cortège set out to the house of the Supper, only to find that Jesus and His Eleven were gone. The crowd became suspicious; was this Judas Iscariot, one of the Twelve, evidently by nature not to be trusted, leading them on a fruitless errand? If he were, he would pay for it, of that he might be certain. But Judas reassured them; there was still hope. He knew that Jesus had made no arrangement to stay in Jerusalem that night; therefore it was certain that He would have gone back, as usual, to His resting-place in Bethania. On the road to Bethania, as they all knew, was an olive grove; it was the regular custom for Jesus to break His journey at that grove before He went over Olivet. If they would come with Him quickly they would certainly catch Him there. But let them come quietly; let them make no noise on the way, or they might give the alarm. When they arrived let them take Him by surprise; for in addition to Jesus there were others who might be more violent, and if there were a scuffle Jesus might escape them, as He had escaped them before.

'Now Judas also who betrayed him
One of the Twelve
Knew the place
Because Jesus had often resorted thither
With his disciples
Judas therefore
Having received a band of men and servants
From the chief priests and the Pharisees
The scribes and the ancients of the people
Cometh thither
While he was yet speaking
And with him a great multitude

With lanterns and torches and weapons
Swords and clubs and staves.'

Such, then, was the motley rabble that gathered round the garden gate that night under the guidance of Judas Iscariot. It was an army worthy of himself; it was in no way representative of the people of Jerusalem. It was typical of the mobs by which revolutions are made; reckless, violent, cruel, without an idea of their own. And Jesus knew they were there. He knew that again and again through the ages scenes like this would be repeated; that again and again His own would be taken, always in the name of justice, and of the people, and of law and order, and would be handed over to the refuse of mankind for them to do with them what they would. That night He had warned His own that it would come; He had encouraged them to face it with the assurance that the same had been done to Him:

' If the world hate you
Know ye that it hath hated me before you
If you had been of the world
The world would love its own
But because you are not of the world
But I have chosen you out of the world
Therefore the world hateth you
Remember my word that I said to you
The servant is not greater than his master
If they have persecuted me
They will also persecute you.'

John xv, 18–20.

' These things have I spoken to you
That you may not be scandalized
They will put you out of the synagogues
Yea the hour cometh
That whosoever killeth you
Will think that he doth a service to God.'

John xvi, 1–2.

Only a few days before, when they had sat together on Olivet looking down on the city for the last time, He had uttered the same warning:

' Then shall they deliver you up to be afflicted
And shall put you to death

And you shall be hated by all nations
For my name's sake.'
                    Matthew xxiv, 9.

Nay, further back, when He had first sent them out to preach, He had given them the advice :

'Behold I send you
As sheep in the midst of wolves
Be ye therefore wise as serpents
And simple as doves
But beware of men
For they will deliver you up in councils
And they will scourge you in their synagogues
And you shall be brought before governors
And before kings
For my sake
For a testimony to them
And to the gentiles.'
                    Matthew x, 16–18.

Now, therefore, He would give them another example, one they would never forget. He had just said :

'Rise up
Let us go
Behold he that will betray me is at hand ' ;

nevertheless He Himself showed no sign of going. As a child in Bethlehem an angel had saved His life from the sword of a brutal tyrant. At Nazareth in the early days, when His own fellow-townsmen had thought to make away with Him, He had passed through their hands and had saved them from the crime which would have stained the fair name of His beloved Nazareth for ever. In the Temple, more than once, when His enemies had thought to lay hands on Him or to stone Him, He had simply 'passed from their midst'. His hour had not yet come, and His Father's house, though they had made it a den of thieves, should not be further smeared with the blood of the Son. Often in other places the same danger had beset Him ; from the very beginning there were those who had decided on His death, and had only been waiting for their opportunity. He had avoided them all, He defied anyone to lay hands on Him, even 'that fox' Herod in Peroea who had done the

Baptist to death, and they had only feared Him the more.
Now, therefore, though the time had come

> 'To pass out of this world
> To the Father',

yet would He prove that He was still the same. Though
they were at last to have their way, yet should it only be
because He would surrender Himself into their hands.
Here in the garden, before anything were done to Him,
He would have this truth convincingly proclaimed.

Jesus was standing, already stained with blood, over
Peter, James, and John, as they lay overcome with sleep
beneath the olive tree. While He stood there the pur-
suivants had gathered round the gate, but had not ventured
in ; if He was to be taken, it was evident that He must go
Himself to meet them. He left the Three behind Him ; He
walked deliberately down the narrow path towards the
entrance ; while the gathered crowd stood silent, awaiting
the sign that would tell them they might begin their work,
His voice came through the darkness to them :

> 'Jesus therefore
> Knowing all things that were to come upon him
> Went forward
> And saith to them
> Whom seek ye ?'

It was a question that had often been asked before.
Down by the Jordan, on the first day the disciples had gone
after Him, they had been greeted by these very words :

> 'And Jesus turning
> And seeing them following him
> Saith to them
> What seek ye ?'

Indeed the one aim of His whole life had been that men
should seek Him, and in the end should find Him. He had
invited them to come, He had complained that they would
not come, He had promised all manner of good things to
those who would :

> 'Come to me
> And I will refresh you.'
> 'Come after me
> And I will make you fishers of men.'

> ' If any man thirst
> Let him come to me and drink.'
> ' I am come a light into the world
> And men will not come to me.'

And when at last one, who had been with Him for already a long time, had discovered and declared Him for what He was, His joy and His generous reward had known no bounds. But what a different seeking was this ! He had promised them that if they would seek Him He would give them life ; now they came seeking that life indeed !

The crowd was ready with its answer. The sign had not yet been given. Possibly in the darkness they did not recognize Him ; possibly even at that late date some had never seen Him :

> ' They answered him
> Jesus of Nazareth.'

It was a well-known name by this time ; even those who had never met Him had heard it often enough. Though they knew nothing of all the things that had been done far away in Galilee, here in and round Jerusalem there had been done enough to make the commonest rabble of the city talk. It had been said that He had once healed on an instant a poor, diseased beggar by the well in the North of the city ; that in the South in the quarter where they themselves dwelt He had healed a man born blind ; it was said that a mere appeal in His name never failed to win His favour ; that

> ' Jesus, Son of David
> Have mercy on us ',

had always received what it asked. Long since, men had come to take sides, for or against Jesus of Nazareth.

Jesus welcomed their cry of His name, as He always did. They might call to Him in hatred, yet should they have the same response as the best of His friends ; if they wanted Him, for good or for evil, they should have Him :

> ' Jesus saith to them
> I am he ' ;

And S. John immediately adds the sentence :

> ' And Judas also
> Who betrayed him
> Was with them.'

Judas was there, and heard the declaration of Jesus; at this last moment Jesus would save him from the crime he was about to commit. He would forestall the act of treachery; He would surrender Himself so that there would be no need for Judas to carry out his evil promise. He was there before the rest, already nearest of them all to Jesus. It would be easy for him to get himself free. Let him leave the company with whom he had come; let him join the Three in the darkness; no one, not even the Eleven, need have known what he had done. This surely is the meaning of the sentence of S. John; even at that last moment Jesus was faithful to His own.

But the call, alike for Judas and the crowd, was neglected; the offer, as so often, was thrown aside. But Jesus would still not leave them to their fate. They had called for 'Jesus of Nazareth', and that name meant 'Saviour'; therefore yet again, in another way, He would warn them of the evil thing they were about to do. He had scarcely spoken, when the power of His word was felt:

> 'As soon as he had said to them
> I am he
> They went backward
> And fell to the ground.'

Years after, S. Paul would thus extol the name of Jesus:

> 'He humbled himself
> Becoming obedient unto death
> Even to the death of the cross
> For which cause
> God also hath exalted him
> And hath given him a name
> Which is above all names
> That in the name of Jesus
> Every knee shall bow
> Of those that are in heaven
> On earth and under the earth.'

One cannot help asking oneself whether the Apostle had in mind the scene of which we are here told.

But it was enough that the lesson should be taught them; at this moment, in this 'their hour', He would not drive the lesson home. The time would come when 'in the name of Jesus of Nazareth ', men would be made to 'rise and walk'; now they would be made to fall to the ground, but no more. There would be a time when whatsoever they asked of the Father in that name would be given to them; now, since they sought Him, no matter for what purpose, He would give them Himself. But He would give them no more; He would not give them His own whom He had with Him, not though His own had already offered to die with Him. It was more than enough that He had lost one. The last act of His commanding power before He surrendered to the traitor should be exercised for their protection. Only a few hours before He had asked the Father to keep them in the future in His name; now once more, even at this absorbing moment, He would show them how He loved them as the apple of His eye. The crowd recovered from its rebuff; it stood there inactive, not knowing what was next to be done. Jesus had taught it its lesson; now He would take up the scene where it had been interrupted, and let come what might.

> ' Again therefore he asked them
> Whom seek ye?
> And they said
> Jesus of Nazareth
> Jesus answered
> I have told you I am he
> If therefore you seek me
> Let these go their way ';

and the Evangelist sees in this another careful fulfilment of the prophecy made in the supper-room:

> ' That the word might be fulfilled which said
> Of those whom thou hast given me
> I have not lost any one.'

(b) *The Betrayal.*

Thus had Jesus of His own accord given Himself up to His enemies. He had protected His own, and had separated Himself from them. He had given Judas the means to avoid his crime and escape; there was no need of further identification. But Judas by this time was not to be won. His heart had long since been hardened; he had thrown in his lot with the band of Satan and he would not draw back. He had made a promise, and he would keep it; when later he claimed his reward, his promotion, no one should say he had not played his part. As they had come up the road the plan had been arranged. Jesus would be easy of access to Judas, as He had always been. They had parted friends that night; they would meet as friends again; and the sign of their meeting as friends would be to his followers the sign that they might take Him. But they must be careful; they must be sure they held him safe; they must be cautious and wary, allowing Him no way of escape. Often before He had eluded His captors; if they were careless He would elude them again:

> 'And he that betrayed him
> Had given them a sign saying
> Whomsoever I shall kiss
> That is he
> Lay hold on him
> Hold him fast
> And lead him away cautiously.'

Now was the moment for Judas to fulfil his contract. Jesus stood there alone, the light from the lanterns picking Him out from the darkness. He would have saved Judas, if Judas had chosen to be saved; but He would not compel him; never yet had He compelled anyone, nor would He ever do so. Judas should now be allowed to do his worst; that terrible worst, which had haunted Jesus from the beginning, which, whenever He had thought of the Passion, had always stood out as the greatest shame of all. Judas came forward through the lighted space, he spoke to Jesus as a friend; on his face there was the smile of glad welcome; he threw his arms round Him, he put his lips to His cheek, he spoke to Him as to one whom he held very dear:

> 'And when he was come
> Immediately going up to Jesus he said
> Hail Rabbi
> And he kissed him.'

It was the action of a moment; but it was the most terrible moment in the history of man. Away by Cæsarea Philippi, not a year before, Judas had heard Simon proclaim, in the name of them all:

' Thou art the Christ
The Son of the Living God ',

and he had not protested. Jesus could not say of him, as later He could make Himself say of His executioners :

' Father forgive him
For he knows not what he does.'

He could warn him ; He had done so again and again, during the whole of that last year. He could use all manner of endearments to win him from his evil way ; He could keep him closer with Him than others, He could trust him as He had not trusted them, He could give him counsel all his own, He could wash his feet, He could call him not a servant but a friend, and allow him to call Him the same, He could give him the power of miracles, send him to preach in His name, see to it that men were won by his preaching, that he shared all honour with the rest of His chosen Twelve. But He could do no more. If the will of Judas would not bend, if he would abide by his choice, if malice could so possess him, Jesus must let things take their course ; it were better for Judas had he never been born. Still even then would Jesus not condemn ; condemnation belonged to the Father. He was there to save, not to destroy ; He would yield not one tittle of His saving right, not even under such provocation. Judas, traitor as he now was, was still His own, one of those ' whom He had chosen Himself', whom the Father had given Him out of the world, who had once stood with Him in His temptations ; whom having loved He would love to the end. Whatever Judas did to Him, Jesus would not of Himself annul that friendship. He would make a last appeal, even at this eleventh hour. Secretly, as He had done before ; affectionately, as He could not but always do ; with that love which sought not its own, which endured all things, He answered Judas. While the hands of betrayal still clung about Him, while the sense of the indignity surged within Him, while all nature seemed to cry out against the deed of shame that was being done, Jesus whispered to Judas, the last words he was ever to hear from His lips :

' And Jesus said to him
Friend
Whereto art thou come ?

> Judas
> Dost thou
> Betray the Son of man
> With a kiss?'

It was a terrible indictment; there was not a word too much or too little. Jesus has been often revealed as the master of human language, but nowhere is He more complete, more concise, at once human and divine, than here. He who said those words, who held those thoughts in His heart, for such a man, at such a time, under such provocation, was more than man.

The deed had been done, the signal had been given; Jesus could now submit to whatever was to follow. The plan of Judas had succeeded; Jesus had clearly been deceived. His success gave the rabble courage; Judas now could disappear and leave the rest to them. At once the silence of the night was broken; the mob that till then had been held in check, first by Judas, then by Jesus, now resumed its noisy clamour, that clamour that turns cowards into mock heroes. They came up and pressed upon Jesus of Nazareth; they laid their hands upon Him, and this time He showed no inclination to escape. At last His magic power was gone; the kiss of the traitor had undone Him, as the caresses of Delilah had undone the mighty Samson. Now in His presence they could be very brave indeed:

> 'They then came up
> And laid hands on him
> And held him.'

But for the companions of Jesus this was indeed a new situation. Let it be remembered that, for most of them at least, the action of Judas need not have appeared as anything strange. He had gone out from the supper-room, as they had presumed, upon an errand, some commission given to him by Jesus. He had come back to them here in the garden; he had gone to salute his Master, and tell Him that the commission had been done, nay more, he had owned Him before this threatening crowd. It was a noble act, a good act, a brave act; as before they had always tended to follow the lead of Judas, so they would follow it now. They, too, would renew their courage and be brave. Now they remembered that at the Supper Jesus had forewarned them that they should have swords in readiness for what was to happen that night; and they had said that they would go with Him even to death. Against all these odds they would fight for their Master. On other occasions He had tested their courage, and blamed them for their want of faith and trust; it might be that He was only testing them now. Simon Peter especially; he had been tried before as none of the others, rewarded for his faith and trust as none of them. That night he had committed himself further than the rest, protesting that he would not deny his Lord, that he would die with Him; he must be their leader in courage now.

> ' And they that were about him
> Seeing what would follow
> Said to him
> Lord
> Shall we strike with the sword?
> Then one of them that was with Jesus
> Simon Peter
> Stretching forth his hand
> Drew his sword
> And striking the servant of the high priest
> Cut off his right ear
> And the name of the servant was Malchus.'

The story is so naive as almost to cause a smile. These uncouth men from Galilee, easily stirred to a fray, had heard their Master tauntingly called 'Jesus of Nazareth'. A few hours before, in the supper-room, they had been discussing among themselves who should be the foremost in the kingdom; during all that week, since the Sunday's triumphal march, they had been telling themselves that at last the kingdom was at hand. Now was their opportunity to show their prowess; kingdoms must be won by battle. It was true they had but two swords among them. But they would be brave none the less. If once upon a time, when they were fighting the waves and the storm, they had shown themselves afraid, they would not be afraid now; if then He helped them, He would come to their aid again.

Simon Peter drew the first sword. He struck, it did not matter how or where; he struck one in the vanguard of the crowd, an official in the high priest's household. The blow was partly averted; it cut off the man's right ear.

We are told that the man's name was Malchus; if we may judge from other cases, we may conclude that Malchus was later a disciple of Peter, a member of the Christian Church.

But this daring deed received a very different reward from that which they had expected. Jesus did not seem willing to encourage them; on the contrary He held them back. He came forward between them. Peter had done foolishly and might suffer for it; Jesus would still care for His own.

'Suffer ye thus far',

He said; the words were gentle, they did not blame, they merely told His would-be defenders that now they had done enough. Then He turned to Simon Peter, who stood there wondering at himself, what he had done and what he should do next. Jesus had a last lesson to teach Simon; one which in later years the Apostle would put into practice with wonderful effect. The kingdom of Jesus Christ did not, and never would, depend upon the sword; if the sword were ever to be drawn, in misguided zeal, to spread it, there would be left on the battle-field the seeds of its own undoing. It had other weapons for its defence and for its conquests, far more effective than the sword; weapons which were not of this world. It had other armies to fight for it; not twelve recruits from Galilee, but twelve legions of His Father's angels were at His command should He call for them. For the enemies of the kingdom were not men, not even the men arrayed before Him at that moment. These were but poor creatures, poor misguided creatures who knew not what they did, as were all the others who failed to see 'the things that were to their peace'. His warfare was not, and never would be, against men; it would be only against the spirits who deluded them:

'Principalities and powers
The rulers of the world of this darkness
The spirits of wickedness in the high places',
Ephesians vi, 12.

and against such enemies other weapons than the sword were needed. For the present let men have their way; by doing what they did they would only confirm the truth of the word of God. Since the Father willed it, let Him suffer; since the chalice had to be drunk, He had the strength to drink it:

> 'Then he said to Peter
> Put up again thy sword into the scabbard
> For all that take the sword
> Shall perish with the sword
> Thinkest thou that I cannot ask my Father
> And he will give me presently
> More than twelve legions of angels?
> How then shall the Scriptures be fulfilled
> That so it must be done?
> The chalice which my Father hath given me
> Shall I not drink it?'

He who spoke was the same self-possessed Jesus Christ that we have always seen; restraining, not Himself, for indeed He needed no restraint, but the over-eager zeal of those who would fain imagine they could fight and die for Him. He had set the example of submission and service; He proclaimed them blessed who suffered persecution, for theirs would be the kingdom. He Himself had conquered His own by service; by the service of men, not by violence, His kingdom would be spread. He suited the deed to the word. He had said:

> 'Love your enemies
> Do good to them that hate you
> Bless them that curse you
> And pray for them that calumniate you
> And to him that striketh you on the one cheek
> Offer him also the other.'

He would show that even at this moment He was what He had always been; nay, more, for here was a wound received on His own account, from one of His own disciples. He went forward to the wounded man. He put His hand on the stricken ear, thereby, it may have been, mingling the sufferer's blood with His own. He took away His hand and the wound was healed.

Such was the first act of Jesus in His Passion; strong and masterful, tender and gentle, every word and deed worthy of a king, yet in perfect harmony with that other side of Him which would gather men to Him 'as a hen gathers her little ones under its wing'. Then He turned once more to the multitude before Him. Now for the first time we hear that besides the servants and rabble that made up that multitude there were others there of more account. We had been told that the chief priests and elders had gathered a rabble together to go with Judas, now we find that some of these same ancients had followed in the rabble's wake. Curiosity had got the better of them; hatred had driven them; the darkness would conceal them; they had been unable to wait, but had come themselves to see how their design would prosper. They stood behind the crowd in the lane, however they used these people they would not touch them; had they not said of them and their likes:

'This multitude
That knoweth not the law
Are accursed'?

John vii, 49.

They stood behind the crowd, but the darkness did not hide them from the eyes of Jesus. As on a former occasion at Capharnaum, when their allies in the North had stood behind the crowd, and had first suggested that He worked by Beelzebub, so now He called across to them, leaving their deluded followers aside, and made His first address to them alone. They were soon to put Him on His trial; He would first put them on theirs. They were soon to trump up false charges against Him, of His having threatened to destroy their Temple and the like; He would first show them how faithful He had been to that Temple and its spirit, how they themselves had paid Him respect when He had been there. In that very Temple, but three days before, some of them had come to Him and said:

'Master
We know that thou art a true speaker
And teachest the word of God in truth';

what defence, then, could they make of the deed that they were doing now? He would not condemn them; He would but ask them a question, which was always His method when He complained; in the answer to that question they would condemn themselves, long before they passed sentence on Him.

> ' In that same hour
> Jesus said
> To the chief priests and the magistrates of the Temple
> And the ancients and the multitude
> That were come to him
> Are you come out
> As it were against a robber
> With swords and clubs and staves
> To apprehend me ?
> I sat daily with you
> Teaching in the Temple
> And you did not stretch forth your hand against me.'

No, even then He would not condemn. He would look for an excuse even for such as these ; and He found it in the knowledge that by this road He must enter into His glory, by defeat He must win His triumph. Therefore, pitying them rather than blaming them, as if the fault were less theirs than that of a power that drove them, He added :

> ' But this is your hour
> And the power of darkness.'

(c) *The Desertion.*

It was evident by now to the Eleven, or to such of them as were still there, that Jesus, their Master and Lord, would this time do nothing for Himself. Hitherto, on like occasions, even in broad daylight, He had always passed out of the hands of His assailants ; this night, though the darkness was about Him, and escape through the garden was an easy matter, He stood there and allowed men to handle Him as He had never done before. Moreover, He had forbidden them to defend Him ; He had even hinted that they might go. It was a new and strange experience ; it was the climax of a series of strange happenings that day. In Bethania in the early afternoon, when He had sent Simon and John into the city to prepare the Pasch, they had noticed the mixture of authority with sadness that had seemed to come upon Him. In the supper-room all through the night He had spoken in mystery, things that they half understood, stirring them to new enthusiasm; yet also forebodings, and warnings, and assurances of trials and failures, which they had almost resented. After the Supper, along the road to the garden, He had shown Himself so broken that they were glad to leave Him to Himself. In the garden Peter and James and John had seen Him coming to them, and pleading with them, as if He could no longer endure to be alone. It was true, even now, in spite of all this, He still spoke 'as one having authority'; He still held His enemies at bay till His own part was played. Nevertheless it was now clear what the issue would be; that in the end He meant to yield to them was evident. What then could they do? He had already told His captors that His own must first be allowed to go their way; perhaps then it was His wish that they should go. Conscience, on the other hand, told them that they should stay; they had promised to stand with Him, even though that meant that they should die by His side. Nevertheless fear had begun to dictate; fear greater than that which had once overcome them on the lake, greater than that which, in Capharnaum, had prompted them to warn Him to be more upon His guard, greater than that which they had felt in Peræa, when He had asked them to return with Him into the danger zone of Judæa. In those days, under all those anxious circumstances, they still had Him always to lead them, and in His strength they, too, could be strong. Had He not this very night praised them for their constancy? Had He not said :

> 'You are they who have stood with me
> In my temptations'?

Now that strength was gone; they had nothing on which they could rely. This kind of fear was a new thing to them; and it broke them. While the hustling crowd renewed its courage, while the din and commotion grew more threatening and came nearer, a panic seized them. They turned and fled, back into the darkness of the olive grove where escape would have been easy even for Him, each one to whatever place he chose :

> 'Then his disciples leaving him
> Fled away.'

He knew it would be so; He had foretold it an hour or more before. The first loneliness of Jesus Christ had come upon Him, the second and greater was yet to come:

> ' Behold the hour cometh
> And now is come
> That you shall be scattered
> Every man to his own
> And shall leave me alone
> And yet : I am not alone
> Because the Father is with me.'

S. Mark here adds an incident which seems to have little connection with the rest of the story of the Passion, and therefore is all the more stamped with the evidence of historic fact. Of all the Evangelists S. Mark is the most concise; though his narrative is in many ways the most dramatic and full of colour, most like the narrative of an eye-witness, still he would seem to be the most economic in his choice, both of words and of subject matter. This has led commentators to believe that in this incident he describes his own part in the scene at the garden gate that night. Mark, we know from other evidence, was of the richer class; it may well have been that he was the owner, or the son of the owner, of the house in which the Supper had been held. He may have noticed that something unusual was happening in the street that evening, above all if, as has been already suggested, Judas and his band had first visited the house before they came to the Garden of Gethsemane. In that case we need not be surprised if he followed after, to see what was afoot. He would have been close behind the crowd, yet apart, and not with those elders and other dignitaries who by their presence were giving the proceedings their countenance. When the mob turned it would easily have noticed him, and that he was not one of its number; indeed his very presence, aloof from the rest, would have been a stab to a guilty conscience. But by this time its blood was up; the more guilty it knew itself to be, the more reckless it became. It was now prepared for any cruelty on any victim, innocent or guilty, such cruelty as is always the mark of cowardice joined to licence. And as nothing is so cruel as an incensed mob, it was prepared to vent its spite on anyone. It had lost the disciples, here was one who might take their place. If this be so, the story of S. Mark is an incident in keeping with the rest; he is the forerunner of many an innocent sufferer that has fallen a victim to a senseless rabble :

> ' And a certain young man followed him
> Having a linen cloth cast about his naked body
> And they laid hold on him
> But he casting off the linen cloth
> Fled from them naked.'

CHAPTER VII

18. Jesus before Annas.

JESUS now gave permission to His captors to do their worst. He had asserted His authority; He had declared how He could defend Himself if He would, He had already beforehand rendered good for evil; He had made His appeal to the best that was in them, their memory of their former freedom with Him. For the rest the Scriptures must be fulfilled; the will of His Father must be done, and He had no other will of His own but to do it. He had a baptism wherewith He must be baptized, and until it was accomplished His own work on earth would not be completed, His heart would not be satisfied. He would let men do with Him what they would; every vilest instinct that dwelt in man, the worse than beast of which he was always capable, should be let loose and be allowed to vent itself upon Him. Love had been trampled underfoot, truth had been slighted, hatred had been given the reins; the world should see for all time, if it chose to see, to what extreme hatred would always drive. The mob, given its way, gathered like a pack of ravenous wolves around Him; in their midst the police and their tribune, the guardians of law and order, assumed a pompous authority, as if the capture belonged by right to them. A few months before they had been sent to take Him prisoner, and had been beaten by His mere word:

> ' And they said to them
> Why have you not brought him?
> The ministers answered
> Never did man speak like this man.'
>
> John vii, 45–46.

Now that voice was silenced, that eye no longer made them fear; instead, Jesus had given them permission to do what they had come to do, and they could proceed.

> 'Then the band and the tribune
> And the servants of the Jews
> Took Jesus and bound him.'

In these few words we are told of the first act of violence done to Jesus in the Passion. The moon was full, lighting up the scene with a light that invited to silence, and making the shadows beneath the trees the darker. The hands of Jesus were bound with cords behind Him; a rope was tied about His waist, for from what follows we know that He was dragged from one place to another. The captors set out down the hill, noisy in the night, boasting to themselves because of their easy victory, brave enough now that it was clear that their prey would offer no resistance. There had been no need after all for the swords and clubs and sticks; no need for the warning of Judas, that they should be cautious and secure in what they did. Their victim's magic powers had deserted Him, if they had ever really existed; with the kiss of a friend His strength had failed Him, and they need not fear Him any more. They crossed again over the brook Kedron, in which some would see a prophecy fulfilled, up the slope once more and by the lower gate into the city, along the same road and down the same street that both He and they had traversed a short time before.

Officially the captors had been sent by Caiphas and his council; therefore officially they were to hand over their prisoner to them. But on their way they passed the house of Annas; and Annas, though no longer holding office, yet was, and had been for years, the 'power behind the throne', the ruling spirit of Jewry. He had himself been high priest; five of his sons were high priests after him, as well as a son-in-law, Caiphas, and a grandson. He was a Sadducee by profession, and was hard; an unbeliever in spite of his dignity, as were others of his class; one who had evolved a creed of his own, satisfying all his requirements in this world, since he did not believe in another, and not believing in another, then even in this world he believed in none but himself; Annas was his own god, his own beginning and end, cool, calculating, determined, successful, wise with the wisdom of the children of men. Indeed he was the wise man of Jerusalem; the independent man who was never ruffled; the prudent man who would always in the end secure his own way, who could promote men to office, and let them govern as they would, yet somehow through it all his own will was done. He was the father-in-law of Caiphas, the ruling high priest at that time ; both history and the Gospels indicate that Caiphas owed his priesthood to Annas. It was common, almost natural, especially if it was known that Annas wished it, to bring important cases before him for a preliminary judgment, and the case of Jesus of Nazareth was surely one of these.

For this reason, when they came to the gate of Annas' court, the guard almost instinctively turned in. By this time Judas had gone, for he had done his work, and no one gave him further thought ; the soldiers had no one now to guide them. They could scarcely have been surprised to find the old man waiting for them. Of all the elders of Judæa none could have known the significance of Jesus Christ and His teaching better than Annas. Whether he believed or not, he was well acquainted with the Law and the Prophets ; of the practice of the Temple, and the meaning of that practice, he was the first exponent in the land, indeed he had made good use of his prerogative for the enrichment of himself and his family. He knew well that according to the prophets, and according to the firm belief of the people, there would one day come a Messias. He knew that His coming, if there was any truth in Judaism at all, was destined to inaugurate a new Law, a new kingdom, a new ceremonial ; in a true sense it was not so much Jesus Christ of Nazareth that he and his following had need to fear, as the new thing that He might found and leave behind Him. What had alarmed Herod the King when Jesus was born, made Annas suspicious now ; Annas was the true successor of Herod. To him the mere death of Jesus was a secondary matter ; of what use would that death be if, nevertheless, followers were left to propagate His doctrine ? If with Jesus the guards had also brought His disciples, Annas would have been better pleased.

Therefore at this preliminary trial we may notice a sharp contrast with all that followed. Here were no witnesses brought, no sentence was passed. Jesus was not asked to pronounce His own condemnation ; He was questioned only about those things in which Annas himself was interested. Jesus stood bound before this merciless, masterful, far-seeing, calculating man. That He would be ultimately condemned, Annas had no doubt at all; he could safely leave that to his more eloquent and self-righteous son-in-law, who knew well enough already what was Annas' mind. But his own examination went deeper; he looked through Jesus, as it were, and beyond Him, making nothing of Him, making much of what might follow after He was dead. Hence the nature of his questions; who Jesus actually was, whether indeed He were or were not what He was said to be, what were the charges to be brought against Him—all these things were of no account to Annas. What mattered more was the influence He possessed, the sway over other men that was pitted against his own; who, and how many, and of what kind, were His followers; what was the secret of His teaching which gave Him His power, not only over friends but also over enemies. Annas called for no other evidence; he wanted only the secret of the Man Himself, and that only Jesus could give him:

'The high priest therefore asked Jesus
Of his disciples
And his doctrine.'

But Jesus 'knew what was in man', and He knew Annas. If He could so easily sum up 'that fox' Herod, if He could so boldly and convincingly accuse 'the scribes and Pharisees, hypocrites', if He could silence the Sadducees by a single question, so that they could harass Him no more, He needed not that any man should reveal Annas to Him. Moreover, Annas was not one to whom He was bound to reply. He was no official judge, he had no authority to put questions to anyone on his trial; Jesus was in no sense his subject, before the Law they were equal men. To Caiphas, when the time came, He would reply as was His duty; to the questionings of Annas He would give no positive answer. All through the Passion we shall notice this exact attention to the claim of the Law on the part of Jesus; never for a moment was He anything but the Master, even of those who held Him their prisoner:

'Jesus answered him
I have spoken openly to the world
I have always taught in the synagogue
And in the temple whither all the Jews resort

> And in private I have spoken nothing
> Why askest thou me?
> Ask them who have heard
> What I have spoken to them
> Behold they know what things I have said.'

Which of these two was the judge of the other? As Jesus in the garden had held the crowd till such time as He chose to let it have its will, so now He held Annas, and Annas could do no more. As of old, on many an occasion, He had defied Pharisees and Sadducees till they could make no answer, but could only retire to plot against Him, so now He silenced Annas. Least of all would He answer Him anything which might betray any one of His own. Had Annas lived in Galilee he would have long since learnt how futile would be any question that might lead to injury ' of His disciples '. Had Annas lived in Galilee he would have known how tenderly He had cared for them, how He had defended them when they were accused of gathering corn on the Sabbath, how He had spoken for them when their customs at table had been blamed, how, when one of them had been too bold about paying the tribute, He had worked a miracle to save him from embarrassment. Though men might injure or accuse Himself, never a word uttered against them went unrebuked.

Annas was silenced and had failed; for once he had met one who dared to defy and challenge him. He could do no more. He could not condemn, for that was not within his office; even if he could he would not, for that might compromise him. But his sycophants in the room read the mind of their master well, and willingly supplied what he was too cautious of himself to do. They saw that he had been worsted, and they would avenge him; be he right or wrong, that this lord of theirs should be defied was not to be endured. Honest defence there was none; there remained only that of brutality, that commonest resort of might and cowardice in high places. A guard was standing by; it is the duty of a guard to defend his ward from injury, not only to hold him that he may not escape. But here it was manifest what would please the master of the court. Annas would not demean himself, would not even show a sign of discomfiture, but brutality in another would be easily condoned. The guard raised his soldier's strong arm ; with his fist he struck Jesus on the mouth ; it was the second of the deliberate injuries of which we are expressly told.

> ' And when he had said these things
> One of the officers standing by
> Gave Jesus a blow
> Saying
> Answerest thou the high priest so ? '

If we need a proof, beyond His own unhesitating words, that Jesus was the Master in the interview with Annas, we have it in the soldier's anger. So much was He the Master that His guard could interpret His attitude as arrogance ; and in reward he offered Him an insult, the greatest insult one man could offer to another in those days, so great that a Greek philosopher had declared it unforgivable, whatever else a man of honour may allow himself to forgive. Yet had Jesus long since said how such a blow should be received. When they were struck upon the face, He had told His own what they should do ; and what He said was very different from anything that had been said before Him :

> ' You have heard that it hath been said
> An eye for an eye
> And a tooth for a tooth
> But I say to you not to resist evil
> But if one strike thee on the right cheek
> Turn to him also the other
> And if a man will contend with thee in judgment
> And take away thy coat
> Let go thy cloak also unto him.'
> Matthew v, 38–40.

If, then, Annas would have an answer ' concerning His doctrine ', he should have it by example more than in words.

Jesus recovered Himself from the staggering blow ; though the mark of it would remain, blue and black, across His face to the end, yet was He unmoved. One thing only He would do, as He had often done before when He had been hurt or injured. He would complain, He would defend plain justice, but, as on so many occasions before, His complaint and His defence would be put as a simple question that could not be answered. He turned from

Annas to the guard; meekly, yet no less 'as one having authority',

> 'Jesus answered him
> If I have spoken ill
> Give testimony of the evil
> But if well
> Why strikest thou me?'

It was the same Jesus then, in word and in manner, as He had always been:

> 'Will you also go away?'
> 'Were not ten made clean?
> And where are the nine?'
> 'Which of you shall convince me of sin?
> If I speak the truth to you
> Why do you not believe me?'
> 'Many good works have I done among you
> For which of them do you stone me?'
> 'So long a time have I been with you
> And have you not known me?'
> 'Friend
> Whereto art thou come?'
> 'Judas
> Dost thou betray the Son of Man
> With a kiss?'
> 'Have you come out as it were against a thief
> To apprehend me?'

A grim silence fell upon the court. The rebuke was just and there was no answer. But that meant no conversion or remorse; malice is not convinced or converted, it suffers no repentance. It was only clear now to Annas that he could gain no more from this Man who, by His simplicity and truth, was more than equal to all his astuteness. He, too, like his colleagues in the Temple, three days before 'durst ask Him no more questions'. He would dismiss Him to those who were less subtle than himself, and therefore would be less cautious; they would at least have authority which he had not and he knew well how they would use it. With that easy contempt which falsehood in high places can assume when it is beaten, he dismissed the prisoner and His guard; the business after all was not his concern, it did not even interest him. He went into his palace as if nothing had been brought before him ; we do not hear of Annas any more till long after Jesus had been dead and buried, and then once more we find him busy :

> 'About his disciples
> And his doctrine.'

19. Jesus before Caiphas.

(a) *The Witnesses.*

By this time it was well into the night. Even at the Supper it had been already dark, and later the pursuers of Jesus had come to the Garden with lanterns. The Law indeed forbade that trials should take place after nightfall, but this night all law and justice were scattered to the winds. The occasion was exceptional, indeed unique, and every law had its exceptions. So unlooked for had been this capture, so well thus far had the plan succeeded, it must not be allowed to fail because of some trivial formality ; unless they hurried forward this Man might yet in some mysterious way escape them. They feared Him, they hated Him, and they had much to avenge. His judges, then, could easily forget all convention, all order and form ; they could find excuses in abundance that they might have their will. Long since they had decided that He must die. They had proved to themselves that to compass His death was a holy act and patriotic ; then that the holy act might be done they must not stand too much upon such a trifle as the keeping of the letter of the Law. Many writers have shown in how many ways justice was violated during the course of the Passion ; some have gone further and said that the violations are so many as to prove the whole story untrue. We know there is another conclusion ; in any case we are concerned, not with the law and the breakers of the law, but with Him on whose account they broke it.

Contrary to all justice, then, there were gathered together in the house of Caiphas that night :

> 'The priests and the scribes
> And the ancients.'

We can see them as they waited for their prey, seated in order in a semicircle round the council chamber. What was to be the issue of that trial they had long since decided ; all that was needed now was that they should give the sentence the appearance of justice. Therefore witnesses must be called, men who would give evidence sufficient to allow them to condemn; in the East witnesses of that kind are easily forthcoming. Jesus was led in before that assembly; still bound, still a prisoner, an onlooker might have said that His very degradation, as He stood there, was evidence of His guilt. Was this the Man who had once defied the rulers of the Temple in their very stronghold, and had accused them before the world of making His Father's house a den of thieves? Was this He who had told them to their faces, in that same Temple area, that they were degenerate sons of Abraham, and that the devil was their father? Was this He who had accused them of sin which should never be forgiven? Who had challenged their most sacred ceremonial, who had spurned their demand for 'a sign', had called them 'a wicked and adulterous generation', had warned men against their hypocrisy, had put them to shame and confusion before their own disciples, had called down 'Woe' upon them as He had told all the world of the evil of their ways? Was this He who had ridiculed their fasting and almsgiving, who had repudiated their manner of prayer, who had set up publicans, and Samaritans, and even public sinners, as being better men than they? Was this He who had said they would die in their sin, and that others, not of the race of Abraham, would go into the kingdom before them? Surely if anyone deserved to be condemned for contempt of court it was this Jesus of Nazareth, miracles or no miracles, good works or not, let His teaching of truth, and justice, and mercy, and forgiveness be what it might.

Now after so many vain attempts that they had almost despaired of taking Him, at last they had Him in their hands. They made Him stand in all His wretchedness before them, the blue marks from the blow upon His face, His clothing already fouled and bedraggled, His hands helpless within their bonds. They could scarce believe their eyes; they could scarce refrain from leaping from their seats upon Him. But they must remember; they must restrain themselves; they were the models of order and observance for all Jewry, and above all things else they must behave like rulers of the synagogue. All must be done, outwardly at least, as became their time-honoured court. Witnesses were brought in to give evidence, even at that hour of the night they were there in abundance. The old charges were renewed ; that He broke the Sabbath, that He was the friend and boon-companion of publicans and sinners, that He ignored and held up to contempt the sacred ceremonial of the Law, that He sat down to table with unwashed hands, that He insulted the name of Abraham, that He was a Samaritan at heart, a heretic, an unbeliever, that He was possessed by a devil, that He cast out devils by Beelzebub, the prince of devils, that only by the devil's means could He do the things He did, or have such fascination for the multitude. Evidence was brought in from all sources ; from Galilee, for Pharisees had been sent there to spy upon Him in the early days, from Judæa, from Jerusalem most of all ; the volume was overwhelming, and surely would convince any court of the Prisoner's villainy. And yet it was not enough. As these witnesses told each his story, first one contradiction appeared, and then another, which made their evidence worthless. He who had broken the Sabbath, had shown how they themselves would do the same for far less urgent reasons. He who was the friend of publicans and sinners had quoted the prophet's words in His defence. He who had been accused of working by Beelzebub, had nevertheless empowered their own children to go and do likewise. One by one the charges brought up fell to the ground ; and even had they stood examination, still were they not enough, taken all together, to justify sentence of death.

> ' And the chief priests
> And the whole council
> Sought false witness
> For evidence against Jesus
> That they might put him to death
> For though many false witnesses did come in
> And bore false witness against him
> Their evidence did not agree.'

But at last there came two witnesses whose charges promised to provide the evidence that was needed. They had been in the Temple that day when He had made His first public appearance in the place. They had witnessed His driving the traders from the Court, and the unseemly confusion He had caused ; they themselves had suffered from His insolent aggression, and were eager to have their revenge. They remembered how that day had closed, and what He had said to justify His action. It had happened at the foot of the steps leading up to the Holy of Holies. The priests and Pharisees were there; doubtless some of those present would recall the scene, and would be able to confirm the evidence now being given. From the top of the steps they would have witnessed what had gone on before their eyes; the stampede of men and cattle on God's holy ground, the injustice and injury done to poor people earning an honest livelihood, the hindrance caused to the celebrations of the feast, above all at the solemn Paschal season. They would recall how the priests and Pharisees had restrained themselves, in spite of the provocation. They had not retaliated; they had not attempted to arrest or suppress this upstart mischief-maker from Galilee; they had simply asked Him, as responsible officials, by what authority He did these unwarrantable things.

And what had Jesus said or done in His own defence? They remembered His words well. Like any uneducated upstart, He had gone on from insolence to insolence. Not content with causing such confusion in the sacred place, such desecration of all that was most holy, He had proceeded to threaten the very existence of the Temple itself. He had said that one day He would destroy it. He had done more. He had ridiculed the time, and labour, and devotion that had been spent upon it. He had said that He would bring it all to nothing, and in three days would build it up again. More than forty years the Temple had taken in building; with His hand on His heart He had said He would raise it up within a week. He had claimed magic powers, and that in defiance of the holy place. He was indeed a magician; other events in His career went to confirm it; for this alone He was worthy of death.

> ' And last of all there came two false witnesses
> They rising up
> Bore false witness against him saying
> We heard him say
> I will destroy this temple of God
> Made with hands
> And within three days I will build another
> Not made with hands.'

At first it seemed that something could be made of this charge. Some of the judges remembered, only too well, what the insolent Nazarene had said to them that day. They remembered how by look and act He had held them paralysed upon the Temple steps; how beneath His glance their indignation had been turned to fear; how in feeble self-defence they had asked Him for His authority to act in the Temple as He did. And they remembered the answer He gave; they had never been able to forget it. He had stood still in front of them. He had raised His hand and had pointed to Himself. He had told them that even if they vented their wrath upon Him and killed Him, yet in three days He would come to life again. He had put it in His own way, but they had known well what He had meant; though since then they had tried to forget His declaration, yet had they often discussed it among them. On the whole at this moment it were better forgotten or ignored; later, when He was actually dead and buried, would be time enough to recall it, and provide against any fraud it might occasion. The evidence might lead to awkward conclusions, therefore it was proved to be unconvincing. The witnesses were dismissed till a more convenient time.

And Jesus listened while His words and deeds were twisted and turned and interpreted to His own condemnation. These things, or something like them, He had said; these things He had done, enough at least to give ground for the slanders poured out upon Him. There is no lie like half a lie; no calumny more cruel than the false use of a good deed. Such slander, such calumny is unanswerable; for he who utters them, and he who accepts them, have other ends in view than the truth. They will only reply, to any defence, *Qui s'excuse s'accuse;* and will find in that defence only further proof of guilt. There are wounds which can be healed, by time at least if by no other way; there are others which admit of no healing, except in the knowledge that Jesus Christ Our Lord has endured them before us. He bore this half-truth slander, and He answered not a word; He passed it by, and never again did complaint pass His lips about it:

'Blessed are ye
When they shall revile you
And persecute you
And speak all that is evil against you

> Untruly
> For my sake
> Be glad and rejoice
> For your reward is very great in heaven
> For so they persecuted the prophets
> That were before you.'

To those to whom He said this, He immediately added :

> ' You are the salt of the earth
> You are the light of the world ' ;

as if He would show them by what process the true apostle is made. And the Acts of the Apostles confirm it, for they tell how they

> ' Went rejoicing
> That they were accounted worthy
> To suffer reproach
> For the name of Jesus
> And every day they ceased not
> In the temple and from house to house
> To teach and preach Christ Jesus.'
>
> Acts v, 41–42.

(b) *The Question of Caiphas.*

The trial dragged on and all to no avail. It was evident that, by suborned witnesses at least, no conclusion would be reached. But Caiphas, as we have long since learnt, was not one to be beaten by a circumstance so trifling. Already in private conclave, without need of a single witness to support him, he had convinced his fellow-judges that Jesus of Nazareth must die ; now, in spite of the conflicting evidence, he knew a way to be no less convincing. On one thing he knew he could rely ; he could rely on his Victim's utter truthfulness. Jesus had called Himself the very Truth, in the Temple itself, and no one had contradicted Him. He had demanded who could convict Him of sin, and no one had ventured a single accusation. Only three days ago some of the very judges there present had addressed Him :

> ' Master
> We know that thou art a true speaker
> And teachest the way of God in truth
> Neither carest thou for any man
> For thou dost not regard the person of man.'

Yes, Caiphas the high priest could rely on this; if the worst happened, if every other witness failed, a clever question could be put which would make his Prisoner bear witness against Himself. On another occasion, it was true, these very men had said, to this same Jesus Christ:

'Thou givest testimony of thyself
Thy testimony is not true.'

It was true, moreover, that their Law forbade condemnation on the evidence of less than two witnesses:

'By the mouth of two or three witnesses
Shall he die that is to be slain
Let no man be put to death
When only one beareth witness against him.'
Deuteronomy xvii, 6.

'One witness shall not rise up against any man
Whatsoever the sin or wickedness be
But in the mouth of two or three witnesses
Every word shall stand.'
Deuteronomy xix, 15.

Still, for the moment the first of these objections could be forgotten, the second could be waived. This was an exceptional case; the Prisoner had already been condemned for the sake of the people, and in such a circumstance even the Law must be rightly interpreted.

But Caiphas would at least abide by the form of law; if he must break the letter, he would preserve what he would call its spirit. He was the judge, not the accuser; therefore from the beginning to the end he would take care that he himself made no formal accusation. Should anything at any time go wrong, should the trial fail in any way and the sentence be frustrated, should there come later a reaction against this Man's condemnation, he himself at least would be safe. Many charges had been made already; though they had conflicted, though none had been proved, still even a merciful judge could assume that something in them all must be true. He would first play that part. He would ask the Prisoner to say what He could in His defence. From what He said further evidence might be gained, if it were only evidence of contempt of court. He rose from his seat, as one who held authority:

> ' And the high priest
> Rising up in the midst
> Asked Jesus saying
> Answerest thou nothing
> To the things that are laid to thy charge
> By these men?
> But Jesus held his peace
> And answered nothing.'

From which we know that from the time He had been brought before that court Jesus had spoken not a word. In the house of Annas He had spoken twice, but nothing He had said had been positive. Annas had questioned Him, and He had bidden Annas go and question others; the guard had struck Him, and He had merely asked why He had been so treated. Now Caiphas put his question from his seat of office; but it was a question to which Jesus, by the provisions of the Law itself, was not bound to give an answer. No prisoner was compelled to incriminate himself; he was not compelled even to defend himself. Moreover, the charges that had been made had already received their sufficient refutation; what remained to reply was best done by silence:

> ' Jesus held his peace
> And answered nothing.'

Once more by His simple manner, meek yet commanding, He proved to these men that He was their Master, even as He was Master of Himself.

But such silence did not please Caiphas any more than it pleased the priests and judges who sat about him; it did not please them that the only self-possessed man in that assembly was the Prisoner before them. They became restless; His silence was beginning to cast a spell upon them, as His words had often held them in the Temple court. Already the witnesses had been beaten by it; soon, if they did not break the spell, the whole court would slink away ashamed, as some of them had slunk away ashamed that day when He had stooped down before them, and had silently written on the ground. The spell must be broken, and Caiphas knew well how to break it. He had hoped there would have been no need to use this last device; he had hoped that some other charge would have been

found on which this hated Man might have been condemned.
something which would have proved that He died 'that
the whole nation might not perish'. He was loth to
betray to all the world the real accusation which burnt
within the souls of all present. But there was now no
escape. They had tried every means, and Jesus had beaten
back all their charges; without any doubt, and that
without uttering a word, He was the Master of them all.
Therefore Caiphas must play his last card; he must ask
the question which, he knew, would convict Jesus before
that assembly If He still refused to answer, then He
could be held up to ridicule as an impostor; if He answered,
then Caiphas knew well what that answer would be.

> 'Again the high priest asked him
> And said to him
> I adjure thee
> By the living God
> That thou tell us
> If thou be the Christ
> The Son of the blessed God.'

Did ever malice more betray itself than in this question
of Caiphas? There are many enemies of Jesus Christ, as
of other men, now as well as in His own time, but their
hatred is founded chiefly on ignorance; twice at least, in
the scenes that are to follow, we shall find Him speaking
of them, however cruel they may be, in terms of pity and
mercy. But there is a hatred which is founded on the
opposite. It hates the truth because it knows it to be true;
and such hatred is merciless, cruel unto death. Such is the
hatred of Satan himself; such was the hatred of Caiphas;
such is the hatred of those enemies of Jesus Christ who will
persecute Him because He is not of their mind. They will
not have this Man ruling over them, no matter what His
right, no matter what may be the blessing of His rule:

> 'Let us therefore lie in wait for the just
> Because he is not for our turn
> And he is contrary to our doings
> And upbraideth us with transgressions of the law
> And divulgeth against us the sins of our way of life
> He boasteth that he hath the knowledge of God
> And calleth himself the Son of God

> He is become a censurer of our thoughts
> He is grievous unto us
> Even to behold
> For his life is not like other men's
> And his ways are very different
> We are esteemed by him as triflers
> And he abstaineth from our ways
> As from filthiness
> And he preferreth the latter end of the just
> And glorieth that he hath God for his father
> Let us see then if his words be true
> And let us prove what shall happen to him
> And we shall know what his end shall be
> For if he be the true Son of God
> He will deliver him
> From the hands of his enemies
> Let us examine him by outrages and tortures
> That we may know his meekness
> And try his patience
> Let us condemn him to a most shameful death
> For there shall be respect had unto him
> By his words
> These things they thought
> And were deceived
> For their own malice blinded them
> And they knew not the secrets of God
> Nor hoped for the wages of justice
> Nor esteemed the honour of holy souls.'
>   Wisdom ii, 12–22.

Such was the hatred and malice of Caiphas, for his question showed that he knew, knew perhaps better than any other man in that assembly. He knew that Jesus claimed to be the Christ; that when He had been called the Son of God, by friend or enemy, He had never denied it or repudiated it. He knew that He had said and done things which only a true Son of God could say or do; Caiphas was skilled in sifting such evidence. He knew that Jesus had given proofs of His title, even to those who had long since determined not to take them. He knew that on that account, and on no other, because He claimed to be the true Son of God and nothing less, because they had taken Him at His word without equivocation, Jesus stood before that court, on trial for His life, incurring the hatred of them all. He knew, moreover, that because He was the Son of God, the very Truth who could not speak otherwise, if He answered the question put to Him He would not deny.

But we are not concerned with Caiphas and his accomplices; we are concerned only with Him to whom at last the crucial question had been put. It is true the suspicion, and even the charge, was not altogether new. Quite early in His career, when He had healed the beggar at the pool in the North of the city, we are told, as a sequel to the story:

> 'Hereupon therefore
> The Jews sought the more to kill him
> Because he did not only break the sabbath
> But also said God was his Father
> Making himself equal to God.'
>
> John v, 18.

On another occasion He had openly challenged them, and they had betrayed themselves. They had taken up stones to stone Him:

> 'Jesus answered them
> Many good works have I shewed you from my Father
> For which of those works do you stone me?
> The Jews answered him
> For a good work we stone thee not
> But for blasphemy
> And because thou
> Being a man
> Makest thyself God.'
>
> John x, 32, 33.

Indeed when had He come into collision with the masters of the Temple and the controversy had not arisen?

Still, never before had the question been put to Him so formally, with such authority, by the appointed high priest of the Old Observance, under solemn oath. On other occasions He had been asked to speak more plainly; He had been asked for signs; He had been asked to prove His authority. Now He was asked as He had always wished to be asked, by the high priest, in his full capacity of high priest, without any possibility that question or answer should be misinterpreted, and with His life depending on the answer, that He should tell them whether He was or was not that which He had come into the world to declare. Caiphas, as high priest and as judge, had the right to ask the question ; then at last, to him, and to the Old Law, and for all the world to hear, Jesus would answer him, plainly and without reserve, as He had never answered anyone before. Here, as He stood on His defence, knowing that His answer sealed His doom, He would speak so that He could not be misunderstood ; more than that, He would confirm it by a prophecy which none of those present would be able to misunderstand. Again in every word it is Jesus the Master who speaks, and every man who hears Him cannot but know it :

> ' And Jesus said to him
> Thou hast said it
> I am
> Nevertheless I say to you
> Hereafter you shall see the Son of Man
> Sitting on the right hand of the power of God
> And coming in the clouds of heaven.'

Such calm, such dignity, such sureness of word and tone! The false calm and dignity of Caiphas broke down before it. He had known what confession his demand would extort ; he had not known the nobility with which it would be made. His mind went back to that noble prophecy of the Psalmist :

> ' The Lord said to my Lord
> Sit thou at my right hand
> Until I make thy enemies thy footstool
> The Lord will send forth the sceptre of thy power
> Out of Sion
> Rule thou in the midst of thy enemies
> With thee is the principality
> In the day of thy strength
> In the brightness of the saints
> From the womb before the day-star I begot thee
> The Lord hath sworn
> And he will not repent
> Thou art a priest for ever
> According to the order of Melchisedech
> The Lord at thy right hand hath broken the kings
> In the day of his wrath

He shall judge among nations
He shall fill ruins
He shall crush the heads in the land of many.'
>> Psalm cix, 1-6.

The prophet Daniel, too, had said :
' I beheld therefore in the vision of the night
And lo one like the Son of Man
Came with the clouds of heaven
And he came even to the Ancient of Days
And they presented him before him
And he gave him power and glory
And a kingdom
And all peoples, tribes and tongues shall serve him
His power is an everlasting power
That shall not be taken away
And his kingdom shall not be destroyed.'
>> Daniel vii, 13-14.

Caiphas knew the terms in which Jesus spoke. He knew their significance in his own regard, that the sentence was his own condemnation. The rôles had been reversed, and he, not Jesus, was the accused and convicted. But he must not yield to fear, he must preserve appearances, and the honour of his court ; though anger and hatred were now roused beyond control, yet must he give them a show of righteousness. He would gladly have torn his Victim limb from limb ; instead he would tear his own garments, the customary mark of indignation when blasphemy was heard :

' Then the high priest rent his garments
Saying
He hath blasphemed
What further need have we of witnesses ?
Behold
Now you have heard the blasphemy
What think you ? '

It was the same Caiphas that we have long known. When the priests and elders had before been bewildered because all the world was going after this Man, he had solved their problem for them. He had proved to them that to compass His death was a holy and a patriotic act. Now he guided them again along the road they wished to go. They had listened to all the witnesses, and the evidence had come to nothing. They had heard this last solemn declaration. They were bewildered by the Speaker's sincerity and truth; the words of the prophets were ringing in their ears; they knew not what to say or think. But once more Caiphas came to their aid. He supplied the needed word: 'Blasphemy'! Given the word he emphasized it; having emphasized it, he asked the question which could have only one answer. Once more Caiphas had removed their tender scruples, and they were able to satisfy their souls:

> 'But they all answering
> Condemned him and said
> He is guilty of death.'

But, be it noted, Caiphas did not give the final word himself. He asked what further need there was of witnesses; he asked the rest what they thought; though it was his function to pass sentence, he took care that he himself, in a trial that from beginning to end was illegal, should be safe. If Jesus in spite of all were yet to survive, it should not be said that Caiphas the high priest had condemned Him. That was done by others, and it was done by them with one voice; behind that screen Caiphas would shield himself, whatever came. Caiphas knew his trade.

Once the sentence was passed the gates of hell were let loose. Those elegant upholders of the Laws, those models of all that should be, had held themselves in long enough; they would endure no more. Till this moment, with all their authority, He had proved Himself their Master; now that the sentence had been passed, knowing well the will of him who presided, they could wreak their vengeance on their Captive at their will. It was indeed 'their hour and the power of darkness'. They let themselves go; that reserve with which the worldling surrounds himself, and calls it self-command, broke down beneath the strain. Every one of us knows the wild beast chained within him; there comes an occasion when no natural power will keep it back. These men descended to indignities which, to their dying day, whether they repented or not, they would never forget. They would remember the night when their self-control broke down before Jesus of Nazareth, and for a terrible hour they behaved like inhuman beasts. And their sycophants took their cue from them. The trial was over; the sentence had been passed, at least enough to suit their purpose; the Man in their hands had been declared 'guilty of death', and therefore was deserving of no mercy. He had been declared guilty on no evidence but His own; all the more must His guilt be proved by the ignominy poured upon Him. They came up to Him one by one; they spat in His face, they mocked His silent and commanding manner. They struck Him where He stood, His hands tied behind His back, unable to defend Himself. They took a common rag and tied it over His eyes, they covered His face with the same; as He was thus covered they struck that face, with whatever they held, or with the flat of the hand. And since He still stood silent among them, since nothing could break His peace, they endeavoured to provoke Him. He who had spoken with authority, He who had been said to read men's hearts and thoughts, who, on their own confession, had spoken as never man had spoken, had uttered always the word of God in truth, was now as a lamb before them, and would not open His mouth. They were now at their ease in His company, but it was a restless ease; they could challenge Him as they would, but their challenges came back to them in blasphemies:

> 'And the men that held him
> Began to spit in his face
> And mocked him
> And buffeted him
> And they blindfolded him
> And covered his face
> And smote him in the face
> And the servants struck him
> With the palms of their hands
> And they asked him saying
> Prophesy unto us
> O Christ
> Who is he that struck thee?
> And many other things blaspheming
> They said against him.'

Thus began that course of sheer brutality which was to continue to the very end.

20. The Denial of Peter.

But gross injustice and indignity from those who hated Him was not the only suffering that Jesus Christ Our Lord had to endure in the house of Caiphas that night. Though all His disciples had fled away from Him at the garden gate, still it was no wonder that some of them at least could not leave Him altogether alone. Their thoughts could not but follow Him through the night. They sought to learn how He fared; they hoped against hope that when the trial came He would vindicate Himself as He had often done of old; that in their council chamber He would put to shame the men who sought His ruin, as He had put them to shame in the Temple court. Simon Peter especially, the daring one among them, even while also on occasion the most timid, could not resist the fascination. He had fled with the rest, after it was clear that Jesus refused to be defended; perhaps more frightened than the rest, seeing that he had been rebuked for his deed of daring. But he had not fled far. He had hidden himself in the darkness close by; he had stopped to see what would happen. The procession had begun its march back to the city and he had followed after; in such a turmoil concealment was easy. On the way he had met with another follower of Jesus, one who was known in Jerusalem, who was familiar even with Caiphas and his court. Together they came to the house of Caiphas; at the gate a guard was kept, the usual guard who admitted only those who for any reason had a right to claim access. Peter's companion was one of those; when Jesus was brought in he was able to enter with the rest. Peter had no passport; he was compelled to wait among the crowd outside.

But his companion was able to use influence. He could not hide the fact that Simon Peter was a Galilæan; still he could claim him as an acquaintance of his own, a man from the country, come up for the Paschal festival, a harmless individual, only interested in the fate of his fellow Galilæan, and likely to do harm to no one. With arguments such as these he persuaded the portress at a side entrance, and Simon Peter was admitted. The woman eyed him as he entered; Simon's tongue was active while he passed through the doorway, and she was quick to detect his Galilæan dialect. She noticed, too, a certain eagerness, a certain anxiety, about Simon, which told her at once that his coming in was not due to curiosity alone. As he turned his back upon her she smiled to herself in contempt ; what she had observed about Simon might be useful later on.

It was cold in Jerusalem that night. If we except the two storms on the lake of Galilee, this is perhaps the only place in the Gospels where we are actually told the condition of the weather. We are told that it was cold, yet it was the month of April, and April in Palestine is not usually cold. But in the East the hottest days may have very cold nights, especially in high or dry districts ; as soon as the sun goes down the temperature falls suddenly, and a cold wind will begin to blow. So was it that night. It had been a warm day ; earlier in the night, in the Garden of Gethsemane, which was down in the valley and sheltered, there had been no inconvenience from the cold. But here up in the city, on its high plateau, the attendants in their light garments, standing about the flagged courtyard, felt the change of temperature more keenly. They had therefore done according to their custom on such nights ; a fire was lit in the middle of the courtyard, and the men were squatting round it, careless of all that was going on in the open court beyond, content that something had brought them together.

In the midst of this careless group Simon Peter gradually found a place. No sooner had he gained admission at the door than all his courage left him, as it had left him that night in Galilee, when, at his Master's bidding, he had stepped out boldly on the waves. But this time, on these troubled waters, there was no Master present to whom he could appeal ; there was no ship behind him to which he might retreat. He had entered the courtyard with his usual impetuosity ; now as he stood there he was terribly alone. To find some companionship he mingled with the rest ; he sat down with them by the fire and warmed himself, doing as they did, choosing a place from which he could observe what went on in the court beyond. There was no one there who knew him, no one would care about him ; the more he stayed with the crowd the safer he would be.

But he had miscalculated. Besides the men hanging round the fire there were others passing to and fro, some sauntering from one group to another, others serving the soldiers with liquor or whatever they might need. Among these was the servant-maid who had admitted Peter at the gate. She chanced to pass by the fire; the light was shining full on Peter's face. She recognized the Galilæan; she detected the fear in his face, seeking to hide itself beneath a show of swagger and bravado; it was a sight that provoked the woman in her to taunt him. Besides, if she told what she had discovered about him, it would cause ribald laughter from those about the fire; and that was a pleasure too good to be resisted. She stopped in front of him, the fire between them; she looked on him with a contempt that made him shrink before her. She pointed at him with her finger; presently, in a shrill, hard voice, which none could fail to hear, she said :

' Thou also wast with Jesus of Nazareth
The Galilæan.'

With her finger still pointing at him, she turned to those about her and went on :

' This man also was with him.'

Then, again looking at him, she challenged him :

' Art not thou also
One of this man's disciples ? '

It was indeed a trying moment for Simon Peter :

' Thou art Simon
Thou shalt be called the Rock.'
' Thou art Peter
And upon this rock
I will build my church
And the gates of hell shall not prevail against it.'

After such promises as these could it be that Simon should fail his Lord, or that his Lord should fail him? If the gates of hell should not prevail against him, could he be beaten by a girl keeper of the gate of Caiphas? Simon, chosen from the beginning, assured that one day he would be made a great fisher of men, the first among the Twelve, who had worked miracles in the name of Jesus, who had cast out devils in His name, who had walked on the waters of the lake and had not sunk, whose very ship had been singled out from among the rest, for from it Jesus had preached, from it He had commanded the draught of fishes, in it He had slept, that night when they had come to Him and He had calmed the storm—after all this could Simon waver now? Or again, in the past had he not played his part well, and had not his Master praised and rewarded him for the way he had played it? He had been welcomed at the Jordan and had made one of the company. By his home on the lake-side at Bethsaida he had been called and had followed promptly, leaving his ship and his nets; and the Lord had expressly told him that for that surrender he would one day sit upon a throne, judging the twelve tribes of Israel. One day, when all others were deserting, he had stood by his Master and said:

> 'Lord
> To whom shall we go?
> Thou hast the words of eternal life.'

On another day, when Jesus had chosen to put them to the test, he had proclaimed before them all:

> 'Thou art the Christ
> The Son of the Living God',

and had been blessed above all the rest for his confession. In proof of his election he had been taken by the Master into the holy mountain, there to see and hear what it was not given to others to see and hear. He had been taken aside and had witnessed miracles which not even all the Twelve had been permitted to witness. Nay, this very night, in presence of them all, Jesus had chosen him out from all the rest for special care, had told him of coming temptation, had assured him of His prayers, had bidden him after his ordeal to strengthen the others:

> 'Simon, Simon
> Behold Satan hath desired to have you
> That he may sift you as wheat
> But I have prayed for thee
> That thy faith fail not
> And thou being once converted
> Confirm thy brethren.'

After all this, how could it be that in a moment like this he should fail?

Recollections such as these galloped through Simon's brain as he listened to the woman's taunt and challenge.

Beyond her in the court he could see his Master, where he stood before His judges, His hands bound behind Him, no longer able to lift His trembling disciple up as he sank beneath the wave. He could hear the witnesses pour out their false charges; yet Jesus no longer looked about Him and asked:

> 'Will you also go away?'

There was no voice now from heaven which proclaimed him:

> 'This is my beloved Son
> In whom I am well pleased.'

He who had spoken 'with authority and not as the scribes' was now dumb; He whom no man could accuse of sin was now a criminal on His trial; He who had challenged and defied all the world was now the world's helpless victim. His thoughts went back to that day in Capharnaum when He had warned the Master to be more careful, and not to exasperate these men in power who were plotting even then to have His life. If only Jesus had listened to him, and had taken his advice, perhaps these things would not have happened. But now what could he do? He could draw no sword to defend Him; not even any word of his could be of any avail. The doom had come upon them all; in less than an hour the hopes of years had come to nought. Was it then all a failure? The kingdom, the banquet in the kingdom, the thrones and high places from which they were to judge the tribes of Israel, the hundredfold in this world, the life eternal, were they all castles in the air? What was secure, what could be believed? Where was the rock immovable, against which not even the gates of hell were to prevail, on which all was to be built?

So, far more quickly than they can be told, did the doubts and questions rise and fall, chasing each other in Simon's fevered soul, like the waves on the tossed waters that stormy night when he had walked on them alone. Meanwhile the woman's words were ringing in his ears; their sting was piercing his heart. 'Nazarene', 'Galilæan', 'One of them'; at one time he had thought he would never have heeded, now they made him wish the earth would open and swallow him up. Leering eyes were turned upon him; jeers were on the tip of every tongue; what good could Simon do, to himself, to his Master, to anyone, by standing up now in His defence, even by acknowledging the truth about himself? There were two men suddenly struggling within him. There was the Simon that still loved, that still believed though the clouds had gathered round and all was black, that still pleaded to him to be true ; and there was that other Simon, impetuous in word and act, brave to dare yet fearful in a crisis, overawed by the opinions and conventions of men. The first Simon bade him at least say nothing, to leave this place of danger ; the second Simon wavered, argued with himself, begged that he would be a man among men.

And the second Simon won. The woman had asked :

'Art not thou also one of this man's disciples ? '

As soon as he could gain his speech, not allowing himself time for reflexion, the fatal answer came :

' But he denied before them all saying
Woman
I am not.'

Having once denied, the rest was easy ; it is the first step in evil-doing that is hard. He could now emphasize what he had said ; indeed what else could he now do ? Was he one of this Man's disciples ? He did not even know Him :

' Woman
I am not
I know him not
I neither know nor understand what thou sayest.'

Was the voice his own that spoke ? Were the words he heard words coming from his own mouth ? Simon listened to himself and wondered what he had said. He had spoken to avoid the shame of men whom he might well have despised ; he incurred his own shame, he could not endure the thought of himself. He had been ashamed and humbled before, but this was something altogether new ; a sense of unfitness for the company of men, a clammy sense of foulness, a craving to hide himself away from the sight of men, even of such men as these about him. He rose from the fire and went away. He passed out by a gate into the garden,

into the night, that he might get alone. As he walked
aimlessly to and fro the sound of a cock-crow broke on his
ear, a common thing at night in the East. He had heard it
often in the night before, in his own country-side in Galilee,
and it need have meant nothing to him. But this night it
seemed to catch his ear; it seemed to bring some recollection
to his mind. It sounded like a note of warning, bidding him
beware lest worse things befall him. That he should be
troubled by a trifle annoyed him. Anything annoyed him
at that moment, and he was in no mood to be annoyed.
To stifle his annoyance he went back into the noise of the
court.

Scarcely had he done so than he was again accosted.
He had put himself apart; his coming in from the garden
alone drew the gaze of a group standing by upon him.
They had been speaking of this Jesus and His followers;
they had abused the first, it was natural to abuse the others.
Suddenly Simon came upon them, out of the darkness.
Another serving woman looked at him. She told herself
she had seen that man before. She remembered; she had
seen him once upon a time with Jesus of Nazareth. She
cared little what she said; she spoke before them all the
thought that was passing through her mind:

> ' And again another maidservant saw him
> And she began to say to the standers-by
> This is one of them
> This man also was with Jesus of Nazareth.'

Then, encouraged, with a look of scorn she turned upon
him:
> ' Thou also art one of them.'

By this time Simon's defences were all broken down. He
had uttered a denial once; to repeat it was no hard thing.
The voice of conscience was now but dimly heard; the
warnings that before had rushed through his soul were all
gone, or else were so confused that they meant almost
nothing. He had betrayed himself once; it mattered little
now what he said or did. Not waiting a moment to weigh
his words, caring nothing whether they were true or not,
catching up the ribald language of the men about him, he
answered them after their own manner. He avoided the

gaze of the woman ; he spoke to a man in the group ; surely after this, he seemed to say, he would be left alone.

'And again he denied with an oath
O man I am not
I do not know the man.'

For a time Simon was not troubled any more. He turned away from his accusers, and lost himself in the crowd that filled the hall. He had said that he was not 'one of them', he had said that he did not 'know the man'. There in the court beyond him, within sight and hearing, 'the Man' whom he 'did not know' was still undergoing His ordeal, and Simon had come in expressly that he might 'see the end'. But now he scarcely dared to allow his eyes to wander towards Him. Instead he would try to forget Him ; he would try to forget himself. He would mingle with the rest and would be one of them. He would do anything to escape the sense of guilt that spread over him as very slime. By noise, and garrulity, and boasting, he would lay the spectre that now pursued him whichever way he turned.

For an hour or more Simon went among the crowd, careless as any one of them without, trembling and wretched within as any beaten creature. Meanwhile in the upper court the trial went on, and now was drawing to an end. He heard the evidence of the witnesses, and he knew the reply that could be made to each ; but he could not speak, his tongue was tied, he did not wish even to listen. At length, at a solemn moment, he saw the high priest stand up. The hall became deadly silent ; he heard the terrible question :

'I adjure thee
By the living God
That thou tell us
If thou be the Christ
The Son of the blessed God.'

The words were an echo of Simon's own confession long ago. He heard the answer to that question, yet more clear than ever he had heard it before, spoken with yet more authority :

'Thou hast said it
I am.'

Strive as he might, in that awful silence, Simon could not forget the question that had been put to him hard by Cæsarea Philippi :

' Whom do you say that I am ? '

still less his own spontaneous answer :

' Thou art the Christ
The son of the living God.'

He recalled the reward he had received for that declaration ; he had been made Peter, the Rock, against which nothing should prevail. Till that night he had lived in the glow of that promise. He had heard his own words confirmed on the mountain :

' This is my beloved son
In whom I am well pleased ',

and had cried out, in an ecstasy of joy, that it was good to be there. He had discussed since then with his companions, again and again, when at length the kingdom would be founded ; that very night they had hoped it would have begun.

For a moment that hope came back to him ; would Jesus seize this occasion ? Would He be surrounded with the clouds of heaven, as He had foretold ? Would the legions of angels come to His rescue ? Never before had He permitted Himself so to fall into the hands of His enemies ; now that He had asserted His claim, in words that not even Simon had ever heard before, could He suffer Himself to be beaten and put to shame ? Simon stood there in suspense, expecting he knew not what ; if the earth had opened beneath them and swallowed them all up, himself included, if the hall had fallen down upon them, if an angel with a sword of fire had come down to vindicate the honour of the Son of God, he would not have been surprised. And yet how differently did the wheel turn ! No angel came to help his Master, no voice was heard from heaven to glorify His name ; instead the high priest, with all the dignity of his office, pronounced Jesus Christ a blasphemer, and the wrath of hell was let loose upon Him. It grew from worse to worse. Simon watched the ribald crowd, one by one, come up to his Master and strike Him ; he watched them spit in His face ; he watched them as they put a rag

about His eyes, he heard them bid Him prophesy. He was
paralysed with horror; he could not move. He remembered now the prophecies that all this would be, prophecies
which he had always refused to believe, which more than
once he had contradicted. He had come 'to see the end';
it indeed seemed to be the end of everything for Simon;
faith and love, and hope—what of them had he left in his
poor, laden heart?

Presently the court began to move. It was now far into
the night; the sentence, or what would stand for a sentence,
had been pronounced; the prisoner was 'guilty of death',
and it remained only to wait till morning to put the sentence
into execution. They dared not do that themselves; for
it the permit of the Roman governor was needed. They
must put their prisoner in gaol till dawn, and then their
demand for His blood would be satisfied. A procession
began to be formed; as it passed down through the courtyard
it threatened to come near to Simon. Simon pressed back
into the crowd; he would not be seen; now with far
greater reason might he have uttered that prayer of his
earliest days:

'Depart from me
For I am a sinful man
O Lord.'

But his movements attracted attention. That while all the
rest pressed forward one should press backward could not
but be noticed. His neighbours looked at him; they
noticed the fear in his eyes, that harmonized ill with the
affected bravado in his manner. They heard his speech, and
his accent was not that of Judæa. It was that of the North;
it was that of the Galilæan Himself; little provocation was
needed to make this mob turn upon any Galilæan. One
of the crowd framed the charge, as one in a crowd will;
the rest took it up, careless whether it were true or false, so
long as it gave an opportunity for baiting:

'Surely thou also art one of them
For even thy speech doth discover thee
Thou also art a Galilæan.'

Had the mocking accusation ended there Simon might yet
have escaped. But no such fortune was to befall him. The
mockery attracted the attention of one who had been with

THE DENIAL OF PETER

the captors of Jesus that night at the garden gate. He had some rank among his fellows, for he held an office in the high priest's household. Moreover he was something of a hero among them, for he could boast of being a kinsman of the man who had been wantonly injured by one of Jesus' company. This man now looked at Simon; he thought he recognized his face. In the light of the lanterns on the hill-side impressions were doubtful, on the other hand Simon's were features that were not easily forgotten. The mob was hooting; he would join his witness with the rest:

> ' Did not I see thee, he said
> In the garden
> With him? '

It was a charge which Simon was unable to escape. The hounds were upon him and he was at bay; they were hot with triumph over their first victim, they would not scruple now about a second. Simon was compelled to act at once; if he would save himself he must not hesitate. By now he had got used to denial, to add a third to the two before was now an easy matter. Moreover through the night he had listened to the language of blasphemers; now that same language came from his own mouth easily enough. He cursed as they cursed; he swore as they swore; he would swagger and be brave as the rest of them, as is the manner of a coward. And his courage found expression. Scarcely thinking what he said, he added to his oaths:

> ' Man
> I know not what thou sayest
> I know not this man of whom you speak.'

And some approved him for a brave fellow, and some claimed him as one of themselves; and all in their hearts were convinced that he lied and despised him.

But for Simon himself, the words had not escaped his lips when he heard from the yard outside the crowing of a cock. He had heard it before during that night, but it had only confused his thoughts; now he heard it, and at once the memory of what his Lord had said came back to him:

> ' Amen I say to thee
> To-day even this night
> Before the cock crow twice
> Thou shalt deny me thrice.'

Worse still, as he stood there paralysed, the procession that was bearing Jesus away passed him by :

' And the Lord turning
Looked on Peter.'

Jesus turned aside and looked at Peter. Their eyes met and they knew each other ; and they knew each other as friends. Then Jesus had heard what Simon Peter had said ; He had heard it and yet had not forsaken or abandoned him. It was the same look, however saddened by this last experience, which He had always bestowed upon him ; on that first day by the Jordan when Simon had come to judge of this new Prophet and had been conquered ; by the lake when he had been called, and without a word had followed ; in the boat when the draught of fishes had been given him, and he had pleaded to his Lord to leave him ; on the lake that night when Jesus had bid him come to Him across the water ; in the synagogue at Capharnaum, when men deserted Him, and Simon had said they would not go away ; by Cæsarea when He had asked Simon for his confession and he had made it ; on the mountain when Simon had been frightened, and Jesus had leaned down and touched him and all had been well ; on the roadside in Judæa, when He had taught him lessons of humility, and forgiveness, and prayer ; that very night in the supper-room, when He had given Simon his last warning and had assured him of His prayers ; in the garden, when in distress He had come and pleaded to him to watch and pray with Him ; at the garden gate when He had bid him put up his sword, and then had secured that he should go away free. It all came back on Peter now. Jesus had always been the same, in praise or in blame, in success or failure ; He was the same now, even under this ordeal. Had Simon lost his faith in Jesus ? This only he now knew ; in spite of what he had done Jesus had not lost His faith in Simon. He still would trust him ; He still would love him ; Simon was still His own ; all this was shown to Simon in that single look :

' And the Lord turning
Looked on Peter
And Peter remembered the word
That the Lord Jesus had said to him
Before the cock crow twice
Thou shalt deny me thrice.'

It was all over in a moment. None but Simon Peter had noticed that look ; as with Judas, so with Peter, Jesus would not betray His own. The procession passed through the courtyard. Soon the Master was out of sight and Peter was alone ; alone in that throng of ribald men. He must get alone ; he must hide himself from every human eye. Why did not the earth gape open and swallow him ? It was no longer fear that possessed him ; it was love that had revived ; and with love sorrow unto death, and with sorrow yet more love, till Simon no longer cared who stood about him. He forced his way to the door ; even as he went the tears were brimming in his eyes and he could not stay them.

'He began to weep' ;

when he was at last alone he wept bitterly. Tradition tells us, but we scarcely need the witness of tradition, that from that day Simon Peter never ceased weeping for that deed, till the tears he shed wore lasting furrows on his face.

CHAPTER VIII

21. The Morning Trial.

IT was well after midnight before the assembly in the court of Caiphas broke up. Of this we have abundant evidence. When Judas left the supper-room it was already quite dark; therefore it must have been not earlier than eight o'clock, according to our reckoning. The supper had continued, perhaps for an hour. There had been the walk to the Garden of Gethsemane, a short half-hour. The agony is spoken of as lasting at least an hour, probably longer; the betrayal, the capture, the journey back to the courts, first of Annas, then of Caiphas, could scarcely have taken less than an hour more. Hence, even if we shorten these estimates, the trial before Caiphas would have begun not earlier than an hour before midnight. The trial itself seems to have lasted some two hours; between the second and the third denials of Peter we are expressly told that there was an interval of about an hour. Jesus, then, would have gone to His prison, and the judges to their beds, between one and two o'clock in the morning.

What happened during the remainder of that night we are not expressly told. Many commentators take the insults offered in the court of Caiphas as an account of the treatment meted out to Jesus during all the early morning hours. It may well have been so; but it would rather seem from the Gospel story that what was done by the soldiers and the rabble was done in the sight of the priests and elders, following the example which these leaders set, and with their full approval. Once the sentence had been passed, once the passions of the judges had been let loose, the mob had crowded into the open room from the yard below and had joined in the abuse and confusion. It was only when they had wearied of their sport that the guard at length had led their victim out, and consigned Him to the narrow cell where He was to await the more formal and final sentence of the court next day.

In any case there could have been but little sleep that night either for Jesus, or for His gaolers, or for those most concerned in the tragedy. These last were up betimes. The meetings overnight, with whatever pomp and circumstance Annas and Caiphas had carried them through, could not, by any reading of the Law, be accounted official trials; the Law forbade that trials should be held during the night. Therefore for even a show of legal justice it was essential that a council should be held in the morning. But moreover, if they would have their work completed that day, they must set about it early. For the next day was the Pasch, 'a great sabbath day'; and before it began, that is, before sunset that evening, Jesus of Nazareth must be condemned, not only by themselves but by the Roman court, and put to death, and buried out of sight, then and for ever.

They came together in the court of Caiphas as soon as it was day; so well had their plans succeeded in that meeting-place, they could well take up the threads where they had laid them down. They gathered in their numbers, that the full weight of their authority might be brought to bear later upon the Roman judge. Since Jesus had been tried and condemned the night before, since the witnesses had been heard and the sentence had been pronounced, there was no need to go back upon the trial; all that was required was a formal sanction of the informal proceedings they had gone through:

> 'And straightway in the morning
> As soon as it was day
> The chief priests and ancients of the people
> And scribes
> Came together
> And held a council against Jesus
> To put him to death
> And they brought him into their council
> Saying: If thou be the Christ
> Tell us.'

It was indeed to them only a formality, but it was necessary, even now, that no mistake should be made. They must act together; they must agree beforehand what should be done. Caiphas had long since proved to them the end they were to achieve; last night he had shown them how they might most speedily achieve it. There was no further need of witnesses ; Jesus, if He were asked, would condemn Himself out of His own mouth. Then they might take Him forthwith to the Governor, Pontius Pilate ; he was one who, with his contempt of the Jews, and with the evidence of this court before him, would without doubt grant them their request. Then Jesus could be put away at once, and they could return to their preparations for the Pasch, and could receive the homage due to their rank in the Temple, without any further trouble of mind. Indeed this would be for them a great sabbath day, with their enemy dead in His tomb.

But for Jesus this morning trial was much more than a formality. The night before, until He had been questioned directly, and that by the high priest himself, He had not deigned to answer anything ; for that was not a lawful trial, and only when Caiphas had spoken as high priest, when he had called upon his prisoner ' in the name of the living God ', had Jesus deigned to give even him an answer. But this morning all was different ; now, with all their show of formalities, this was the true judicial court, and these were responsible judges. Last night one overweening man alone had swayed the rest, and in a heated moment, by a single adroit question, had won from them their sentence ; now the sentence would be passed of the court's own accord, without the excuse of passion or haste, deliberately and with full knowledge. Therefore, as was His duty, Jesus would answer them ; and His answer would be no less clear to these masters of the Law and the Prophets than before. But first He would also warn them ; if in His pity He had warned Judas, if He had warned Peter and the others, no less, even at this moment, would He warn these poor men of the evil thing they were about to do, and save them if He could from their shame. He would appeal to their common sense of justice ; He would ask for that fair dealing which they would grant to any man, and yet were refusing to Him. Let them condemn Him if they wished, but let them not refuse Him the hearing to which He had a right :

> ' And he said to them
> If I shall tell you
> You will not believe me
> And if I shall ask you

You will not answer me
Nor let me go.'

Nevertheless, though they would not hear Him, in spite of the storm which He knew His words would arouse, now more than ever it was His right and duty to speak. They might not believe Him; indeed, whether they believed or not they would most certainly condemn Him. But they should hear, and that in terms which, from their knowledge of the Sacred Books, they could not mistake:

' But hereafter
The Son of Man shall be sitting
On the right hand of the power of God.'

. . . .

' I beheld therefore in the vision of the night
And lo one like the Son of Man
Came with the clouds of heaven
And he came even to the Ancient of days
And they presented him before him
And he gave him power and glory
And a kingdom
And all the peoples, tribes and tongues
Shall serve him
His power is an everlasting power
That shall not be taken away
And his kingdom shall not be destroyed.'
Daniel vii, 13–14.

' The Lord said to my Lord
Sit thou at my right hand
Until I make thy enemies thy footstool
The Lord will send the sceptre of thy power
Out of Sion
Rule thou in the midst of thy enemies
With thee is the principality
In the day of thy strength
In the brightness of the saints
From the womb before the day-star I begot thee
The Lord hath sworn
And he will not repent
Thou art a priest for ever

> According to the order of Melchisedech
> The Lord at thy right hand hath broken kings
> In the day of his wrath.'
>
> > Psalm cix, 1–5.

Prophecies such as these were familiar to these men, and could not fail to be recalled by the words He used. They were words of majesty, spoken now before the lawful court as they had been spoken before the unlawful court of Caiphas the night before. The cruelties and hardships of the night had in no way bent Him; the long fast and the sleeplessness had not weakened His spirit; in spite of all they did to the body of this Man there was that within which they could not break. From beginning to end He kept before them all the iniquity of their deed; He kept it unflinchingly before them, He appealed to evidence with which they were familiar. While they brought against Him either deliberately false witness or none at all, He brought against them the witness of the prophets, in whom they had always believed; while they affected to judge Him He let them clearly see at every step that in reality He was their judge. In the end He would have the last word, when He was seated,

> 'On the right hand of the power of God.'

Now it was their hour and the power of darkness, and in the blind passion of that hour they might refuse to look beyond; but the time would come when He would be in His rightful place, and with 'the power of God' would pass sentence upon them.

And yet He would not say, He would not even hint, what that sentence would be. The Son of Man had come to save the world, not to destroy it; not to condemn but to win sinners to repentance; and so long as there was hope for one in that crowd of evil men He would not utter, He would not even threaten, a word of condemnation. He had spared them so often in the past, He would spare them then. Nay more, in the past He had upbraided them; they should hear no word of accusation now. The nearer He came to His kingdom the more He would have pity on the blinded folly that did Him to death.

But these men were not to be beaten, either by His forbearance or by His warnings; they hated Him and hatred knows no reason, hatred will never yield. Let Him say what He would, they had learnt from the trial of the night before the test question, the answer to which would prove His doom; for they knew what answer this Man would give, who on their own confession but three days before, was:

'A true speaker
Who teachest the way of God in truth
Neither carest thou for any man
For thou dost not regard the person of men.'
Matthew xxii, 16.

Caiphas, who long ago had soothed their consciences concerning what they did, had also found for them this further key; they had only to repeat his test. Again, therefore, ignoring what Jesus had just said, as if it had no bearing on the case, as deliberate injustice always will:

'Then said they all
Art thou then the Son of God?'

Jesus answered as they wished. He had said all that He had to say in His own defence; it remained only that He should give witness to the truth, before this court that alone had the right to ask Him and judge Him:

'And he said
You say that I am.'

The answer was received with the same assumption as that with which it had been received at the trial in the night; these judges had well learnt from their leader how to play their part. Besides, they were in need to hurry with their work; Jesus must be put out of the way before the day was over, and there was much yet to be done. Somewhere that morning, at a preliminary meeting, almost certainly before Jesus had been brought in to them, it had been decided to take Him to be condemned by the Roman court. No doubt they might themselves have condemned Him to be stoned to death for blasphemy; but they recalled that they had attempted this before, on more than one occasion, and always He had escaped them. Moreover, that He should die as a public malefactor and criminal would serve their purpose better than that He should be put to death for blasphemy. Stoning to death might make

Him a hero; death for religion's sake might invest Him with the halo of a martyr; if they, the Sanhedrin, alone condemned Him, when the reaction came, when the city awoke to what had been done, they would have reason to 'fear the people', as they had so often feared them before. But the death of a public criminal, the degrading death of crucifixion, no man's reputation could survive; even the Law of Moses would bury the name of such a one in oblivion.

> ' When a man hath committed a crime
> For which he is to be punished with death
> And being condemned to die
> Is hanged on a gibbet
> His body shall not remain upon the tree
> But shall be buried the same day
> For he is accursed of God
> That hangeth on a tree
> And thou shalt not defile thy land
> Which the Lord thy God shall give thee in possession.'
> Deuteronomy xxi, 22–23.

The trial was quickly over, yet surely was it the critical moment of the whole story of the Passion. Now definitely, in a council which could no longer be called illegal or in any way invalid, Jesus was rejected and condemned by the judges of His own people. No wonder they wished to make haste; though conscience no longer troubled them, yet the sense of degradation and shame because of what they did hung about them, and the eyes of Him whom they had condemned to die followed them about the hall. There was no need now to go through any further form; there was no further need of witnesses. Before the highest court in the land He had made His confession of guilt and they could proceed.

> ' Then they said
> What need we any further testimony?
> For we ourselves have heard it
> From his own mouth.'

There was nothing more to delay them, not even the formalities of the Law. Their plans had been carefully laid and they were free to act at once. The house and council chamber of Caiphas, where these things had been done, were in the lower part of the city; Fort Antonia, where Pilate kept his court, was at the upper end beyond the Temple. All that remained was to take Him there and have their sentence formally confirmed and carried out by the Roman Governor; if all went as they wished and expected, the sentence would be completed long before midday. Pilate was a man of moods and they knew him well; arbitrary in his manifestations of power, with no understanding of Jewish prejudice, contemning and flouting religious form of any kind, a man of the world who had no use for religion, especially for that antiquated ceremonial in which the Jews were steeped. Moreover, he was careless of Jewish life, as became a dominant Roman; and much as the accusers of Jesus hated him for it, yet on this occasion they felt they could use it for their purpose. They had but to show Pilate that they were in earnest and he would yield; they had but to prove to him that unless he yielded there would be trouble in the city, and he would condemn. Pilate was in Jerusalem at that time precisely to keep order in a troubled season, and he would not care, for the sake of a single Jew's life, to add to his worries. There were others to be put to death that day, for executions usually took place before the great festivals, and to add one more to the number would be of little moment to Pilate.

Nevertheless all must be properly staged. The priests and elders were cooler now than they had been the night before, and they knew the importance of first impressions on the judge whom they were about to face. Jesus must be bound again. Everything that could mark their decision as to His guilt must be laid upon Him; He must be brought before the Roman judge as an undoubted criminal. Moreover, they must themselves be unanimous in decision and action; a dissentient voice must not be heard. It was still very early in the morning, scarcely six o'clock, as we would say. There would be few about at that early hour to protest, even if they wished it; if they hurried with their work, all might be completed before the city awoke to what was being done; for even yet it must not be forgotten that, more than Pilate or his soldiers, those priests and elders 'feared the people'.

> 'And the whole multitude of them rose up
> And binding Jesus
> Led him from Caiphas to the Governor's hall

And brought him bound
And delivered him to Pilate the Governor.'

The street from the house of Caiphas to the court of Herod led up through the deep valley which cut the city of Jerusalem in two. On their right as the accusers with their Victim went, towered up the wall of the Temple; on their left, also high up above them, was the thronged part of the town, a confusion of palaces and hovels, with the bazaar towards the North. Over their heads, at intervals, stone arches carrying streets joined the city to the Temple courts. The road up the valley was a thoroughfare joining North and South, little more; to-day it is buried many feet beneath the surface, filled with the debris of ancient Jerusalem, when it was beaten 'flat to the ground' and there was left of the city 'not a stone upon a stone'.

It would seem that Pontius Pilate, the Roman Governor, had been forewarned of what was in store for him that day, and of what would be expected of him; moreover, the Romans were glad to have the business of litigation done with as soon as possible. Accordingly, even at this early hour, he was awaiting the crowd that gathered round his door. At the north-west corner of the Temple wall the road turned sharply to the right, running along the northern boundary. On the other side, to the North, soon appeared the barracks and courts of the Roman soldiery, with the threatening Tower of Antonia raised above them, overlooking, commanding, and threatening, in case of trouble, the court of the Temple below. This street was far more narrow than that along which the crowd had come up through the city. It led past the prætorium out to the north-eastern gate; in front of the Governor's hall an archway spanned it, connecting the Roman quarters on either side. The stones of that archway are still preserved, spanning the altar of Our Lady of Sion built upon the spot.

On ordinary occasions the accusers with their victim would have gone up the steps leading to the Governor's hall, and would have pleaded their cause before the Roman judge in the place of justice, where the judge would sit upon his marble throne. But on this occasion they would not go in; instead they handed Jesus over to the Roman guard, and demanded that Pilate should come out to them. For the morrow was the Pasch, even Pilate knew that, or he would not have been at that moment in the city; and the good Jew must be careful that he prepared for the great day with due solemnity. He must not contaminate himself beforehand; he must do nothing that would make him unclean, or guilty in the eyes of the Law. But to enter the house of an unbeliever would at any time contaminate him for that day; much more then must he be careful on a day when ceremonies were to be performed. Therefore on no account, not even to ensure that in this case of all cases his end was gained, would he cross the threshold of the unbeliever Pilate, on this day. He might hate but, outside his own court, he must have due regard to ceremony; he might advocate injustice, but it must be covered by the letter of the law. He might do an innocent man to death, he might commit the most terrible crime that ever man had committed on this earth; still, if he did 'what was done', if he conformed to convention, if he claimed on his side the maintenance of law and order and righteousness, whatever crime he did he might satisfy himself that all was well, and the world that thought with him would applaud.

> 'And they went not into the hall
> That they might not be defiled
> But that they might eat the pasch.'

22. The Despair of Judas.

We must leave Jesus and His accusers here at the door of Pilate's court, to record the dread event of which S. Matthew, and later S. Luke, have kept the memory. We left Judas with the crowd at the gate of the Garden of Gethsemane; from the way he there disappears altogether from the scene we may make our conjectures. First the crowd, once he had done his work, had no further use for him, and he was made to recognize it; secondly, as with every first offender, no sooner had he done his deed than he realized his own deep shame. When the mob had taken Jesus, and had passed with Him across the valley, Judas stood alone in the lane outside the gate. He had stood there often before, and he knew the place well, but always till now it had been with a companion. Now there was not one who would be with him, not a friend, not an enemy; not Jesus, not any of the Twelve, not a fellow-countryman,

not any man at all, once he realized what he had done.
The curse of Cain was upon him, and he could only say
with Cain :

> 'My iniquity is greater
> Than that I may deserve pardon
> Behold thou dost cast me out this day
> From the face of the earth
> And I shall be hidden from thy face
> And I shall be a vagabond
> And a fugitive on the earth
> Everyone therefore that findeth me
> Shall kill me.'
>
> Genesis iv, 13, 14.

There is no need to go back with Judas on all that had happened during that night from the time he had played the traitor. Judas even more than Simon had followed it all; with a fascination he could not resist he had gone with the crowd, he had entered the hall, he had witnessed all that had been done to the Master and Friend whom he had betrayed. He had heard the sentence of Caiphas and the rest; in the morning he had again been present in the court and with his own ears had heard the condemnation. Jesus had been judged worthy of death, by the highest authority of Jewish law, without a shadow of convicting evidence; Judas alone was the cause. He had been hurried away through the city that the sentence might at once be carried out, and had offered no resistance; the deed of Judas seemed to have paralysed Him from the beginning. What had he done? The blood of Jesus was on his hands, the voice of God thundered out against him, nature would cast him away as unfit any longer to live, hatred had come into his soul and he hated himself:

> 'What hast thou done?
> The voice of thy brother's blood
> Crieth to me from the earth
> Now therefore cursed shalt thou be upon the earth
> Which hath opened her mouth
> And received the blood of thy brother
> At thy hand.'
>
> Genesis iv, 10, 11.

He was a traitor, and for what? A murderer, and for what? A traitor and murderer of One who had loved and trusted him, and for what? For thirty silver coins, which a few days ago had seemed reward enough, but now were worse than worthless. All the rest had gone; the friendship of Jesus Christ, the company of the Eleven, the tender love of that woman whose Son he had betrayed. All the rest had gone; the joy in life that had been his long ago, the high ambitions, the desire to be and to do great things, the yearning after God. All had gone; instead he carried in him a dead soul, a heart icy cold, a life degraded below the life of any beast. He looked at the coins in his pouch and he cursed them. They were as burning coals to his fingers as he touched them, heated with the fire of hell itself. He would have none of them any longer; he would fling them back at the accursed men who had tempted him with them. There were still some of them in the Temple; not all had been able to go with Jesus to the court of Pilate, for the business of the Pasch had still to go on. Scarcely reckoning what he did, goaded on by the knowledge of his crime, and of all he had forfeited thereby, aware that he was no longer fit to be called a human being, 'a fugitive and a vagabond upon the earth', Judas hurried from the house of Caiphas. He rushed into the Temple, with all the signs of a madman, of one possessed. He burst into the hall where the rulers of Jerusalem were sitting, the hall where the contract had been made two days before; no longer the cringing, petitioning Judas whom they had then received, but now defiant, reckless of their high dignity, with hatred hissing through his teeth, danger glaring in his eyes, seeking only to throw on them some at least of the misery that overwhelmed him.

> 'And Judas who betrayed him
> Seeing that he was condemned
> Repenting himself
> Brought back the thirty pieces of silver
> To the chief priests and the ancients
> Saying
> I have sinned
> In betraying innocent blood.'

It was a confession, but a confession of despair; repentance, but without hope or love; and it was made, not to God, of whom he no longer thought, but to those whose hearts had been long since hardened. If Judas was guilty, they were no less, and they knew it as well as he; but if Judas was so foolish as to lose his self-control and confess his guilt, that was no reason why they should follow his example. Decorum must be kept; there were rules of self-respect which no man of honour would break, and that Judas broke them only proved that he was a country boor and beneath their notice. He was doubly contemptible. As the damned in hell confess their guilt to the devils their masters, so did Judas confess his sin before these men; and in like manner was his confession heard. They looked down upon him from their higher platform; they despised him for a traitor and a coward; they looked at one another and were becomingly indignant at this unseemly intrusion. The bargain had been struck; they had fulfilled their part of that bargain; what followed after was no concern of theirs nor, for that matter, what had gone before. Let Judas keep to the terms of his contract, and they would keep to theirs; whatever else they were, these masters of the Law must be gentlemen, truthful, and honest, and law-abiding. Therefore once more, with that same show of justice with which they had before proved to themselves the justice, the necessity, the duty of seeking the death of Jesus of Nazareth, these whited sepulchres now repudiated Judas Iscariot. He had not come there for sympathy but out of hatred; he had not come for forgiveness and pardon but to accuse; he could expect neither from those who had already said that He who claimed to forgive sins was a blasphemer, He who was the friend of publicans and sinners was a danger to the nation.

> ' But they said
> What is that to us?
> Look thou to it.'

Judas could have expected nothing else from a court such as this. The contract could not be cancelled, the sentence passed on Him whom he had betrayed could not be revoked; already, even as he spoke, probably somewhere hard by, Jesus was being done to death, so triumphantly thought these ancients and chief priests. There was nothing left for Judas but to go; and since to live, with this burthen upon him, the outcast of God and men, would be worse than any death, it was better now that he should end his life and be done with it. It were better for him had he never been born; it were better for him had he never known this Jesus of Nazareth. Why had God made him? Why had Jesus given him His favour, only to take it away again? He emptied the contents of his purse on the ground. The thirty silver pieces fell jingling on the stone floor, many of them rolling to the feet of the men who had paid them. He hurried out as he had come in, caring nought for anything or anyone about him. Next morning, a pilgrim coming up the valley outside the southern city wall, saw a man hanging from a tree, and his body burst asunder.

> ' And casting down the pieces of silver
> In the temple
> He departed
> And went and hanged himself with a halter.'

S. Matthew concludes his story with an account of the fate of those thirty pieces of silver. When all was over, and the chief priests no less than Judas, but after their own manner, had realized what they had done, they were unwilling to have anything to do with this blood-money, much less dared they put it back into the Temple treasury. It had done its work, and now like the scapegoat it must be cast out and carry their sin with it. They held a consultation regarding what should be done with it. The price of blood made them think of the dead. There was need of a burial-place near the city for such strangers as came and died there, especially during such times as the Paschal season. It might be well to use the money for that purpose. Outside the city to the South, across the valley and up the slope of the Mount of Evil Counsel was a derelict piece of land which once had been a potter's field. It was cheap; the thirty pieces would suffice; it would serve their purpose very well. Nevertheless it was never forgotten by the people whence had come the money that had bought that field, and for long years after it was known as the Field of Blood. S. Matthew sees in this the fulfilment of a prophecy, which he quotes as from Jeremias, but the passages seem to be adapted from the prophet Zachary :

> ' But the chief priests
> Having taken the pieces of silver said

It is not lawful for us
To put them into the corbona
Because they are the price of blood
And having consulted together
They bought with them the potter's field
To be a burying-place for strangers
For which cause that field was called Haceldama
That is the Field of Blood
Even to this day
Then was fulfilled
That which was spoken by Jeremias the prophet
Saying
And they took the thirty pieces of silver
The price of him that was prized
Whom they had prized of the children of Israel
And they gave them unto the potter's field
As the Lord appointed to me.'

23. Jesus before Pilate.

(a) *The Accusations.*

The crowd of the accusers of Jesus and their satellites had gathered round and on the steps of Pilate's palace. Jesus stood bound at the summit of those steps, between the Roman guard, rejected by His people ; what was to greet Him when the Gentile governor opened his door ? He stood between two worlds, as did His apostles after Him ; the old one was that day ending, the new one had already begun, but the door as yet was closed. The crowd below was not a large one. It was still very early in the morning, and though the city was already awake there was much to be done by everyone that day in preparation for the Pasch. The street in which the crowd had assembled was narrow, for a single arch spanned it ; this gave the impression to one standing on the balcony of a much larger number than was actually there. There were the chief priests and ancients, with the men who had come up with them from the house of Caiphas ; these were the main body, loud and clamorous and insistent, but it would seem, from the very nature of the case, that their actual number could not have been great. As they had proceeded through the city some few may have joined them, curious to see what was going forward, at so early an hour, and on such a day ; but the elders expected no strong support from the ordinary people, whom they feared, and were anxious to avoid.

Pilate the Governor was within his hall waiting for them; as we have seen, he had been prepared for their coming. But the accusers disdained to enter into his palace; their Victim might enter, for He was already doomed, but for themselves in a cause of justice, they clamoured that Pilate who governed them must respect their religious scruples. And Pilate yielded, he committed his first act of weakness; from that moment the leaders were conscious that, whatever opposition the Roman Governor might make, they had but to persevere and in the end they would win. It was a clever beginning; on more than one occasion before, they had beaten Pilate in a contest concerning religious observance, and Pilate was unwilling to contend with them again on what was to him a trifle. But his first surrender was followed by a second. He looked at the Figure before him, silent and unmoved, yet stained with blood, bespattered with spittle and filth, with bruises marked across His face, obviously already the object of gross maltreatment and abuse. Justice should have said that here was one who had been grievously treated before He had yet been condemned; before the charges were considered, something was needed to explain why these men had so taken the law into their own hands.

But Pilate set this aside. When, at his appearance on the balcony, the howling of the mob had been silenced he turned to them and asked:

'What accusation
Bring you against this man?'

He said nothing of the 'Man's' condition; nothing by way of rebuke to those who had treated Him so roughly. His question, almost apologetic in its tone, gave the accusers courage. They could assume a defiant attitude; though he had spoken as one who wished to go through at least the forms of law, they would let this weak Governor know that their Victim was already condemned, and that all that was needed was his consent to proceed with the execution. There was no need to formulate their charge as there is seldom need to formulate a charge when hatred is the accuser. They would demand justice and their rights; they would claim that all there present held Jesus to be guilty, and that was evidence enough; since Jesus had so many enemies, a whole streetful of them calling for His death, it was the duty of Pilate to pass sentence according to the law of the land.

> ' They answered and said to him
> If he were not a malefactor
> We would not have delivered him up to thee.'

This, then, was the first charge these accusers of Jesus had to bring before the court of human justice. In their own court it had been quite otherwise. There He had been accused of threatening to destroy the Temple, and to build it up again in three days; He had been challenged to say in open court whether or not He was

> ' The Christ
> The Son of the living God.'

Once in the Temple it had been openly acknowledged that He was no malefactor; that indeed it was His very good works that they had been compelled to own:

> ' Many good works I have showed you
> From my Father
> For which of those works do you stone me?'
> ' The Jews answered him
> For a good work we stone thee not
> But for blasphemy
> And because that thou being a man
> Makest thyself God.'
>
> John x, 32-33.

Another time He had dared them to convince Him of a single evil deed He had done, and they had been able to answer nothing. And now there is no charge; Jesus is to be condemned on an assumption, the common justice of the street. ' If he were not a malefactor!' Since the leaders of men gave Him this name, what remained for the rest but to believe that something in it must be true?

But Pilate was not so easily to be induced to yield; weak as he had already shown himself, he had also the subtlety of weakness. He had to defend himself from the charge of miscarriage of justice; he had to defend the honour of the Roman court. Perhaps, too, there was another power coming to support him if he would accept it; the presence

of the Man who stood fettered and helpless at his side.
But for the moment Pilate had no interest to consider
this; at such a crisis the form of justice would suffice
for him. These clamouring men before Him were obstinate
and determined; they would stop at nothing to gain their
end; and he was there to keep the peace. Whoever this
Jesus was, already His presence was telling upon the Roman
Governor. The leaders of these Jews were clearly inflamed
with deadly hatred against Him; they were in no mood to
consider right or wrong, justice or injustice, observance
of law or its violation. He had but to let them have their
way, and he would be freed from all responsibility; he had
but to shut his eyes, and they would take the matter into
their own hands. By what they had just said they had
implied that they had already tried and condemned the
criminal who stood before him; in their eyes He was
'a malefactor', and the judgment of a malefactor came
within the scope of their courts. He could leave it to them
to finish the work they had begun. Thus would he save
himself; his words would be non-committal; should this
rabble later go too far, and violate the law, then, if it were
needed, he would be able to proceed against them and act as
an upholder of justice should.

> ' Pilate said to them
> Take him you
> And judge him according to your law.'

The leaders heard him, but were not satisfied. The
subtle and experienced Roman was no match for the far
more subtle and astute Asiatic. With all the implication
that his words conveyed, the acknowledgment of their
rights, the willingness to accept their decision, they saw
very well that they failed to cover all that they coveted.
For the words omitted the death-sentence; above all the
sentence to that death on which they had set their hearts.
A less sophisticated mind might have assumed that they
implied it, and Pilate hoped that they would be so understood; but the expounders of the Law were too trained
in word-splitting to be so easily deceived. They would let
the Governor see that they were not content. Pilate had
seemingly accepted without question their decision that
this Man was a malefactor; they would make him accept
their further decision upon the sentence they expected him

to pass. For that sentence belonged to him alone. Jesus was a malefactor ; so they had proved, or rather had assumed, and Pilate had asked for no further evidence. Jesus was a malefactor, and malefactors were not stoned to death ; which alone was within the powers of their courts of justice. He was fit only for the gibbet, stoning to death was too good for Him ; this also they would declare, or rather would again assume, and would see what this weak-kneed Roman would do :

> 'The Jews therefore said to him
> It is not lawful for us
> To put any man to death.'

As the evangelist S. John records this cry, it brings back to his mind the many occasions on which Jesus had foretold His death to His own. They had never understood what He had said ; least of all had they understood the prophecy as to the way He would die. For if He were to perish at the hands of the Jews, who alone were His enemies, it would be by stoning ; several times the attempt had been made and had failed. But death by crucifixion ? That was the method of the Romans, and with the Romans Jesus had never any quarrel. Now S. John sees the meaning of the Jewish protest. Jesus must not die as a blasphemer ; that might make Him a martyr, as many a prophet had been made. He must die as a malefactor, that His name might be stained for all time :

> 'That the words of Jesus might be fulfilled
> Signifying what death he should die.'

But the effect of this second demand was very different from that which the accusers of Jesus had anticipated. Weakness will yield to a point, but weakness driven to a corner will turn and retaliate. From this last cry Pilate saw that he must be drawn into the affair ; the would-be shedders of blood would act only on his responsibility, with his consent, insisting on a kind of death which he alone had the power to inflict. At once, then, he began to harden. If he was to sanction the death of this Man he must be given reasons. The leaders of the Law saw the change, but they were ready ; hatred and malice find arguments to justify any situation. In their own courts Jesus had been condemned because He had made Himself the Son of God ; in the eyes of Pilate, for the present at least, this would not count for much. It would not prove Him a malefactor; it might only make Pilate take Him for a harmless fool. That they might find acceptance by a Roman official the charges they preferred must be political. They must show that this malefactor was the enemy of law and order, that He interfered with the Roman revenue, that He was a danger to the Emperor's authority. It was no difficult matter. Had there not been occasions when He had so stirred the people that they had risen like one man and had tried to proclaim Him King? Had He not been known to question Rome's right to impose tribute money? Had He not said that He and His disciples were free from the obligation of the taxes? Had He not Himself spoken of His kingdom, of those who belonged to it, of the conditions for admittance to it? Surely out of all this they could discover cause enough to make even Pilate suspicious. They were quick to seize the situation. One charge followed another; so long as the Governor was given reason for his sentence he would certainly pronounce it, if only to free himself from further trouble:

'And they began to accuse him saying
We have found this man
Perverting our nation
And forbidding to give tribute to Cæsar
And saying he is Christ the King.'

These were surely charges serious enough to make any provincial governor pause. Perverting the nation, that is, a sedition-monger? Forbidding to pay the taxes? Calling himself a king? Before such a judge His enemies could scarcely have chosen their accusations more astutely. That none of them had been so much as thought of in the courts of Annas and Caiaphas mattered nothing; there they had condemned Jesus of Nazareth for reasons of their own, here they were but seeking confirmation of their sentence, and any charge would suit their purpose. But by the first two at least Pilate was little moved. Like other Roman governors he had his own means of information; and he knew his province well enough to value such charges at their proper worth. If there had been danger of a rising anywhere, if there had been any refusal to pay taxes, he would long since have been informed. But the last charge was

more serious ; at least it roused his curiosity. No one could
have lived long in Palestine in those days, and have come
to understand much of the Jewish mind, without learning
the place this dream of kingship held in the hearts of the
people. They sang continually the songs of David ; they
clung without shadow of doubt to the belief that one day
would come a son of David who would set them free ;
though the very word kingdom had almost perished from
the Roman reckoning, here it was always on men's lips.

(b) *The First Examination.*

Recollections like these were roused in Pilate's mind
by the last accusation. This Man said He was Christ the
King. He turned and looked at the Victim of hate who
stood before him. He was a pitiable sight enough. If He
had claimed to be the King of this people, He had already
paid dearly for His false pretension ; if He were a king
He had certainly been dethroned. Still there might be
something in what had been said. 'Christ the King' : the
words meant more than mere kingship, as he, though only
a Roman, could well guess. Moreover there was something
in the Man Himself, as He stood there at the mercy of them
all, that made the Governor pause. Mean and bespattered
as He was, alone and apart from all the world, with not a
hand to defend Him, not a sword that could be drawn on
His side, still it was against Him that all this fury was raging,
it was He who had roused all this bitter hatred. Such a man
could be no mean creature. There might then be something in the charge. Even in some sense which meant
nothing to a Roman, which implied no danger to the
Empire, this Man might be what they said He claimed to be.
If He was, He would acknowledge it ; if He did not, His
denial would put Pilate at his ease, and would be ample
reason to give Him His freedom. Pilate would challenge
Him to speak :

> 'And Pilate asked him saying
> Art thou the king of the Jews ? '

The answer was not unexpected, and yet it was given
with a firmness, a directness, which made Pilate hesitate.
There was no word of self-defence, no circumlocution ;
no counter-accusation against those who had brought Him

to this pass; no explanation, as yet, that the word had another sense from that which Pilate had in mind. Jesus had been asked a simple, lawful question by one who had lawful authority to ask it, and He gave the simplest reply:

> 'And Jesus answered him and said
> Thou sayest it
>
> .   .   .   .
>
> Render unto Cæsar
> The things that are Cæsar's.'

We look back on the life of Jesus and notice but few occasions when He has come in contact with the ruling Romans; yet always there has been a deference, a friendliness, which cannot be mistaken. The second miracle recorded at Cana, the cure of the official's son, may well have been wrought on the son of a Roman. In Capharnaum, after the Sermon on the Mount, He had healed the servant of a Roman officer, and on that occasion had broken out in praise of the Roman's faith. He had said that many would come after, from East and West, and would enter the Kingdom when the natural heirs would be cast out. He had been the friend of the tax-collectors, men disliked because of their service of Rome; one of them He had made a chosen disciple. When His enemies had come tempting Him about the tribute, He had taken in His hand a Roman coin, and had bidden men give to the Roman Emperor his due. They had tempted Him again, because of a slaughter by Roman arrows in the Temple court. But Jesus had said not a word against the Romans; He had only turned the occasion to speak to the Jews themselves. In His parables He had spoken of princes and kings, of merchants and foreign powers; He had always spoken of them with respect. Only at the Supper that night had He warned His disciples, the future princes of His own kingdom, that their standards were not to be as were the standards of other rulers; but even then He spoke with no word of complaint or criticism.

Now, when we find Him before Pilate, from beginning to end His attitude is the same. He treats Pilate always with respect; He calls upon him no woe; He will warn him, but He will not blame him; in His manner throughout there is a consideration for Pilate which would have made one more sensitive to truth realize that he was dealing, not with a criminal on his trial, but with a friend. Indeed one might think that Pilate himself realized it. What Roman governor, with a despicable Jew, a Jewish criminal, before him, would have condescended to such lengths as Pilate condescended in his conversation with Jesus that day? Yet as the hours of the morning dragged on, the Judge and the Criminal became only the more intimate. At first Pilate had before him just a Jew for whom he cared nothing; at the end he passed sentence on One who had won not only his esteem but a place in his heart. But a little more courage, a little further response to the affection stirred within him, and not Pilate and Herod, but Pilate and Jesus might have been intimate friends from that day. Such, even under this ordeal, was the heart of Jesus Christ.

The Prisoner had given His answer, so plainly that there was no room for further questioning; He had spoken to Pilate as He had spoken to Caiphas the night before. Meanwhile the uproar in the street below became ever louder. The crowd by this time had increased, and its leaders had made it plain which way it should act. Let it be recalled once more that a crowd has little conscience or will of its own. It is more easily led by the powers that rule it than are the individuals who make it up, and it is far more merciless, and thoughtless, and cruel. This will account for much that happened that weird morning. As Pilate hesitated after the answer of Jesus, as he leaned over to the stricken Man who stood before him, cries came up from the mob below, voicing ever-new accusations. What they were mattered little; many were terms of abuse and nothing more; what mattered most was that it should be brought home to Pilate that nothing but the blood of the Man before him would appease them. Still the Man made no reply. He let them clamour on, He was unmoved, He showed no sign that He would defend Himself in any way; He seemed to be in another world.

What could Pilate do or say? If the Man were so submissive, if He would do nothing to defend Himself, how could Pilate defend Him? There were no witnesses on His side; no advocate had His cause in hand; if He said nothing for Himself His cause might be lost by default. He would stir Him to speak; His answers would no doubt give some evidence on which he could act, since clearly His accusers were not disposed to be cross-examined.

'And the chief priests and ancients
Accused him in many things
And when he was accused
He answered nothing
Then Pilate again asked him
Answerest thou nothing ?
Behold in how many things
They accuse thee
Dost thou not hear
How many things they allege against thee ? '

This time Pilate received no reply ; to such questions silence was answer enough. As before Annas and Caiphas Jesus had declined to defend Himself by so much as a word, so He declined before Pilate ; before both, He would confine Himself to the simple truth and no more. None the less Pilate wondered at His silence :

' But Jesus still answered him not
To any word
So that the governor wondered exceedingly.'

For there stood Jesus, between him and that howling mob ready to destroy Him if Pilate would give them leave, and He was unmoved, He seemed careless of what would be. Already, if He were a king, they had done that to Him which should have stirred His indignation and vengeance, but He was still unmoved. That in the end His life would be spared was now more than doubtful, yet He remained there silent as if it were of no concern to Him, rather as if it were a fate He expected. Jesus began to fascinate Pilate ; He stirred his admiration. Pilate must see this Man alone, apart from the clamour of the crowd, and judge of Him more for himself.

Pilate then left the balcony where hitherto he had faced the crowd, and went back into the hall behind him. He made a sign ; and Jesus was brought in after him. Others, forsooth, would not step across that threshold lest they be contaminated ; but for Jesus, who was already ' reputed with the wicked ', who already ' bore the sins of many ', this further contamination could matter little. Within the hall Pilate sat upon his marble chair, the arbiter of justice ; Jesus stood before him, silent, in His very silence seeming to command. Pilate had not forgotten the one confession that Jesus had made to him on the balcony outside; whatever else He had passed over, He had plainly said that He was a king, the King of the Jews, King of these very people who were hounding Him to death. He would test Him further on this point; clearly the rest could matter nothing. If he could but understand what this kingship meant he would be on safer ground:

> 'Pilate therefore went into the hall again
> And called Jesus and said to him
> Art thou the King of the Jews?'

There have been many occasions in the life of Jesus when men have come to Him to judge Him, yet have always gone away knowing that He, not they, was the Judge. We have seen it with Simon and Nathaniel, in the early days by the Jordan. We have seen it, again, with the Pharisee, Nicodemus, who came to Him by night; with the elders and chief priests on many an occasion; with Annas and Caiphas on this very night. So was it now with Pilate. The Governor repeated a question to which already Jesus had given a plain and sufficient answer. It was now the turn for the Prisoner to ask; and it would be, not a timid question, as of one who stood on his trial and pleaded for his life, but of one who was Himself the master. It would be a question which would tell Pilate, if he chose to hear, that the Man before him was not a criminal only at his mercy; He was a reader of Pilate's own heart. It would tell Pilate that Jesus knew that he had a double purpose in his question. Before, on the balcony outside, in presence of the accusers, he had asked only because the charge had been made against Him that He had claimed to be 'Christ the King'; now in the privacy of that hall he asked for another reason. He was interested for his own sake. A light had been given him and he had accepted it; it was one more of the many occasions in the life of Jesus when a light accepted had led to another. Indeed at this moment Pontius Pilate was very near the truth; he was 'not far from the kingdom of God'. That moment was the turning-point, not of the trial of Jesus only, but of Pilate's whole life. In Peræa, a few weeks before, a rich young man had come very near and then had turned away; at this secret meeting Pilate was given a like offer and he failed.

But with what patience and even love he was treated!

In spite of His own distress, in spite of all that depended for Himself on this cross-examination, the Lover of men laid His own care aside. He would treat this hard Roman as He would treat the tenderest child. Pilate had much against him: his Roman upbringing, his Roman contempt for the Jew, his Roman assumption that what was not Roman was of little account. Jesus knew all this. He would not urge this Roman; He would only induce him to reflect; once more, as always in like cases, Jesus by a simple question would draw him to think upon himself. Was He the King of the Jews?

'Jesus answered
Sayest thou this thing of thyself
Or have others told it thee of me?'

It was as if He would have said: 'Pilate, out there before My accusers thou didst ask this question because others brought it as a charge against Me. Now thou dost ask Me, though thou hast not reflected on it, for another reason. Thou dost ask, not because of what men say, but because in thy heart thou dost begin to believe that it is the real truth. Flesh and blood are not revealing Me to thee, but My Father who is in heaven.'

Jesus had indeed read and interpreted the mind of Pilate far more truly than Pilate wished. He had hoped to keep his secret to himself; he had hoped to discover more about this Man while still he remained the Roman Governor. And here was one, a criminal on trial in his hands, who read his secret, and with that knowledge dared to reverse their positions. Pilate was no longer examining Jesus; Pilate was no longer the judge of Jesus; Jesus was coming very near to being his Judge. And yet how gently, how considerately, giving him if he would take it opportunity for how much! By His question He was appealing to him to be true to himself, not merely to the Roman within him; if he would be true to his real self, there was behind that question an offer of light, of grace, such as Pilate could never have imagined. If he accepted it, if he would but answer that simple question, if he would only say that, for his own sake, he wished to know the truth, what light, even in that council chamber, would he not have received! Pilate would have been added to that noble list of the conquests of Jesus—Nicodemus, the woman of Samaria, the woman of Magdala, Levi, the Roman soldier in Capharnaum, the many more who had learned to know, and love, and follow the Friend of publicans and sinners.

But Pilate recoiled. As before, in the presence of the Jewish rabble, consciousness that he was being overcome made him act with a show of strength, so now, in the presence of this King, he was too weak to yield. A question had been put to him; he would not answer it. He would still play his part; he would be the man of the world he professed to be; he would pretend he did not care. What was Jesus to him? What were Jesus and His kingdom to a Roman like himself? Let others be interested if it so pleased them, as it pleased a Jew; for himself, he was a Roman judge, and a Roman judge he would remain. The light had been given and had been rejected; and at once it went out.

> ' Pilate answered
> Am I a Jew?
> Thy nation and the chief priests
> Have delivered thee up to me
> What hast thou done? '

So, by another question, Pilate thought to recover the position he had lost. Whether Jesus were a king or not, He had enemies clamouring for His blood; whether He were a king or not, He must have done something to provoke this hatred and bitterness. But Jesus, the Hunter of souls, was not so easily to be turned aside. Pilate himself had come to Him and asked Him for ' the things that were to his peace ', and he should not because of a single refusal be rejected. With the love of the Good Shepherd risking all for one lost sheep, while out in the street the wolves were howling, He would press His appeal more home. Pilate had shown that whatever befell he would be a Roman; Jesus would assure him that from His kingship and His kingdom the Roman need not fear. These would bring no danger to the Empire, no danger to himself; the follower of Christ the King would be no less loyal to Tiberius the Emperor. Were it not so, were Christ a rival of Tiberius, the battle between them would not last long:

> ' Jesus answered
> My kingdom is not of this world

> If my kingdom were of this world
> My servants would certainly strive
> That I should not be delivered to the Jews
> But now my kingdom is not from hence.'

Pilate, in his fancied strength which in reality was weakness, had already rejected one grace proferred by the Man whom he feared to reverence ; he now rejected another. Gradually the darkness was closing around him ; for he chose to 'love darkness rather than the light'. From a doubter who, nevertheless, suspected where the truth lay, he was fast degenerating into a mere sceptic. He harked back to his former question. Jesus had drawn him away into depths he was unwilling to fathom ; Pilate would save himself from being led further.

> ' Pilate therefore said to him
> Art thou a king then ? '

This time Jesus would reply clearly and without cavil. He had declared it before when the question had been put merely as an accusation ; He would declare it again, that Pilate might understand it in the added light he had received. For still would Jesus fight for the soul of Pilate. He had already appealed to him that he should listen to the voice that spoke within him, that he should be true to himself. He had assured him, further, that to follow the light and accept Him would imply no disloyalty to an earthly chief ; he could still be a Roman and yet believe. He would now urge His cause from another angle, the angle from which the heart of a Roman might be most surely reached. For the Roman honoured nobility of character ; the grandeur of Rome herself cast her shadow on all her citizens ; and nobility of character is nowhere more manifest than when it pursues a noble cause. Jesus would make this last appeal, to the finest things in Pilate ; though twice He had failed He would not be the first to yield. We can see the beaten figure rise to its full stature, expressing kingship in every gesture despite the bonds and the foulness, as

> ' Jesus answered
> Thou sayest that I am a king
> For this was I born
> And for this I came into the world

> That I should give testimony to the truth
> Everyone that is of the truth
> Heareth my voice.'

For a third time Jesus had appealed to the natural honesty of Pilate. From the very nature of His words we may judge what was the character of the Roman Governor; for here as everywhere else Jesus adapted Himself to the one to whom He spoke. Jesus who had always shown Himself equal to all, to the simplest and the most subtle in the land, was no less the equal of the Roman. He saw in Pilate one who before all else would be what the world would call, then as now, a gentleman; with a high sense of honour, as men would measure honour, with a desire to be what men would call just and true, strong in the virtues that would make him stand well with his fellow-men, but on that very account stricken with a fatal weakness. Because other men were his standard, because other men were his judges, nothing must be suffered to make him fail in men's eyes; on the one hand no dishonourable act as they would understand it, on the other not even Truth itself, if it spoke in language different from that which was spoken in his circle. When that came to him, when the voice of Truth threatened to put him out of harmony with the world that was his ideal, then the voice of Truth must be silenced. And that was never difficult. If Truth cannot be contradicted, she can usually be questioned; if she cannot be denied, she can at least be made matter of controversy; above all if a question is asked and we do not wait for an answer.

Such was Pilate, eager to stand well before men, and for that ideal willing to sacrifice the one thing that was for his peace. He listened to this King of truth; he felt again the impulse for higher things within him. But as twice before he had failed, so now he escaped by the subterfuge common to his kind. Truth?

> ' Pilate saith to him
> What is truth?'

and without waiting for a reply he rose from his seat of justice, passed the King of justice by, and went forth again to the din of the crowd outside. How many are those who, through the ages, have imitated Pilate! It is an easy way to kill conscience, an easy escape from the call to all that is noblest, but in the very act we prove that we are cowards. Thus, in another way, is conscience apt to make cowards of us all.

Pilate left Jesus alone in the inner room, lamenting this His third failure to win a human soul since His prayer in the garden. He came out again before the crowd. While he had been with the Prisoner, the leaders of the people had not been idle. By this time the crowd had grown, and the new-comers, no longer their own on whom they could rely, must be attuned to their purpose. Jesus of Nazareth, the contemptible Galilæan, had been unmasked at last. Whatever He had seemed to them before, now His power was clearly beaten; whatever miracles He had seemed to work, now His power of magic had deserted Him. Those who before had believed in Him might now see how mistaken they had been; the elders and chief priests, their lawful leaders, had been right after all, and the people responded. They had reason to be ashamed of their former allegiance; they were annoyed that they had been so deceived; they were only too ready to have their revenge, to vent their wrath on this manifest impostor. The chief priests and elders had indeed good ground on which to sow their seed, and during this interval had made good use of their opportunity. When Pilate again appeared on the balcony above them, he found before him a mob, larger in numbers, more stirred to fury, more determined than ever not to be baulked of its prey.

Still he would make another stand. The cross-examination in the private room had had a peculiar effect; question as he would, it had been an examination of himself, rather than of the Nazarene. And he had come away convinced of one thing. If he admired truth, Jesus of Nazareth was true; if he honoured nobility, Jesus of Nazareth was noble; if he respected strength, without any doubt Jesus was strong and void of fear. To condemn such a Man was surely impossible; He could be accused of nothing. Then he, too, would be a man. He would pull himself together; he would defend this Jesus; this clamouring mob should not overcome him; he would tell it plainly that he found the Accused not guilty.

> ' And when he had said this
> He went forth again to the Jews
> And said to them
> I find no cause in him.'

It was indeed a feeble defence, and the accusers were not slow to recognize it. It was almost a half-confession that he was on their side, that if he could find cause he would condemn. They must press their case against such feeble opposition. Of all things Pilate would be most affected by the charge of disturbing the peace. They would urge that point; they would show the Governor that the mischief made was not confined to Judæa only. It was also spread through the tetrarchies, where his own authority was limited. Jesus was a danger to Rome; His influence was greatest among the troublesome people of Galilee. If Pilate were not careful to crush Him, Jesus of Nazareth might one day descend on Jerusalem from the hill country in the North :

> ' But they were more earnest saying
> He stirreth up the people
> Teaching throughout Judæa
> Beginning from Galilee
> To this place.'

24. Jesus before Herod.

Once more the vehemence of the chief priests and elders overreached itself. The shifting Pilate, eager for any escape from the necessity of making a decision, seized on the mention of Galilee. He enquired further, how came Jesus to ' begin from Galilee ' ? Did He belong to that province ? Yes, He was Jesus of Nazareth ; He had made Capharnaum ' His own city ' ; His followers were all Galilæans ; it was in Galilee that He had worked most of His miracles, that He had preached the Sermon on the mountain, that He had promised eternal life to those who would eat His flesh and drink His blood, and had been rejected. It was in Galilee that He had claimed the power to forgive sins, and had made the Pharisees and Herodians come together to plot His death. It was in Galilee that He had done most of His good works ; from Galilee that He had been compelled to fly ; it was against the towns of

Galilee, Corozain, and Bethsaida, and Capharnaum, that in the end He had been driven to pronounce words of doom, a greater doom than even that of Sodom and Gomorrha. Yes, indeed, in Galilee He had 'stirred up the people', so that in Nazareth itself they had sought His life, in Capharnaum they had 'laughed Him to scorn'. He had been convicted of 'casting out devils' by Beelzebub, the prince of devils, He had been the Friend of publicans and sinners, the refuse of the land. It was in Galilee, and this was worst of all, that some had cried :

> 'A great prophet hath risen up among us
> And God hath visited his people';

it was people from Galilee who had wished to make Him their King.

The charges were poured out for Pilate to hear, and in them he saw an unexpected escape. If all this could be said against the Galilæan, then let Him be judged by a Galilæan judge. He knew that Herod, the tetrarch of Galilee, was in the city; Herod had come there like the rest to be present at the Pasch, as became a dutiful son of the builder of the Temple. Pilate would send the Galilæan to Herod. Though he was no friend, though at this moment they were bitter rivals, though in Jerusalem Herod had no jurisdiction whatsoever, but was only there as any other stranger, still on this occasion he might serve Pilate's purpose, and the rest could be overlooked. Pilate knew the character of Herod, the opposite of his own, and he contemned it; capricious, impetuous, cruel, eaten up with self-indulgence that knew no bounds, dealing out death on the whim of a moment, loving none and loved by none, a stranger to love from his infancy. Such a man, surely, above all with a hint from the Roman Governor, might solve this morning's problem. If he did, then all would be well; Pilate would find excuse for all that followed.

> 'And Pilate
> Hearing of Galilee
> Asked if the man were a Galilæan
> And when he understood
> That he belonged to Herod's jurisdiction
> He sent him away to Herod
> Who himself was at Jerusalem in those days.'

A messenger was quickly despatched across the city to the palace of Herod. A Galilæan had been brought before Pilate, called Jesus of Nazareth, or some such name. There was against Him some charge or other of sedition. It appeared that the seat of the trouble was in Galilee. No doubt Herod knew better than Pilate what this accusation meant ; no doubt he would know how to deal with it. Pilate was aware of Herod's strictness in matters of this kind ; if then he would judge the Man, and condemn Him should He be found guilty, and see to it that He received the due punishment of treason, Pilate would owe Herod a debt of gratitude, as a lover of justice and order. Herod was made to understand what line would most please the Roman Governor.

Herod was honoured by the message ; never before had such deference been paid to him by a Roman, least of all by Pilate. Besides, it was true he already knew much about the case. Since the day when John the Baptist had been imprisoned for a similar offence, it was known that Jesus had only followed in his footsteps. Indeed He had gone further ; the Baptist had once rebuked the tetrarch for his unlawful marriage, Jesus had publicly defied him in the open road.

' Go and tell that fox ',

He had once said, in presence of the people in Peræa, when He had been given warning of Herod's machinations :

' Go and tell that fox
Behold I cast out devils
And do cures to-day and to-morrow
And the third day I am consummated
Nevertheless I must walk to-day
And to-morrow and the day following
Because it cannot be
That a prophet perish out of Jerusalem.'

All this evidence, common talk among the spies of Herod, made a presumption that the charge of sedition against Jesus of Nazareth was true ; in his own court at Machærus Herod would have asked for no further evidence. But there was for Herod another interest in the case of this Galilæan. He had not only taught as the Baptist had taught; it was known all over Herod's tetrarchy that He was some kind of magician, and that He won men to follow Him by His tricks. Herod had heard of Him from many sources. At one time, after the murder of the Baptist, when remorse and fear had almost driven him mad, he had lived in dread of this Man's name and power; he had suspected He might be his murdered victim's venging spirit, come back to hunt him down. Since that time, during the year or more that had elapsed, seeing that nothing had happened, his fears had died away; encouraged by his friends, his old craving for novelty had revived. He had long wished to see this Man; he had hoped to see Him work some magic trick; now he would have a golden opportunity, for Jesus would be at his mercy. He would compel Him to display some of His conjuring, to save His life.

> ' And Herod
> Seeing Jesus
> Was very glad
> For he was desirous for a long time to see him
> Because he had heard many things of him
> And he hoped to see some miracle
> Wrought by him.'

Herod called his court together; his eastern bodyguard, his courtesans, his sycophant attendants, a very different court from that of Pilate. One asks oneself whether Herodias and her daughter were there, with the blood of the Baptist still upon their hands; and there seems no reason to doubt it. But whatever misery was in their hearts, nay, the more because of their misery, Herod and his court loved a merry time; and to-day they would have a spectacle altogether interesting, something quite novel even to this satiated crew.

Jesus was led down the steps from the balcony where He had stood to be tried by the Roman Governor. He made no protest, not even against this gross and manifest injustice; He submitted to be taken wherever these men of blood chose to take Him. Had He resisted, it is possible that His very accusers would this time have supported Him; for the death of Jesus at the hands of Herod was not according to their plan. Still, the whim of Pilate must be obeyed; a guard was placed around the Prisoner, even in this gathering the formalities of law and order must be obeyed. Men might howl at Him as He passed; they might throw at Him the refuse and garbage of those filthy Eastern streets; but the Law must do its ceremonious duty. For Jesus was now in Roman, not in Jewish, hands; and the Roman guard would see to it that He reached the court of Herod in safety. There He was ushered into Herod's sumptuous hall; and this time, since Herod was, in name at least, a Jew, the elders and priests could enter with Him without fear of contamination.

The trial began with much merriment on the part of Herod and his courtiers. Jesus was a sorry sight in their eyes, fit only for jeering and laughter; mean, sordid, in every way contemptible, they could afford to make sport of such a creature as this. No doubt if He were tempted, if He were offered His release on condition of a display of His magic, He would easily yield; that a man should refuse, under such conditions, was unthinkable. Besides, Herod was not one to be thwarted, and all the world knew it; Jesus could not have forgotten the fate that had befallen His predecessor and friend. Herod therefore began with many questions. In the court of Annas the questioning had been about His doctrine and His disciples; but Herod cared for neither of these. His questions were prompted by curiosity. He was eager to know this Man's secret if He had one; His secret fascination, which made all poor men and women gather round Him, His magic secret, which He used so freely. Also, for his own sake, Herod would gladly know whether or not there was any connexion between this strange Man and the murdered John the Baptist; though that ghost had long been laid, still the memory of it would revive. He put to Jesus all manner of conundrums, and the giddy creatures round his throne assisted him:

'He questioned him with many words.'

But it was not long before the whole tone of the trial began to change. To all Herod's questions, to all the laughter of his courtiers, Jesus replied not one word:

'But he answered him nothing.'

He had spoken in the end both to Annas and Caiphas; He had spoken at greater length to Pilate; but to Herod

He had not a word to say. He seemed almost to ignore the whole assembly; He seemed almost not to notice they were there. He had spared nothing to save even Judas; He would still do more to rescue Pontius Pilate; He would at the last moment befriend a dying criminal; but for Herod and his kind, this Friend of publicans and sinners had nothing to say. His very enemies, the scribes and Pharisees, the chief priests and elders, had received His appeals, His warnings, His denunciations; but Herod and his company received nothing, not even a threat such as had been given in the Jewish courts the night before. To Jesus Herod was as one dead; a dead body, a dead soul, his whole life eaten away by luxury, by concupiscence of the flesh, by that cancer which destroys not only men but whole nations. Against that evil there was no appeal; to speak would have been a waste of words, though Jesus longed for Herod no less than He longed for Pilate, yet could He do nothing more:

'He answered him nothing.'

Under such treatment, very soon the gaiety began to die down, the laughter became forced and artificial, soon both turned into annoyance and anger, for no one is more easily roused to anger than a man of Herod's type. In Herod's own court this mountebank was defying them; He was insulting their tetrarch, He was behaving as if He, not Herod, were the master in that hall. He must be taught His place; if He would not do what Herod and his courtiers demanded of Him, then He must be punished. They were not accustomed to be challenged by such canaille as this. The atmosphere was thickening and a storm threatened, and the chief priests and elders were quick to notice it. Herod was becoming grave; he might now be roused to do something fatal; now at least was the moment to induce him to listen to their charges. He was becoming conscious of defeat; he had thought to make a fool of this criminal, he was perilously near being befooled. He would be ready to give ear to any accusation they might make; what those accusations were, before such a judge, could matter nothing. Before Pilate they had need to be careful what they said; before Herod and his crew anything would serve. The evangelists have not troubled to record the charges that were made:

> 'And the chief priests and elders stood by
> Earnestly accusing him.'

They might have spared themselves their trouble. Herod 'the fox' soon found a means to restore the balance, at least to save himself from discomfiture. Since Jesus of Nazareth would not play the fool to please His lord, His lord would make Him a fool. Since He presumed to make Herod himself appear foolish before Herod's own courtiers, Herod would prove Him a fool before all the world. This unbending Jesus, this tongue-tied Jesus, this deaf mute, this paralysed mountebank, had at last been exposed. He would not work a miracle, therefore He could not; if He could, under such conditions, with so much at stake, none but a fool would refuse. Let Him work one, and He would save His life; let Him work one, and He would put His enemies to confusion; let Him work only one, and Herod and his court would applaud, would protect Him, would let Him go free to preach as He would in Galilee. Who but a fool could refuse such an opportunity?

> 'But he answered him nothing.'

Evidently, therefore, He was a fool; a greater fool than even Herod had suspected; and like a fool, not like a criminal, He must be treated.

For in spite of Pilate's flattery, Herod had no mind to be caught by his words. Herod was more astute than Pilate; he had not lived his crafty life for nothing. From the beginning he had had no mind to pronounce sentence on Jesus; he knew the limits of his powers in Jerusalem. This turn in the game gave him the means to end it; the tetrarch and his courtiers renewed their old courage. The laughter was renewed, but there was bitterness in its hard note; the merriment revived, but it was restless, and obviously, terribly, cruel. Worship of pleasure is seldom kind; nothing more develops the mere brute, and we have long since learnt, from another scene, how brutal Herod and his gentry and ladies could be. The bodyguard caught the temper of their master; they were practised in that art, and knew how to behave in his presence. This Jesus the Fool was beyond contempt; He was unfit even to be guarded; they could treat Him only as He deserved, this stolid, stupid, silent piece of stone. But yes, they could do more; there occurred to a jester among them a happy thought. The garb of a lunatic was a white tunic; in such a dress they would clothe Him and send Him back to Pilate. It would tell Pilate without words what the judgment of Herod had been; this Fool was not worth the sentence of a court of law. A white sheet was found and was thrown round Jesus; all the court of ribald men and women shrieked their laughter at this wonderful display of cleverness. And Jesus, in the garment of a fool, was dragged back through the streets to the court of Pilate :

> ' And Herod with his soldiers despised him
> And mocked him
> Putting on him a white garment
> And sent him back to Pilate
> And Herod and Pilate
> Were made friends together that same day
> For before they were enemies
> One to another.'

CHAPTER IX

25. The Second Trial before Pilate : Barabbas.

PILATE could scarcely have been much disappointed when he heard the howling cortège coming up the street, bringing its Victim back to him. He knew Herod well and his cunning ; when he sent to him the Galilæan it was only as a forlorn hope. He had thought that, perhaps, in a moment of impetuous anger, possibly helped by excess, with a little encouragement from others, Herod might have acted with Jesus as he had acted before, and might have done his Prisoner to death. But again his strategy had failed, and he must shoulder the responsibility. He would do it as became a Roman. He would pull himself together, he would begin all over again from the beginning. He would sum up the evidence as it stood, prove to these men the injustice of their cause, and see whether he could not bring them to their senses. Not that Jesus was of much concern to him ; he would betray no sign of that. It was the formality of justice that must be observed, and he would see that all observed it. On the present evidence a compromise was possible. No doubt, indeed quite evidently, the Accused had given some cause for all this animosity : therefore some kind of punishment might reasonably be dealt out to Him. If that were sanctioned, perhaps these bloodhounds would be satisfied ; and as for Jesus, in the end, to punish Him would be to save Him, and that would be the greatest service Pilate could render.

In these terms Pilate soothed his conscience, satisfied his sense of justice, and prepared his address. It was surely sound common sense, such as any thinking man would accept ; justice, but not bigotry ; mercy, but not softness ; judicious compromise, a little to be yielded to and from both sides. It was a perfect sentence in a complicated case, according to all the standards. He went out again upon the balcony ; he called the leaders to him, as near as they would come, and began his oration. There was a sense of boredom in his manner, as if the matter did not concern him; as if he were making this concession merely to humour those whom he wished to placate:

> ' And Pilate
> Calling together the chief priests
> And the magistrates and the people
> Said to them
> You have brought this man to me
> As one that perverteth the people
> And behold I
> Having examined him before you
> Find no cause in this man
> Touching those things wherein you accuse him
> No nor yet Herod
> For I sent you to him
> And behold
> Nothing worthy of death is done to him
> I will chastise him
> Therefore
> And release him.'

'Therefore'! Because He is not guilty, He shall be chastised. Because no man can accuse Him of sin, He shall be scourged. Because for His good works no man can blame Him, He shall be punished. Because He did all things well, because this great Prophet has risen up among them, and God hath visited His people, because this is indeed the Prophet that was to come into the world, because He is a good man, because everything that John said concerning Him is true, His people must look on Him with hatred, must chastise Him, must let Him know that He is an intruder into this world which belongs to man. Pilate's argument was strange, but it was nothing very new; it was childishly false, but it is acted on to this day. And Jesus stood there, listening to this first sentence passed upon Him, and said no word:

> ' Who did no sin
> Neither was guile found in his mouth
> Who when he was reviled
> Did not revile
> When he suffered
> He threatened not

> But delivered himself to him
> That judged him unjustly.'
>
> 1 Peter ii, 22–23.

At this point in the trial there occurred a diversion which Pilate thought he might use to advantage. Besides those who had come to his door with the chief priests and elders demanding the blood of Jesus, there were others there who had come for an opposite purpose. For the Pasch was the festival that kept alive the memory of the people's release from their Egyptian bondage ; in keeping with that memory the custom had grown up for the Governor to release some prisoner that day at the people's request. It was taken as symbolic ; it was an empty implication that after all, in spite of the Roman domination, the Jews were their own masters, were free. The ceremony took place on this day, the eve of the Pasch ; and there was always gathered round his door a group of the people, both to make the petition and to receive the released man from the Governor's hands.

Such a group had come together while the enemies of Jesus had been away at the house of Herod. When they returned they naturally overwhelmed the former, but in the interval after Pilate's declaration the petitioners succeeded in making themselves heard. His words had set the accusers thinking. They were apparently final, they had been spoken as a definite decision ; it would seem that in their absence the weak man had nerved himself to act with strength and do his duty. But when the new cry was raised by the second party, that the custom of the Paschal season should be observed at once, the innate fickleness of Pilate was revealed. After all he had not wholly meant what he had just said. The demand was made that a prisoner should be released, one whom the people themselves might name. Here was another opportunity. He would offer Jesus to them ; though he had already said he would release Him, if he did it at their demand his reputation would be the better saved. This group seemed more humane than the other ; probably in it were some of the Prisoner's friends ; he would appeal to it in opposition to the clamourers for blood. He would do more ; he would give them a choice between two such as would almost compel them to decide for Jesus. There was in the prison under guard one criminal who had of late made himself specially notorious, whose execution was only too eagerly desired by the people. He was a highwayman, a dacoit; and on that account alone, in the eyes of the inhabitants of Judæa, death was only his long-merited reward. He was a convicted murderer; and for those whose law was 'an eye for an eye and a tooth for a tooth', he could look for nothing else but to die. He was a sedition-monger, who had found occupation in 'stirring up the people'; and since this was the charge, preferred but not as yet proven, against Jesus, there could be no choice between Him and one whose guilt was notorious. Pilate's confidence was renewed. He would bring this man out and put him by the side of Jesus. He would ask them to choose between the two. Jesus the Nazarene might indeed be hated, but none would deny that Barabbas was indefinitely more worthy of hate.

There was another consideration, which had now become more clear in Pilate's mind, and which further led him to hope for victory. With all their clamour against Jesus as a maker of sedition, he knew these leaders of the Jews too well; he did not trust this new enthusiasm for the cause of Rome. If they cried out against the Kingship of Jesus, against His winning the people, it was not because of the Roman Emperor, it was because of themselves, because they saw in Him a challenge to their own jurisdiction. This had been brought home to him the more by what his Prisoner had said about Himself. He had confessed that He was indeed a King, but no enemy to Cæsar for all that. He had a kingdom, but it was not a kingdom of this world. All this coincided with what he knew already of the difficult, bigoted enthusiasts whom he had to govern; these visionaries who had little use for the comforts and luxuries of Rome, yet who could live in a wealth of luxury that would dazzle any Roman; these students who cared almost nothing for the culture of the Empire, because they had an ascetic culture of their own; who would look with contempt on the comfortable gods of Rome and Greece, worshipping instead a hidden, intangible Being, in whom they professed to live, whose sway they recognized as that of any overlord, with whom it were wiser, even for a Roman Emperor, not to come into conflict. All this Pilate knew, as every Eastern Governor knew it; and he had been warned from headquarters to leave all questions of religion discreetly alone. But though he left it alone, it was clear that this Jesus of

Nazareth did not. He had interfered; He had called Himself a King; He had called Himself Christ, the anointed King; as such He had put Himself above the elders and priests. It had begun to grow upon Pilate; whatever the words of their charge, this, he knew full well, was their real cause of grievance.

Pilate was determined to use this, possibly his last, opportunity. He would see whether he could put the people, who called for the release of a prisoner, against their leaders, who called for the death of one Man. He had before them the evident contrast between Jesus and Barabbas; he would strengthen this by what he now knew of the spiritual side of the One he hoped to save. If the leaders were not to be influenced, the people at least might yield.

> ' And when the multitude was come up
> They began to desire
> What he had always done to them
> And Pilate answered them and said
> You have a custom
> That I should release one unto you at the Pasch
> Will you therefore
> That I release unto you the King of the Jews?
> Whom will you that I release to you
> Barabbas
> Or Jesus who is called Christ?
> For he knew that through envy
> The priests had delivered him up.'

This was a new kind of offensive, and for a moment there was silence in the crowd. Jesus stood there in bonds before them all, the convict Barabbas beside Him: now indeed the prophecy was being fulfilled:

> ' He was reputed with the wicked.'
> Isaias liii, 12.

He was being held up, before His own people, side by side with the worst of criminals, that they might make their choice between the two. Had they been left to themselves, it can scarcely be doubted which they would have chosen; they who, a few months before, despite the efforts of the Pharisees, had decided in His favour on the witness of John the Baptist:

> 'John indeed did no sign
> But all things whatsoever John said
> Of this man
> Were true
> And many believed in him.'
>
> John x, 41-42.

But they were not left long to decide for themselves; this was a vital moment, and their leaders dared not let it slip by. Pilate had weakened his sentence; in spite of his decision he had opened the question again. At once they were busy among the crowd, whispering here, boasting there, cajoling some, threatening others; in every way imposing their authority, their superior knowledge, their science, their art, on a poor, ignorant mob that knew no better, that stood in awe of these keepers of the Temple. Jesus had been found guilty by their own high priest; was not that evidence enough? He had been treated with contempt and put to shame, and had been unable to speak a word or perform one act to witness in His own defence; did not that prove that, in spite of all He had said and done before, He was a deceiver? Herod had shewn Him up as a fool; Pilate the Roman was evidently in His favour; did not this show that there was collusion between them? That this Jesus, breaker of the Law of Moses as He had always been, scorner of the true sons of Abraham, was secretly too an ally of the Romans? And as for Barabbas, culprit as he was, was he not also a victim of Roman tyranny? What loyal Jew would hesitate to choose between them? With all his crimes, let the good Jew Barabbas be preferred; with all His seeming innocence, let the dangerous, magnetising Jesus be sent to His death.

Pilate waited while the decision was being made; he sat on his seat of judgment hoping against hope. Meanwhile as he waited a strange thing occurred. The wife of Pilate was within, in the seclusion of the women's quarters; but she well knew what was going on outside. She had known overnight what was impending that day; not unlikely she had heard it from Pilate himself. And the knowledge had made her restless; she feared what evil might come of it for Pilate her husband. She had heard enough of Jesus to believe Him true; she knew enough of the Jewish elders to suspect them; her woman's instinct did the rest. All the night she had been unhappy; the trouble had brought weird dreams; she woke in the morning determined, if she could, to draw Pilate out of the whole affair. She cared for Pilate, which is not the least thing in his favour; she had influence over him, which is more; she had the courage and confidence to use this influence even in the midst of a judicial trial. As Pilate sat waiting for the answer of the people, a tablet was put in his hands on which were written these words:

> 'Have thou nothing to do
> With that just man
> For I have suffered many things this day
> In a dream
> Because of him.'

From first to last, from the Garden to Calvary, this was the only voice raised in the defence of Jesus. We do not wonder the evangelist S. Matthew records it; we do not wonder that tradition has wished to honour the wife of Pilate.

At length it was time for an answer to Pilate's question. While he had waited, the chief priests had done their work, and this time there was no one to check them. In the Temple courts Jesus had always opposed their malice, and always some had stood by Him; here the enemy had it all their own way; it was their hour and the power of darkness. They had argued from presumption, which the ignorant could not deny; presumption grew into assertion, and the sorry sight of Jesus before them seemed to confirm it. What the elders said might be true; probably it was true; there were good reasons why it should be true; it was safer and wiser to say that it was true; then surely it was true. Common opinion became a common voice; if any still hesitated, their resistance was broken by the louder cries of the more reckless multitudes. After due time Pilate stood up once more and renewed his question:

> 'Which will you have of the two
> To be released to you?'

There was only one answer to be heard; violence is always louder-mouthed than meekness, and the loud mouth speaks with a tongue infallible, which will brook no opposition:

'But the whole multitude
Cried out at once saying
Away with this man
And release unto us Barabbas.'

It was a momentous choice. It was the turning-point of the whole tragedy. Now the die was cast; even for the people who had joined in the cry there was now no looking back. Pilate had opened a fresh sluice, and it only remained for him to be overwhelmed by the torrent.

Still like a drowning man he would catch at any straw; common justice compelled him not yet to yield. As he had himself declared, he had seen enough to know that the Man before him was not guilty. He had spoken with Him and had learnt to respect Him, almost to revere Him. Behind Him, too, there was a strength which made the Roman Governor fear; a strength which nothing His enemies said or did could bend, a strength and certainty in Himself and in His own just cause, a strength, moreover, in something which Pilate could not fathom, which was not of this world, which gave to Jesus a peace beyond the reach of men's abuse. For other reasons, therefore, more than for those of common justice, Pilate would save Jesus if he could; he did not know what god he might be offending, whose wrath he might incur, if he injured that god's favourite. If Herod was made a coward from fear of a ghost, Pilate the Roman had no less the fear common among his fellow-countrymen.

He must make yet another attempt. He would appeal to those deeper things which had made so great an impression on himself, and which, he knew, meant so much more to the Jewish people. He could affect contempt in what he said; he could pretend it was not his concern; yet in his heart he knew it was not all contempt. Jesus 'the Christ', 'the Anointed'—the word clearly had a meaning to the Jew, for the chief priests and elders had flung it at Jesus with exceeding bitterness. Jesus 'the King of the Jews'—whatever it might signify, he was sure by now that the title was no empty name. The accusers had been enraged because their Victim had claimed these titles for Himself; if they meant nothing, neither could the charge they contained have any meaning. No man could be put to death for claiming a title that meant nothing; no man could rouse against himself such bitter hatred by the mere adoption of a foolish, empty name. He would press these titles home ; if the elders and priests rejected them, nevertheless the people might yet be moved. He would imply that, as judge, not only did he declare Jesus innocent of any crime, but also he believed Him to be what He claimed to be. If still they would have His life, then, in the final judgment of the independent Roman court, it would not only be because Jesus claimed to be ' Christ the King ', but because He was ' Christ the King ' in very truth.

> ' And Pilate spoke to them again
> Desiring to release Jesus
> What will you then that I do with Jesus
> Who is called Christ
> The King of the Jews ? '

And again he failed. Once more the reminder of the truth did but aggravate them ; the will not to believe is hard to convince, the determination not to accept what is known to be true is invincible. Indeed to attempt to convince is to rouse the most violent kind of enmity. Hitherto the accusers had only clamoured for the condemnation of Jesus. They had asked that somehow He should be put to death, apparently it mattered not how ; now, since they had been taunted with His being their Christ, their anointed King, they went to a further extreme. He must not only die ; He must die the most shameful death that even the Roman world knew. He must die the death of a guilty slave, of a convicted criminal ; though to be a Roman citizen would save even a criminal from such a fate. Their Anointed ? Let Him be crucified. Then it would be known what they thought of Him, then even such men as Pilate would check their sarcastic tongues :

> ' But they all again cried out
> Crucify him, crucify him
> Let him be crucified.'

This was indeed a climax of hatred, so that more than ever Pilate was amazed. He had seen passion roused to blind fury before ; in his own city it was cultivated as an amusement. He had seen, in Rome, eyes glittering and faces taut, as women round the arena turned down their thumbs demanding a gladiator's death. He had seen his own soldiers, brutalised and hardened till they were scarcely human any longer, laughing and turning to sport the slaughter of the helpless. He had watched an Asiatic mob, more deliberate and merciless than any European, show its white teeth and express dread purpose in its eyes as it pursued some deed of callous cruelty. He had himself a heart hardened enough to pass suffering by, to inflict it if need be, and to be moved no more than if he plucked a lily. But this sight before him was different from all these. It was not fury, it was not blind ; it was cold, deliberate, determined. There was too much hatred now even for mockery or laughter. Never before had a Jew, or a Jewish mob, demanded that a Jew should be crucified, no matter what might have been his crime.

Pilate himself feared ; if he persisted, he himself might incur their vengeance, for this was a hatred that would not be baulked, that would not count the cost of its deeds. Weakly he repeated what he had said before. The Man was innocent ; He had done nothing in any way deserving death ; if He were chastised it would be punishment enough :

> 'And Pilate said to them the third time
> Why ?
> What evil hath he done ? '
> I find no cause of death in him
> I will chastise him
> Therefore
> And let him go.'

The words, the repeated sentence, the unjust concession, the yet feebler opening question, only confirmed to the enemy that their case was won. They had only to persist in their demand and all would be secured according to their will. Legality was now thrown to the winds ; its very forms could now be set aside. They had found a formula which admirably suited their purpose, and they needed but to repeat it till the very sound would seem its vindication.

> ' But they were the more instant
> With loud voices
> Crucify him
> Let him be crucified
> And their voices prevailed.'

26. The Sentence.

'Their voices prevailed!' Pilate had gone through many phases before he had come to this. Never before in his life had he been so utterly tried and found wanting. He was Roman Governor of Palestine; he had held the office for years; in the eyes, then, of the authorities in Rome he was suited for the purpose. Judæa was a province not easy to rule, yet with all his mistakes Pilate had succeeded in ruling it. On other occasions he had done as he would with this people and they had submitted; he had learnt to despise them, as he had deemed a strong Roman should. When that morning they had brought Jesus before him he had treated them with that same contempt; when they had urged their demand, he had sent them to another, a more petty judge, to settle their claim for them. Yet all the time he had wavered; something had told him from the first that this was no ordinary mob affair. He had seen Jesus alone, and the interview had convinced him that he was dealing with a just and innocent Man. Then his contempt had begun to change to fear. Then he knew that this was a case, not of justice but of hatred; and hatred is always unjust, and merciless, and cruel.

During all this time Jesus had stood before them all, submissive till submission became weird, saying not a word on His own behalf, making no sign that showed indignation, or protest, or insult, or weakness, scarcely even concern; He stood there, the only one calm and self-possessed in that gathering. By His manner alone a keen judge would have known Him to be guiltless; it seemed to prove more, that there was within Him a power which He could use if He would, but which, for some reason that Pilate could not understand, He refused to exercise. Pilate feared the mob howling in the street beneath him; he feared too this silent Being standing on the steps beside him, the like of whom he had never had to judge in all his experience of men. He dared not yet pass the final sentence; before he yielded he must save himself from the consequences of an unjust act, whether from Cæsar in Rome, or from this mysterious King whose kingdom was not of this world. Like all unbelievers, Pilate was superstitious; brave it as he might, in his heart he feared he knew not what.

Meanwhile the clamour in the street grew louder. It

had risen so as to be threatening, and must needs be appeased. It was true he could have turned his soldiers on the crowd and dispersed it, but he hesitated. He had done something of the kind before, and had been made to repent his indiscretion; these Asiatics were a people that did not forgive or forget. Somehow he must humour them; at the same time he must justify himself in his own mind. So far as he could he would free himself from all responsibility. This he had endeavoured to do during all the morning; since there now seemed no escape, since in the end it seemed inevitable that he must speak the final word, he would throw the responsibility for that word on others. He argued with himself. These violent disturbers of the peace insisted. It was his duty to keep the peace, especially at such a time as this, when Jerusalem was full of strangers from everywhere, and was not the public peace of far greater importance than the life of any single man? Let Jesus go free, and many lives might be lost in the disturbance; almost certainly the life of Jesus Himself, in any case. Let Him die, and many would be saved, peace would be restored and the Paschal season would pass off tranquilly. He would yield, it would be better in the end; thus did Pilate, by another route, arrive at the conclusion of Caiphas:

'It were better
That one man should die for the people.'

But his yielding should be with all the formality that became one in his position. A Roman judge, whatever he might decree, must not be accused of injustice; a Roman judge could do no wrong. So he went through an empty form. As Caiphas long ago had settled the scruples of the priests by the invention of a formula, so would Pilate settle the scruples of his own worldly conscience by the invention of a form. He would wash his hands of the whole affair; he little dreamt that his act would establish a metaphor for all time to come. He called an attendant boy; he bade him bring water and a basin, as if for some ablution which would have seemed nothing strange. As he put his hands into the water, he spoke words which made his action symbolic. He had already declared his Prisoner innocent; now he would absolve himself also from all guilt. If guilt rested on anyone, it lay on those who were driving him to do what he abhorred.

> ' And Pilate
> Seeing that he prevailed nothing
> But rather that a tumult was made
> Having taken water
> Washed his hands before the people saying
> I am innocent
> Of the blood of this just man
> Look you to it.'

Pilate the poor worldling, keeping up appearances at any cost before the eyes of men ! The coward affecting to be brave, the anxious affecting to be careless, the grossly cruel affecting to be just, the brutally cruel affecting to be humane, the guilty affecting to be honest, the self-seeking affecting to be eaten up with zeal for law and order ; whatever he may be in his own heart and conscience, outwardly his hands must be clean, he must stand well and be approved before the tribunal of men. We cannot hate Pilate, he is too weak and worldly-wise for hatred. But it is hard not to despise him for a cunning self-deceiver, one who in the end might persuade himself that any evil deed was good. Yet when we condemn him, how many of us at the same time pronounce in some degree our own condemnation? The world is a liar and a deceiver; in nothing more contemptible than in its constant affectation of truth and honesty, and the service of men. Of all the characters in the Passion Pilate has always had most imitators.

Yet even Pilate little suspected the response his self-exculpation would evoke. He had declared himself innocent in the eyes of men ; his victorious adversaries in the street below had no such scruples. Let men think of them what they liked ; they would have this Man's blood at any cost, though it were to be upon them for all time. If that were all Pilate wanted that he might pass the final sentence, let him have it. He had shifted the guilt upon their shoulders ; they had understood the travesty he had gone through well enough. They would willingly accept the burthen. The cry they poured out is one of those terrible prophecies which cannot have been invented ; its significance is too deep for any man to have dared, its fulfilment too manifest for anyone to doubt.

' And all the people answering said
His blood be upon us
And upon our children.'

The words were the closing of another act in the drama. For a moment there was a dread silence, as if the crowd itself were appalled at the self-condemnation it had uttered :

' What hast thou done ?
The voice of thy brother's blood
Crieth to me from the earth.'

It was misery indeed, cold and clammy, that enshrouded their hearts. It must be killed ; the drama must go on ; by noise, if by no other means, the cry in the heart must be stifled in the crowd. Men talked loudly to one another, boasting, careless, losing themselves in ribaldry ; what mattered any consequence, they had gained their end. Up above, around the seat of judgment, officials moved to and fro ; documents were produced and duly signed. Barabbas was brought out and handed over to the crowd, wondering what this confusion meant, how he came to be the hero of this heated moment. He knew himself to be a convicted murderer, and therefore the hand of every man should be against him. He knew himself to have been condemned as a provoker of sedition, and therefore could expect no mercy from the Roman Governor. He had been cast into prison, tried, proved guilty, and condemned, and could only await the hour of his execution, probably that very day. Yet now on a sudden he was told that his people had demanded his release, and that the Roman Governor had consented. What had happened ? Had a revolution come about while he had been in prison ? Had the Roman been made to yield before the threats of Jewry ? Had the kingdom come ? But even if it had, what could have made his people choose him for its favour ? Murderers were never forgiven, highwaymen were always feared. Such kindness could be nothing but a mockery. Barabbas : the son of the Father ! Was there no one who noticed the significance of that name ?

27. The Scourging and Crowning.

Barabbas, the highwayman and murderer, and promoter of sedition and revolt, was set at liberty, and Jesus, the way, the truth, and the life, who had done all things well, whom no man could convict of any sin, of whom His enemies had said that for His good works they accused Him not, was delivered over to the servants of the law. There was nothing now left to be done but for the preliminaries of the execution to begin. First He must be scourged, both because Pilate had consented to it, and because such was the ordinary treatment of one condemned to death. But in the scourging Jesus, the Son of David, was not to enjoy the benefit of the Jewish Law. According to that Law, even in the worst of cases, scourging was confined to ' forty stripes save one ' :

> ' And if they see
> That the offender be worthy of stripes
> They shall lay him down
> And shall cause him to be beaten before them
> According to the measure of the sin
> Shall the measure also of the stripes be
> Yet so
> That they exceed not the number of forty
> Lest thy brother depart
> Shamefully torn before thy eyes.'
> Deuteronomy xxv, 2, 3.

According to the Jewish Law the punishment was limited ; it was to be inflicted in the presence of the judges ; to the end they were to remember that the criminal was a fellow-man, and that his body was as sacred as their own. The Roman law had no such limits ; moreover, the Prisoner was no Roman citizen, a title which alone would have saved Him from the degradation. He was only a Jew, only a Galilæan, only one of those hill-country people who were for ever giving trouble ; He was one of those on whom these Roman soldiers could vent their cruelty and contempt to their heart's content. The evangelists, one and all, pass the scene over ; they mention the fact of the scourging and no more, either because there had been no witness to give them the details, or, more probably, because the scene was too terrible, too horrible, too painful, to be described. But Jesus Himself had not passed it over. Again and again in His prophecies of the Passion He had come back to it, as if from the beginning it had been something from which His human nature had shrunk :

> 'They shall condemn him to death
> And shall deliver him to the Gentiles to be mocked
> And scourged
> And crucified.'
>
> Matthew xx, 18–19.

> 'They shall condemn him to death
> And shall deliver him to the Gentiles
> And they shall mock him
> And spit on him
> And scourge him.'
>
> Mark x, 33–34.

> 'He shall be delivered to the Gentiles
> And shall be mocked
> And scourged
> And spat upon
> And after they have scourged him
> They will put him to death.'
>
> Luke xviii, 32–33.

In the spirit of the Gospels we may also be reticent. Jesus Christ, the Son of God, the Son of Mary blessed among women, the most beautiful among the sons of men, declared by His enemies to be sinless, declared by His judges to be free from fault, 'therefore', because He was all this and no more, was handed over to the soldiers of Pilate to be scourged. Thus far there was no real sentence of death:

> 'I will chastise him therefore
> And let him go.'

At the command of both Jews and Romans, Jesus Christ was stripped of His clothes; He was tied to a whipping-post; He was beaten till His whole body became one gaping wound, till it fell exhausted to the ground, till brutalized men, brought up to cruelty, revelling in it as sport, boasting of it as if it were a mark of bravery, restricted to no limit, were satisfied. Jesus Christ, the Son of God, was left in their hands that they might vent their brutality upon Him unrestrained.

Yet even this was not enough; and here the evangelists take up the story once more, as if for what follows they have the evidence of eye-witnesses. The 'soldiers of the Governor' had carried out their orders; they had done their work of scourging, but Jesus was still upon their hands. One might almost suspect that Pilate delayed to bring his Prisoner back into his presence for the final sentence with a special purpose; perhaps he hoped that to pass that sentence might not be needed. Many a slave had before died beneath the lash, and he knew the temper of his soldiers; if he left Jesus long enough at their mercy, perhaps they, too, might do Him to death. But they were cautious; like Annas and Caiaphas, like Herod and his satellites, like the priests and elders clamouring at that moment before Pilate's door, they would not risk the reactions of their capricious Governor. They would have good sport of their own, but they would be careful that Jesus should not die. During the trial Pilate had repeatedly said that this Man claimed to be a king; the people shouting in the street below had abused Him for claiming the title. It would be a fine game, suited to the occasion. If He were in truth a king, so much the better; they had no such scruples as those of their Governor, they would let this King see how they thought kings like Him should be treated. If He were in truth a king, and evidently the Governor had his suspicions that He was, then they could pour out on Him, with the greater zest, their utter contempt, both for Him and for these Jewish malcontents whom they despised with all their hearts. There was excitement, and a new interest in the soldiers' courtyard. Some stopped their gambling, others their alea; all came together to take part in this new burlesque. They would crown this Jesus a king indeed, and they would be His courtiers; every man should play what character he would in the solemn farce.

> ' Then the soldiers of the governor
> Taking Jesus into the court of the palace
> Gathered together unto him the whole band
> And stripping him
> They put a scarlet cloak about him.'

Thus they began the performance. Once upon a time loving hands had wrapped that tender body in swaddling clothes and laid it to rest in a manger; and angels had told shepherds that by that sign they would know

> ' The Saviour
> Who is Christ the Lord
> And this shall be a sign unto you

You shall find the infant
Wrapped in swaddling clothes
And laid in a manger.'
                              Luke ii, 12.

Wise men had come to that same place from afar and had found Him, and had 'rejoiced with exceeding great joy'; they had

'Falling down
Adored him
And opening their treasures
They offered him gifts
Gold frankincense and myrrh.'
                              Matthew ii, 11.

So the Prophet had foretold, so John the Baptist had announced, the coming of the King:

'And he shall rule from sea to sea
And from the river unto the ends of the earth
Before him the Ethiopians shall fall down
And his enemies shall lick the ground
The kings of Tharsis and the islands shall offer presents
The kings of the Arabians and of Saba shall bring gifts
And all kings of the earth shall adore him
And all nations shall serve him
For he shall deliver the poor from the mighty
And the needy that had no helper
He shall spare the poor and needy
And he shall save the souls of the poor
He shall save their souls from usuries and iniquity
And their name shall be honourable in his sight
And he shall live
And to him shall be given of the gold of Arabia
For him they shall always adore
They shall bless him all the day.'
                              Psalm lxxi, 8-15.

Yet what a contrast to this and other prophecies was here! Herod the tetrarch had 'wished for a long time to see Jesus': he had seen Him that morning, and all he had done had been to clothe Him in the garment of a fool:

'And Herod with his army
Set him at nought

> And mocked him
> Putting on him a white garment
> And sent him back to Pilate.'
>
> Luke xxiii, 11.

Now these Roman soldiers prepared to treat Him no better; to Herod He was no more than a mountebank, to them He was a puppet in a show. A second time they stripped Him; this King must first be clothed in royal robes. They threw a scarlet cloak across His naked and scarred shoulders, some cast-off garment of an officer of the guard. They set Him against the wall, upon a tub for a throne, Him of whom an angel had said:

> 'The Lord shall give unto him
> The throne of David his father
> And he shall reign in the house of Jacob
> For ever';
>
> Luke i, 32.

Him who had promised to His followers:

> 'Amen I say to you
> That you who have followed me
> In the regeneration
> When the Son of man shall sit on the seat
> Of his majesty
> You also shall sit on twelve seats
> Judging the twelve tribes of Israel.'
>
> Matthew xix, 28.

Yet so He was now enthroned, and He must needs be crowned; with what should they crown Him? In a corner of the courtyard was a heap of prickly bramble, put there to supply the fire. A soldier had a happy idea. He took his sword, cut away some of the twigs, beat them into a ball between his sword and his staff, for they were too thorny to be handled, and clapped them down upon the head of Jesus, hammering them about till they fitted like a helmet.

> 'Thou hast given him his heart's desire
> And hast not withholden from him
> The will of his lips
> For thou hast prevented him with blessings of sweetness

> Thou hast set on his head
> A crown of precious stones.'
>
> Psalm xx, 3-4.

Thus was Jesus crowned, seated on His throne of shame. The enthronement had suggested coronation; the crowning suggested a sceptre. There were rushes strewn about the floor, to serve as a carpet. Another soldier picked up one of these, and pushed it between the fettered hands, and behold Jesus Christ, the King of the Jews, crowned in state in the very court of the Roman Pilate, by Pilate's own Roman bodyguard! Were not His ambitions now satisfied?

> ' And platting a crown of thorns
> They put it upon his head
> And a reed in his right hand.'

One idea followed another. The King had been crowned; He must now be duly honoured by His courtiers and devoted subjects. They knew how this was to be done; often enough they had stood on guard when men had paid obeisance to monarchs, when local chiefs and petty kings had done homage to their overlord. They had watched them approach in solemn order, one by one, clad in all the glory that became their rank, kneel to the mighty and offer him their sword, pay him their homage as to one who held their lives in his hands, utter the one salutation that was permitted to them. It was an easy thing for them to go through the mock ceremonial; what one did another imitated, in solemn, derisive procession.

> ' And they came to him
> And bowing the knee before him
> They mocked him
> And began to salute him saying
> Hail King of the Jews.'

There was special bitterness in the choice of the salutation they used. In ordinary life these Roman soldiers would have paid no such honour to any Oriental monarch, not even to Herod, the tetrarch appointed by Cæsar; what they did was an act of contempt, not to Jesus only, but to all His race. And it was shown by what followed. In the court of Caiphas the evangelists had for a moment let us see the treatment meted out by the Jewish sycophants;

here once more, for a like brief moment, the veil is lifted. As each man rose from his knee, he invented some new device, vying with those who had gone before him, by which he might pour ridicule and insult on the Man who sat, clothed in scarlet, crowned with thorns and with a sceptre in His hand, silent and unmoved against the wall of the court. One, as he stepped aside, would raise his arm and strike Him, and a soldier's blow is heavy. The next would look up at Him after his humble salutation, and as he rose from the ground would cast his spittle in His face. A third, doing further homage by touching the sceptre with his fingers, would seize the reed from the hands of Jesus and strike Him with it on His thorn-pierced head. Then all together, in Asiatic not in Roman fashion, knowing well that the cause of all this trouble against Jesus was a matter of religion, would gather together around Him, would put their fingers to their lips, would bow profoundly to the ground before this God, bidding Him ' live for ever ', the Lord and Master of them all.

> ' And they gave him blows
> And they did spit upon him
> And they took the reed and struck his head
> And bowing their knees
> They worshipped him.'

This was the homage Jesus received when at last He had declared His title before men. Prophets and kings had foretold His coming; they had rejoiced that they had foreseen His day; and yet it had come to this. In Bethlehem, when He was born, angels had seen in that birth glory and joy both in heaven and on earth :

> ' Glory to God in the highest
> And on earth peace to men of goodwill.'
>
> Luke ii, 14.

> ' Good tidings of great joy
> For this day is born to you a Saviour
> Who is Christ the Lord
> In the city of David.'
>
> Luke ii, 10, 11.

So they had sung, that ' multitude of the army '. Before He left that city of David His ancestor, Gentiles had come and looked for Him saying :

> ' Where is he
> That is born King of the Jews?
> For we have seen his star in the east
> And have come to adore him ',
> Matthew ii, 2.

and yet this was the issue. When He first appeared in the sight of men, after He had sent His herald before Him, to prepare His path as was the way of kings, one had come to Him and said :

> ' Thou art the Son of God
> Thou art the King of Israel ',
> John i, 49.

and in reward for his confession he had been assured that he would see great things :

> ' Amen, amen I say to you
> You shall see the heavens opened
> And the angels of God
> Ascending and descending upon the Son of man.'
> John i, 51.

But always there had been the other side. Not only had there been from the beginning a mighty Herod, who had spared nothing to compass this Child's death, and whose successors had sworn within themselves that they would have none of Him ; on a famous occasion another king, who had seen more than any of these, and had learnt and feared, had offered terms to this new claimant to the throne of all the world. He had come and parleyed with Him ; by show of power he had hoped to impose upon Him ; but behind that parleying there was hidden fear and hatred :

> ' And he shewed him all the kingdoms of the world
> In a moment of time
> And he said to him
> To thee will I give all this power
> And the glory of them
> For to me they are delivered
> And to whom I will I give them
> If thou therefore wilt adore before me
> All shall be thine.'
> Luke iv, 5-7.

Since that attempt had failed, he had tried it in another way. On the mountain of temptation the king of the world had begun with the temptation of bread, and had ended with that of the kingdom ; once, on the plain beyond the lake of Galilee, Jesus had Himself given a sign of bread, whereupon His followers had risen up and cried :

> ' This is of a truth the prophet
> That is to come into the world ',
>
> John vi, 14.

and had rushed forward to make Him their king :

> ' Jesus therefore when he knew
> That they would come to take him by force
> And make him king
> Fled again into the mountain
> Himself alone.'
>
> John vi, 15.

Seated on His throne in the soldiers' court, with the scarlet cloak across His shoulders, the crown upon His head, the sceptre in His hand, the courtiers paying their homage to Him, the red blood running down His face, Jesus could look back on all that had been, and count the friends, and count the enemies, that had gathered round His title of kingship. It was indeed, and would ever be, the battle of all time ; He had come

> ' To send not peace
> But a sword.'
>
> Matthew x, 34.

And, as He had forewarned His own, it was a battle in which it would seem that He was for ever beaten. But at the same time He had reassured them, again and again ; in defeat and shame would lie victory and honour. In the Temple court, when His work had been wellnigh done, on the last day of His preaching as He looked forward to the doom about to fall upon Him He had said :

> ' Now is the judgment of the world
> Now shall the prince of this world be cast out
> And I
> If I be lifted up from the earth
> Will draw all things to myself.'
>
> John xii, 31–32.

In the supper-room the night before He had repeated the same assurance:

> 'Let not your heart be troubled
>
> . . . .
>
> Peace I leave with you
> My peace I give unto you
> Not as the world giveth
> Do I give unto you
> Let not your heart be troubled
> Nor let it be afraid
>
> . . . .
>
> If the world hate you
> Know ye that it hath hated me before you
>
> . . . .
>
> Remember my word that I said to you
> The servant is not greater than his master
> If they have persecuted me
> They will also persecute you
>
> . . . .
>
> They will put you out of the synagogues
> Yea the hour cometh
> That whosoever killeth you
> Will think that he doth a service to God
>
> . . . .
>
> Amen, amen I say to you
> That you shall lament and weep
> But the world shall rejoice
> And you shall be made sorrowful
> But your sorrow shall be turned into joy
>
> . . . .
>
> In the world you shall have distress
> But have confidence
> I have overcome the world.'
>
> John xiv–xvii.

Not long hence He would come back to His own, victorious and triumphant, a King indeed; and with the authority of a king He would issue His mandate:

> 'All power is given to me
> In heaven and in earth

Going therefore
Teach ye all nations ' ;
Matthew xxviii, 18–19.

and they would understand the meaning of the battle He had fought and won. His apostle, perhaps with the scene we have just witnessed in his mind, for he was fond of contrasts, would write in triumph, for all the world to read in all time to come :

' He humbled himself
Becoming obedient unto death
Even to the death of the cross
For which cause
God also hath exalted him
And hath given him a name
Which is above all names
That in the name of Jesus
Every knee should bow
Of those that are in heaven
On earth and under the earth
And that every tongue should confess
That the Lord Jesus Christ
Is in the glory of God the Father.'
Philippians ii, 8–11.

It was all worth while. These poor men who played their game served Him and His cause better than they knew. They would have their imitators throughout all time, no less than Annas, and Caiphas, and Pilate ; but because of what He had endured He would have His followers as well. They too would be stripped and scourged, they too would be crowned with thorns ; but the sight of their King crowned before them would turn their sorrow into matter of thanksgiving :

' For this is thankworthy
If for conscience towards God
A man endure sorrows
Suffering wrongfully

. . . . .

If doing well you suffer patiently
This is thankworthy before God
For unto this are you called

Because Christ also suffered for us
Leaving you an example
That you should follow his steps
Who did no sin
Neither was guile found in his mouth
Who when he was reviled did not revile
When he suffered he threatened not
But delivered himself to him that judged him unjustly.'
1 Peter ii, 19–23.

In this light, through the blood that blinded His eyes, He could look into the future and know that the kingdom would be won. The prophecy would be fulfilled:

' He shall reign in the house of Jacob
For ever
And of his kingdom there shall be no end.'
Luke ii, 32–33.

' Jesus Christ
Yesterday and to-day
And the same for ever.'
Hebrews xiii, 8.

28. The Surrender of Pilate.

(a) ' *Behold the Man !* '

Meanwhile Pilate sat apart in his hall, wondering what next he should do. What was his duty, as a judge and as a man, he knew very well; but the justice of a judge, and the rights of a single man, were not the only things to be considered by a Roman governor of Palestine. The mob in the narrow street outside was becoming more restless than ever; even this delay caused by the scourging was making the priests and elders yet more imperious in their demands. Every moment now was of importance. If Jesus was to die and be put away before the Sabbath, the end must come and all must be over that same afternoon; if He was to die upon the cross, which would be a lingering death of at least some hours, then the permission must be granted and He must be put upon His gibbet without any further delay. If Pilate had hoped that his Prisoner, like many another criminal or slave, might have perished beneath the lashes of the soldiers, he was disappointed. A messenger was sent down to the courtyard, to bring news of what was being done. The scourging was over, but Jesus still lived. The executioners had been careful not to go beyond their instructions; if Pilate so wished he could now carry out his second decision and let his Prisoner go. To fill up their time, knowing well the wishes of their master, and his contempt for kingship in any form, the soldiers had performed a mock ceremony about their Victim. They had reduced this Jesus of Nazareth to a condition that became Him; He was now a spectacle that would move a heart of stone. He was a worm and no man; from head to foot there was no soundness in Him; in His present plight, with a tangled mass of thorns upon His head, blood and spittle streaming down His face, body bent double beneath the filthy rag that covered Him, hands and feet so shackled that He could scarcely stand or walk, one had to look again before one could be sure that the creature was a man at all.

The description moved even Pilate; with all his cruelty, as his literature shows, the Roman of his day was not wanting in human sympathy. The thought occurred to him that the sight of Jesus in His present plight would move His would-be murderers no less; he made the mistake which many a Western makes when dealing with an Asiatic crowd. But it seemed his last hope and he must try it. The people and the priests should see for themselves the mangled state to which Jesus had been reduced; surely the very sight would silence them, there must be something short of death which would satisfy their hatred. He rose from his seat of justice and strode out again to the balcony. He would remind them of the sentence he had already passed: Jesus was not guilty, and other courts beside his own had confirmed it. In spite of that sentence they should see what he had done to humour them; they should be compelled to acknowledge that he had done enough, more than enough, and need do no more.

> ' Pilate therefore went forth again
> And said to them
> Behold I bring him forth to you
> That you may know
> That I find no cause in him.'

The order had gone down to the court below that the Prisoner should be brought up to Pilate in His present condition with nothing altered. The helmet of thorns was not to be taken from His head; He was not to be given His own clothing, but He must come in His half-naked state, with the red cloak covering His shoulders. The reed was to remain in His bound hands; the spittle and blood were not to be removed from His face; for His own sake, that men might at last be moved to pity for Him, and spare Him, everything that could make Him appear foul, contemptible, repugnant, in the eyes of His own people, was to be left upon Him. And Jesus Christ obeyed. At the word of command, He rose from the wooden seat against the wall, every movement a torture to that aching, thorn-pierced head. In the garden He had fallen flat upon the ground, the Victim of the enemy of the human race; now He was the Victim of the human race itself, and there was no angel to strengthen Him. He stumbled across the paved floor, bent double by the pain in His whole body, by the wounds that reopened as He moved, by the thorns that pierced afresh with every motion. He climbed the stone steps leading to the balcony where Pilate awaited Him, every step drawing blood from the naked feet that dragged along the ground. He stood before the people, an outcast and a reproach, by the side of Pilate, despised and rejected; if He could feel it when Galilæans walked with Him no more, if the apathy of Jerusalem could draw tears from His eyes, what did He feel and endure as He looked down, if He was able to look down, on the crowd gathered beneath Him? We have seen the picture so often that we have become used to it; the words have been so repeated that they tend to be echoes without meaning; human nature itself so shrinks from the sight that it gladly substitutes a thing of beauty for the terrible truth; the eyes lost in long clots of blood, the mouth opened, for the Sufferer dared no longer close it, the face, so much as could be seen, blackened and bruised till one might well question whether it were human, the thorns piled up on the head confirming the question, for that was no human head-dress. Even Pilate could call the attention of those who gazed upon Him to the change that had come over Him within the last hour. They had demanded the life of Jesus; was it not enough that He had been so stripped of His humanity, that He was as a hunted beast before them, scarcely to be recognized any longer as a man?

' So Jesus came forth
　　Bearing the crown of thorns
　　And the purple garment
　　And he saith to them
　　Behold the man ! '

And yet even a sight so terrible was of no avail to win a little pity, let alone pardon, from the hatred that looked upon it. On the contrary, the effect was the opposite. Having gained so much, the hunters for blood were now convinced that the prey was theirs. Hitherto they had doubted whether Pilate might yet elude them, and the death they sought might not be inflicted after the manner they had chosen. In spite of his repeated assurances of the innocence of Jesus, Pilate had consented thus far ; they had now but to persist and he would do the rest of their will. Scourging, crowning, degradation, punishment of any kind would not satisfy them, even an ordinary death would not satisfy them now. Jesus must die the death of the worst of criminals ; He must die the death of an enemy of the State ; He must die as the enemy of man :

' When the chief priests therefore and the officers
　　Had seen him
　　They cried out saying
　　Crucify him
　　Crucify him ! '

and the crowd that stretched down the narrow street, maddened with the sight of blood, took up the cry.

Once again the ruse of Pilate had failed. Hatred had conquered cruelty ; malice had no use for compromise. Had Jesus Himself but compromised all would have been well ; but as He stood there, nay, the more because of His plight, He was ' a censurer of their thoughts, He was grievous unto them, even to behold.' But if they were so blinded, and so determined in their blindness, perhaps Pilate might again attempt to shift the responsibility for the crime on them. They affected to believe Jesus guilty and for all he knew, so Pilate told himself, He might have broken their Law ; according to Roman justice He certainly was not. They were determined that Jesus should be crucified, and should not merely die the death of an ordinary breaker of their Law ; if this were all, if this would satisfy them and restore order in the city, could he not, for once, acquiesce, and allow them to crucify their criminal themselves ? In their excitement, in their blind fury, they had already declared that they would take His blood upon themselves and their children ; surely, then, since they were so determined to attain their end, they would accept the offer that he made. They had claimed the right to judge their fellow-countryman ; let them judge Him, Pilate had allowed it. They had claimed that He should die ; let Him die, Pilate, for peace' sake, had allowed it. They claimed now that He should be crucified ; let them crucify Him if they chose, what further concession could they ask ?

> ' Pilate saith to them
> Take him you
> And crucify him
> For I find no cause in him.'

But with the cunning of madmen the chief priests and leaders of the people were not to be deceived. Though they might now go and crucify Jesus if they would, that would not be the gaining of their end. He would then die as their Victim only ; He would not die the shame and scandal of all the world. That the guilt of Jesus might be utterly unquestioned, that His good name might be stained beyond recovery, that all men for all time might know His utter falsehood, Jesus of Nazareth must die at the hands, not of a party, but of the highest authority in the civilized world. If a Jew put to death a Jew, what would the Gentile care ? If a Jew's condemnation were confirmed by the Roman judge, by the just, impartial, disinterested Roman, then would all the world know that indeed their own sentence was right, that Jesus had a devil, and that they were the true sons of Abraham.

Even as their thoughts went back to their original purpose and motive, at the same time some strange instinct told them that now was the moment to prefer the original charge ; the charge which had brought about the condemnation before Annas and Caiphas, on which alone sentence had been passed in the lawful court of the Sanhedrin that morning :

> ' I adjure thee
> By the living God

That thou tell us
If thou be the Christ
The son of the blessed God
And Jesus said to him
Thou hast said it
I am

.   .   .

Then they said all
Art thou then the Son of God ?
And he said
You say that I am.'

Hitherto no charge of the kind had been laid before Pilate. Before him Jesus had been declared :

A malefactor,
A perverter of the people,
A defier of the ruling of Cæsar,
A foolish claimant to the throne of David.

Pilate had disregarded every charge but one, but that one he had taken seriously : Jesus claimed to be a King. Indeed Pilate had gone further; he had shown an inclination to believe that the claim was not without foundation. He had implied that according to their Law and their traditions Jesus might indeed be the hereditary King of the Jews ; malefactor or not, perverter of the people or not, He might still be the lawful descendant of the house of David. But since he had thus inclined to turn the charge against them, since he saw no ' cause of death ' in a mere matter of descent, since he had half-taunted them with their Law and their pretensions, they must teach him what that Law really contained. They would make him understand what was really implied in that title ; that behind all they had said was something deeper down, which would prove beyond a doubt that they had justice on their side. That broken Man before them, that worm and no man, claimed not only to be a King ; He claimed not only to be a son of David ; He claimed God as His Father, in very truth and without equivocation. Such a claim, according to the strictest theology, was blasphemy, such a claimant was worthy only of death. True, this was no charge that came within the scope of the Roman court, but what did that matter to them now ? Hatred had reached its climax and could restrain itself no longer, it had shot its every bolt and had failed. Even in the presence of this unbeliever Pilate, it must pour out its venom; it must let him see all the more that, no matter how he twisted and pleaded, pardon for this offender was impossible:

> 'The Jews answered
> We have a law
> And according to that law he ought to die
> Because he made himself the Son of God.'

(b) *The Last Trial of Jesus.*

The whole truth was out at last, and behind it was a determination, a finality that could no longer be contemned. Pilate looked down on those upturned faces, hard, merciless, unyielding, and was genuinely afraid; he listened to this new, mysterious charge and 'feared the more'. How was he to judge in such a case? Sons of gods and of goddesses he knew of in abundance in his mythology, but this was something more than myth; there was evidence of truth and reality, whatever that might be, in the very bitterness of those who brought the charge. To them, at least, sonship of God, in the case of Jesus, meant more than metaphor; it implied a truth that to them was matter of life and death. Now he seemed to see further than he had seen before. Already he had been given some inkling of the truth when, in his former examination, Jesus had told him that His kingdom was 'not of this world'; and all that He had said, all that in fact He had shown Himself to be as He had stood unmoved during all these hours between His judge and His accusers, implied a power within Him different from anything Pilate had ever known in any man before. Was this another of those eastern mysteries, of which he had heard in Rome, and which, by their claim to divine communications, were threatening to oust the ancient Roman gods from their seats and temples? But this was something more even than those rites and mysteries. For they, too, rested on myth; they were fostered by strangely-clad priests with weird, mystic rites; they caught the fancy of women, and led their votaries to delirium. This was far more real. The claim of Jesus rested on no myth or ceremonial; He bore no mystic cap, He was clothed in no magician's robe;

His head-dress was this helmet of thorns, His garments were dyed in His own blood. According to this new charge Jesus claimed to be, not a king only, not a miracle-worker only, not only a priest of a new rite, but an actual descendant of God Himself. If He were a son of God—and how was Pilate to discover this?—then by God He would be loved and protected; if He were put to death, then by God He would be avenged, and Pilate would have reason to beware of His wrath.

So did Pilate's superstitions give colour to the charge that was now preferred, and superstition always leads to fear. The trial had now taken on a new phase, and he, the judge, must examine the case afresh; he must learn more of this strange Man's origin. He must decide for himself, without pressure from the howling mob outside, whether this new charge were a mere form of words, or whether it contained a solemn truth.

> ' When Pilate therefore had heard this saying
> He feared the more
> And he entered into the hall again
> And he said to Jesus
> Whence art thou ? '

We have already noticed how Jesus, by His speech and by His silences, was careful in every trial to conform to the rights of the law; when it was His duty to speak He spoke, when questioned unjustly He was silent, no matter what might be the consequences. Before Annas He said nothing; He replied to the high priest Caiphas. He accepted the challenge of the Sanhedrin, to Herod He answered never a word. So was it now in this last examination before Pilate. This was a question which in no way concerned the Roman Governor. Before Caiphas, before the Jewish court of justice, where the title had a meaning sanctified since the days of David, Jesus had been openly and legally challenged, and had openly declared His Sonship, and for that declaration He had been condemned to die. Before Pilate He might have made the same declaration and it might have saved Him. But the matter was not Pilate's concern. He was there to pass sentence on Jesus, not in things spiritual, but in things that concerned Roman law and order. He was there to decide whether or not Jesus were a malefactor, whether He were a disturber of the peace, even, perhaps, whether He were a king; but as to His Sonship of God, Pilate had no jurisdiction whatsoever. Jesus would render to Cæsar the things that were Cæsar's, but Cæsar had no authority to ask or to judge in such affairs as this. Abruptly, therefore, with an abruptness that at once seems to make that mangled figure stand up in all its dignity, we are told that in answer to the judge's question:

'Jesus gave him no answer.'

Pilate understood full well what this silence meant. Annas had understood it, and had escaped by passing Jesus on to Caiphas; Caiphas and Herod had evaded the rebuke by contempt. But Pilate had no such escape. Again it was brought home to him which of the two was the stronger, which the master, which the judge; not even the ordeal through which Jesus had already gone, the mockery from Herod, the scourging from the Roman soldiers, the howling of the mob that He should be crucified, had broken His spirit, had altered the relation between them. Still Pilate could not yield; he was seated in the seat of justice, he represented Rome that brooked no rival, and he must needs assert his authority. He had recourse to that favourite device of the weakling in power who knows himself to be in the wrong; he would play the tyrant and the bully. Jesus would not speak to him? Would ignore him? Would by His silence give him to understand that he acted beyond his rights? Pilate in his turn would let Jesus see which of the two had the power to strike, on which side rested the authority of the sword.

'Pilate therefore saith to him
Speakest thou not to me?
Knowest thou not
That I have power to crucify thee
And I have power to release thee?'

It was a bullying threat and nothing more, an attitude unworthy of Pilate, which almost at once he seems to have recognized and to have wished to put right. With all Pilate's weakness, with all his cruel concessions to the Jewish rabble, he had always hitherto treated Jesus personally with respect. Whoever Jesus was He was true, whatever He had done to engender this hatred He was innocent of any crime; and from the beginning to this moment Pilate had consistently honoured Him as such. It was part of his good breeding that he should do so; it belonged to him as a Roman, as one superior to this Asiatic crew, that he should preserve his dignity, that he should keep the code of right behaviour, even when he dealt with a criminal on trial for his life. But now even Pilate's self-respect had broken down; the moment had come for the collapse of his dignified demeanour, as it had come for the self-respecting priests and elders in the court-house of Caiphas, as it comes some time or other to every man whose standard is that of convention alone. Pilate, no doubt, was true to type; he was a typical Roman of his day. There were things which his code allowed, lashing a slave to death was one of them, showing contempt for an eastern mob was another. There were other things which it did not allow; and one of these was to browbeat a fellow-man whom he held within his grasp. Yet this Pilate had just done; he had been piqued by the silence of this Man who so evidently was greater than himself, and he had uttered a threat of which he was ashamed as soon as the words had been spoken.

But Jesus 'knew what was in man', and took pity once more on this creature of big words. He did not fear him and his threats; Pilate knew at once that they had made no effect on this Man whom nothing could break. At the beginning of His career, on the first sign of danger, He had said that if men destroyed the temple of His body He would build it up again. Long ago He had encouraged His own not to be afraid of those who killed the body, but after that had no more that they could do; such a Man was not to wince under the threat of one like Pilate. Long ago and often He had defied His bitterest enemies when they had threatened to have His life; He had told them that when He would He would let them have it, and not a moment sooner. Herod had sought to catch Him, and He had called him a 'fox' in return; if He had no fear for any of these, neither could He fear the threat contained in Pilate's empty words. And since He could not fear Pilate, He could pity him; He could be sorry for this poor worldling, whose conventional dignity could so suffer eclipse. Since He pitied him, He would take the judgment into His own hands; He would give Pilate another and a last lesson in the art of government. He would remind him again, as He had reminded him before, that, Roman ruler as he was, with the Empire of Rome behind him and the wings of Roman eagles shielding him, nevertheless he was not almighty, he might not use his authority as he pleased.

But the pity of Jesus for this poor arbiter of His life and death would take Him much further. It was evident that Pilate was afraid; afraid because of what he had already done, his conscience making him every minute more and more a coward; afraid of what he might yet be driven to do by the merciless mob that goaded him to further injustice. He was weak rather than malicious; ignorant, and Jesus well knew how to use this shield for the fallen; He would give then to Pilate this consolation that he was not wholly, he was not even chiefly, to blame in this affair. Yes, in failing to be just, Pilate did grievous wrong; but far worse were those who had dragged him into it, who were driving him whither he would not, who were moved by hatred and hatred only, who knew in their hearts that there was truth in the claim of Jesus Christ, the Son of God, and hated Him the more because of it.

> 'Jesus answered
> Thou shouldst not have any power against me
> Unless it were given thee from above
> Therefore he that hath delivered me to thee
> Hath the greater sin.'

These are the last recorded words spoken by Jesus to the Roman Governor. Pilate had already done Jesus grievous injury, yet Jesus has no word of remonstrance or blame. He vaunted that he could and might do more; Jesus pays no heed to the threat, He does but warn him of his limitations. Pilate knew, his whole attitude from the beginning of the trial betrayed it, that he was guilty of grave injustice; Jesus passes sentence upon him, but it is a sentence tempered with sympathy and mercy. Pilate is guilty, yes, but guilty in great part from ignorance and weakness; guilty, but not so guilty as those who have driven him to this pass. We have elsewhere noticed the courtesy and forbearance of Jesus Christ; when He placed the boy whom He had raised to life into his widowed mother's arms; when He gently dismissed the woman who was a sinner, and gently handled the man who had Him at his table as a guest; when He asked that something to eat should be given to the little child of Jairus ; and many a time besides. All through this weary Passion the same characteristic courtesy is marked, no matter what may have been the provocation. He is courteous to all, whoever they may be, and whatever they may do ; to the man who betrayed Him, to the soldier who brutally struck Him, to the apostle who denied Him, to His accusers who raged about Him, most conspicuously to this Roman magnate who feebly tried to save Him yet did Him so much wrong. He had spoken to Pilate more than He had spoken to all the rest since He had been taken in the Garden ; always with dignity, as an equal to an equal, yet always with respect, as to a lawful authority. He had given the Roman to understand that He was more than the Roman's subject, to be dealt with as any common serf ; yet never a word that He had said had fallen short of the honour due to Pilate, or had shown the least arrogance or assertiveness in Himself. He had given him light beyond that given to others ; He had explained to him His kingship and His kingdom so that Pilate the judge might make no mistake, might have no misgivings ; He had drawn him on, step by step, to seek the real truth, not the shadow of it ; even now when He had failed He dismissed him, He gave him leave to proceed with his business, but not without a kindly word, a word of pity and condonement, certainly a word which Pilate would remember with gratitude to his dying day.

The reply of Jesus only revived in Pilate the desire to win his Prisoner's release :

> ' He that hath delivered me to thee
> Hath the greater sin.'

But if their sin was the greater, yet was his own sin great ; if hitherto he had striven to settle all the guilt on the shoulders of others, now he heard with his own ears that this Man whom he feared, and could only affect to despise, held him in part responsible. He could say no more to this strange Man who at every turn proved Himself his master. He could examine no further One who would do nothing, would not even answer a question, on His own behalf. Even the threat which Pilate had uttered, and which he now would gladly have retracted, had fallen away like water through a sieve. Jesus had never been one to be threatened, and Pilate in his heart had long since discovered it; instead there was that about Him which of itself 'spoke as one having authority', which told Pilate that if He wished He might at any moment begin to command and to threaten. Two years ago, in Capharnaum, another Roman officer had come to Him, had acknowledged Him to be too great to come under his roof, had recognized His majesty while he himself was but a man among men; had Pilate but yielded to the same light clearly shining on him, to the same appeal, repeated and repeated during all that morning in spite of all he had done, to the dictate of his own conscience which would not permit him to escape, once more the joy of the Lord might have been heard, crying:

> 'Amen I say to you
> I have not found so great faith
> In Israel
> And I say to you
> That many shall come from the east and the west
> And shall sit down with Abraham and Isaac and Jacob
> In the kingdom of heaven.'
> Matthew viii, 10-11.

But Pilate was a man of the world; and though the 'kingdom not of this world' was within his reach if he would have it, he preferred to keep that which he thought he possessed, convention rather than the truth, power rather than greatness, bubble reputation rather than surrender to a noble, but to him less tangible, ideal. He made his choice and, once he had made it, to stay alone in the company of this Man became an agony. At all costs he must save Him if he could; His truth, His innocence, His greatness, His independence of soul, had impressed themselves on him more than ever. Moreover, there was something else about this 'Son of God' which added fear to respect in the Roman's heart, and fear was an evil not to be endured by a Roman. He went out again to the crowd below the balcony; he parleyed with the enemy yet again; he repeated his belief in the innocence of Jesus; one thing he did not do, and that was to act in the only way a just judge could have acted. But while he parleyed, the enemy prepared their last bolt. That Jesus claimed to be a king had not been enough; that He had 'made

Himself the Son of God' had apparently fallen on deaf ears; then must Pilate himself be threatened, he must be made to choose between the life of his Prisoner and, perhaps, his own.

The accusers of Jesus could not forget how Pilate had continually turned against them the charge that Jesus had claimed to be a king. He had almost taunted them with that claim; he had affected at least to believe in it; he had bestowed it upon their Victim, as if it were His by right; he had made it a reason why He should be released, not why He should die; since he had so made light of it, they would now use it as a warning and a charge against Pilate himself. It was their last bolt, but they had reason to believe that it would reach its mark. More than once during his long period of office complaints had gone to Rome against Pilate, and every time his tenure had been threatened; it was well known that of all things he feared this the most, the charge of disloyalty to the Roman Emperor, or of compromising Roman authority. Here, then, was their final opportunity. Pilate had affected to acknowledge the kingship of Jesus, even though His kingdom were not of this world; to acknowledge a king independent of Cæsar, even though his kingdom were not of this world, was, or could be interpreted to be, an act of treason against the all-ruling Emperor, the Saviour of his people, the Pontifex Maximus, who would tolerate almost any creed within his fold, but would tolerate none that were independent of him. Hitherto hatred had vented itself on Jesus alone, now it threatened to include Pilate also. What Judas had rejected, what Simon Peter had denied, what all His own had thrown away, that same now was offered to Pilate if he would have it, the glory of being the first to be hated by men for the sake of Jesus Christ:

> ' But the Jews cried out saying
> If thou release this man
> Thou art not Cæsar's friend
> For whosoever maketh himself a king
> Speaketh against Cæsar.'

It was an argument worthy of the emptiest of sophists. Moreover, Pilate knew well the hollowness of this sudden pretence of loyalty. Of all the nations which the vast empire of Cæsar included, none had accepted his sway with such sullen grace as the Jews; none had more resisted and even defied the assimilation brought about by Roman culture. Other nations had submitted, and in a generation had blended their interests with those of Rome. They had given their men to make up her armies, they had even taken pride in being called Roman citizens. The Jews had always held aloof; even in the heart of Rome itself they had kept themselves a race apart. When they had come under the imperial sway they had declared for what they called their Law, and Rome had been compelled to humour them; though they had accepted perforce obedience to Rome, yet Rome had found it wiser to leave them to themselves as much as she was able. Others had even united their religious worship with that of the city of the Cæsars; and Rome had accommodated them with temples within her walls. Rites and mysteries passed from East to West, more than from West to East; young Rome had found a new interest and excitement in novelties such as these. But the Jews had always held aloof. Wherever they had gone they had always remained a nation within a nation, carrying their boundaries with them into every city. In Rome itself their capital was not Rome but Jerusalem. They would tolerate nothing Roman in their synagogues, much less in their Temple, to which all eyes turned; they would worship their one God in their own traditional way, they asked for no friendship, and gave none; whoever was not a Jew was a Gentile, there was no other distinction or class. True, they had been subdued, and had been compelled to accept the rule of the Roman Cæsar; but it was only an external acceptance, and since they could not have a monarch of their own they would, in spite of Cæsar, make God Himself in some way their King and Lord.

Something like this was the impression which Pilate, in common with other Romans of his class, had formed of the Jewish people, long before he had been sent to govern them. Since that time it had only been deepened. He had learnt, sometimes to his cost, that he must not interfere with Jewish prejudice, especially in matters of religion. Now when the final moment drew near, and it seemed that the irrevocable sentence must be passed, he still felt he could rely upon it. These people, in their hatred, had preferred Barabbas to Jesus; but then even Barabbas was a Jew, and religious sentiment had not been injured. What would they do if Jesus, the Jew, were set over against a Gentile? If Jesus, the King, though they hated Him, were balanced against the hated yoke of Cæsar? Once they had chosen Barabbas, whom certainly they had not loved; now, when the alternative was set before them, would they not prefer Jesus whom they hated?

This would seem to explain Pilate's next and final manœuvre. The trial had now dragged on from sunrise till the middle of the morning; one way or the other it must now be concluded. Beyond the Temple wall close by him the courts had long since filled with buyers and sellers, and worshippers from many lands; the streets of the city were already thronged with the pilgrims that pressed in from their camps outside the city walls. It was time that this business should conclude; the longer he delayed the greater might be the tumult should things go wrong. Moreover, his own good name was now at stake; this last cry, this threat that he was no friend to Cæsar, made it essential that a decision should be reached. Therefore he would parley no longer. That Jesus was a malefactor, a disturber of the peace, was a charge so groundless that His accusers themselves had forgotten it; that He was the Son of God did not concern him. Of all the charges that had been brought, one only came within his cognizance; the charge that Jesus claimed to be a king. In the eyes of His accusers that claim was either true or it was not. If it was not, if Jesus had not a single follower or subject that acknowledged Him, where was the point in putting Him to death? Better to let Him go free, a self-deluded madman, as had been so many before Him. But if He were in truth a king, if these men knew in their hearts that they owed Him some allegiance, then perhaps at the last moment they might be brought to relent.

With great formality, therefore, Pilate went about his last move. The crowd was silent below; the tension proved that they knew that the decisive moment had come. Pilate took his place on the stone seat of judgment; the definite seat of justice. By his act he gave the mob to understand that this was indeed the end; this time there would be no going back. He gave orders that Jesus should be brought out once more before them all; once more the blood-stained figure, thorn-crowned, robed in filthy red, the outcast alike of Jew and Gentile, yet there was not one among them all, Gentile or Jew, but felt the strength, the dignity, the power to command of this Man who yielded to them, saying not a word :

> ' Now when Pilate had heard these words
> He brought Jesus forth
> And sat down in the judgment seat
> In the place that is called Lithostratos
> And in Hebrew Gabbatha
> And it was the Parasceve of the pasch
> About the sixth hour
> And he saith to the Jews
> Behold your king ! '

Never has even S. John spoken with such solemnity as this ; Pilate had before declared Jesus innocent, now he declares much more ; he declares his belief, as a Roman and impartial judge, that Jesus is indeed what He claims to be, a king. Before, he could find no cause in Him why He should die ; now he finds good cause why He should live. Before, he had washed his hands, and they had taken the blood of this Man upon themselves and their children ; now it would almost seem that he would remind them of the content of their words, the curse that was on those who touched the anointed of the Lord :

> ' David said to him
> Why didst thou not fear
> To put out thy hand to kill the Lord's anointed ?
> And David calling one of his servants
> Said : Go near and fall upon him
> And he struck him so that he died
> And David said to him
> Thy blood be upon thy own head
> For thy own mouth hath spoken against thee
> Saying : I have slain the Lord's anointed.'
> 2 Kings i, 14-16.

Again and for the last time the strategy of Pilate failed. Whatever their religious instincts told them, whatever was written in the Law or the Prophets, the priests and elders before Pilate's house had committed themselves too far to draw back. They would be satisfied now with nothing but the last extreme, let the cost be what it may, yes, though it be the one thing that was theirs, their kingdom that was not of this world, their sonship of Abraham, their inheritance as the chosen people of God. Mercilessly, with no mercy left even for themselves or their posterity, flinging all charges to the winds, no longer even finding an excuse for their malice, guiltily, accepting the doom of their own guilt,

> 'They cried out
> Away with him
> Away with him
> Crucify him!'

(c) *The Defeat of Pilate.*

Yet for another moment Pilate hesitated. In all this multitude of men was there not one who would stand with him on the side of common justice? This was not a public show in an arena, where victims were done to death to please a populace maddened with the sight of blood. This was not his own pagan Rome, where life was held of light account and where men were trained to die. This was no slave that stood bound before them, whose master could crucify him almost at his pleasure. This was a court of justice; this was a city whose law made much of the life of any man, whether slave or free; this was a free man among free men, a Jew among the Jews, whose innocence was proved, whose nobility was manifest, a king in mien in spite of His condition, a Son of God, whatever that title might imply. Was there not one who saw the truth as he clearly saw it? Or rather, for he knew that they knew and understood better far than he, that it was because they knew and were envious of this Man that they would have Him die, was there not one who would at last relent, and suffer common justice to be done? Perhaps beyond the howling crowd there were some who were silent; some who did not belong to these leaders, to this 'generation of vipers'; who had come only to witness a prisoner's release, or who had followed 'that they might see the end'. Pilate would appeal to them. If only a few would support him he might yet at this last moment be empowered to save this innocent Victim of a mob. He raised his voice higher; he called to those who stood on the outskirts of the crowd;

in the tense silence that followed the last cry, the voice of the Roman Governor rang down the narrow street :

'Pilate saith to them
Shall I crucify your king?'

It was his last attempt. It was put as a distinct challenge, and the chief priests knew it. 'Behold your king!' he had just said, and though they had called for His death they had not denied that He was. Hence this new question had a further meaning :

'Shall I crucify your king
Because he is your king?'

was its implication. What were His enemies to answer? They had clamoured for a Roman condemnation and a Roman punishment; that Jesus might be put to death they had submitted thus far, of their own free choice, to the hated Roman yoke. But now Pilate drove them further. They had just challenged his loyalty to Cæsar, now he challenged theirs to their own King. They would have Jesus crucified; they would have their King crucified; they would have Him crucified who claimed to be their King, and because He claimed it; who, then, was their King? And they made their choice. They renounced not Jesus only, but the whole inheritance that was theirs. Openly, before Pilate, before all the world, they chose the kingdom of this earth ; the evangelist is careful to notice that this time it was not the people, it was their leaders the chief priests, that made this last decision :

'The chief priests answered
We have no king
But Cæsar.'

There was nothing more to be done. Formally the Jewish hierarchy had surrendered the one claim that made them a people, the one and only bond which Pilate had thought could never be broken, and on which he had relied to save his Prisoner. Never before had they spoken so clearly, never before in all Jewish history had the people of God accepted so whole-heartedly an alien yoke. Perhaps after all Pilate had now reason to be satisfied. Caiphas had said that it was

> 'Expedient
> That one man should die
> For the people
> And that the whole nation should not perish';

now, of its own free choice, the nation had destroyed itself If Pilate had lost his fight for Jesus, at least he had conquered in another way. When the story of what he had done was told in Rome, this issue of the conflict would save him. He could surrender now with less uneasiness:

> 'Then therefore
> He delivered him to them
> To be crucified.'

CHAPTER X

29. The Way of the Cross.

(a) *Simon of Cyrene.*

THE battle was over, the enemy had won, and nothing now remained but that the execution should be carried out as quickly as might be. He of whom it had been said, before He was yet born, that He would sit on the throne of David His Father, and that of His kingdom there would be no end, was about to be put to death. He whose life, as an infant, Herod the Great had failed to destroy, who had openly defied the lesser Herod, saying He would die where and when He would, was at last at the mercy of His murderers. He whom at Nazareth, at Capharnaum, then in Jerusalem, men had planned to annihilate and had failed, now at length was delivered into their hands. They had wished to cast Him down from the mountain, and He had passed through their midst; they had taken up stones to stone Him, and He had gone out of their sight; they had sent guards to take Him, and the guards had returned empty-handed; they had plotted and devised schemes, and yet He had come in and gone out as He would, and no one had dared to lay a hand upon Him. Now He stood before them, on the steps between them and Pilate, 'to the Jews a block of stumbling, to the Gentiles foolishness', not only helpless to resist, but almost seeming that He would not resist even if He were able. He was to be led as a lamb to the slaughter; He would not open His mouth. The guilt of the world was upon Him and He would carry it. The sentence had been passed, by His Father, by Himself, and by man; it was for Him now to complete the greatest act of love that man has ever done, for man or for God, upon this earth.

There were other executions appointed for that day, for executions were common on the eve of a great feast. Jesus, then, need not be sent back to prison to await another day. He could be put to death at once with the other criminals;

one more in the group would be of no account. There was little time left for further mockery or insult; the sanction had been gained, His blood was already upon the accusers and their children, and a silence of dread determination fell upon the crowd. Indeed from now till He is actually raised upon the cross we hear no more of cries and accusation; the task is hurried through without a further word, even the evangelists themselves catch the spirit of the scene, and pause only twice in their story. All this time Jesus had stood before the people as He had left the hands of the Roman soldiers; the red robe of mockery still covered His shoulders, the helmet of thorns was still upon His head, the cords were still about His wrists, the blood flowed down His face, hiding it like a veil. Now these things were torn once more from His body, opening the dried wounds afresh. His own clothing was brought up from the barrack yard, and meekly He covered Himself with it. In this He should traverse, for the last time, the streets of His beloved city; as He went along it should be known without a doubt to every onlooker who was the Criminal that was going to receive the reward that was His due. It was Jesus of Nazareth, the Jesus whom many knew, whom till that moment many had professed to revere; who would reverence Him now?

They took Him down the steps from the balcony where He had stood all this time by the side of Pilate. The Governor's work was done and he could retire to his next diversion: Israel had no further use for the despicable Gentile. At the foot of the steps executioners were waiting, holding the wooden beams to which the condemned man was destined to be nailed. The beams were put upon His shoulders, the bed on which He was to die; meekly He put His arms about them, He pressed them to Him, for they were to be His standard through the ages. Two years before, not far from that very spot, He had stood over a begging cripple and had bid him arise, and take up his bed and walk; in that very street His deed had roused a controversy. He had saved others, Himself He refused to save. There was no delay; the usual procession was formed, the herald leading, the Roman guard with the prisoners in their midst, the crowd making way, pinned against the walls of the narrow street.

> 'And bearing his own cross
> He went forth to that place
> Which is called Calvary
> But in Hebrew Golgotha.'

From Fort Antonia to the knoll of Calvary the distance was barely half a mile. The route wound in and out among the narrow lanes across the North of the city, almost due west from the house of Pilate, creeping first along the northern wall of the Temple, dropping down into the Tyropœan valley, then up again by a street of many steps, and through the bazaar towards the Tower of David. At ordinary times it was at most a walk of a quarter of an hour; with Jesus in His present plight, weakened by the loss of blood and with the weight of the wood upon His shoulders, it may well have been a little more. As the procession moved through the crowded streets, the rest of the city went about its ordinary business. It was the eve of the Paschal Sabbath, and preparations of all kinds had to be made. Many pilgrims from abroad filled every quarter, and the sellers of food, the money-changers, the dealers in whatever might attract a stranger's notice, could not lose the opportunity. There were droves of animals being brought into the Temple from the country; altogether this was not a day on which much interest would be taken by ordinary people in such a thing as a common execution. Not even the attendance of so many priests and elders would avail to attract them; as he looked at them lazily and unconcernedly from his booth or counter, many a squatting shopkeeper would tell himself, with a hidden sneer though his face remained a blank, that here was another victim of these merciless men, this time being hounded to death. Some would ask their neighbours who was this Man who was evidently so hated; and they would be told that He was one who had called the scribes and Pharisees 'a wicked and adulterous generation', who had cried 'Woe' upon them for their injustice and hypocrisy, who had said that their power would be taken from them, and would be given to another. This was He who had called Himself the Light of the World, the Good Shepherd, the Life of men, the Son of God; who, it was true, had done nothing but good, but who had claimed for Himself such rights and titles as no scribe or Pharisee could tolerate.

x

He had been accused of perverting the nation, of stirring up the people, of making all the world go after Him; the Roman Governor had condemned Him for making Himself a king. Such men were better out of the way; they disturbed the peace, they interrupted trade. Commercial Jerusalem had its own working creed; it had little use for fanatics or bigots.

So we may be sure the talk passed from mouth to mouth as the procession moved through the streets. It turned into the main thoroughfare which came into the city by the Damascus Gate. How often had Jesus come to and gone from Jerusalem by that route! It was the ordinary road from Nazareth, through Samaria and the Judæan upland; when He had come annually to the Temple, when He had gone through Samaria to Cana, and had met the woman at the Well of Jacob, when He had returned for the great assault upon the city at the Feast of Tabernacles the year before, He had come and gone by that gate and road. It had memories for Him now; not least the memory of her who, twenty years before, had passed down that street searching for Him, that first time a sword had pierced her heart. Tradition says that it was at the corner of this street that she met Him on His way to Calvary. Now at last the end had come, the end which she had always known must come, and which she had seen always hanging over Him, in the cave at Bethlehem, in the home at Nazareth, in the market-place of Capharnaum.

Beyond this thoroughfare the route turned to the right, and a narrow street of many steps had to be climbed, leading up to the thickly populated portion of the city and the bazaar. At the foot of this ascent there was a pause. The officers of the law looked at their Prisoner. In His broken condition, with the weight of the wood lying heavy on Him, they might well wonder whether He would be able to climb the many steps of the street unaided. The danger must not be risked; Jesus must be given help to carry His cross. But who should help Him? Not one of themselves; rather let Him die on the road than that a Roman soldier should relieve Him. Not one of the following crowd; to have asked or compelled a Judæan to assist a criminal would have put him to lasting shame. As they hesitated, perhaps as Jesus lay upon the ground gathering strength for the ascent, it chanced that there came down the road from the Damascus Gate one who by his dress was clearly no Judæan. Evidently he was a stranger from abroad, come, no doubt, like so many others, for the festival. He was seized and examined; he was a native of Cyrene; that was in North Africa, beyond Egypt, beyond Alexandria, far enough away to save him from losing caste. He would serve the purpose; let him help the Prisoner with His burthen.

Simon of Cyrene resisted, as well he might, but the elders and soldiers were not men to be contradicted; they forced the wood upon his shoulders, and bade him follow Jesus up the hill. At first he was crushed with the shame; he was indignant beyond words. The very stones beneath his feet seemed to echo words flung by Jesus at His enemies only a few days before:

' They bind heavy and insupportable burdens
And lay them on men's shoulders
But with a finger of their own
They will not move them.'

Matthew xxiii, 4.

But soon there came another refrain. This Man whom Simon was assisting was not one to be outdone in generosity. Never had anyone helped Him but he had received more in return; never had a grace been accepted from Him but another had instantly followed. Whether Simon knew it or not, this Man had said winning things to those who would share His burthens.

' Take my yoke upon you ', He had said,
' And learn of me
Because I am meek
And humble of heart
And you shall find rest to your souls,
For my yoke is sweet
And my burden light.'

Matthew xi, 29, 30.

So He had enticed men to follow; and when they came, and would be His men, it was by the same standard that He chose to test them:

> 'If any man will come after me
> Let him deny himself
> And take up his cross
> And follow me.'
>
> Matthew xvi, 24.

> 'He that taketh not up his cross
> And followeth me
> Is not worthy of me.'
>
> Matthew x, 38.

> 'Whosoever doth not carry his cross
> And come after me
> Cannot be my disciple.'
>
> Luke xiv, 27.

By these words alone we may judge what passed through the mind of Simon of Cyrene. Jesus was one who kept His word; He turned sorrow into joy; not only was His burthen light, it became a glory. Long afterwards, when the story of the Passion was retold, the sons of Simon of Cyrene, Alexander and Rufus, were proud to recall the favour that had been done to their father by Jesus the Lord that day.

> 'And as they led him away
> They found a man of Cyrene
> Named Simon
> The father of Alexander and of Rufus
> Who passed by
> Coming from the country
> Him they forced to take up his cross
> To carry after Jesus.'

(b) *The Mourning Crowd.*

But there were many others in Jerusalem that Paschal season of whom something must be said. The Gospel of S. John, which alone tells at length the story of Jesus in Jerusalem, is, and is intended to be by the evangelist, for the most part a record of rejection. Nevertheless it contains abundant proofs that among the people of the city, and of the whole province of Judæa, there were very many who in their hearts, some even openly, believed in Him.

' What do we ?
For behold all the world goes after him ',

the elders had said on a memorable occasion ; and we have seen how they feared to hasten His capture, or to take Him openly :

' Lest perhaps a tumult arise
Among the people.'

There were those of an older and faithful generation, represented by Zachary and Elizabeth, by Simeon and Anna, in the early days, good and earnest, far-seeing and long-suffering souls, who continued to ' wait for the consolation of Israel ', and indeed knew that it had come. There were many, not of the humbler classes only, exploited by the pharisaic rulers, as Jesus Himself had said in His memorable denunciation of them :

' Who departed not from the temple
By fastings and prayers serving night and day.'
Luke ii, 37.

There were the faithful followers of John the Baptist who, under his direction, had transferred their allegiance from their beloved John to Jesus :

' And many resorted to him
And they said
John indeed did no sign
But all things whatsoever John said
Of this man
Were true
And many believed in him.'

There were those who had been influenced by His miracles, especially the two great miracles in Jerusalem itself, the healing of the beggar at the Pool at Bethesda, in the North of the city, and the healing of the man born blind at the Pool of Siloe in the South :

' But of the people many believed in him
And said
When the Christ cometh
Shall he do more miracles
Than those which this man doth ? '
John vii, 31.

And again :

> 'These are not the words of one that hath a devil
> Can a devil open the eyes of the blind ?'
>
> John x, 21.

There were the crowds who had taken His side in the many disputes in the Temple court, especially during the last days ; who had risked the displeasure of the priests in so doing, and yet whose numbers had made the priests afraid :

> 'Of the multitude therefore
> When they heard these words of his
> Some said
> This is the prophet indeed
> Others said
> This is the Christ' ;

to whose conclusions the Pharisees were only able to retort :

> 'This multitude
> That knoweth not the law
> Are accursed.'

There were men of higher station, such as Nicodemus and his friends, or such as Gamaliel and his school, who followed in secret and were not few in number :

> 'However many of the chief men also
> Believed in him
> But because of the Pharisees
> They did not confess him
> That they might not be cast out of the synagogue.'

And besides those dwellers in Jerusalem, there were also at this time many more, who had come into the city from elsewhere for the Pasch, from Galilee, from Peroea where He had never been unfavourably received, even from Syria and beyond, who had gone long journeys to Jesus in Capharnaum and had learnt to believe in Him, and love Him, and follow Him, no matter what His enemies might say.

To many of these the news of the events of Thursday night had quickly spread. If on the occasion of a lesser feast He had been looked for, and had been missed when He had failed to come, now that He was known to be in the city He was not for long out of their sight. On the Friday morning what had been done, and what was being done, was soon made known to them all. He in whom they had believed apparently had failed; He was in His enemies' hands and was being done to death; if the Apostles were scandalized in Him that day, much more were these poor people who knew no better. They had seen no Transfiguration, they had heard no prophecies of the Passion; the Bread of Life had not yet been given to them, they had still to wait before they knew of the coming of the Holy Spirit. And yet not all; if many, like the Apostles, feared and remained in hiding, waiting for the turn of events, there were many more who had no such fears. These were drawn to Jesus now as they had been drawn to Him before; they had loved Him in life more than they had known, and now love drove them to follow Him that they might 'see the end'. As the procession passed through the narrow streets the accompanying crowd had been forced to stand back and follow after. They came to a crossing of two streets; it was not far from the end of the journey. There a large group had gathered, awaiting Him; no sooner did He appear than loud lamentations broke out.

For indeed what an end was this to all their expectations! What a doom for one whom they had learnt to take for their ideal! Was this He of whom the Baptist had said:

> 'There shall come one mightier than I
> The latchet of whose shoes
> I am not worthy to stoop down and loose
> He shall baptize you with the Holy Ghost
> And with fire
> Whose fan is in his hand
> And he will purge his floor
> And will gather the wheat into his barn
> But the chaff he will burn
> With unquenchable fire?'

Was this He whom John had pointed out to them, saying

> 'Behold the Lamb of God
> Behold him who taketh away the sins of the world?'

Whom John had boldly defended before he himself was struck:

> 'He must increase
> But I must decrease
> He that cometh from above
> Is above all'?

So those poor followers, who had known the Baptist by the Jordan, argued among themselves. But there were others from Galilee, who remembered the happy days when

> ' The fame of him
> Went out through the whole country
> And he taught in their synagogues
> And was magnified by all.'
>
> Luke iv, 14, 15.

When men cried :

> ' What word is this ?
> For with authority and power
> He commandeth the unclean spirits
> And they go out
> And the fame of him was published
> Into every place of the country.'
>
> Luke iv, 36, 37.

When His wonder-working brought back to their minds the words of the Prophet :

> ' He took our infirmities
> And bore our diseases.'
>
> Matthew viii, 17.

They remembered the time when they lost Him, and sought for Him, and found Him alone in prayer on the mountain-side :

> ' And the multitudes sought him
> And came unto him
> And they stayed him
> That he should not depart from them.'
>
> Luke iv, 42.

When, again,

> ' He could not openly go into the city
> But was without in desert places
> And they flocked to him from all sides.'
>
> Mark i, 45.

They recalled that evening in the cottage at Capharnaum when He had first forgiven sins, and had proved His right by a miracle ; and

> ' All were astonished
> And they glorified God
> Saying : We have seen wonderful things to-day.'
>> Luke v, 26.

They could not forget that other time when His enemies had first laid definite plots to catch Him. Then He had gone away from Capharnaum, but they had followed ; and they had recalled to themselves the prophecy :

> ' Behold thy servant
> Whom I have chosen
> My beloved
> In whom my soul hath been well pleased
> I will put my Spirit upon him
> And he shall show judgment to the gentiles
> He shall not contend
> Nor cry out
> Neither shall any man hear his voice in the streets
> The bruised reed he shall not break
> And smoking flax he shall not extinguish
> Till he send forth judgment unto victory
> And in his name the gentiles shall hope.'
>> Matthew xii, 18–21.

This was He who had taught them on the mountain-side, as no other had taught them, the blessedness of poverty, the blessedness of mourning, the blessedness of persecution :

> ' And it came to pass
> When Jesus had fully ended these words
> The people were in admiration
> At his doctrine
> For he was teaching them as one having power
> And not as the scribes and Pharisees.'
>> Matthew vii, 28, 29.

This was He whom they had proclaimed outside the gate of Naim :
> ' A great prophet is risen up among us
> And God hath visited his people.'
>> Luke vii, 16.

And again, on the green plain beyond the lake, at the Paschal season of last year :

> 'This is of a truth the prophet
> That is to come into the world.'
>
> John vi, 14.

These memories, and many more like them, were still fresh both in Judæa and Galilee when Jesus came back from His exile in Syria in the latter days; and a sudden collapse such as they were witnessing that day could not immediately destroy them. Indeed it revealed to them something new within themselves which they had not realized before. In the past they had been won by this Wonder-worker, this Prophet who spoke as no other man spoke, this Man fit to be their King. They had put their faith in Him, and even when they saw Him in this plight they would not take it back. They had admired Him, they had acclaimed Him, but not till now had they discovered how He had found His way into their hearts. Now the glamour was all gone; the tongue, it seemed, was silenced for ever; the wonder-working power was paralysed; He whom they had wished to make their king was on His way to death with that title held before Him for His shame. Still was He Jesus Christ; though stripped of all He was still their Jesus of Nazareth; now in His sorrow they discovered, what they had never discovered in the days when all went well, how much they loved Him. To see Him in this plight was an agony, but also it was a fascination. They crowded towards Him as He passed; the sight of Him drew from them sympathy that refused to be restrained; even the Roman guard could only yield to such a tide of sorrow.

> 'And there followed him a great multitude
> of people and of women
> Who bewailed and lamented Him.'

Jesus, bent beneath His load, saw and heard this gathering of friends and sympathisers, and the effect on Him was characteristic; it was in keeping with all we have known of Him before. If He could not pass a weeping widow but He must do something to console her, neither could He pass by mourning such as this without a word. If many a time He had shown pity for a devoted multitude, because it was as a flock of sheep without a shepherd, how could He but feel pity for this flock, whose Shepherd was so sorely struck? Whatever might befall Himself, He must think of them; such had always been His nature, never more manifest than during these hours of agony, insult, and injustice. In the Garden one had betrayed Him, and He had pleaded to the traitor as to a friend; when the mob had seized Him, He had thought first of His own, and had secured them from harm. In the house of Caiphas He had thought of His judges before all else, and had warned them of the judgment that would come to them because of all that they were doing. When the Apostle denied Him, 'Jesus turning looked on Peter', thinking more of unhappy Simon Peter than of the injury done to Himself. In the house of Pilate He had regarded only the Roman Governor, warning him, instructing him, drawing him, finding excuse for him, till the judge himself had been disconcerted. Before this weeping multitude it was the same. Even at such a moment, whatever cruelty might be shown to Him, there was the same gentle courtesy which He had often shown to women in distress: to the widow of Naim, to the woman who was a sinner at Magdala, to the woman who touched Him in the crowd by the landing-place at Capharnaum, to the wife of Jairus, to the Syro-Phœnician woman on the coast-land by Tyre, to the woman taken in adultery in Jerusalem, to the two beloved sisters in Bethania; there was the same ignoring of Himself, no matter what He suffered as He thought of the suffering that was theirs, both present and to come.

Moreover, what He said to these mourners was couched in language worthy of one who spoke as no man spoke. It was the mystic language of the prophets of old, the coloured language of the poets, as if the very suffering He underwent did but sharpen the more the keenness of His vision and His power to express it. Saints have dwelt upon the dignity of Jesus throughout the Passion, in spite of all that was done to Him, though He was crushed till He seemed a worm and no man; never does that dignity appear more than at this moment. It was their reward who mourned for Him; in the future years they should bear this portrait of Him, stamped upon their souls. He stood still in the road, commanding again when He would, however the Roman guard and the pressing enemy might urge the procession to go forward. He looked upon these weeping women and these silent men; He looked from them into the future. There He saw other women, weeping in these selfsame streets, in misery so great that this world has hardly seen the like. Twice at least before, during this very week, He had warned Jerusalem of the doom that awaited it, because of its rejection of Him ; and each time it had been, not in the language of an angry avenger, but in that of one who loved the very stones of the city of His choice. When others had gloried, He had only wept ; when others had sung : ' Hosanna to the Son of David ', He had only stood where David himself had once stood, an exile from his own city, and said :

' If thou hadst known
And that in this thy day
The things that are to thy peace
But now they are hidden from thy eyes
For the days shall come upon thee
And thy enemies shall cast a trench about thee
And compass thee round
And straiten thee on every side
And beat thee flat to the ground
And they shall not leave in thee a stone upon a stone
Because thou hast not known
The time of thy visitation.'

Luke xix, 42–44.

On the Tuesday following, when at last He had been driven to pronounce ' Woe ' upon the scribes and Pharisees, love made Him end with the cry to the very walls of His beloved city :

' Jerusalem Jerusalem
Thou that killest the prophets
And stonest them that are sent to thee
How often
Would I have gathered together thy children
As the hen doth gather her chickens
Under her wings
And thou wouldest not ?
Behold your house shall be left to you
Desolate.'

Matthew xxiii, 37, 38.

Before that day of doom came He had bidden His own flee from the city. Now He spoke to these women with His thoughts occupied with them alone ; if He thought of

Himself, He thought only of the sorrow that must come to others because of the injury done to Him.

> ' But Jesus turning to them said
> Daughters of Jerusalem
> Weep not over me
> But weep for yourselves
> And for your children
> For behold the day shall come
> Wherein they shall say
> Blessed are the barren
> And the wombs that have not borne
> And the breasts that have not given suck
> Then shall they begin to say to the mountains
> Fall upon us
> And to the hills
> Cover us
> For if in the green wood they do these things
> What shall be done in the dry ? '

So beautifully, even in the midst of all this day of horror, could Jesus Christ, the Son of Man, both think and speak. It was no strange thing, the story is not extravagant, it was Jesus Christ as we have always seen Him, as He is to the end of time.

(c) *The Arrival at Calvary.*

As we have already noted, a strange dulness, almost a silence, seems to come over the story of the Passion at this point. Since the procession left the house of Pilate, we have heard nothing of the cries of the pursuing crowd. Simon the Cyrenian could easily be picked up in the street in spite of it, Jesus Himself, in spite of the guard about Him, could easily be reached by the multitude of mourners on the road. It would almost seem that the mob with its leaders, exhausted with all they had done that morning, had vanished for the moment, to appear again when their Victim was secure on the cross. Indeed this may well have been so. The cortège made its way through the crowded streets of the bazaar, to the place of execution outside the city wall in the north-western corner. In the vanguard the soldiers pushed the people aside ; in the centre the three condemned to die carried their burthens, of interest to very few ; the seekers of blood followed in the rear, too eager to reach their goal to hinder the proceedings by too much confusion. As they watched the procession move along, now for the first time the evangelists tell us that 'two other malefactors' were being taken to die along with their Lord. They speak of it as nothing extraordinary ; as we have already seen, executions were commonly fixed for the eve of festivals, and these men, not improbably with Barabbas in their midst, would have been crucified that day, whether Jesus had been with them or not. His condemnation had not hastened theirs ; nowhere is there any hint of this, either in the narrative itself, or in the later charges hurled by the criminals against Him. According to the agreement between Pilate and the priests, Jesus had only taken the place of another ; the Son of God in the room of Bar-Abbas, the Son of the Father. It may be noticed that when the release of Barabbas was demanded, then for the first time the cry : 'Crucify Him !' was heard.

One other event only on the way to Calvary the evangelists consider worthy of mention. It was a common custom to give some stupefying drink to one about to be crucified ; a sympathiser on the road might offer it, or the executioners themselves, less out of sympathy, more that the cruel nailing might be more easily performed. A victim half-stupefied would be less able to resist or shrink. We are told that a drink of this kind was offered to Jesus. He took it, touched it with His lips, but did no more. To do thus much was to show His gratitude to one who did Him this passing kindness ; but the only chalice of which He would now drink was that which His Father had given to Him.

> 'And they gave Him to drink
> Wine mingled with myrrh
> And when He had tasted
> He would not drink.'

30. The Crucifixion.

(a) *Jesus Crucified*.

A death-bed is always a solemn and impressive sight, no matter to whom, or how, or when it may come. But when it is the death-bed of someone we know it is still more impressive ; we feel it then as if somehow we ourselves were sharing it. And more, again, if it be one we care for who is dying; then the sense of loss and separation is our own, we realize the blank that must come after, in one part at least of ourselves the finger of death has touched us.

If that death-bed is one of great suffering, the fascination increases. It hurts us ourselves as we look on; with one part of our nature we turn away, looking for relief; with the other we are fixed to the spot and nothing will move us. But if that suffering in death has been caused by ourselves; if the dying man has come to this, let us say, by some careless act of ours, or because of an attempt to save us from some disaster, then the suffering will enter into us as our own, as well as his who is dying. We share the suffering with him; every spasm strikes through us as we witness it in him. We long to relieve him; we would help him in any way we could; cost what it may, to give the sufferer some respite, we would gladly put ourselves in his place.

In some such spirit as this we come to the death-bed of Jesus Christ Our Lord. We know Jesus Christ, we care for Him, as we care for no one else. We look on a death-bed whose suffering is beyond words to describe, beyond human senses to feel. We know that we are its cause; that because of us He has endured, that by our own hands it has been intensified, that if justice alone were done we, not He, should be lying on that bed of agony and death. We are unable to leave Him, even though human nature sickens at the sight and resents it all; we have a great longing to help Him, to share the suffering with Him, if in no other way, at least by companionship. Though nature resents, we would feel His suffering yet more; though the agony grows in us even unto death, yet because it is His agony, because it draws us nearer to Him, because it proves that we are sincere in our love and compassion, the greater the suffering we ourselves endure, the greater our satisfaction and joy.

' And when they were come to the place
They crucified him there
And the robbers
One on the right hand
And the other on the left
And Jesus in the midst
And the Scripture was fulfilled which saith
And with the wicked he was reputed

And Pilate wrote a title also
And he put it upon the cross
Over his head
And the writing was
This is Jesus of Nazareth
The King of the Jews
This title therefore many of the Jews read
Because the place where Jesus was crucified
Was near to the city
And it was written
In Hebrew in Greek and in Latin
Then the chief priests said to Pilate
Write not The King of the Jews
But that he said
I am the King of the Jews
Pilate answered
What I have written I have written.'

Thus, with almost terrible brevity, as if they could not induce themselves to dwell upon it, the story of the Crucifixion is told by all the four evangelists together. S. Matthew scarcely dares to mention it at all ; he passes it over, dwelling rather on the crucifixion of the other two :

' Then were crucified with him
Two thieves
One on the right hand
And one on the left.'

S. Mark speaks rather of the hour when the deed was done ; he turns aside from the scene to tell us that it was nine o'clock in the morning :

' And it was the third hour
And they crucified him.'

S. Luke passes over it as quickly as he may ; he has dwelt on other scenes of suffering more than any of his fellow-evangelists, but for this one word is enough :

' There they crucified him
And the evildoers
One on the right hand
And one on the left.'

S. John was the only eye-witness of the four; he is more vivid, he sees everything in its place, yet he adds nothing to the facts and a single sentence suffices:

> ' Where they crucified him
> And with him other two
> On this side and on that
> And in the middle Jesus.'

As with the scourging, to which not so much as a single complete sentence was given by any one of the sacred writers, so with the actual crucifying of their Lord, they seem to long to hurry past it all, to say no more than they must, and to distract themselves from the recollection of the Central Figure by a comparatively minor trifle. The position of the crosses and the burthens they bore, the fulfilment of prophecy, as if to find in that some palliation for the horror of it, in the way that Jesus Himself had done before them, the title set above the Cross in three languages, the dispute of the priests with Pilate—they will dwell on any of these rather than on the cruel act itself, the greatest crime that was ever committed on this earth. Of that they will only say, and not a word more:

> ' They crucified him there.'

But love has succeeded to horror; the unspeakable has become a treasured memory; the deed of hatred and human cruelty has been made the one great glory of the world, because of Him who permitted and endured.

> ' Greater love than this no man hath
> That he lay down his life for his friend.'

> ' When I shall be lifted up from the earth
> I will draw all things to myself.'

> ' Far be it from me to glory
> Except in the cross of Our Lord Jesus Christ.'

Even if, by impossibility, the Resurrection had never followed; had the story of Jesus, as handed down to us, ended with that single sentence:

> ' They crucified him there ',

still would that one deed have stood out among all deeds in the history of men. It was the deed in which the two have met, man at his worst, the Man-God at His best. We would have looked to it as the one transcending act of heroism, the triumph of human love, the single model and inspiration that has called forth greatness from the generations that have followed, the supreme sacrifice that has transformed the world, that has given a new meaning to life.

'They crucified him there.'

Tradition, history, archæology, art, meditation in many forms, philosophy and theology, have all dwelt upon those simple words, and have tried to fathom them for us. They have spoken of the glory, they have vied with each other in portraying the beauty of the Cross, they have brought it forward as the hall-mark of all that is best in man; the chivalry of knighthood, the mercy of the hospital, gallantry on the battle-field, even the monarch's crown, have all been stamped and rewarded with the sign of the Cross. In this sign Christianity has conquered; in it and by it Christendom has expressed its own noblest ideals; because of Him who hung upon it, the Cross has become a solace to the poor and downtrodden, an inspiration to the young, a reward to all, whether in life they have succeeded or failed.

But we must first see that Cross and its burthen as best we may. The procession passed out of the city gate to the common place of execution; the Law forbade that such things should be done within the city walls. There the crowd was brought to a standstill; the executioners with their charges passed alone up the slight ascent, while the guard kept the howling mob back. Holes in the rock were already there, prepared for all executions; the upright beams of the crosses were firmly fixed, the cross-beam securely nailed above it. The victims were stripped of their clothing, then were hoisted by ropes each to his own cross. The arms were drawn out along the upper beam, stretched to their fullest extent, the better to support the weight of the body. A hole was pierced through the palm of each hand and a nail driven through it, fixing it to the wood. Then the body was dragged down to its full length, and a nail through each foot fixed it to a board on which it rested; sometimes the legs were bent, and the feet were nailed flat against the beam of the cross. A cord round the body, and others round the arms, held the man's frame in its place; otherwise the twitching and writhing of the body in torture, or its falling forward by its sheer weight, might have torn the hands from the nails that held them. The crosses were not high; the hanging men would have been but little above the heads of those who stood on the rock around them; later a soldier was able to reach the lips of Jesus with a reed of hyssop, which is seldom much more than a foot long. If the sufferer spoke, even in a whisper, he would have been easily heard by anyone standing by.

Such was the death-bed of Jesus Christ; the death-bed to which He had looked forward from the beginning, and towards which He had walked without flinching throughout His life. We have evidence in plenty that He had kept it always consciously before Him; often He had spoken of it, to Himself, to His Father, to His enemies, to the disciples about Him, even, in the solemn ecstasy of the Transfiguration, to Moses and Elias:

> 'And they spoke of his decease
> That he should accomplish in Jerusalem.'
>
> Luke ix, 31.

From Bethlehem, and the bloodshedding there, to Calvary, the shadow of the Cross had never left Him; when we look back upon His life, this alone throws a new light on everything He said and did. For instance, when He had said:

> 'If any man will come after me
> Let him deny himself
> And take up his cross daily
> And follow me',

though to those who heard Him that Cross was no more than a metaphor, an accident of everyday life, to Him, even as He spoke, it stood out on the skyline, an actual reality. When in the earliest days He said to Nicodemus:

> 'As Moses lifted up the serpent in the desert
> So must the Son of Man be lifted up',
>
> John iii, 14.

He showed how clearly He realized for Himself, not only the meaning of that scene in the wilderness, but every other type in the Old Dispensation that pointed to the shedding of His blood. Nazareth had tried to destroy Him, but it was not thus nor there that He was to die. Herod and his minions had plotted against Him, but His consummation was not to be at their hands. Jerusalem would have stoned Him, but that was not to be the manner of His death. Always the Cross had stood out on the horizon, showing Him the goal He would one day reach, at once His defeat and His triumph.

The same had been manifest in all the signs He had given; not merely in the explicit prophecies He had uttered to His own, but in countless others He had kept the vision of this day before Himself and those who heard Him. His enemies had asked Him for a sign, and He had replied:

> ' Destroy this temple
> And in three days I will raise it up.'
>
> John ii, 19.

He had spoken of Himself as the Good Shepherd, but the chief characteristic of His shepherding was one which none would have expected:

> ' The good shepherd giveth his life
> For his sheep.'
>
> John x, 11.

Once in the midst of persecution, as if to encourage Himself, He had said:

> ' If I be lifted up from the earth
> I will draw all things to myself ',
>
> John xii, 32.

and though He dwelt on the fruit of the conquest, nevertheless He saw it through the medium of that terrible ordeal:

> ' Now this he said
> Signifying what death he should die.'
>
> John xii, 33.

To encourage His own He had looked, and had made them look, at the cross they would one day have to bear:

> ' Fear not those who destroy the body
> And afterwards have no more that they can do ';

or again:

> ' If the world hate you
> Know ye
> That it hath hated me before you ' ;
>
> John xv, 18.

or yet again :

> ' They will put you out of the synagogues
> Yea the hour cometh
> That whosoever killeth you
> Will think that he doth a service to God.'
>
> John xvi, 2.

In all this He knew well that the hatred for Himself would be more terribly inhuman, and more terribly effective, than ever it would be for them ; if they were to follow, then He must lead by an example that none should surpass :

> ' That the word may be fulfilled
> Which was written in their law
> They hated me without cause.'
>
> John xv, 25.

Now at last, with full permission to do its worst, that hatred, more than human hatred, was being poured out upon Him in all its merciless vindictiveness and malice. The perfect Man was dying a perfect death ; He was being crucified, not in body only, but in every part of body and soul. And yet through it all His majesty shone without mistake, for anyone who wished to see. It exasperated His enemies the more, it drew His own the closer about Him, it made His executioners declare at the end that indeed He was the Son of God. If in His lifetime the human character of Jesus baffles us, so full is it of everything noble, so abundant in every human quality that makes for greatness, how much more must it baffle us in this last hour ! If it is impossible for any man, for all men together, to fathom the content of the life of Jesus, and to draw even an adequate portrait of Him who lived it, how much less may we hope to fathom the content of the hour of His death ! S. Paul leads the way in acknowledging the impossible. He knows that what he says of his crucified Lord will seem only foolishness to many, but he cannot say more :

> ' For the word of the cross
> To them indeed that perish
> Is foolishness
> But to them that are saved
> That is to us
> It is the power of God.

> For both the Jews require signs
> And the Greeks seek after wisdom
> But we preach Christ crucified
> Unto the Jews indeed a stumbling block
> And unto the Gentiles foolishness
> But unto them that are called
> Both Jews and Greeks
> Christ the power of God
> And the wisdom of God.'
>
> 1 Corinthians i, 18–24.

There he stops, having but touched the fringe of his subject, but despairing of human power to say more. Saints have followed him, and have done the same. They have seen Jesus crucified before them, at once their delight and their agony unto death. They have spoken some tiny word, but the more they have seen the more they have despaired of speaking:

> ' That which we have seen
> And have heard
> We declare unto you ',
>
> 1 John i, 3.

is in the end all they have cared to say; content to be called fools, if this is foolishness; to be called unwise, if this is want of wisdom; but knowing, in spite of the wisest of men's judgments, that with God it is power and glory.

> ' For the foolishness of God
> Is wiser than men
> And the weakness of God
> Is stronger than men.'
>
> 1 Corinthians i, 25.

If S. Paul, if the saints, saw so much, yet were able to say so little, what can we other creatures do? We can but join the tiny group that looked on apart from the rest at the foot of Calvary, and, while all the world seemed to howl about them, were themselves speechless and still. He who stands with them will see more in that bleeding body before him than he can ever hope to express; nay more, the moment will come when he will have no wish to express it. *Secretum meum mihi:* ' My secret to myself'. He will see as Jesus saw; through the blood an infinite beyond, through the shame an infinite glory, through the suffering a joy inexpressible, which none but Jesus Christ Himself can understand, but which through His eyes we can discern. There cross and throne are one, spittle and blood are priceless diamonds and rubies, thorns are the shining rays of light about a crown, death passes into life, death is absorbed in victory through the pathway of love. We cannot wonder that the evangelists, when the years had passed, and the truth had grown upon them, and they had understood the triumph of the Cross, were content to sum up the crucifixion in the simple, uncoloured sentence :

' They crucified him there ' ;

and that, without another word, they turned aside to other things more within the scope of human language to describe.

(b) *The Title.*

Thus we find them turning their eyes from the Central Figure, looking at the two between whom He hung. They were criminals, both of them, convicts of whose guilt there was no doubt, justly condemned and executed ; and the evangelists recognized the fulfilment of yet another prophecy :

' And with the wicked he was reputed.'

Indeed it was more ; it was a fitting ending to one aspect of His whole life's history. Before He was born He had been called, by a messenger sent from heaven,

' JESUS
Because he shall save his people
From their sins.'

This was the first task given to Him by His Father, and the last. When He had first appeared before the world, John the Baptist had announced Him to his followers as

' The Lamb of God
Who taketh away the sin of the world.'

Once, when He had raised a dead child to life, He had been acclaimed by all those who witnessed it :

' A great prophet hath risen up among us
And God hath visited his people.'

When He had fed a hungry multitude, it had cried out in gratitude :

> 'This is indeed the prophet
> That is to come into the world.'

Once, beyond the Lake of Galilee, the crowd had again gathered about Him on the mountain-side and cried :

> '**He hath done all things well**
> **He hath made the deaf to hear**
> **And the dumb to speak.**'

Only a few days ago, in the Temple court, these His very enemies had come to Him, and openly acknowledged :

> 'Master
> We know that thou art a true speaker
> And teachest the way of God
> In truth
> For thou dost not regard the person of men.'

All during this day of suffering His one challenge had been, stated expressly by Him at the outset :

> 'If I have done evil
> Give testimony of the evil' ;

and in response the declaration had been again and again repeated :

> 'I find no cause in him.'
> 'Why what evil hath he done !'
> 'Behold I bring him forth to you
> That you may know
> That I find no cause in him.'
> 'I am innocent of the blood of this just man.'

Often enough in the past, in one form or another, He had appealed to the evidence of His life, and had demanded :

> 'Which of you shall accuse me of sin ?'

and no one had ever dared to accept the challenge. Yet here and now, before the eyes of all men, for all generations to see,

> 'He was reputed with the wicked.'

And all generations have seen it, but have drawn from the sight a conclusion very different from that which was intended. He who had been sent 'to save His people from their sins' had long since submitted to be called 'the Friend of publicans and sinners'. He had declared that He had come,

> 'Not for the just
> But to call sinners to repentance';

that He had been appointed to win back to the Father,

> 'The lost sheep
> Of the house of Israel.'

Now on His death-bed He would not desert them. They were His own; and for them as well as for the Twelve the saying of S. John was true:

> 'Having loved his own that were in the world
> He loved them unto the end.'

As in life He had risked, nay sacrificed, influence and reputation that He might be with them, so in death He would allow His name to be joined with theirs, let posterity say of Him what it would.

The title, 'Friend of publicans and sinners', has been kept to the last; the evangelists next turn to another. Above the Cross, set there by the express order of Pontius Pilate, that all the world, whether Jew, Greek, or Roman, might read it, was the cause of His condemnation. Since Pilate had been driven to put the Man to death, none should be in doubt about the cause for which He died. Friend of sinners He might have been, yet He was no malefactor; though He 'stirred up the people' He was no sedition-monger; of all the charges that had been brought against Him two alone were true. Jesus was a 'king'; Jesus made Himself the 'Son of God'. The second did not concern Pilate though he had known very well that, whatever it might mean, it was at the root of all the hatred. But the Jews had refused to 'judge Him according to their law'; therefore only on the first charge could He be condemned. Jesus died because in very truth He was a king, and because Pilate believed it. He died because He was the King of the Jews, and Pilate knew that deep down in their hearts 'those who had the greater sin' knew it also. They might protest to him against the title; Pilate knew that their very protest condemned them. If Jesus were not a king, then the name so given would be but an added mockery. So the Roman soldiers had used it; they had proclaimed Him King in their barrack-yard, and had clothed Him in purple and crowned Him. Had the Jews believed as the Romans believed, they would have joined with the Romans in their ribaldry. But they could not forget all that had gone before. Three days ago, at their last meeting with Jesus in the Temple, He had

> ' Asked them, saying
> What think you of Christ?
> Whose son is he?
> They say to him : David's.
> He saith to them
> How then in spirit doth David call him Lord
> Saying
> The Lord said to my Lord
> Sit on my right hand
> Until I make thy enemies thy footstool?'

And no man was able to answer Him a word. Now they might demand that the title should be changed; Pilate, beaten hitherto at every point, now that it was too late could turn upon them. What he had written he had written, and it should not be changed. If Jesus Christ was to be 'reckoned with the wicked' for all time, nevertheless all posterity should also know that the judge who condemned Him declared Him most certainly to be,

> ' Jesus of Nazareth
> King.'

31. The First Word : ' Father, forgive them.'

While the enemy wrangle with each other at the house of Pilate, the evangelist brings us back to the foot of the cross, that we may hear the first words that fall from the lips of Him who hangs upon it. Two characteristics of Jesus have already been summed up, Jesus the Friend of sinners, Jesus the King; we have now a third. In all the teaching and practice of Jesus nothing had been so striking, nothing, if we may so express it, so new, as His constant forgiveness. The Paralytic at Capharnaum, the woman who was a sinner in Magdala, the adulteress in Jerusalem, the Samaritans who refused Him, His enemies at every turn, all these scenes had all but shocked His followers; He had seemed to them to sacrifice justice for mercy, honour for meekness, strength for peace, almost truth itself, that sin might be forgotten and the sinner might go free. Yet in His teaching He had but emphasized the lesson of His deeds. 'Forgive and you shall be forgiven.' 'Forgive us our trespasses, as we forgive them that trespass against us.' 'Seven times?—Seventy times seven times.' The refrain had run through all His life:

> 'I say to you
> Love your enemies
> Do good to them that hate you
> And pray for them
> That persecute and calumniate you.'

Still there was a limit even to forgiveness. In Galilee He had pronounced 'Woe' on Corozain and Bethsaida; He had said that Capharnaum should go down even to hell, because they had not heard Him nor received His kingdom as they ought. Over Jerusalem, too, He had wept; Jerusalem would perish because it would not have Him. It would look for Him and it would not find Him; the day would come when there would be left of it not a stone upon a stone. On the Tuesday evening of that very week, when for the last time He had left the Temple and its battles behind Him, as He sat with His Twelve on the Mount of Olives looking down on the beauty of the city below Him, He had foretold to them the doom that was to come. He had added that one day the Son of Man would return in all His majesty, and would pronounce on those who had shown themselves His enemies the sentence:

> 'Depart from me
> You cursed
> Into everlasting fire
> Which was prepared for the devil
> And his angels.'

Surely now the time for the fulfilment of that prophecy had come. He had run His course. He had declared Himself, and had been declared, a king; openly at last He had claimed to be the Son of God; and while Pilate crucified Him for the first, His own people crucified Him for the second. Should He now die unavenged, unvindicated, with all this ignominy heaped upon Him, would not His death, unworthy of a king, utterly unworthy of a Son of God, prove His enemies to be right, and His own claims wrong? In the face of such a scandal, what disciple, no matter how devoted, would be able to uphold Him in the future? Moreover, what provocation could be compared to this? He had offered these men the kingdom, and they had refused it; life, and they had rejected it; light, and they had loved darkness rather than the light; Himself, and they had crucified Him. He had warned them of what they did; of the consequences that would come to them; plainly in words, clearly enough in parables, so that

> ' When the chief priests and prophets
> Had heard his parables
> They knew that he spoke of them.'

Nay, with that irony which He knew so well how to use, once He had led them on unwittingly to pronounce judgment on themselves:

> ' Last of all he sent to them his son
> Saying: they will reverence my son
> But the husbandmen seeing the son
> Said among themselves
> This is the heir
> Come let us kill him
> And we shall have his inheritance
> And taking him
> They cast him forth out of the vineyard
> And killed him
> When therefore the lord of the vineyard shall come
> What will he do to those husbandmen?
> They say to him
> He will bring those evil men to an evil end
> And will let out his vineyard to other husbandmen
> That shall render him the fruit in due season.
> Jesus saith to them
> Have you never read in the Scriptures
> The stone which the builders rejected
> The same is become the head of the corner?

> By the Lord hath this been done
> And it is wonderful in our eyes
> Therefore I say to you
> That the kingdom shall be taken from you
> And shall be given to a nation
> Yielding the fruits thereof.'
>   Matthew xxi, 37–43.

If then He now came down from the cross, if at this dramatic moment He pronounced on these His murderers the doom with which He had already threatened them, would not all posterity applaud the magnificent act of justice? Would not all the world resound with hosannas to the Son of David, who had so vindicated His own honour? Would it not be said that once more the prophecies and types had been fulfilled, the floods of Noe, Sodom and Gomorrha, the destructions in the desert, the exile of the Chosen People themselves in foreign lands?

Maybe the world would have applauded; maybe even the Christian world would have bowed in homage before a proof of divine justice, but such was not the way of Jesus Christ. The prophets had said of Him that He ' would not break the bruised reed', and He had said of Himself that He had

> ' Come not to judge the world
> But that the world might be saved
> Through him.'

He had preached forgiveness as no other man had ever preached it before Him. He had said that if a man be struck in the face he should not retaliate; that vengeance belonged not to men, not even to Himself, but to the Father who knew all things and to Him alone. He had said that He would be the example of men, in this as in all things else; He was

> ' The way, the truth and the life.'

If, then, He had so taught forgiveness, that greatest of virtues in so far as it is the hardest, the most opposed to human nature, of all the things that He taught, then as Man must He give a supreme example. If, as He had said, forgiveness makes man most akin to God the Father, then, to prove Himself indeed the Son of that Father, must He put forgiveness before the world as His own last manifestation. From the throne to which He was nailed, lifted up at last so that He might draw all things to Himself, at the solemn moment when He was to be declared the Redeemer of the world, He must set an example of forgiveness beyond which no man could go. He had told men to forgive that they might be

> 'The children of your Father
> Who is in heaven.'

This, then, would be the way He would prove He was the Son of that Father, not the way men expected, or these His very enemies demanded of Him. He would be

> 'Perfect
> As the heavenly Father is perfect.'

He looked, not at men and their judgments, not at His enemies and their defiances, but upwards to the Father Himself. He spoke, not as the Judge that He was to be, not as the Master that He had always been, but as the Redeemer that at that moment He was. He searched for a reason to forgive, and even in that vast ocean of evil His infinite love found it, as love always finds it when it seeks. He allowed the words to be heard, by some at least around Him. That they were words of prayer did not surprise them; those who knew Him were accustomed to His prayer. But this was a prayer to be ever remembered; the prayer of Jesus crucified, for these His executioners, in such a place, at such a time, under such conditions.

> 'And Jesus said
> Father
> Forgive them
> For they know not what they do.'

32. The Second Word : 'This Day.'

We may pass quickly by the incident that follows; evidently the evangelists record it because of the fulfilment of prophecy that it contains. Indeed the twenty-first Psalm dominates much that we are now told of the scene on Calvary; it would seem that the writers have it chiefly in mind when they select the events they choose to mention. The Psalm begins :

THE SECOND WORD

> ' O God, my God, look upon me :
> Why hast thou forsaken me ? '

Later it takes up the theme :

> ' I am a worm and no man :
> The reproach of men and the outcast
> of the people.
> And they that saw have laughed me to scorn :
> They have spoken with the lips and
> wagged the head.
> He hoped in the Lord, let him deliver him :
> Let him save him, seeing he delighted
> in him.
>
> . . . .
>
> Many dogs have encompassed me
> The council of the malignant hath besieged me.
> They have dug my hands and feet
> They have numbered all my bones.
> They have looked and stared upon me :
> They parted my garments among them,
> And upon my vesture they cast lots.'

In the light of this prophecy we may read what the evangelists next tell us. It was about midday :

> ' Then the soldiers
> After they had crucified him
> Took his garments
> And they made four parts
> To every soldier a part
> Casting lots upon them
> What every man should take
> And also his coat
> Now the coat was without seam
> Woven from the top throughout
> They said then to one another
> Let us not cut it
> But let us cast lots upon it
> Whose it shall be
> That the word might be fulfilled
> Which was spoken by the prophet
> They have parted my garments among them
> And upon my vesture they have cast lots

And the soldiers indeed did these things
And it was the third hour
And they crucified him
And they sat down and watched him
And the people stood beholding.'

So briefly, yet with so much detail, have the evangelists put the scene before us; here, more than anywhere else in all the Gospels, the story takes on the action of a drama. Upon the rock by the three crosses are the Roman soldiers, four in number as we are carefully told, behaving in such a way as would seem to show that the crowd was kept from gathering too near. These four men had done their work; for the rest they were too callous to care. Suffering in other men afforded them amusement, as it had amused them an hour before when Jesus lay bleeding beneath the scourge. If they were Romans, their betters could find a Roman holiday in the butchering of gladiators, and they could follow their example; if they were Syrians, for the Roman army in the East was recruited from them, they were trained in a school of cruelty even more appalling. Besides, they had other things to occupy them than the mere agony of criminals. The Victim's clothes lay on the rock where He had been stripped; they were the perquisite of His executioners. They shared the clothes among themselves, shaking their dice over them for him who should have first choice. The long robe was too good to be torn in pieces. They tossed their dice for it apart from the rest; that seamless garment which has meant so much, in fact and in symbol, to succeeding Christian ages.

Below the rock, between it and the city wall, ran the narrow road from the hill country of Judæa, and Samaria and Galilee beyond, to the city gate. Within the gate was the bazaar; there was therefore much coming and going by that route, but chiefly at that hour, and on that busy day, there was more coming than going. Along that road the crowd that had come out of the gate following the procession had been made to halt; now that the worst had been done it could say and do no more. But there were the passers-by, men who cared little for these commotions, men to whom religion of any kind was only a nuisance; intent on their own affairs, their business and their merchandise, they were still not sorry to hear that another religious mischief-maker had been silenced. They cared nothing for the Kingship of Jesus, it had no money value; the title of the Son of God meant little to them, it was not in their vocabulary. They were busy men and practical; good Jews it was true, but Judaism meant to them, for the most part, the paying of dues, and the social status attached to belonging to the synagogue. But though they made nothing of religion, they could willingly take part in the cry against one to whom it meant much, and it was easy to find words to revile Him. This Man, so they were told as they passed through the crowd, had threatened to destroy their Temple, their national monument, one of the glories of the world, worth untold gold. Whatever other charges were brought against Him, such a one deserved to be crucified; and they passed Him by, each hurling his own particular insult, joining in the abuse of the mob, careless of justice or injustice, for justice was suspended when religion was concerned. Justice was a matter of business.

> ' And they that passed by blasphemed him
> Wagging their heads and saying
> Vah thou that destroyest the temple of God
> And in three days buildest it up again
> Save thy own self
> If thou be the Son of God
> Come down from the cross.'

But apart from the common herd, which here, as everywhere, knew little what it did, and whose numbers, from many indications, were not overwhelming, there were those who had been most responsible for that morning's work,

> ' The chief priests
> With the scribes and ancients.'

These were gathered, some by the rock, but not too near lest they should be contaminated; others on the city wall beyond, from which they could look down on their Victim as He hung in His agony beneath them. They, too, had at last achieved their heart's desire and could do no more. It had all come so suddenly, the collapse of their enemy had been so complete, they could scarcely yet trust in their success. For long they had sought His death and He had always escaped and defied them. He had told them plainly that He would lay down His life when He chose, and not one moment sooner. He had called them, openly before all men, 'a wicked and adulterous generation'; He had pronounced 'Woe' upon them, and warned others against them, because of their hypocrisy. In their own domain, the Temple court itself, He had defied their authority; in that same court He had fought them with their own weapons, till they dared ask Him no more questions. Once He had warned them that they saw, however they affected not to see. They saw, but they would not believe, and the fault, the guilt was theirs:

> 'If you were blind
> You should not have sin
> But now you say : we see
> Your sin remaineth.'
>
> John ix, 41.

Now at last they had Him wholly at their mercy, and the mockery they had not dared to use before they poured out upon Him, 'full measure, flowing over'. Not even in the court of Caiphas had they been so bold; then He had still warned and threatened. But He would not answer them now; of that, by this time in the day, they were confident. He would not come down from the Cross; the way He had submitted to them, all that day and all the night before, assured them that at last His power had been broken. He had worked miracles before, that could not be denied; now they had proof enough that all were mere tricks. For if He saved others, much more should He be able to save Himself. They had asked Him for a sign, and He had refused to give it; now, if He so chose, He might give one which would compel all the world to believe. If He were the Christ, if He were the King of Israel, if He were the Son of God, let Him give a sign which would be beyond all question. He had spoken of the sign of Jonas the Prophet; He had used empty words about rebuilding the Temple in three days; here was a sign more tangible, more convincing; let Him save Himself from death. Let Him come down from the Cross and they would believe; they did not add that if He raised His dead body from the tomb they would not. Or again He had called God His Father. He had said the Father was always with Him; He had claimed the protection of that Father and His legions of angels; in the security of the Father's care He had put Himself above their own father, Abraham. He and the Father were one. Now was the occasion to vindicate His claim ; now, surely, or never. If God the Father had a special care for Him, let God the Father deliver Him from His death-bed of shame. That would be a miracle indeed ; that would be a sign that none could controvert.

> ' In like manner the chief priests
> With the scribes and ancients
> Mocking derided him saying
> He saved others
> Himself he cannot save
> If he be the Christ
> The King of Israel
> If he be the Christ
> The Son of God
> Let him now come down from the cross
> That we may see
> And believe
> He trusted in God
> Let him now deliver him
> If he will have him
> For he said
> I am the Son of God.'

So the cries continued, even from these usually self-controlled men ; and they were all the more vehemently uttered because behind them there was still the haunting fear that this Man whom they had crucified might yet accept their challenge. But in answer to all their cries the King of Israel, the Son of God, said and did nothing. Who does not know that man is at his noblest, or has the opportunity of being at his noblest, when he is most beaten and down ? Then may he prove, as at no other time, his endurance, his magnanimity, the depths of his generosity and love. And if the ages to come were to be stamped with this ideal, if His elect, the greatest of the sons of men, were to be persecuted even unto death by their brethren, then it behoved the Leader of them all to give them an example, to go before them all in shame and suffering. Not by coming down from the Cross, but by remaining on it till the last drop of blood was shed ; not by yielding to His enemies' demands, but by fulfilling to the last iota the will of His Father, would He prove Himself the first among the children of men, the Lord and Master of the world, the Son of God. Not Jesus the Judge and Vindicator, but Jesus the Lover and He crucified, would be the glory of His saints, and the power that would transform the world.

Lastly the Roman soldiery, the executioners and the guard, took up the insults hurled at Jesus by these leaders of Israel about them. Already in the courtyard of the Prætorium they had had their sport with this King; the title they had fixed above His head gave them cause for endless merriment. Death such as this was the only fate that pseudo-kings deserved. Indeed it was good to see Him in agony; to watch His face turned upward, as if the sight of this sordid and unfeeling world were too much for Him, to trace the streams of blood that flowed from Him and bespattered the ground. They lifted their goblets to the King as they sat on the rock beneath Him; they invited Him to share their liquor with them; He who had eaten and drunk with publicans and sinners might not disdain to drink with soldiers of the guard. They held a cup before His lips as the blood flowed from between them, shouting the while in His face:

'King of the Jews
Save thyself.'

But perhaps the abuse that cut deepest into the heart of Jesus on the Cross was that which came from the crosses on either side of Him. From Roman soldiers He could expect no better treatment, though even from them, before the tragedy was over, He was to receive His meed of honour. From the elders and the leaders of Israel He was reaping only that which He had reaped from the beginning; though by them, too, by friend and enemy alike, He would be treated worthily at the end. But there was one class to whom He had always been drawn, for whom He had always had a peculiar fascination. He had been known in life as 'the friend of publicans and sinners'; He had risked His very reputation for their sakes; only this morning He had been classed with them, 'a malefactor', as if the fact had required no proof. Often in His life by word and deed He had defended them; He had declared that such as they would enter the Kingdom when the more self-righteous would be cast out. He had spoken parables which had all proclaimed His predilection for the downtrodden; for the prayer of the Publican, for the broken Prodigal, for the Lost Sheep that He would seek at whatsoever cost to Himself. And in return, though in His lifetime He received insult from others in plenty, there is no record that He was ever insulted by publicans, or sinners, or the outcast. As, at the beginning, men of this type had gathered round John the Baptist, so had they come to Him. There had always been understanding; whatever their state, they had always known Him as a friend.

And yet at this moment even that consolation seemed to be denied Him; for the first time these His beloved turned against Him.

> ' And the selfsame thing the thieves
> That were crucified with him
> Reproached him with
> And reviled him.'

If He was, as men reported, ' the friend of sinners ', if He had said :
> ' Come to me
> All you that labour and are burthened
> And I will refresh you ',

had He not now an unmatched occasion to prove the truth of His words? As they, too, writhed in their agony on each side of Him, though stupefied in part by the drink that had been given to them, they joined in the cursing of the crowd :

> ' If thou be the Christ
> Save thyself
> And us.'

Still, as from others, so from sinners, recognition came at last; indeed, since in life and in death He had given most to them, so from them He received the one consolation of Calvary. One of the convicts continued his abuse; the other grew silent. He had heard the prayer :

> ' Father
> Forgive them
> For they know not what they do.'

They were strange words to come from the mouth of a condemned and convicted criminal; stranger still from one who was said to be a King. But they were words of prayer, and prayer became a dying man: would that he, too, could pray, and could go to the God of his fathers, to the bosom of Abraham, with some sort of contrition in his heart, with some word of hope on his lips. He ceased his own raillery; if he could, he would check the abuse of his comrade. His arguments might not be convincing; they might be confused, but his soul was in his words and they would say what he had in mind.

> ' And one of these robbers
> Who were hanging
> Blasphemed him saying
> If thou be the Christ
> Save thyself
> And us
> But the other answering rebuked him saying
> Neither dost thou fear God
> Seeing thou art under the same condemnation.'

It has often been noticed in the life of Jesus how a grace accepted has been the harbinger of another. Jesus led His own to Himself step by step. We have seen it in Simon and Nathanael, in the first days by the Jordan; in the Roman centurion at Capharnaum, after the Sermon on the Mount; in the Woman who was a sinner at Magdala; in the Rich Young Man who came to Him in Perœa, even though at the final step he failed. Nay, more; when He was asked for anything, when any confessed Him as He would be confessed, how generously Jesus poured Himself out, beyond the suppliant's dreams! A paralytic came to Him to be healed; Jesus sent him away, healed in both soul and body. A poor creature fell at His feet penitent; He made of her an intimate friend. An apostle confessed Him to be the true Son of God; He made him the head of His universal church.

So, most conspicuously of all, as if He would set this last seal on all He had said and done for sinners, was it here with this dying criminal. The man had seen and had felt compassion for the dying Sufferer beside him; he had felt compassion and had defended Him. At once he received his reward; there came to him the sight of his own guilt, and the grace of contrition came with it. And with contrition his eyes were opened:

> 'Blessed are the clean of heart
> For they shall see God.'

He saw his own guilt and the justice of his sentence; he saw the injustice that was being done to the Man beside him. Then came another grace, another vision, revealed to him 'not by flesh and blood, but by the Father who is in heaven', as, long ago, it had been revealed to Simon Peter. Not only was Jesus innocent; being innocent, He must indeed be that which He claimed to be. He was a King, of a kingdom not of this world, of a kingdom which He would enter, even through the gates of death. Others had asked that they might sit, the one on His right hand, the other on His left, in that kingdom; the penitent criminal had no such ambitions. He was hanging on His right hand now, that was honour enough. For the rest, if afterwards in His kingdom this King would but remember His companion in death, he would be more than glad to die. Already he knew in whom he believed, he knew in whom he trusted; even on the cross He who was sent 'for the lost sheep of the house of Israel' had not failed the sinner who looked up to Him, had gone after one and had found it. We may watch the growth of grace, step by step, from light and understanding to yet further light, as the crucified penitent continues:

> '(1) And we indeed justly
> For we have received the due reward of our deeds
>   (2) But this man hath done no evil.
>   (3) And he said to Jesus
>   Lord
>   Remember me
> When thou shalt come into thy kingdom.'

It was indeed a tremendous act of faith, of the kind specially dear to Our Lord Jesus Christ, and in a special way it must be rewarded. As He had rewarded His Mother's faith long ago at Cana; as He had praised and crowned the Roman soldier's faith at Capharnaum; as the Syro-Phœnician's faith had been honoured by Him in the country about Tyre; as Simon's, for his brave confession; so now, for this unique recognition of Him, this solitary voice among all the execration, Jesus would reward this man in His own lavish way, full measure, flowing over. 'Remember him?' That alone would have been much; it is all that a dying man will often ask of a friend. But it was not enough for the heart of Jesus Christ. 'Remember him in the kingdom?' The very word 'kingdom' no longer satisfies Him. Jesus turned His aching head towards His companion in suffering. He spoke with that emphatic introduction which He had always been wont to use whenever He proclaimed a solemn truth. From His throne on Calvary He spoke and acted and bestowed His largess like a King.

> 'Then Jesus said to him
> Amen I say to thee
> This day
> Thou shalt be with me
> In paradise.'

It was language worthy of a conqueror, spoken on a field where a battle had been won; it was a reward worthy of Jesus Christ, the King of Israel, the Son of God. From a criminal, in an instant, to a saint, the first of the New Dispensation; with this unique distinction granted to no other, that he was canonized before his death.

33. The Third Word : 'Behold thy son.'

By this time the crowd, as is the wont of crowds, was becoming weary of its own ribaldry. We have noticed how throughout the morning its number could never have been overwhelming; during all this turmoil in the upper quarter of the city, business in the streets went on as before. Since the final condemnation by Pilate the mob had dwindled still more; the morning was advancing, there was much to be done that day, the chief interest in this trial was over, many did not care to be involved in what was to follow. Both before the Roman Governor, and here round the knoll of Calvary, they were the cries of the leaders of the people that were chiefly heard; the rest followed after, taking up the cry from them, with that brutal, irresponsible cruelty which is common with a mob, but with thoughtlessness more than with malice.

But even the leaders, too, were beginning to tire of their work. They had attained their end; they had seen their Victim crucified before their eyes; they had secured the death of His body, and there was no more that they could do. At once there had come that sense of satiety, of disgust, of self-contempt, which is the sequel of realized guilt. They awoke from their delirium of hatred, and they despised themselves for what they had done. Jesus of Nazareth had been put to shame before all the world, but in their hearts they knew well with whom the shame lay. For a time, as we have seen, they made a brave show, but their very vehemence betrayed them. They shouted and blasphemed round Calvary more violently, more recklessly, than ever they had done before, even during all that day, but the bravado could not endure. The Figure on the cross that deigned no reply, not even recognition, made all their insult hollow. Already many had begun to leave the scene; they hastened to distract themselves with other things from the thought of the ghastly spectre that now haunted them. It was the eve of the great Sabbath Day; both in the Temple and in the bazaar there was much to be done before evening, prayers to be offered in thanksgiving, offerings to be purchased and made, for the fulfilment of the Law and the honour of Jehovah.

Hence the crowd around Calvary soon became less turbulent; there was a lull, and the hours began to drag as the onlookers waited for the end. The guard became less careful; they had done their work, which could not be undone, and it mattered little now who approached the criminals. Gradually a group drew near. It consisted chiefly of women; among them S. John mentions three, or it may be four.

> ' Now there stood by the cross of Jesus
> His mother
> And his mother's sister Mary of Cleophas
> And Mary Magdalen.'

We might dwell long on the composition of this group, and the forces that brought them to witness this scene of horror. That His mother should be there does not surprise us, though we may well wonder that such a thing could have been permitted by the most callous of men; a mother, and such a mother, witnessing her Son, and such a Son, bleeding to death before her eyes, dying as a common criminal, with blasphemies hurtling around her, and she could do nothing. It had come at last. During all the three-and-thirty years before she had known that the end would be something terrible. Since the day when she first nursed her Child in the rock-chamber at Bethlehem, and swathed His helpless body, and laid it in the hay in the manger, she had known that through many tribulations her Son must win His way to the throne of David His Father. She had never forgotten what the holy man had said, that day when, in accordance with the Law, she had offered Him to the Father in the Temple.

> ' And Simeon blessed them
> And said to Mary his mother
> Behold this child is set
> For the fall and for the resurrection of many in Israel
> And for a sign which shall be contradicted
> And thy own soul a sword shall pierce
> That out of many hearts
> Thoughts may be revealed.'
>
> Luke ii, 34–35.

She had fled with that Child away into a foreign land, with bloodshed in her wake ; almost from the first the joy of motherhood had been marred by this agony. Her own Child's life had brought death to many children, desolation to many mothers. She had brought Him back from exile in fear and trembling, longing to live in Bethlehem, the home of David, but they dared not ; hiding at last in Nazareth, the village of no repute, lest evil men might again discover Him and seek His life. Once she had lost Him for part of three days ; the memory of that could never be forgotten, it remained as a warning to her, a foreshadowing, of the greater separation that one day must be. Always she had kept it in mind, pondering it in her heart ; always she had feared when and how the end would come. This woman of few words but deep understanding had often prayed :

> ' Father
> If it be possible
> Let this chalice pass from me ' ;

but not before she had also said :

> ' Behold the handmaid of the Lord
> Be it done to me
> According to thy word
> Not my will
> But thine be done.'

When at length after thirty years He had left her, and had gone out to preach the kingdom, her agony had only increased. Twice at least she had been made to wonder whether the end was there. Once in Nazareth His fellow-citizens had sought to take His life, men whom she had known in her daily intercourse, men who had spoken of her as being nothing worth; and she had trembled with fear in her cottage as an angry, blood-seeking crowd hustled Him past her door. Again one day in Capharnaum, when He had been first charged with working 'by Beelzebub, the Prince of devils', there had been trouble in the town, and she had run out to Him, fearing the worst. Since that time she had seen Him, now in exile beyond Galilee, because even there men plotted His death and He was no longer safe; now delaying in Peroea, to avoid His Judæan enemies; now hiding in Ephraim or in the wilderness; when He came up to Jerusalem, never spending a night within its walls. She had noticed all these things; even had no other light been given to her, her mother's heart could not but notice them. Her own Son was hated, by her own people; her own Son's life was in danger; her own Son wept because He was rejected, and her heart bled for Him. She said not a word of her sorrow and her fears to others, as she had said not a word to Joseph of her earliest joys; still within herself

> 'Mary kept all these words
> Pondering them in her heart.'
>
> Luke ii, 19.

Indeed she had long since seen what the inevitable end would be; she had no delusions, like those of the apostles, concerning the founding of a kingdom. If one such as Judas foresaw the coming doom, Mary, the lover of humanity, foresaw it even more. She who had read the Scriptures so well could not fail to have discovered the repeated warnings concerning her Son. Still she had followed wherever He had led; silently waiting in Nazareth, silently watching in Capharnaum, pierced to the heart by every rejection till the last rejection should come. She had followed Him in this last journey to Jerusalem, and now even to Calvary, knowing that so it must be. And it had come at last, here, in this terrible way; and she, the mother who had nursed Him and clothed Him as a Child, could only stand there and do nothing.

There were other women at her side, some at least of those who had been her constant companions during the last two years. They had followed her Son in Galilee, ministering to His wants; now, when they could minister no more, they would at least stay with Him while He died. Among them, we might have been sure beforehand, was Mary Magdalen. A week ago, at the supper in Bethania, she had poured out her precious spikenard upon Him; and when men who understood not complained, He had read her heart more truly. She had done it for His burial; her name should never be forgotten to the end of time. With the group was also the disciple John, the Son of Thunder, the one who claimed for himself that Jesus loved him, and who could presume upon that love. Little more than a week before, on the way up from Peræa, his mother had come to the King that soon was to be; she had petitioned of Him that her sons might sit, the one on His right hand, the other on His left, in the kingdom. He had warned them what such an honour might imply; He had told them that it was not His to give, but that it belonged to the Father. Still would He give them what He could; He would give them a share in His chalice. Now He was fulfilling that promise to His beloved John; and even as John drank, though he realized it not, he was standing with his King, on His right hand, in the kingdom.

It would not have been possible for this mighty Lover of mankind to ignore this group of His own that had come so near to be His companions as He lay stretched on His bed of death. Cost what it might to His tortured body, though the blood streamed down and almost blinded Him, His eyes opened and looked at them. We have seen often enough the human love of Jesus Christ; He who had come 'not to destroy but to perfect', had not destroyed the love of man and woman by making it divine. He had dear friends in Bethania:

'Now Jesus loved Martha
And her sister Mary.'

In Peræa, when a young man had come to Him, we were told:

'Jesus looked on him and loved him.'

When Lazarus lay dying, his sisters had appealed to the human heart of Jesus in their message :

'He whom thou lovest is sick' ;
John xi, 3,

and when at length He came to His dead friend's grave, His weeping made those who stood by say :

'Behold how he loved.'
John xi, 36.

During all the early part of this day of suffering we had proof of the love of Him who 'loved His own who were in the world', and 'loved them unto the end'. He had called them 'not servants, but friends' ; He had called them His 'little children'. He had asked them for their love, He had bid them love one another ; when the torrent of sorrow broke over Him, He had asked them, as a friend might ask a friend, not to leave Him, to stay with Him. Even when the worst befell Him, when one of His own turned traitor, even then His human love would not die, but would still call the traitor 'Friend.'

Now on Calvary that human heart was still the same. He saw His mother standing before Him, the 'valiant woman', erect, motionless, almost expressionless, with scarce a tear in her eye. There are 'griefs that lie too deep for tears', and a mother's broken heart is one. If Jesus could say :

'The Father and I are one',

He could say something akin of His relation with His mother. If He could pray, for His own whom He had chosen, that

'They all may be one
In me',

and could ask that where He was they also might be with Him, among them all of none was this more true than of His chosen mother. If He could say :

'Greater love than this no man hath
That he lay down his life for his friend',

He knew that in no one could this be more proved than in His mother. She had given Him life ; she had lived wholly for Him, 'the handmaid of the Lord'; gladly now would she die for Him. Not only would she gladly die ; during these three-and-thirty years they had so lived together, their lives had been so intertwined, the union of mother and son, of son and mother, had been so complete, that, if we speak of nature only, even in death they would not be separated. We have known of those who in life have so grown together that the death of one has been the death of the other. We have known of those whose death has been so terrible that it has caused the death of another. Both of these were being illustrated here. With His death the mother's life was surely ended ; seeing Him die this awful death, when the moment came how could she but die with Him ?

But Jesus would not have that to be ; Mary's hour was not yet come. Though He died for many, yet would He have her live for many, 'that out of many hearts thoughts might be revealed'. There was work yet to be done by her in this valley of tears, and for the sake of that work He would have her live in it yet a little longer. Then must He devise some means to save her. Without Him her life would be a lonely life, lonely unto death unless some object worthy of her love were given to her. He must fill up the void in that mother's heart which His own death would inevitably make ; He must transfer that mighty mother's love to another, give her a foster-child, whom she might cherish, and who in his turn might cherish her, when He was gone. There was John at her side ; John whom He had loved with a special love, whom also He had held to His heart. He would give them to each other. At the Supper He had said to His own :

'In this shall men know that you are my disciples
'If you have love
One for another';

but this love should be even more. He had given a new commandment :

'That you love one another
As I have loved you
That you also love one another.'

Further than this He could not go, but in these two it should be perfectly fulfilled. They should find in each other the love they had hitherto found in Him ; they should give to each other what they could of the love they had hitherto given to Him. Mary's love for John, because of, built upon, like to, the love she gave to Jesus, her Son ; John's love for Mary, because of, like to, his love for Jesus his Lord—it was the perfect consecration, and the consummation, of human love. So, by a new interchange of love, would His mother be saved to live among men yet a little longer ; if she would die of love, by means of love would she survive. So, too, would the disciple whom He loved have, even in this life, an ample reward for all the love he had shown his Master :

> ' Having loved his own that were in the world
> He loved them unto the end.
> When Jesus therefore saw his mother
> And the disciple standing whom he loved
> He said to his mother
> Woman, behold thy son
> After that he saith to the disciple
> Behold thy mother
> And from that hour
> The disciple took her to his own.'

The gift of John to Mary, and of Mary to John, was the last will and testament of Jesus Christ Our Lord. His life He had already given ; His blood He was now pouring out, to its last drop, for all men. In this last gift He gave the only possession that remained ; He bestowed on Mary the motherhood of all mankind, He bestowed on men His own mother, to be theirs, like His Father, through all the coming ages. The type had been fulfilled ; Mary, the new mother of men, was made the second Eve. This was the first-fruit of His bloodshedding.

34. The Fourth Word : ' Why hast Thou forsaken me ? '

There was another reason, besides those we have already given, why the crowd had dwindled away as the hours had drawn on. A strange darkness had come over the sky ; the sun had concealed its face, Nature herself had seemed to hide in shame because of what was being done upon the earth. Who did not know the warning of the Prophet ?

> ' Behold the day of the Lord shall come
> A cruel day
> And full of indignation
> And of wrath and fury
> To lay the land desolate
> And to destroy the sinners thereof out of it
> For the stars of heaven and their brightness
> Shall not display their light
> The sun shall be darkened in his rising
> And the moon shall not shine with her light
> And I will visit the evils of the world
> And against the wicked for their iniquity
> And I will make the pride of infidels to cease
> And will bring down the arrogance of the mighty.'
>
> Isaias xiii, 9–11.

Or the scene portrayed by that other Prophet?

> ' At their presence the earth hath trembled
> The heavens are moved
> The sun and moon are darkened
> And the stars have withdrawn their shining
> And the Lord hath uttered his voice
> Before the face of his army
> For his armies are exceeding great
> For they are strong and execute his word
> For the day of the Lord is great
> And very terrible
> And who can stand it?'
>
> Joel ii, 10–11.

Still had he concluded with words of hope:

> ' Now therefore saith the Lord
> Be converted to me with all your heart
> In fasting and in weeping and in mourning
> And rend your hearts and not your garments
> And turn to the Lord your God
> For he is gracious and merciful
> Patient and rich in mercy
> And ready to repent of the evil
> Who knoweth but he will return
> And forgive

> And leave a blessing behind him
> Sacrifice and libation to the Lord your God.'
> Joel ii, 12-14.

But be the cause and significance of this midday darkness what it may, we can see through the gloom the rest of the crowd already beginning to turn homeward; we can hear what remained of noise and clamour dying away, weakening perhaps even to a dread silence. As the evangelist at a later moment tells us:

> ' And all the multitude of them
> That were come together to that sight
> And saw the things that were done
> Returned
> Striking their breasts.'

There seem to have been left on the spot few beside the guard, and the groups of real sympathizers, who, as we have seen, had been permitted now to draw near. The city wall behind them shut them off from the busy world; beyond that wall, a few hundred yards away, there was buying and selling in the bazaar as if nothing unwonted were taking place on the hill of criminal executions. The end was drawing near; those who knew the signs of death could have no doubt of it; though the two by His side might linger on, for Him the loss of blood since the agony in Gethsemane, the fasting since the evening before, the unrest of that night, the torture of that day, the tearing of the body at the scourging, the abuse and mauling by the mob, had utterly exhausted His strength, and death could not be far off.

Suddenly, in the midst of the silence, Jesus raised His face to heaven and was heard to pray. He spoke this time in the ancient language of the Prophets and the Psalms, which, perhaps, most of those within hearing would not have understood. But they would have guessed, and rightly, that He was taking His prayer from the Sacred Books; He was using the beginning of the Psalm which has already been given, that most vivid foreshadowing, even to details, of all He was now enduring. He spoke in a loud voice, louder than could have been expected from one so near to death:

> ' And about the ninth hour
> Jesus cried out with a loud voice saying
> Eloi Eloi lamma sabacthani ?
> Which is being interpreted
> My God, my God, why hast thou forsaken me ? '

But clearly the prayer was more than the mere quoting of a Psalm or the fulfilment of a prophecy ; it was the full expression of His soul, in that open, simple way with which we have long been familiar. In the Temple, early in the week, we have heard Him cry in a moment of weariness :

> ' Now is my soul troubled
> And what shall I say ?
> Father
> Save me from this hour.'

And previously in Judæa, in a similar moment of distress and opposition, He had exclaimed :

> ' Father
> I give thee thanks
> That thou hast hid these things
> From the wise and prudent
> And hast revealed them to little ones.'

That we may understand even a little of the meaning of this prayer of Jesus on the cross, it will be well to recall a feature of His life and character which is easily forgotten. Jesus Christ, throughout His life, was what we would call in our human language a lonely Man. We need not dwell on the years of His upbringing, when, as is sufficiently clear, this Child had no companions of like outlook to His own ; nor on the long years at Nazareth, for thirty years are long, after which the best that could be said of Him by those who had been most with Him was only this :

> ' Is not this the carpenter ? '

All these years He had been to them the ' Carpenter ' and nothing more. Yet were they the years of youth and early manhood, in which He had ' grown in wisdom, age, and grace ', in which He had looked from the hills across Esdrælon to Samaria, and had dreamed His dreams, and had longed to begin His course. They were the years in which He had longed too, as youth will long, that there might be some in Nazareth with whom He could speak about the great things in His soul. But there had been none ; to them He was the ' Carpenter ', and that was enough ; indeed it was reason why He should not be more, so that when at last He revealed Himself

' They were scandalized
Because of him ' ;

and He could only comment, as one who had had long experience of it, that a prophet was not received in his own country. Jesus was a Nazarene ; Jesus was only Mary's son ; Jesus was the village carpenter ; Jesus had had no schooling ; Jesus could not be of any moment ; such was the reception He met with from those with whom He had lived thirty years. Then the life of Jesus in Nazareth had been a lonely one indeed.

In Galilee it had not been much better. Many at first had followed Him, but He was not deceived ; He had told the crowds that they did not realize who He was that lived among them. Some said He was Elias come back ; some that He was a prophet ; some that He was John the Baptist risen from the dead ; even when it almost seemed that they might have realized, when they called Him ' the prophet who was to come into the world ', they proved that they knew Him not when they would have Him proclaimed their King. The sense of lonely disappointment is seldom absent from any page of the Galilæan story ; it reaches its climax when, after all He had done, He stood in the synagogue at Capharnaum and watched the crowds of His hitherto admirers vanish from before Him like snow beneath the sun.

' After this
Many of his disciples went back
And walked no more with Him.'

In Jerusalem from the beginning it had been even worse ; Jesus could never have come into the city without feeling that sense of loneliness which studied ignoring and contempt always provides. To those in authority, so far as they could make it so, He was just nothing at all ; the more His person became manifest, the more He was treated with contempt.

' How doth this man know letters
   Having never learnt ?

   . . . .

We know this man whence he is
But when the Christ cometh
No man knoweth whence he is.

   . . . .

Hath any of the rulers believed in him
   Or of the Pharisees ?

   . . . .

Search the scriptures and see
That out of Nazareth a prophet riseth not.

   . . . .

Do not we say well
That thou art a Samaritan
And hast a devil ?

   . . . .

He hath a devil and is mad
Why hear you him ? '

So the effort to suppress Him by consistent contempt had gone on whenever He had appeared in Jerusalem ; and thus far at least it had succeeded, that if in Galilee He could say He had ' not where to lay His head ', in the Holy City it would seem that He never dared spend a night.

Even among His own, whom He had trained, with whom He had lived night and day, there was always that distance which made Him feel His separation.

' Do you not yet understand ? '

He had said to them once on the Lake of Galilee. How often He had blamed them for their lack of faith, for their presumption, for their misinterpretation of His words. Sometimes there is almost visible in His soul a struggle between love longing for their friendship, and love falling back upon itself disappointed. Even at the Supper He had been compelled to say :

' How long a time have I been with you
And you have not known me ! '

Which was followed in an hour by the lonely appeal :

> ' Stay you here
> And watch with me.
> Could you not watch one hour with me ? '

Nor can it be said that in all this Jesus was above the sense of loneliness felt by ordinary men. Like other men He was hurt by desertion, by slander, by ingratitude, by failure, by treachery ; by any of those things which set a man alone, looking for one to grieve together with Him and there is none. He seldom complained ; yet when this lot befell Him He allowed Himself to speak. When the crowd deserted Him in Capharnaum, He turned to His own and asked :

> ' Will you also go away ? '

and we can easily catch the tone in which the words were uttered. When men found fault with His companionship He asked :

> ' The Son of Man came eating and drinking
> And you say
> Behold a glutton
> And a drinker of wine.'

When He had healed ten together, and only one thought to thank Him, He enquired :

> ' Were not ten made clean ?
> And where are the nine ? '

In the supper-room the night before, we remember the note on which the discourse of love almost ended :

> ' Behold the hour cometh
> And it is now come
> That you shall be scattered
> Every man to his own
> And shall leave me alone.'

Indeed so constant is this sense of loneliness, of disappointment, of separation, that S. John does not hesitate to make it the background of his Gospel, while the others fall back upon it as a characteristic which stands out like a mountain from a plain.

> ' He was in the world
> And the world was made by him

>   And the world knew him not
>   He came into his own
>   And his own received him not.'

So says S. John; and S. Matthew and S. Luke echo it in the cry of pain:

>   'Jerusalem, Jerusalem
>   Thou that killest the prophets
>   And stonest them that are sent unto thee
>   How often would I have gathered together thy children
>   As the hen doth gather her chickens
>   Under her wings
>   And thou wouldst not.'
>   Matthew xxiii, 37.

And yet, through all this disappointment and loneliness, there was one consolation on which He could always rely. If S. John is the evangelist of the rejection of Jesus, he is also the evangelist of the Fatherhood; if he repeats the lesson of man's ingratitude, still a hundred and sixteen times the Father's name is repeated, as the one support against every failure. And S. Matthew, in this point at least most akin to S. John, puts 'the Father' over forty times on the lips of Jesus, His constant and abiding companion when all else left Him.

>   'Father, I give thee thanks.
>   Father, save me from this hour.
>   Father, the hour is come.
>   Father, if it be possible.
>   I and the Father are one.
>   I am not alone
>   The Father is with me.'

So, throughout the whole story of His life do we find Him falling back on this union with the Father; He had reason to be sad, but this certainty that such was the will of the Father, that the Father saw all, that the Father, seeing all, could nevertheless forgive and restore all in Him, was the prayer that had always held Him up, and made Him go on giving, even to this last moment.

But now, for a moment at least, even this support is taken from Him. The night before, at the gate of the garden, with the howling persecutors confronting Him, He had said:

> 'The chalice which my Father hath given me
> Shall I not drink it?'

Now we learn what the dregs of that chalice contained. Other things He had endured since the Agony, and had uttered not a word of complaint. Judas had betrayed Him, and He had responded with a question only; the mob had laid hands on Him, and He had contented Himself with the same; a question, again, was all He gave to the soldier who struck Him in the face. Peter denied Him, and He 'looked on' him, and nothing more; Annas, Caiphas, Pilate had consciously maligned Him, He had been stabbed in the back, He had been stabbed through the heart, and there had been no word of complaint; there had been only an unflinching assertion of the truth. Physical suffering He had endured in plenty; at that moment it racked His torn body from head to foot; but the Man of Sorrows, the Friend of the blind and the maimed, who had invited sufferers to come to Him and He would refresh them, was not one to shrink from physical pain.

There was an agony far worse than pain; one which, had we not His own word for it, we might have judged to have been impossible. It had been anticipated in part in the Garden, where He had identified Himself with the sinner, where He had been 'made sin', as S. Paul boldly puts it; but even there He had been able to appeal to the 'Father' for relief. Now He is permitted to feel the worst consequences of that identification, the agony of hell itself; Jesus Christ is permitted to endure the sense of separation from, abandonment by, the Father. It is no longer 'Father, if it be possible'; it is 'My God, why hast thou deserted me?' He has carried man's griefs to the last degree, He has drunk the cup of man's miseries to the dregs. He has allowed Himself to know by experience all that man endures, even that greatest distress, that 'dark night of the soul', which few souls of prayer escape, but which is known at its worst only by those who have come to closest union with Him. At other times in His life, on fifty occasions and more, we have seen Him the Man of prayer; now, at this last moment, He hangs before us the model of the desolate

> 'Who in the days of his flesh
> With a strong cry and tears
> Offering up prayers and supplications

> To him that was able to save him from death
> Was heard for his reverence
> And whereas indeed he was the Son of God
> He learned obedience
> By the things which he suffered
> And being consummated
> He became to all that obey him
> The cause of eternal salvation
> Called by God a high priest
> According to the order of Melchisedech.'
>
> Hebrews v, 7-10.

35. The Fifth Word : ' I thirst.'

The Roman guard knew no Hebrew, unless it were a word and a phrase which every soldier learns when serving in a foreign land. Still less did they know the language or meaning of prayer. Naturally, then, when they heard their dying Victim call on His Father by the name ' Eloi ', they understood nothing of what He said. They knew something of the myths and fables of these despised Jews about them, and had learnt to laugh at their credulity. There was a fable of a prophet Elias ; the sound they caught from the lips of Jesus brought the story to their minds. Elias, these Jews said, had been taken to heaven in a chariot of fire and perhaps this Man, who had called Himself a prophet, was praying that the same might now be done to Him ; perhaps He was asking that Elias might come as he had gone, and take Him out of His misery.

> ' And some of them that stood there and heard said
> Behold this man calleth for Elias.'

Meanwhile Jesus continued His prayer. Life seemed now to have no further meaning for Him ; this earth had become indeed to Him ' the valley of this death ', and He longed, now, for the moment when He might leave it. But there was another prophecy yet to be fulfilled, one more sign which later His followers might add to the rest, when at last they would see and believe. It had been written by the Psalmist :

> ' Thou knowest my reproach,
> And my confusion and my shame
> In thy sight are all they that afflict me :
> My heart hath expected reproach and misery.

And I looked for one that would grieve together with me,
And there was none
And for one that would comfort me,
And I found none.
And they gave me gall for my food,
And in my thirst they gave me vinegar to drink.'
Psalm lxviii, 20–22.

That last prophecy must now be accomplished and all would be done. He would suggest its accomplishment; by so doing He would remind men for all time of a further agony He endured, perhaps the greatest that man can endure, death from sheer thirst. He had known thirst before; indeed He had been careful to let it be seen throughout His life how He suffered from the needs of the body. Almost the first thing we heard of Him was that He was hungry; so hungry, so craving for food, that Satan himself thought to take advantage of His weakness. He was weary at a well on the roadside; more weary than the companions who were with Him. He had sat down at that well, and had asked a stranger woman to give Him to drink; the only time recorded in the Gospel story when He had asked anyone for anything. In Capharnaum at times the crowds had so thronged upon Him that He had been unable to take His meals; He had slept, weary on a boat, and a storm had not awakened Him. If Jesus could say of Himself that He had ' not where to lay His head ', perhaps, too, He could also have said that He had not where to get food and drink; for these He depended on what men gave Him. For some He would turn water into wine; for others He would multiply bread so that all might eat; for Himself He was content to sit by a well, and say to a passer-by:

' Give me to drink.'

Nor is it without significance that He had often used the relieving of thirst as an illustration in teaching. Men speak of what they know and experience; Jesus then knew thirst in His missionary tours, He knew the agony with which He would die. Hence when He spoke of the torture of a soul condemned, it is this torture of thirst on which He dwells:

' Father Abraham
Have mercy on me
And send Lazarus

> That he may dip the tip of his finger in water
> To cool my tongue
> For I am tortured in this flame.'

When He spoke of charity to others, it was under the figure of 'a cup of water' given in His name. He promised heaven to those who gave Him to drink; in the height of His preaching in the Temple the climax seems to be reached when He cries:

> 'If any man thirst
> Let him come to me
> And drink.'

Of all His sufferings this was the only one of which Jesus spoke during the whole of His Passion. In a true sense it was the greatest of them all, yet was it also one which might easily have passed unnoticed. Travellers tell us of the horrors of thirst, the one torture which drives a man mad; often on a sick-bed, especially where there has been a great loss of blood, we may see the almost insatiable craving to drink. And in the East, in places barren and salt, under a broiling sun, we may taste something of the agony of thirst which will readily bring home to us why Jesus chose the cup of water as His emblem of charity, why He chose the quenching of thirst as the character of His own deep love. Of this, then, He would remind His own at this moment. The loss of blood, the long fast, the all but bursting heart, had indeed produced in Him a thirst almost intolerable. Moreover the scriptures must be fulfilled, and there were yet more things to be done. We recognize the intended deliberation in the evangelist's narrative, as if he would say: this was no complaint, rather was it a command.

> 'Afterwards
> Jesus knowing that all things were accomplished
> That the Scriptures might be fulfilled
> Said: I thirst.'

These at least were words which the soldiers and those about Him understood. But what could His friends do to relieve Him? The women who in Galilee had followed Him, and had ministered to His wants, stood there now, empty-handed. Mary Magdalen, at whose house He had supped in Bethania, would gladly now have left the bleeding feet to which she clung and served Him, but she had nothing now to give. Mary, His mother, at whose prayer, for others' sake, He had once turned water into wine, was helpless now. Only the soldiers might do something. They had with them their own coarse wine, to the Jewish taste more vinegar than wine, with which they regaled themselves during the long hours of watching. There was a sponge lying on the ground; crucifying criminals was soiling work, and executioners needed at times to wash their hands and perhaps their faces. A soldier picked up the sponge and put it in the jar of wine. He took also a stick, a hyssop-stalk of a foot long, not more, and fixed the soaked sponge upon it. He held it up to the blood-stained lips of Jesus, not two feet above him. Jesus sipped a little of the liquor from the sponge; before, when He was offered drink to stupefy Him He had refused it, but this He did not refuse. By accepting it He would reward this last act of charity, even though it came from an executioner, though others about Him might still murmur in contempt:

' Stay
Let us see whether Elias will come
To take him down from the cross.'

Jesus would pay honour to the man who helped Him in His hour of distress; for to have been the last man on earth to serve the dying Lord, was not this honour indeed?

' For whosoever shall give you to drink
A cup of water in my name
Amen I say to you
He shall not lose his reward.'

36. The Sixth and Seventh Words.

All was now completed. The prophecies, one by one, had been fulfilled; the will of His Father had been done to the last iota.

' Did you not know
That I must be about my Father's business?'

had been the first words with which He had begun His career; often He had reminded those about Him, friends and enemies alike, that to carry out the will of His Father was the beginning, and was to be the end, of His whole life. It mattered not whether what He did was to succeed or not; He could look back now from His cross on Calvary, and realize how, in the eyes of men, His life had been one long failure. Nazareth, 'where He had been brought up', was 'scandalized because of Him', and twice cast Him out. Capharnaum, 'His own city', 'walked with Him no more'. Corozain and Bethsaida, 'where He had done most of His miracles', had in the end to be condemned. Galilee was made unsafe for Him, and He had gone out from it into exile. Jerusalem had never received Him; from the very beginning there had always been those in the city who sought His life. He was the outcast of men, He was the scandal of His own; he who would have championed the cause of Jesus Christ at that moment would have been hard put to it to find an argument in His defence.

Nevertheless His work had been done, and He could look on it all with content. His Father had willed that He should be the satisfaction for the race of fallen men, and He had poured out His blood for them all; not one drop only, which would have sufficed, but would never have satisfied His love. His work on earth was over; He had run His course, He had now been baptized with that baptism for which He had longed. Already at the Supper He had prayed:

'Father
The hour is come
Glorify thy Son
That thy Son may glorify thee
I have glorified thee on the earth
I have finished the work
Thou gavest me to do
And now glorify thou me
O Father
With thyself
With the glory which I had before the world was
With thee.'

After that prayer there had still remained the chalice to be drunk, and now He had drunk it to the dregs. He had said all, and could say no more; He had done all, and could do no more; He had given His all, and there was no more to give. He could now lay down His life, the final and supreme act of love; for, as He had proclaimed on many occasions, that, too, should be a deliberate act of His own. He who had commanded life and death for others could command them for Himself; He could lay down His life and could take it up again. And this should be made manifest to those who witnessed His last moments. He would not come down from the cross at their bidding; instead, by the way He died, He would prove to those who were open to conviction that He was more than man. He looked back on the past; it was now 'the fullness of time', the history of the ages converged on that moment. He looked into the future; from the foot of that cross the new world would begin. During the last hours He had successively passed sentence on Annas, and Caiphas, and Pilate; on enemies, on friends, and on all the world; now He would pass sentence on Himself. With the voice of no dying man, but with the loud voice of a conqueror, He would pronounce His own claim, His own right to reward. In spite of the utter desolation through which He was passing, He could trust Himself to His Father.

> ' When Jesus therefore had taken the vinegar
> He said
> It is consummated
> And Jesus again crying with a loud voice said
> Into thy hands
> I commend my spirit
> And saying this
> Bowing down his head
> He gave up the ghost.'

The most tremendous deed that has ever been done upon this earth was completed; the most tremendous crime, turned into the most tremendous act of love, love alike of God and of men. Jesus Christ, the Son of God made man, was dead, and the earth bore His dead body through the infinite spaces. Nature, that had long 'waited for the revelation of the sons of God'; nature, that had 'groaned and travailed in pain even till now' (Romans viii, 19, 22), when all was over, was itself shaken :

> ' And behold the sun was darkened
> And the veil of the temple was rent in two
> In the midst
> From the top even to the bottom
> And the earth quaked
> And the rocks were rent
> And the graves opened

And many bodies of the Saints that had slept
Arose
And coming out of the tombs
After his resurrection
Came into the Holy City
And appeared to many.'

CHAPTER XI

37. The End.

(a) *The Burial.*

WE may glance quickly through the rest of the scene on Calvary, for it has little more to teach us of that which we set out to learn. The crowd has dispersed; for some, insult and blasphemy had no further meaning; for others, remorse was already gnawing at their hearts. They must leave the place and distract themselves with other occupations; they must throw themselves into preparations for the great feast; they must forget their own consciences in the celebrations of deliverance on the morrow's great Sabbath Day. The guards only need remain, the Roman soldiers with their centurion, to whom the morrow meant nothing; if for nothing else, at least they must stay to keep off the pariah dogs and vultures that would soon hover around. Beyond them, at the foot of the rock, a few stragglers still seemed to linger; but these were clearly not of those who had done this 'just Man' to death. These were evidently genuine mourners; these were some who cared for the Man who was dead; the guards need have no fear of them.

We are told how the Roman centurion with his men was affected by the transformation around them. A few moments before all had been turmoil and confusion; now all was quiet, it was more than the peace of death. From His cross above them the Man who was dead seemed yet to reign; His enemies were scattered, His friends were free to draw near, His last words had been words of authority, independent of all that had been said or done to Him. Even these Roman soldiers were moved; they were stirred to something akin to faith as they contrasted this Man with the rabble that had done Him to death. Be He who He might, He was more than they; and they

'Glorified God saying
Indeed this man was the Son of God.'

We may reasonably ask whether this further light and grace, this gift to be the first to confess Jesus Christ after He was dead, was due to the last act of charity these Roman soldiers had done to Him. It had always been the way with Jesus Christ. Had He not said that not a cup of water should be given in His name but it should have its reward? In the early days a Samaritan woman had given Him to drink, and in return He had bestowed on her the light to ask:

'Is not this the Messias?'

Now Roman soldiers had again given Him to drink, and the reward He gave them was the same:

'Indeed this man was the Son of God.'

We are further told how

'All the multitude of them
That were come together to that sight
Returned striking their breasts.'

These were the mere onlookers, the multitude of those in the city who had often heard Jesus and had wondered; who had asked each other questions, as S. John many times points out, and had gone away half convinced. Now the grace won by the death of the Light of the world was already being poured out. The prayer of Jesus was already being heard; already His prophecy was being fulfilled, that when He was lifted up from the earth He would draw all things to Himself. In fifty days from then Simon Peter would be able to appeal to that same multitude, and they would listen to him.

'And there were added in that day
About three thousand souls.'

Lastly we are told of the genuine mourners; of the women who formerly had followed Him and ministered to Him in Galilee; who had come up with Him to Jerusalem, and now from a distance stood and beheld this collapse of all that life had begun to mean to them. Only three women are mentioned by name; but after their names it is added that

> ' All his acquaintance
> And the women
> Stood afar off
> Beholding these things.'

Some of these, as we have seen, had been close by the cross before He died, for the same names appear in both places. In the meantime the guard had removed them to a distance, all the more because of what was about to be done. For it was the eve of the Paschal Sabbath, and before the sun set the criminals must be dead, and their bodies removed. A hurried message was sent across the city to the Governor. Two of the victims lingered on, and there was as yet no sign of their dying; a strong man might hang crucified for two and even three days. It was requested that their deaths might be hastened by the usual process, the breaking of their legs. The permission was given and the cruel act was carried out. But Jesus was already dead; to break His legs there was no need. Only to make sure, perhaps to convince any doubting onlookers that indeed death had come, one of the soldiers raised his lance and ran it through the hanging body, deliberately piercing the heart. S. John is anxious that posterity shall ever have before them this item of the crucifixion. So much did it mean to the disciple whom Jesus loved; to those who have come after him it has meant even more.

> ' And immediately there came out
> Blood and water
> And he that saw gave testimony
> And his testimony is true
> And he knoweth that he saith true
> That you may believe
> For these things were done
> That the scripture might be fulfilled
> You shall not break a bone of him
> And again another scripture saith
> They shall look on him
> Whom they pierced.'

By the side of the mourners whom we have already mentioned was another group, of whom we would gladly have heard more. They were men of mark, some of them even Pharisees, who since the beginning of the Mission of

Jesus had stood, as it were, on the fringe of the crowd uncommitted. That they were by no means a small number S. John has already told us:

> 'However
> Many of the chief men also believed in him
> But because of the Pharisees
> They did not confess him
> That they might not be cast out of the synagogue.'
> John xii, 42

We have met these men often enough in the course of the story of Jesus. There was Nicodemus in the early days, who came to Him by night, and who, there is reason to believe, had a following. It was in the house of Simon the Pharisee, seated at table with him as a guest, that Jesus had welcomed the woman who was a sinner at Magdala; it was in the house of a Pharisee that Mary poured the precious ointment over Him, at the feast given to Him in Bethania. More than once, down in Judæa, we find Pharisees inviting Him to dine with them, even on a Sabbath day; and while there were many there who 'watched Him' that they 'might catch Him in His speech', there were others who had not forgotten the Baptist who had but lately been among them, and what he had said about this Man. These in secret had pondered the evidence, had discussed it among themselves, and had been convinced so far as their will would allow them. Had caste permitted it, they would gladly have given Him their allegiance. But they were Pharisees, they were leaders of the people; for the sake of them they must stand together and not yield. And since they must not yield, it was easy to find reason for their choice. If the Baptist and Jesus were right, so also were Moses and the prophets. If He were greater than Moses, still even He had confessed that salvation came from the Jews; and if the Jews were the people of God, the people of election, was it not well to stand aloof, for a time at least,

'That the whole nation might not perish'?

With arguments like these had these men persuaded themselves that they were sincere, and had stood apart from Jesus during the last two years. But for some among them the events of that day had been a rude awakening. Once Jesus had said, to such men as themselves:

> ' He who is not with me
> Is against me ';

and now that He was dead they might well ask themselves what share of the blame for that murder rested on their shoulders.

From among this group we now hear mention of one for the first time:

> ' And a certain rich man of Arimathea
> A city of Judæa
> By name Joseph
> Who was a senator
> A noble counsellor
> A good and just man
> Who also himself waited for the Kingdom of God
> But secretly for fear of the Jews
> This man had not consented
> To their counsels and doings.'

It is significant that Joseph of Arimathea is mentioned by all the four evangelists. He was a rich man; he was a senator, and a counsellor, that is, he was a member of the Sanhedrin. Moreover, he was a local magnate; he had influence in and around Arimathea, and was therefore one to be considered by the ruling foreigner. On this account he might well have been able to gain access to Pilate, when others less powerful might have been refused admission. With the death of Jesus a new courage had come to him. Before, he had merely looked on and formed his own opinion, convincing himself that the affair of the trial was not his concern; now he was indignant at what had been done. He could not make adequate amends, but he would do what he was able. Jesus was a just man, that Joseph knew, whatever charges had been brought again Him; then He should not be buried in the common ditch with the other criminals. In a garden plot close by Calvary was a tomb cut into the rock, which belonged to Joseph himself. Many a Jew had prepared round the walls of Jerusalem a like resting-place for himself after death. Since there was no other available, Jesus should have that tomb; he himself would secure the body, using his influence with Pilate.

He went across the city to the Governor's palace and boldly demanded an audience ; he had come from the place of execution, and had a request to make. Pilate in his turn was pleased to receive him ; in the first place he was glad to find one of the other side who was not an enemy of Jesus, in the second he was only too anxious to have news of what was going forward. To the end of the trial, as we have seen, Pilate had striven to save Jesus ; even after he had surrendered he still hoped against hope that his Victim might not die. Had Joseph come to make him some suggestion how Jesus might yet be saved ? Had he but spoken at the trial, what a difference to Pilate his single protest would have made ! But perhaps it was not yet too late. Jesus had been crucified, that Pilate knew ; but was it not possible that His life might still be spared ? If remorse had already seized upon the Pharisees, much more had it entered into him who had publicly declared the accused Man's innocence.

But the message and request of Joseph were an end to all these hopes. They were a shock to Pilate, though reason had told him what to expect ; but until he had convincing evidence he was unwilling to believe. An order was sent that the officer in charge at the place of execution should himself come and report ; Pilate would hear the final word from no other witness. The centurion came ; the facts were only too true ; Jesus had died before his eyes, His legs had not been broken on that account, but to prove that He was dead a soldier of the guard had run his spear through His heart.

Thus ended Pilate's last hope. But the respect he had learnt for his Victim lingered on. Though he had suffered Him to die the death of a malefactor, yet he was glad that Jesus was not to be treated as a common criminal after death. If he had not saved the life of Jesus, it was some satisfaction that honour would be done to the body of this Man who to the end had unflinchingly declared Himself a King. Here at least was a Jew, a member of the Sanhedrin, who would give the body honourable burial, and Pilate issued orders that it should be handed over to Joseph of Arimathea. Joseph hastened back and claimed it ; with him by this time was another member of the Sanhedrin, Nicodemus, who since the first coming of Jesus had followed His career with care. With the example of Joseph before him, he, too, had taken courage :

> 'A brother that is helped by his brother
> Is like a strong city.'
> Proverbs xviii, 19.

During all the trouble of the night before he had absented himself from the court; now with Joseph he would do what he could to atone for the deed of his fellow Pharisees. The desire grew to a great longing; esteem had turned into love; to satisfy himself he was lavish in providing all that was of the best for the burial, and that in superabundance.

> 'And Nicodemus also came
> He who at the first had come to Jesus by night
> Bringing a mixture of myrrh and olives
> About an hundred pound weight.'

The best of fine linen was brought; the body was taken from the cross, and His mother received it. She who had once wrapped those living limbs in swaddling clothes and laid them in a manger, now beheld other hands wrap them round and round with the linen strips of death. She gave a last look at the battered face and another piece of linen was drawn over it:

> 'As it is the custom with the Jews to bury.'

The handmaid of the Lord had done her work; the sword had pierced her heart; she no longer asked:

> 'Son
> Why hast thou done so to us?'

though she had abundant cause. Though she 'understood not', she knew more than all the others; but, as S. Augustine well points out, though she knew what would happen in three days, that did not relieve the agony unto death of that terrible Friday.

Then followed the procession to the tomb. It was cut into a rock; a large square chamber some eight feet in depth, and breadth, and height, with a ledge on the rock on one side, on which the body was to be laid.

> 'There therefore
> By reason of the Parasceve of the Jews
> They laid Jesus
> Because the sepulchre was nigh at hand.'

The mourners took their last look at the body, as it lay still and helpless on the ledge where they had laid it against the farther wall of the chamber. He was indeed dead; no hoping that they might be deceived, that it was a nightmare from which they might yet awake, could bring Him back to life. He was dead, and they must leave Him in His tomb; they could not die with Him, they could not be buried with Him, they must return into the city, to a life that was now worse to them than death. The face-cloth was again drawn over the face; the men pressed the other mourners before them, and rolled the huge round stone at the entrance into its socket. There was nothing further to be done, and they went their way, but the women still lingered on.

> 'And Mary Magdalen
> And Mary the mother of Joseph
> And the women that were come with him
> From Galilee
> Following after
> Sitting over against the sepulchre
> Beheld where his body was laid.'

We cannot fail to be struck by the constant presence of the women in the whole story of the crucifixion; moreover, whenever they appear, the picture of them that is drawn is evidently true to life. Early in his Gospel S. Luke had gathered them together, and had given most of their names. It was immediately after the conversion of the 'woman who was a sinner'.

> ' And it came to pass afterwards
> That he travelled through the cities and towns
> Preaching and evangelizing the Kingdom of God
> And the twelve with him
> And certain women
> Who had been healed of evil spirits and infirmities
> Mary who is called Magdalen
> Out of whom seven devils were gone forth
> And Joanna the wife of Chusa, Herod's steward,
> And Susanna
> And many others
> Who ministered unto him of their substance.'
> Luke viii, 1–3.

Since that time we have learnt of others who belonged to the company; we have seen them passing in and out, following where He led, in Galilee and in Judæa, faithful to the last. Already have they been mentioned as on and about the hill of Calvary, silent witnesses of this end of all their heart's desire; now they have joined in the funeral procession, not loudly lamenting as do the professional mourners of the East, but with grief too deep for tears or words. When the men had placed the body on its ledge in the tomb, they sat down apart on the ground, desolate; their eyes fixed on the spot; there was nothing else in the world that could attract them. But vaguely hope lingered on. True, He was dead, and what that meant they were still too numbed by the blow to consider; but He had been their abiding friend and benefactor, what He had done for them could not be measured, and love did not die. Somewhere beyond the gate of death they knew He was their friend and benefactor still; then, since in life He had permitted them to serve Him, now in death they would prove to Him that their love and service were the same. They waited till the men had done their work and gone; then we can see them stealing to the tomb, kissing the stone that separated them from their Beloved; Magdalen bathing it with her tears which at last began to flow, wiping it with her hair in a hungry craving of agony.

But they would see Him yet again, though the morrow was the Sabbath, on which day nothing could be done, still on the next day, the first of the week, they could return and the tomb could be opened; tombs were not finally closed till after three days. They would go at once and make their preparations. There was still time before sunset, when the Sabbath began; they would hurry to the bazaar; at a time like this, when men of every nation were gathered in the city, they would easily pass unknown in the crowd. They would buy more spices, and the other things that were bestowed upon the dead; there was nothing else they could give Him. They had followed Him faithfully while He lived; to be faithful to Him dead was their one remaining consolation.

(b) *The Guarded Tomb*.

Meanwhile elsewhere in the city was a gathering of quite another kind and temper; those who had done the Lord to death now felt the need of still clinging together in their own meeting-house. They had had their will to the last iota; Jesus of Nazareth had been proved a deceiver before all the world, He had been declared accursed by His hanging on the tree, He was dead and buried, and He would never trouble them any more. And yet the reaction had followed; a sense of misery and self-contempt, of cowardice and fear, making them dread they knew not what. It was more than the consciousness of murder and injustice that haunted them; there was the warning still ringing in their ears, that in spite of all they did to Him He would one day come back to them, seated on the clouds of heaven. They could not endure to be alone; they must needs keep together, they must encourage each other with brave words, each must hide his shame in the company of his fellow-murderers.

One thing especially made them restless. Though He had been crucified, though with their own eyes they had seen Him dead, though a lance had been thrust through His heart and He had been put safely in the tomb, were they still sure, even now, that they had done with Him? They recalled His extravagant boasting, which He had not hesitated to repeat:

> 'Destroy this temple
> And in three days
> I will build it up again.
>
> . . . .
>
> A wicked and adulterous generation
> Asketh for a sign
> And a sign shall not be given it
> But the sign of Jonas the prophet.
>
> . . . .
>
> I have power to lay down my life
> And to take it up again.'

At other times they had affected not to understand the meaning of His words. He had threatened to destroy their Temple; He had claimed magic powers; they had brought these charges against Him at the trial, they had flung His words back at Him as He hung on the cross, and He had given no answer. But even on Calvary they had over-reached themselves; the very manner of the taunt had betrayed what lay behind it.

> ' Vah, thou that destroyest the temple of God
> And in three days buildest it up again
> Save thy own self
> If thou be the Son of God
> Come down from the cross.'

In the early days they had asked Him by what authority He acted, and only this had been His answer. Later they had asked Him for a sign, and they had been given only what He called the sign of Jonas. But they had known well what He meant; Jesus had spoken to men who had steeped themselves in the law and the prophets. Jonas, they knew beforehand, was a type as well as a prophet; one day He who was to come would solve the enigma of his story; and now Jesus had affected to solve it. Jonas, after three days, had come back to life; Jesus had said that if men destroyed Him, He, too, after three days would come back to life. Clearly this could not be; dead men did not come back to life, much less did dead men raise themselves from the tomb. Such things did not happen, therefore they could not; they could not happen, therefore they did not; to men determined not to believe the argument mattered little.

Still, it was well to make sure. This Man, as they knew and had proved, had cast out devils by the power of the devil. He had more than the power of the devil, He had been Himself possessed. Had they not declared it long ago?

> Do we not say well
> That thou art a Samaritan
> And hast a devil?'
>
> John viii, 48.
>
> ' Now we know
> That thou hast a devil.'
>
> John viii, 52.

There were men in Samaria, there was especially one called Simon, who did strange things by magic; was Jesus different from him? Moreover, who but one possessed of a devil, who but a madman, could boast as He had boasted, that He could die and live again at His own will? The first part of His boast they had that day proved futile; for they had had their way, He had not been able to save Himself though they had reminded Him and challenged Him to do so, not even Pilate had been able to save Him. They had done Him to death themselves, they had taken the responsibility, they had called down His blood upon themselves and their children; what more was needed to prove that at last they had conquered?

Still there was a haunting dread that all was not yet over. As Herod had once feared the resurrection of his victim, John the Baptist, and could not be persuaded that all was well, so and much more did these murderers of the Son of God grow more and more in fear of what might yet be. Besides the prophecies that He had made in His lifetime, there was His attitude during the whole of that day, which had forced the truth upon them that all the time He had been the master, not they. From the moment they had seized Him in the Garden He had held them; He had told them plainly that they might do what they would only because He allowed it. Often enough before, in broad daylight, and not under the light of the moon, in the open court of the Temple and not under the shadows of an olive grove, He had passed through their midst and escaped them; from the Garden to Calvary they had feared He might escape them again. One who had a devil might do strange things; one who had a devil might work prodigies, though saints might not; after his death the devil himself might do wonders for one who had a devil.

Nevertheless they had succeeded thus far, and they must seal their success. Dead Jesus certainly was, so far as any man could be sure of it, dead He was and buried; it was now all-important that He should be kept carefully fast in His tomb. But how was this to be done? If there was any truth in His boast that He would rise again, for in spite of their assurance the fear would ever recur, then they might expect weird things to happen in the course of the next three days. He had Himself fixed the time; let the three days be safely over and they would need to fear no more. Now suppose that by some devil's trick He did rise again; suppose that in spite of the crucifixion, and of the spear through

His side, and of the blood and water that came from it, He were not really dead. Bodies inhabited by devils are unaccountable. He might then recover; He might awaken in the tomb; He might work another miracle and release Himself from His prison. With such a Man they must be prepared for anything; He must be kept locked in His prison till He was really dead. Even if He did come back to life, care must be taken that He did not escape. The tomb must be sealed and guarded; dead or alive, Jesus must be kept secure in His tomb for ever.

Anxious thoughts like these occupied the minds of these masters in Israel during all the evening after Jesus had been dead and buried. They deliberated long; to contend with the dead was no easy matter. At length it was decided that for the critical three days that were to follow the tomb must be guarded; and as they had secured the sentence of the Roman Governor in proof of the guilt of Jesus, so they must secure that same witness against all talk of His resurrection. They must ask Pilate for a guard. Of course, with him they would need to change their argument, as they had changed it when they had clamoured for their Victim's death. For Pilate was not like Herod; he had no superstitious fears of the dead; to him, even more than to the Sadducees, death was the very end, from which there was no revival. He had certain evidence that Jesus was dead indeed; if they said that they wished to secure that Jesus did not rise again, he would merely contemn them. They must invent another more plausible excuse. They must tell him of a rumour that had been bruited abroad, that this Man of mystery would come back to life. They would relate to him stories of men who had been buried for long periods and yet had lived; these Romans would believe almost any strange tale of Asia. They would remind him that Jesus had seduced many, and had left many followers, hidden it might be for the present, but fanatics every one of them. They were dangerous, very dangerous alike to them and to the state of Rome. One had shown what the rest might do; he had dared to draw a sword, and to fight single-handed the whole band that had been sent to take Jesus in the garden the night before. Unless the tomb were carefully guarded these men would certainly make mischief. They would break it open; they would remove the body; they would give it out that their Master had risen from the dead, and what might follow from such a fable who could say? For the sake of public order it was wise that precautions should be taken; such a nuisance should be forestalled. There had been trouble enough with the tale of Lazarus in Bethania; this tale would be worse. They would see Pilate early next day; Jesus had said He would rise again within three days; they might rest secure for the night. True, the next day would be the Sabbath, on which day no business might be done; but the case was urgent, and if an exception could be made to raise a sheep from a well, then to keep Jesus safe in His tomb they could give themselves a like dispensation.

Thus it was that these meticulous observers of the Sabbath themselves broke the Sabbath on this the greatest Sabbath day of the year. Onlookers must have stared with astonishment upon these masters of the Law as they hurried from the Temple up the street to the house of Pilate that morning. They must have known that nothing but a concern of life and death could have induced them to such violation.

> ' And the next day
> Which followed the day of preparation
> The chief priests and Pharisees
> Came together to Pilate
> Saying : Sir
> We have remembered
> That this seducer said while yet he was living
> After three days I will rise again
> Command therefore
> The sepulchre to be guarded
> Until the third day
> Lest his disciples come
> And steal him away
> And say to the people
> He is risen from the dead
> So the last error shall be worse than the first.'

We listen to this final sentence and wonder what was in the minds of these anxious men. What was 'the first error'? What would be 'the last'? Had they come already to doubt whether, after all, the doing of Jesus to death was a great mistake? Would it have been wiser to follow the caution of Annas, and not the impetuosity of Caiphas? Annas had shown himself more eager to learn 'about His disciples' than about Jesus Himself; would their cause not have been better served by striking at them rather than at Him? But the 'error', if error it was, had been committed; at least they must not commit the further error of leaving these disciples free to do as they pleased.

Pilate was in no mood to receive this embassy with favour. He, too, had gone through his night of remorse, and he had only these men to blame for it. Twenty-four hours before they had come to him with their trumped-up story; they had beaten him, and he had yielded to them. He knew he had done the most shameful deed in his life; and they had driven him to it. He would have nothing more to do with them, these restless Jews, these everlasting makers of mischief, these cunning Asiatics, whose designs no Roman could guess. Already they had complained of the title he had set above the cross; yet they had come to him at first with some charge about Jesus the King. He had ignored them then, he would ignore them now; he would not submit his guard to the humiliation of watching the corpse of a buried Jew. They had their own police: let them look to it themselves; this at least was a matter that could not be said to be outside their rights. If they could not put Jesus to death in the way they would, they had full right to guard His body. He had washed his hands, he would not soil them any more.

> 'Pilate said to them
> You have a guard
> Go guard it as you know.'

The 'chief priests and Pharisees' went their way disappointed; this crowning victory over Pilate would have set the seal on all they had done. But at least they had guards of their own; if their police had failed to take Jesus when commanded, if they had come back empty-handed saying:
> 'Never did man speak
> As this man hath spoken',

at least they could hold Him fast, now that His tongue had been silenced. In spite of the solemn festival more work had to be done; on this Feast of the Great Deliverance, when all Jerusalem rejoiced in God who had visited and saved His people, Jesus of Nazareth must be made secure in His tomb. The stone at the door had to be fastened down and sealed; the guards to be carefully chosen, safe men, loyal men, who would not be open to a bribe, who would not be likely to spread false tales abroad. And yet even then, we may be sure, these leaders of Jerusalem returned to their homes restless and anxious, wondering what the morrow might bring:

> ' And they departing
> Made the sepulchre sure
> Sealing the stone
> And setting guards.'

Meanwhile the King lay in state, with His guard about Him, as became a king.

HARMONY OF THE PASSION OF JESUS CHRIST

2. THE COUNCIL OF THE PRIESTS. Matthew xxvi, 1-5; Mark xiv, 1, 2; Luke xxii, 1, 2.

(Matthew xxvi, 1-5.) And it came to pass, when Jesus had ended all these words, he said to his disciples: you know that after two days shall be the pasch: and the Son of man shall be delivered up to be crucified. Then were gathered together the chief priests and ancients of the people, into the court of the high priest who was called Caiphas; and they consulted together that by subtilty they might apprehend Jesus and put him to death. But they said: Not on the festival day, lest perhaps there should be a tumult amongst the people.

(Mark xiv, 1, 2.) Now the feast of the pasch and of the Azymes was after two days: and the chief priests and the scribes sought how they might by some wile lay hold on him and kill him. But they said: Not on the festival day lest there should be a tumult among the people.

(Luke xxii, 1, 2.) Now the feast of unleavened bread, which is called the pasch, was at hand. And the chief priests and the scribes sought how they might put Jesus to death: but they feared the people.

3. THE COMPACT WITH JUDAS. Matthew xxvi, 14-16; Mark xiv, 10, 11; Luke xxii, 3-6.

(Matthew xxvi, 14-16.) Then went one of the twelve, who was called Judas Iscariot, to the chief priests and said to them: What will you give me, and I will deliver him unto you? But they appointed him thirty pieces of silver. And from thenceforth he sought opportunity to betray him.

(Mark xiv, 10, 11.) And Judas Iscariot, one of the twelve, went to the chief priests, to betray him to them. Who hearing it were glad: and they promised him they would give him money. And he sought how he might conveniently betray him.

(Luke xxii, 3-6.) And Satan entered into Judas, who was surnamed Iscariot, one of the twelve. And he went and discoursed with the chief priests and the magistrates, how he might betray him to them. And they were glad and covenanted to give him money. And he promised. And he sought opportunity to betray him in the absence of the multitude.

(*Harmony*.) And Satan entered into Judas, who was surnamed Iscariot one of the twelve. And he went and discoursed with the chief priests and the magistrates, how he might betray him to them. And he said to them : What will you give me, and I will deliver him unto you ? Who hearing it were glad, and covenanted to give him money. And they appointed him thirty pieces of silver. And he promised. And from thenceforth he sought opportunity how he might conveniently betray him in the absence of the multitude.

4. THE PREPARATION OF THE SUPPER. Matthew xxvi, 17-19 ; Mark xiv, 12-16 ; Luke xxii, 7-13.

(Matthew xxvi, 17-19.) And on the first day of the Azymes, the disciples came to Jesus, saying : Where wilt thou that we prepare for thee to eat the pasch ? But Jesus said : Go ye into the city to a certain man and say to him : The Master saith, My time is near at hand. With thee I make the pasch with my disciples. And the disciples did as Jesus appointed to them : and they prepared the pasch.

(Mark xiv, 12-16.) Now on the first day of the unleavened bread, when they sacrificed the pasch, the disciples say to him : Whither wilt thou that we go and prepare for thee to eat the pasch ? And he sendeth two of his disciples and saith to them : Go ye into the city : and there shall meet you a man carrying a pitcher of water. Follow him. And whithersoever he shall go in, say to the master of the house, The master saith, where is my refectory, where I may eat the pasch with my disciples ? And he will show you a large dining room furnished. And there prepare ye for us. And the disciples went their way and came into the city. And they found as he had told them : and they prepared the pasch.

(Luke xxii, 7-13.) And the day of the unleavened bread came, on which it was necessary that the pasch should be killed. And he sent Peter and John, saying : Go and prepare for us the pasch, that we may eat. But they said : Where wilt thou that we prepare ? And he said : Behold, as you go into the city, there shall meet you a man carrying a pitcher of water : follow him into the house where he entereth in. And you shall say to the goodman of the house : The Master saith to thee : Where is the guest chamber, where I may eat the pasch with my disciples ? And he will show you a large dining room, furnished. And there prepare. And they, going, found as he had said to them and made ready the pasch.

(*Harmony*.) And the first day of the unleavened bread came, on which it was necessary that the pasch should be killed and sacrificed. And the disciples came to Jesus, saying : Where wilt thou that we go and prepare for thee to eat the pasch ? And he sent two of his disciples, Peter and John, and saith to them : Go, and prepare for us the pasch that we may eat. But they said : Where wilt thou that we prepare ? And he said : Behold as you go into the city there shall meet you a certain man carrying a pitcher of water. Follow him into the house where he entereth in. And whithersoever he shall enter in you shall say to the good man of the house : The Master saith to thee : My time is near at hand. With thee I will make the pasch. Where is the guest chamber, where I may eat the pasch with my disciples ? and he will shew you a large dining room furnished ready. And there prepare for us. And the disciples did as Jesus appointed to them, and went their way and came into the city. And they found as he had told them : and they prepared the pasch.

5. THE SUPPER. 6. THE WASHING OF THE FEET. Matthew xxvi, 20 ; Mark xiv, 17 ; Luke xxii, 14–18 ; xxii, 24–30 ; John xiii, 1–20.

(Matthew xxvi, 20.) But when it was evening he sat down with his twelve disciples.

(Mark xiv, 17.) And when evening was come he cometh with the twelve.

(Luke xxii, 14–18.) And when the hour was come he sat down : and the twelve apostles with him. And he said to them : With desire have I desired to eat this pasch with you before I suffer. For I say to you that from this time I will not eat it, till it be fulfilled in the Kingdom of God. And having taken the chalice he gave thanks and said : Take and divide it among you. For I say to you that I will not drink of the fruit of the vine, till the kingdom of God come.

(Luke xxii, 24–30.) And there was also a strife amongst them, which of them should seem to be the greater. And he said to them : The kings of the Gentiles lord it over them : and they that have power over them are called beneficent. But you not so : but he that is the greater among you, let him become as the younger : and he that is the leader, as he that serveth. For which is greater, he that sitteth at table or he that serveth ? Is not he that sitteth at table ? But I am in the midst of you as he that serveth. And ye are they who have continued with me in my temptations. And I dispose to you, as my Father hath disposed to me, a kingdom : that you may eat and drink at my table, in my kingdom : and may sit upon thrones, judging the twelve tribes of Israel.

(John xiii, 1–20.) Before the festival day of the pasch, Jesus knowing that his hour was come, that he should pass out of this world to the Father : having loved his own who were in the world, he loved them unto the end. And when supper was done (the devil having now put it into the heart of Judas Iscariot, the son of Simon, to betray him), knowing that the Father had given him all things into his hands, and that he came from God and goeth to God, he riseth from supper and layeth aside his garments, and having taken a towel, girded himself. After that he putteth water into a basin and began to wash the feet of the disciples and to wipe them with the towel wherewith he was girded. He cometh therefore to Simon Peter. And Peter saith to him: Lord, dost thou wash my feet? Jesus answered and said to him: What I do thou knowest not now: but thou shalt know hereafter. Peter saith to him: Thou shalt never wash my feet. Jesus answered him: If I wash thee not, thou shalt have no part with me. Simon Peter saith to him: Lord, not only my feet, but also my hands and my head. Jesus saith to him: He that is washed needeth not but to wash his feet, but is clean wholly and you are clean, but not all. For he knew who he was that would betray him; therefore he said: You are not all clean. Then after he had washed their feet and taken his garments, being set down again he said to them: Know you what I have done to you? You call me Master and Lord. And you say well: for so I am. If then I being your Lord and Master, have washed your feet: you also ought to wash one another's feet. For I have given you an example, that as I have done to you, so you do also. Amen, amen, I say to you: The servant is not greater than his master: neither is the apostle greater than he that sent him. If you know these things, you shall be blessed if you do them. I speak not of you all: I know whom I have chosen. But that the scripture may be fulfilled: He that eateth bread with me shall lift up his heel against me. At present I tell you before it come to pass: that when it shall come to pass you may believe that I am he. Amen, amen, I say to you, he that receiveth whomsoever I send receiveth me: and he that receiveth me receiveth him that sent me.

(*Harmony.*) Before the festival day of the pasch, Jesus knowing that his hour was come, that he should pass out of this world to the Father: having loved his own who were in the world he loved them unto the end. And when it was evening, when the hour was come, he cometh and sat down, and the twelve apostles with him. And he said to them: With desire I have desired to eat this pasch with you before I suffer. For I say to you that from this time I will not eat it, till it be fulfilled in the kingdom of God. And having taken the chalice he gave thanks and said: Take and divide it among you. For I say to you that I will not drink of the fruit of the vine till the kingdom of God come. And there was also a strife amongst them which of them should seem to be the greater. And he said to them: The kings of the Gentiles lord it over them: and they that have power over them are called beneficent. But you not so: but he that is the greater among you, let him become as the younger : and he that is the leader, as he that serveth. For which is greater, he that sitteth at table or he that serveth ? Is not he that sitteth at table ? But I am in the midst of you as he that serveth. And you are they who have continued with me in my temptations. And I dispose to you, as my Father hath disposed to me, a kingdom ; that you may eat and drink at my table, in my kingdom : and may sit upon thrones, judging the twelve tribes of Israel. And when supper was done (the devil now having put it into the heart of Judas Iscariot, the son of Simon, to betray him), knowing that the Father had given him all things into his hands, and that he came from God and goeth to God, he riseth from supper and layeth aside his garments, and having taken a towel girded himself. After that, he putteth water into a basin and began to wash the feet of the disciples and to wipe them with the towel wherewith he was girded. He cometh therefore to Simon Peter. And Peter saith to him : Lord, dost thou wash my feet ? Jesus answered and said to him : What I do thou knowest not now, but thou shalt know hereafter. Peter saith to him : Thou shalt never wash my feet. Jesus answered him : If I wash thee not thou shalt have no part with me. Simon Peter saith to him : Lord, not only my feet, but also my hands and my head. Jesus saith to him : He that is washed, needeth not but to wash his feet, but is clean wholly. And you are clean, but not all. For he knew who he was that would betray him ; therefore he said : You are not all clean. Then after he had washed their feet and taken his garments, being sat down again he said to them : Know you what I have done to you ? You call me Master and Lord. And you say well ; for so I am. If I then being your Lord and Master, have washed your feet ; you also ought to wash one another's feet. For I have given you an example, that as I have done to you, so you do also. Amen, amen, I say to you : The servant is not greater than his Lord : neither is the apostle greater than he that sent him. If you know these things, you shall be blessed if you do them. I speak not of you all : I know whom I have chosen. But that the scripture may be fulfilled : He that eateth bread with me shall lift up his heel against me. At present I tell you before it come to pass : that when it shall come to pass you may believe that I am he. Amen, amen I say to you, he that receiveth whomsoever I send receiveth me ; and he that receiveth me receiveth him that sent me.

7. THE LAST WARNING TO JUDAS. Matthew xxvi, 21-25 ; Mark xiv, 18-21 ; Luke xxii, 21-23 ; John xiii, 21-35.

(Matthew xxvi, 21-25.) And while they were eating he said : Amen I say to you that one of you is about to betray me. And they being very much troubled began every one to say : Is it I,

Lord? But he answering said: He that dippeth his hand with me in the dish, he shall betray me. The Son of man indeed goeth as it is written of him. But woe to that man by whom the Son of man shall be betrayed. It were better for him, if that man had not been born. And Judas that betrayed him answering, said: Is it I, Rabbi? He saith to him: Thou hast said it.

(Mark xiv, 18–21.) And when they were at table and eating, Jesus saith: Amen I say to you, one of you that eateth with me shall betray me. But they began to be sorrowful, and to say to him, one by one: Is it I? Who saith to them: One of the twelve, who dippeth with me his hand in the dish. And the Son of man indeed goeth as it is written of him: but woe to the man by whom the Son of man shall be betrayed. It were better for him if that man had not been born.

(Luke xxii, 21–23.) But yet behold: the hand of him that betrayeth me is with me on the table. And the Son of man indeed goeth according to that which is determined: but yet, woe to that man by whom he shall be betrayed. And they began to enquire among themselves, which of them it was that should do this thing.

(John xiii, 21–35.) When Jesus had said these things he was troubled in spirit; and he testified and said: Amen, amen, I say to you, one of you shall betray me. The disciples therefore looked one upon another, doubting of whom he spoke. Now there was leaning on Jesus' bosom one of his disciples, whom Jesus loved. Peter therefore beckoned to him and said to him: who is it of whom he speaketh? He therefore, leaning on the breast of Jesus, saith to him: Lord, who is it? Jesus answered: He it is to whom I shall reach bread dipped. And when he had dipped the bread, he gave it to Judas Iscariot, the son of Simon. And after the morsel, Satan entered into him. And Jesus said to him: That which thou dost, do quickly. Now no man at the table knew to what purpose he said this unto him. For some thought, because Judas had the purse, that Jesus had said to him: Buy those things which we have need of for the festival day: or that he should give something to the poor. He therefore, having received the morsel, went out immediately. And it was night. When he therefore was gone out, Jesus said: Now is the Son of man glorified; and God is glorified in him. If God be glorified in him, God will also glorify him in himself; and immediately will he glorify him. Little children, yet a little while I am with you. You shall seek me. And as I said to the Jews: Whither I go, you cannot come, so I say to you now. A new commandment I give unto you. That you love one another, as I have loved you, that you also love one another. By this shall men know that you are my disciples, if you have love one for another.

(*Harmony.*) When Jesus had said these things when they were at table and eating, he was troubled in spirit; and he testified and said: Amen, amen, I say to you, one of you that eateth with me shall betray me. But yet behold the hand of him that betrayeth me is with me on the table. And they being very much troubled began to be sorrowful, and to enquire among themselves which of them it was that should do this thing, and to say to him one by one: Is it I, Lord? But he answering, said: One of the twelve, who dippeth with me his hand in the dish. And the Son of man indeed goeth as it is written of him; but woe to that man by whom the Son of man shall be betrayed. It were better for him, if that man had not been born. The disciples therefore looked one upon another, doubting of whom he spoke. Now there was leaning on Jesus' bosom one of his disciples, whom Jesus loved. Simon Peter therefore beckoned to him and said to him: Who is it of whom he speaketh? He therefore leaning upon the breast of Jesus, saith to him: Lord, who is it? Jesus answered: He it is to whom I shall reach bread dipped. And when he had dipped the bread, he gave it to Judas Iscariot, the son of Simon. And Judas that betrayed him answering said: Is it I, Rabbi? He saith to him: Thou hast said it. And after the morsel, Satan entered into him. And Jesus said: That which thou doest, do quickly. Now no man at the table knew for what purpose he said this unto him. For some thought, because Judas had the purse, that Jesus had said to him: Buy those things which we have need of for the festival day: or that he should give something to the poor. He therefore, having received the morsel, went out immediately. And it was night. When he therefore was gone out, Jesus said: Now is the Son of man glorified, and God is glorified in him. If God be glorified in him, God also will glorify him in himself, and immediately will he glorify him. Little children, yet a little while I am with you. You shall seek me. And as I said to the Jews: Whither I go you cannot come: so I say to you now. A new commandment I give unto you: that you love one another, as I have loved you, that you also love one another. By this shall men know that you are my disciples, if you have love one for another.

8. THE HOLY EUCHARIST. Matthew xxvi, 26-29; Mark xiv, 22-25; Luke xxii, 19, 20 (1 Corinthians xi, 23-25).

(Matthew xxvi, 26-29.) And whilst they were at supper Jesus took bread and blessed and broke and gave to his disciples and said: Take ye and eat. This is my body. And taking the chalice he gave thanks and gave to them, saying: Drink ye all of it. For this is my blood of the new testament, which shall be shed for many unto remission of sins. And I say to you, I will not drink from henceforth of this fruit of the vine until that day when I shall drink it with you new in the kingdom of my Father.

(Mark xiv, 22-25.) And whilst they were eating, Jesus took bread ; and blessing, broke and gave to them and said : Take ye. This is my body. And having taken the chalice, giving thanks, he gave it to them. And they all drank of it. And he saith to them : This is my blood of the new testament, which shall be shed for many. Amen I say to you that I will drink no more of the fruit of the vine until that day when I shall drink it new in the kingdom of God.

(Luke xxii, 19, 20.) And taking bread, he gave thanks and brake, and gave to them, saying : This is my body, which is given for you. Do this for a commemoration of me. In like manner, the chalice also, after he had supped, saying : This is the chalice, the new testament in my blood, which shall be shed for many.

(1 Corinthians xi, 23-25.) For I have received of the Lord that which also I delivered unto you, that the Lord Jesus, the same night in which he was betrayed, took bread, and giving thanks, broke and said : Take ye and eat : This is my body, which shall be delivered for you. This do for the commemoration of me. In like manner also the chalice, after he had supped, saying : this chalice is the new testament in my blood. This do ye, as often as you shall drink, for the commemoration of me.

(*Harmony.*) And while they were eating, Jesus took bread and blessed and broke and gave to his disciples and said : Take ye and eat. This is my body, which is given for you. Do this for a commemoration of me. In like manner having taken the chalice also, after he had supped, he gave thanks and gave it to them. And they all drank of it. And he said to them : Drink ye all of this. For this is my blood of the new testament, this is the chalice, the new testament in my blood, which shall be shed for many unto remission of sins. Amen I say to you, I will not drink from henceforth of this fruit of the vine until that day when I shall drink it with you new in the kingdom of my Father. This do ye, as often as you shall drink, for a commemoration of me.

9. THE COMING FAILURE OF THE TWELVE. Matthew xxvi, 31-35 ; Mark xiv, 27-31 ; Luke xxii, 31-38 ; John xiii, 36-38.

(Matthew xxvi, 31-35.) Then Jesus saith to them : **All you shall be scandalized in me this night. For it is written : I will strike the shepherd : and the sheep of the flock shall be dispersed. But after I shall be risen again, I will go before you into Galilee.** And Peter answering said to him : **Although all shall be scandalized in thee, I will never be scandalized.** Jesus said to him : Amen I say to thee that in this night before the cock crow thou wilt deny me thrice. And in like manner said all the disciples.

(Mark xiv, 27-31.) And Jesus saith to them : You will all be scandalized in my regard this night. For it is written : I will strike the shepherd, and the sheep shall be dispersed. But after I shall be risen again, I will go before you into Galilee. But Peter saith to him : Although all shall be scandalized in thee, yet not I. And Jesus saith to him : Amen, I say to thee, to-day, even this night, before the cock crow twice, thou shalt deny me thrice. But he spoke the more vehemently : Although I should die together with thee I will not deny thee. And in like manner also said they all.

(Luke xxii, 31-38.) And the Lord said : Simon, Simon, behold Satan hath desired to have you, that he may sift you as wheat. But I have prayed for thee, that thy faith fail not : and thou, being once converted, confirm thy brethren. Who said to him : Lord, I am ready to go with thee, both into prison and to death. And he said : I say to thee, Peter, the cock shall not crow this night till thou thrice deniest that thou knowest me. And he said to them : When I sent you without purse and scrip and shoes, did you want anything ? But they said : Nothing. Then said he unto them : But now he that hath a purse let him take it, and likewise a scrip, and he that hath not, let him sell his coat and buy a sword. For I say to you that this that is written must yet be fulfilled in me : And with the wicked was he reckoned. For the things concerning me have an end. But they said : Lord, behold here are two swords. And he said to them : It is enough.

(John xiii, 36-38.) Simon Peter saith to him : Lord, whither goest thou ? Jesus answered : Whither I go thou canst not follow me now : but thou shalt follow hereafter. Peter saith to him : Why cannot I follow thee now ? I will lay down my life for thee. Jesus answered him : Wilt thou lay down thy life for me ? Amen, amen, I say to thee, the cock shall not crow till thou deny me thrice.

(*Harmony*.) Then Jesus saith to them : You will all be scandalized in my regard this night. For it is written : I will strike the shepherd, and the sheep of the flock shall be dispersed. But after I shall be risen again I will go before you into Galilee. And Peter answering said to him : Although all shall be scandalized in thee, I will never be scandalized. And the Lord said : Simon, Simon, behold Satan hath desired to have you, that he may sift you as wheat. But I have prayed for thee, that thy faith fail not : and thou, being once converted, confirm thy brethren. Simon Peter said to him : Lord, whither goest thou ? Jesus answered : Whither I go thou canst not follow me now :

but thou shalt follow me hereafter. Peter saith to him : Why cannot I follow thee now ? I will lay down my life for thee. Lord, I am ready to go with thee, both into prison and to death. Jesus answered : and said to him : Wilt thou lay down thy life for me ? Amen, amen, I say to thee, Peter, to-day, even in this night, before the cock crow twice thou shalt deny me thrice. But he spoke the more vehemently : Although I should die together with thee, I will not deny thee. And in like manner said all the disciples. And he said to them : When I sent you without purse and scrip and shoes, did you want anything ? But they said : Nothing. Then said he unto them : But now he that hath a purse let him take it, and likewise a scrip, and he that hath not, let him sell his coat and buy a sword. For I say to you that this that is written must yet be fulfilled in me : And with the wicked was he reckoned. For the things concerning me have an end. But they said : Lord, here are two swords. And he said to them : It is enough.

10. INTRODUCTION TO THE DISCOURSE. 11. THE DISCOURSE AT THE SUPPER. 12. THE PROMISE OF THE HOLY GHOST. 13. CONCLUSION OF THE DISCOURSE. John xiv, 1–xvi, 33.

(John xiv, 1–xvi, 33.) Let not your heart be troubled. You believe in God, believe also in me. In my Father's house there are many mansions. If not I would have told you : because I go to prepare a place for you. I will come again and will take you to myself : that where I am you also may be. And whither I go you know : and the way you know. Thomas saith to him : Lord, we know not whither thou goest : and how can we know the way ? Jesus saith to him : I am the way, and the truth, and the life. No man cometh to the Father but by me. If you had known me, you would without doubt have known my Father also ; and from henceforth you shall know him and you have seen him. Philip saith to him : Lord, show us the Father and it is enough for us. Jesus saith to him : Have I been so long a time with you and you have not known me ? Philip, he that seeth me, seeth the Father also. How sayest thou : Show us the Father ? Do you not believe that I am in the Father and the Father is in me ? These words that I speak to you, I speak not of myself. But the Father who abideth in me he doth the works. Believe you not that I am in the Father and the Father is in me : otherwise believe for the very works' sake. Amen, amen, I say to you, he that believeth in me, the works that I do, he also shall do ; and greater than these shall he do. Because I go to the Father, and whatsoever you shall ask the Father in my name, that will I do : that the Father may be glorified in the Son. If you shall ask me anything in my name, that I will do. If you love me, keep my commandments. And I will ask the Father : and he shall give you another Paraclete, that he may abide with you for ever : the spirit of truth, whom the world cannot receive, because it seeth him not, nor knoweth him. But you shall know him ; because he shall abide with you and shall be in you. I will not leave you orphans, I will come to you. Yet a little while and the world seeth me no more. But you see me : because I live, and you shall live. In that day you shall know that I am in the Father : and you in me, and I in you. He that hath my commandments and keepeth them ; he it is that loveth me. And he that loveth me shall be loved by my Father : and I will love him and will manifest myself to him. Judas saith to him, not the Iscariot : Lord, how is it that thou wilt manifest thyself to us and not to the world ? Jesus answered and said to him : If anyone love me he will keep my word. And my Father will love him : and we will come to him and will make our abode with him. He that loveth me not keepeth not my words. And the word which you have heard is not mine ; but the Father's who sent me. These things have I spoken to you abiding with you. But the Paraclete, the Holy Ghost whom the Father will send in my name, he will teach you all things and bring all things to your mind, whatsoever I shall have said to you. Peace I leave with you ; my peace I give unto you : not as the world giveth, do I give unto you. Let not your heart be troubled : nor let it be afraid. You have heard that I said to you : I go away, and come unto you. If you loved me, you would indeed be glad, because I go to the Father. For the Father is greater than I. And now I have told you before it come to pass, that when it shall come to pass you may believe. I will not now speak many things with you : for the prince of this world cometh, and in me he hath not anything. But that the world may know that I love the Father and as the Father hath given me commandment, so do I : arise, let us go. I am the true vine : and my Father is the husbandman. Every branch in me that beareth not fruit he will take away : and every one that beareth fruit he will purge it, that it may bring forth more fruit. Now you are clean, by reason of the word which I have spoken to you. Abide in me, and I in you. As the branch cannot bear fruit of itself, unless it abide in the vine, so neither can you, unless you abide in me. I am the vine, you the branches : he that abideth in me, and I in him, the same beareth much fruit : for without me you can do nothing. If any one abide not in me, he shall be cast forth as a branch, and shall wither : and they shall gather him up and cast him into the fire, and he burneth. If you abide in me, and my words abide in you, you shall ask whatsoever you will, and it shall be done unto you. In this is my Father glorified : that you bring forth very much fruit, and become my disciples. As the

Father hath loved me, I also have loved you : abide in my love. If you keep my commandments you shall abide in my love : as I also have kept my Father's commandments, and do abide in his love. These things I have spoken to you that my joy may be in you, and your joy may be filled. This is my commandment, that you love one another, as I have loved you. Greater love than this no man hath, that a man lay down his life for his friends. You are my friends, if you do the things that I command you. I will not now call you servants : for the servant knoweth not what the master doeth : but I have called you friends, because all things whatsoever I have heard of my Father I have made known to you. You have not chosen me, but I have chosen you ; and have appointed you, that you should go, and should bring forth fruit, and your fruit should remain : that whatsoever you may ask of the Father in my name, he may give it you. These things I command you, that you love one another. If the world hate you, know you that it hath hated me before you. If you had been of the world, the world would love its own : but because you are not of the world, but I have chosen you out of the world, therefore the world hateth you. Remember my word that I said to you : The servant is not greater than his master. If they have persecuted me they will also persecute you. If they have kept my word, they will keep yours also. But all those things they will do to you for my name's sake : because they know not him that sent me. If I had not come and spoken to them, they would not have sin : but now they have no excuse for their sin. He that hateth me hateth my Father also. If I had not done among them the works that no other man hath done, they would not have sin : but now they have both seen and hated both me and my Father. But that the word may be fulfilled which is written in their law : They hated me without cause. But when the Paraclete cometh, whom I will send you from the Father, he shall give testimony of me. And you shall give testimony because you are with me from the beginning. These things have I spoken to you, that you may not be scandalized. They will put you out of the synagogue : yea, the hour cometh, that whosoever killeth you will think that he doeth a service to God. And these things will they do to you ; because they have not known the Father nor me. But these things I have told you, that when the hour shall come, you may remember that I told you of them. But I told you not these things from the beginning, because I was with you. And now I go to him that sent me, and none of you asketh me : Whither goest thou? But because I have spoken these things to you, sorrow hath filled your heart. But I tell you the truth : it is expedient that I go. For if I go not, the Paraclete will not come to you : but if I go, I will send him to you. And when he is come, he will convince the world of sin and of justice and of judgment. Of sin, because they believed not in me. And of justice: because I go to the Father, and you shall see me no longer, and of judgment because the prince of this world is already judged. I have yet many things to say to you: but you cannot bear them now. But when he, the Spirit of truth, is come, he will teach you all truth. For he shall not speak of himself: but what things soever he shall hear he shall speak. And the things that are to come he shall show you. He shall glorify me because he shall receive of mine and show it to you. A little while, and now you shall not see me: and again a little while, and you shall see me: because I go to the Father. Then some of his disciples said one to another: What is this that he saith to us: A little while, and you shall not see me; and again a little while and you shall see me: and because I go to the Father? They said therefore: What is this that he saith, a little while? We know not what he speaketh. And Jesus knew that they had a mind to ask him. And he said to them: Of this do you enquire among yourselves, because I said: A little while, and you shall not see me: and again a little while, and you shall see me? Amen, amen, I say to you, that you shall lament and weep, but the world shall rejoice: and you shall be made sorrowful, but your sorrow shall be turned into joy. A woman, when she is in labour, hath sorrow, because her hour is come; but when she hath brought forth the child, she remembereth no more the anguish, for joy that a man is born into the world. So also you now indeed have sorrow: but I will see you again and your heart shall rejoice. And your joy no man shall take from you. And in that day you shall not ask me anything. Amen, amen, I say to you: if you ask the Father anything in my name, he will give it you. Hitherto you have not asked anything in my name. Ask, and you shall receive: that your joy may be full. These things I have spoken to you in proverbs. The hour cometh when I will no more speak to you in proverbs, but will show you plainly of the Father. In that day you shall ask in my name: and I say not to you that I will ask the Father for you. For the Father himself loveth you, because you have loved me, and have believed that I came out from God. I came forth from the Father and am come into the world: again I leave the world and I go to the Father. His disciples say to him: Behold now thou speakest plainly, and speakest no proverb. Now we know that thou knowest all things, and thou needest not that any man should ask thee. By this we believe that thou camest forth from God. Jesus answered them: Do you now believe? Behold the hour cometh, and it is now come, that you shall be scattered every man to his own and shall leave me alone. And yet I am not alone, because the Father is with me. These things I have spoken to you, that in me you may have peace.

In the world you shall have distress. But have confidence. I have overcome the world.

14. THE SACERDOTAL PRAYER. John xvii, 1-20.

(John xvii, 1-20.) These things Jesus spoke : and lifting up his eyes to heaven, he said : Father, the hour is come. Glorify thy Son, that thy Son may glorify thee. As thou hast given him power over all flesh, that he may give eternal life to all whom thou hast given him. Now this is eternal life ; that they may know thee, the only true God, and Jesus Christ, whom thou hast sent. I have glorified thee on the earth ; I have finished the work which thou gavest me to do. And now glorify thou me, O Father, with thyself, with the glory which I had before the world was, with thee. I have manifested thy name to the men whom thou gavest me out of the world. Thine they were : and to me thou gavest them. And they have kept thy word. Now they have known that all things which thou hast given me are from thee : because the words which thou gavest me, I have given to them. And they have received them, and have known in very deed that I came out from thee : and they have believed that thou didst send me. I pray for them. I pray not for the world, but for them whom thou hast given me : because they are thine. And all my things are thine, and thine are mine ; and I am glorified in them. And now I am not in the world, and these are in the world, and I come to thee. Holy Father, keep them in thy name whom thou hast given me : that they may be one, as we also are. While I was with thee, I kept them in thy name. Those whom thou hast given me I have kept : and none of them is lost, but the son of perdition, that the scripture may be fulfilled. And now I come to thee : and these things I speak in the world, that they may have my joy filled in themselves. I have given them thy word, and the world hath hated them : because they are not of the world, as I am not of the world. I pray not that thou shouldst take them out of the world, but that thou shouldst keep them from evil. They are not of the world, as I also am not of the world. Sanctify them in truth. Thy word is truth. As thou hast sent me into the world, I also have sent them into the world. And for them do I sanctify myself, that they also may be sanctified in truth. And not for them only do I pray, but for them also who through their word shall believe in me. That they all may be one, as thou, Father, in me, and I in thee ; that they also may be one in us ; that the world may believe that thou hast sent me. And the glory which thou hast given me, I have given to them : that they may be one, as we also are one. I in thee, and thou in me : that they may be made perfect in one : and the world may know that thou hast sent me and hast loved them, as thou hast also loved me. Father, I will that where I am, they also whom thou hast given me may be with me : that they may see my glory which thou hast given me, because thou hast loved me before the creation of the world. Just Father, the world hath not known thee : but I have known thee. And these have known that thou hast sent me. And I have made known thy name to them and will make it known : that the love wherewith thou hast loved me, may be in them, and I in them.

16. THE AGONY IN THE GARDEN. Matthew xxvi, 30 ; xxvi, 36-46 ; Mark xiv, 26 ; xiv, 32-42 ; Luke xxii, 39-46 ; John xviii, 1.

(Matthew xxvi, 30 ; xxvi, 36-46.) And a hymn being said, they went out unto mount Olivet.

Then Jesus came with them into a country place which is called Gethsemani. And he said to his disciples : Sit you here, till I go yonder and pray. And taking with him Peter and the two sons of Zebedee, he began to grow sorrowful and to be sad. Then he saith to them : My soul is sorrowful even unto death. Stay you here and watch with me. And going a little further, he fell upon his face, praying and saying : My Father, if it be possible, let this chalice pass from me. Nevertheless, not as I will but as thou wilt. And he cometh to his disciples and findeth them asleep. And he saith to Peter : What ? Could you not watch one hour with me ? Watch ye, and pray that ye enter not into temptation. The spirit indeed is willing but the flesh is weak. Again the second time he went and prayed, saying : My Father, if this chalice may not pass away, but I must drink it, thy will be done. And he cometh again, and findeth them sleeping : for their eyes were heavy. And leaving them, he went again : and he prayed the third time, saying the selfsame word. Then he cometh to his disciples and saith to them : Sleep ye now and take your rest. Behold the hour is at hand : and the Son of man shall be betrayed into the hands of sinners. Rise, let us go. Behold he is at hand that will betray me.

(Mark xiv, 26 ; xiv, 32-42.) And when they had sung a hymn, they went forth to the mount of Olives.

And they came to a farm called Gethsemani. And he saith to his disciples : Sit you here, while I pray. And he taketh Peter and James and John with him : and he began to fear and to be heavy. And he saith to them : my soul is sorrowful even unto death. Stay you here and watch. And when he was gone forward a little, he fell flat on the ground : and he prayed that, if it might be, the hour might pass from him. And he saith : Abba, Father, all things are possible to thee : remove this chalice from me : but not what I will, but what thou wilt. And he cometh and findeth them sleeping. And he saith to Peter :

Simon, sleepest thou ? Couldst thou not watch one hour ? Watch ye : and pray that you enter not into temptation. The spirit indeed is willing, but the flesh is weak. And going away again, he prayed, saying the same words. And when he returned, he found them again asleep (for their eyes were heavy) : and they knew not what to answer him. And he cometh the third time and saith to them : Sleep ye now and take your rest. It is enough. The hour is come : behold the Son of man shall be betrayed into the hands of sinners. Rise up, let us go. Behold he that will betray me is at hand.

(Luke xxii, 39-46.) And going out he went according to his custom to the mount of Olives. And his disciples also followed him. And when he was come to the place, he said to them : Pray, lest ye enter into temptation. And he was withdrawn away from them a stone's cast. And kneeling down, he prayed, saying : Father, if thou wilt, remove this chalice from me : but yet not my will but thine be done. And there appeared to him an angel from heaven, strengthening him. And being in an agony, he prayed the longer. And his sweat became as drops of blood, trickling down upon the ground. And when he rose up from prayer and was come to the disciples, he found them sleeping for sorrow. And he said to them : Why sleep you ? Arise : pray : lest you enter into temptation.

(John xviii, 1.) When Jesus had said these things he went forth with his disciples over the brook Cedron, where there was a garden, into which he entered with his disciples.

(*Harmony*.) And when Jesus had said these things, and they had sung a hymn, he went forth with his disciples, according to the custom, over the brook Cedron to the mount of Olives, where there was a garden. Then Jesus came with them to a country place, a farm, which is called Gethsemani. And he said to his disciples : Sit you here, till I go yonder and pray. Pray, lest ye enter into temptation. And taking with him Peter, and James and John, the two sons of Zebedee, he began to grow sorrowful and to be sad, to fear and to be heavy. Then he said to them : My soul is sorrowful even unto death, stay you here and watch with me. And when he had gone forward a little, and was withdrawn away from them a stone's cast, kneeling down he fell flat on the ground upon his face : and he prayed, saying : Father, if thou wilt, remove this chalice from me, nevertheless not my will but thine be done. O, my Father, if it is possible, let this chalice pass from me. Nevertheless not as I will, but as thou wilt. Abba, Father, all things are possible to thee. Take away this chalice from me. But not what I will, but what thou wilt. And he cometh to his disciples and findeth them asleep. And he saith to Peter : Simon, sleepest thou ? What ! Couldst thou, could you, not watch one hour with me ? Watch ye, and pray that ye enter not into temptation. The spirit indeed is willing, but the flesh is weak. And going away again he went the second time, and prayed, saying the selfsame words : O Father, if this chalice cannot pass except I drink it, thy will be done. And he cometh again and findeth them asleep, for their eyes were heavy with sorrow. And he said to them : Why sleep you ? Arise, pray, lest you enter into temptation. And they knew not what to answer him. And leaving them he went away again, and he prayed the third time, saying the same words. And there appeared to him an angel from heaven, strengthening him. And being in an agony he prayed the longer. And his sweat became as drops of blood trickling down upon the ground. Then he cometh the third time to his disciples and saith to them : Sleep you now and take your rest. It is enough ; the hour is come. Behold the hour is at hand and the Son of man shall be betrayed into the hands of sinners. Rise up : let us go. Behold he that will betray me is at hand.

17. THE CAPTURE OF JESUS. Matthew xxvi, 47-56 ; Mark xiv, 43-52 ; Luke xxii, 47-53 ; John xviii, 2-11.

(Matthew xxvi, 47-56.) As he yet spoke, behold Judas, one of the twelve, came, and with him a great multitude with swords and clubs, sent from the chief priests and the ancients of the people. And he that betrayed him gave them a sign, saying : Whomsoever I shall kiss, that is he, hold him fast. And forthwith coming to Jesus, he said : Hail, Rabbi. And he kissed him. And Jesus said to him : Friend, whereto art thou come ? Then they came up, and laid hands on Jesus and held him. And behold one of them that were with Jesus, stretching forth his hand, drew out his sword : and striking the servant of the high priest, cut off his ear. Then Jesus saith to him : Put up again thy sword into its place : for all that take the sword shall perish with the sword. Thinkest thou that I cannot ask my Father, and he will give me presently more than twelve legions of angels ? How then shall the scripture be fulfilled, that so it must be done ? In that same hour Jesus said to the multitudes : You are come out as it were to a robber, with swords and clubs to apprehend me. I sat daily with you teaching in the temple : and you laid not hands on me. Now all this was done that the scriptures of the prophets might be fulfilled. Then the disciples, all leaving him, fled.

(Mark xiv, 43-52.) And while he was yet speaking cometh Judas Iscariot, one of the twelve : and with him a great multitude with swords and staves, from the chief priests and the scribes and the ancients. And he that betrayed him had given them a sign, saying : Whomsoever I shall kiss, that is he, lay hold on him : and lead him away carefully. And when he was come, immediately going up to him, he saith : Hail, Rabbi. And he kissed him. But they laid hands on him and held him. And one of them that stood by, drawing a sword, struck a servant of the chief priest and cut off his ear. And Jesus answering said to them : Are you come out as it were to a robber with swords and staves to apprehend me ? I was daily with you in the temple teaching : and you did not lay hands on me. But that the scriptures may be fulfilled. Then his disciples, leaving him, all fled away. And a certain young man followed him, having a linen cloth about his naked body, and they laid hold on him. But he, casting off the linen cloth, fled from them naked.

(Luke xxii, 47–53.) As he was yet speaking, behold a multitude : And he that was called Judas, one of the twelve, went before them and drew near to Jesus, for to kiss him. And Jesus said to him : Judas, dost thou betray the Son of man with a kiss ? And they that were about him, seeing what would follow, said to him : Lord, shall we strike with the sword ? And one of them struck the servant of the high priest and cut off his right ear. But Jesus answering, said : Suffer ye thus far. And when he had touched his ear, he healed him. But Jesus said to the chief priests and magistrates of the temple and the ancients that were come unto him : Are ye come out as it were against a thief, with swords and clubs ? When I was daily with you in the temple, you did not stretch forth your hands against me, but this is your hour and the power of darkness.

(John xviii, 8–11.) And Judas also, who betrayed him, knew the place : because Jesus had often resorted thither, together with his disciples. Judas therefore having received a band of soldiers and servants from the chief priests and the Pharisees, cometh thither with lanterns and torches and weapons. Jesus therefore, knowing all things that should come upon him, went forth and said to them : Whom seek ye ? They answered him : Jesus of Nazareth. Jesus said to them : I am he. And Judas also, who betrayed him, stood with them. As soon therefore as he had said to them : I am he : they went backward and fell to the ground. Again therefore he asked them : Whom seek ye ? And they said : Jesus of Nazareth. Jesus answered : I have told you that I am he. If therefore you seek me, let these go their way. That the word might be fulfilled which he said : Of them whom thou hast given me, I have not lost any one. Then Simon Peter, having a sword, drew it and struck the servant of the high priest, and cut off his right ear. And the name of the servant was Malchus. Jesus therefore said to Peter : Put up thy sword into the scabbard. The chalice which my Father hath given me, shall I not drink it ?

(*Harmony.*) Now Judas also, who betrayed him, one of the twelve, knew the place, because Jesus had often resorted thither together with his disciples. Judas, therefore, having received a band of servants from the chief priests and Pharisees, the scribes and the ancients of the people, cometh thither whilst he was yet speaking, and with him a great multitude, with lanterns and torches and weapons, swords and clubs and staves. Jesus, therefore, knowing all things that were to come upon him, went forward and said to them : Whom seek ye ? They answered him : Jesus of Nazareth. Jesus saith to them : I am he. And Judas also, who betrayed him, stood with them. As soon, then, as he had said to them, I am he, they went backward and fell to the ground. Again, therefore, he asked them : Whom seek ye ? And they said : Jesus of Nazareth. Jesus answered : I have told you that I am he. If therefore you seek me, let these go their way : that the word might be fulfilled which he said : Of those whom thou hast given me, I have not lost any one. And he that betrayed him had given them a sign, saying : Whomsoever I shall kiss, that is he : lay hold on him, hold him fast, and lead him away cautiously. And when he was come, immediately going up to Jesus, he said : Hail, Rabbi, and he kissed him. And Jesus said to him : Friend, whereto art thou come ? Judas, dost thou betray the Son of man with a kiss ? Then they came up, and laid hands on Jesus, and held him. And they that were about him, seeing what would follow, said to him : Lord, shall we strike with the sword ? Then one of them that was with Jesus, Simon Peter, stretching forth his hand, drew his sword, and striking the servant of the high priest, cut off his right ear. And the name of the servant was Malchus. But Jesus answering said : Suffer ye thus far. Then he said to Peter : Put up again thy sword into the scabbard. For all that take the sword shall perish with the sword. Thinkest thou that I cannot ask my Father, and he will give me presently more than twelve legions of angels ? How then shall the scriptures be fulfilled, that so it must be done ? The chalice which my Father hath given me, shall I not drink it ? And when he had touched his ear, he healed him. In that same hour Jesus said to the chief priests and magistrates of the temple, and the ancients, and the multitude that were come to him : Are you come out, as it were against a robber, with swords and clubs and staves to apprehend me ? I sat daily with you teaching in the temple, and you did not stretch forth your hand against me. But this is your hour, and the power of darkness. Now all this was done, that the scriptures of the prophets might be fulfilled. Then his disciples, leaving him, all fled away. And a certain young man followed him, having a linen cloth cast about his naked body, and they laid hold on him. But he, casting off the linen cloth, fled from them naked.

18. JESUS BEFORE ANNAS. John xviii, 12-14 ; xviii, 19-24.

(John xviii, 12-14 ; xviii, 19-24.) Then the band and the tribune and the servants of the Jews took Jesus and bound him.

And they led him away to Annas first, for he was father-in-law to Caiphas, who was the high priest of that year. Now Caiphas was he who had given the counsel to the Jews that it was expedient that one man should die for the people.

The high priest therefore asked Jesus of his disciples and his doctrine. Jesus answered him : I have spoken openly to the world. I have always taught in the synagogue and in the temple whither all the Jews resort, and in private I have spoken nothing. Why askest thou me ? Ask them who have heard what I have spoken to them : behold, they know what things I have said. And when he had said these things, one of the officers standing by gave Jesus a blow, saying : Answerest thou the high priest so ? Jesus answered him : If I have spoken evil, give testimony of the evil ; but if well, why strikest thou me ? And Annas sent him bound to Caiphas the high priest.

19. JESUS BEFORE CAIPHAS.   20. THE DENIAL OF PETER.
   Matthew xxvi, 57-75 ; Mark xiv, 53-72 ; Luke xxii, 54-71 ; John xviii, 15-18 ; xviii, 25-27.

(Matthew xxvi, 57-75.) But they holding Jesus led him to Caiphas the high priest, where the scribes and the ancients were assembled. And Peter followed him afar off, even to the court of the high priest. And going in, he sat with the servants, that he might see the end. And the chief priests and the whole council sought false witness against Jesus, that they might put him to death. And they found not, whereas many false witnesses had come in. And last of all there came two false witnesses : and they said : This man said, I am able to destroy the temple of God and after three days to rebuild it. And the high priest rising up said to him : Answerest thou nothing to the things which these witness against thee ? But Jesus held his peace. And the high priest said to him : I charge thee by the living God, that thou tell us if thou be the Christ, the Son of God. Jesus saith to him : Thou hast said it. Nevertheless I say to you, hereafter you shall see the Son of man sitting on the right hand of the power of God and coming in the clouds of heaven. Then the high priest rent his garments, saying : He hath blasphemed. What further need have we of witnesses ? Behold, now you have heard the blasphemy. What think you ? But they answering, said : He is guilty of death. Then did they spit in his face and buffet him. And others struck his face with the palms of their hands, saying : Prophesy unto us, O Christ, who it is that struck thee ? But Peter sat without in the court. And there came to him a servant maid, saying : Thou also wast with Jesus the Galilean. But he denied before them all, saying : I know not what thou sayest. And as he went out of the gate, another maid was him ; and she said to them that were there : This man also was with Jesus of Nazareth. And again he denied with an oath : I know not the man. And after a little while they came that stood by, and said to Peter : Surely thou also art one of them. For even thy speech doth discover thee. Then he began to curse and to swear that he knew not the man. And immediately the cock crew. And Peter remembered the word of Jesus which he had said : Before the cock crow, thou wilt deny me thrice. And going forth, he wept bitterly.

(Mark xiv, 53–72.) And they brought Jesus to the high priest. And all the priests and the scribes and the ancients assembled together. And Peter followed him afar off, even into the court of the high priest. And he sat with the servants at the fire, and warmed himself. And the chief priests and all the council sought for evidence against Jesus, that they might put him to death, and found none. For many bore false witness against him, saying : We heard him say, I will destroy this temple made with hands, and in three days will build another not made with hands. And their witness did not agree. And the high priest rising up in the midst, asked Jesus, saying : Answerest thou nothing to the things that are laid to thy charge by these men ? But he held his peace and answered nothing. Again the high priest asked him and said to him : Art thou the Christ, the Son of the Blessed God ? And Jesus said to him, I am. And you shall see the Son of man sitting on the right hand of the power of God and coming with the clouds of heaven. Then the high priest, rending his garments, saith : What need we any further witnesses ? You have heard the blasphemy. What think you ? Who all condemned him to be guilty of death. And some began to spit on him, and to cover his face, and to buffet him, and to say unto him : Prophesy. And the servants struck him with the palms of their hands. Now when Peter was in the court below, there cometh one of the maid servants of the high priest. And when she had seen Peter warming himself, looking upon him, she saith : Thou also wast with Jesus of Nazareth. But he denied, saying : I neither know nor understand what thou sayest. And he went forth before the court : and the cock crew. And again a maid servant seeing him, began to say to the standers by : This is one of them. But he denied again. And after a while they that stood by said again to Peter : Surely thou art one of them ; for thou art also a Galilean. But he began to curse and to swear, saying : I know not this man of whom you speak. And immediately the cock crew again. And Peter remembered the word that Jesus had said unto him : Before the cock crow twice, thou shalt thrice deny me. And he began to weep.

(Luke xxii, 54–71.) And apprehending him they led him to the high priest's house. But Peter followed afar off. And when they had kindled a fire in the midst of the hall and were sitting about it, Peter was in the midst of them. Whom, when a certain servant maid had seen sitting at the light, and had earnestly beheld him, she said: This man also was with him. But he denied him, saying: Woman, I know him not. And after a little while, another seeing him, said: Thou also art one of them. But Peter said: O man, I am not. And after the space as it were of one hour, another certain man affirmed, saying: Of a truth this man was also with him: for he is also a Galilean. And Peter said: Man, I know not what thou sayest. And immediately, as he was yet speaking, the cock crew. And the Lord turning looked on Peter. And Peter remembered the word of the Lord, as he had said: Before the cock crow thou shalt deny me thrice. And Peter going out, wept bitterly. And the men that held him mocked him and struck him. And they blindfolded him and smote his face. And they asked him, saying: Prophesy: Who is it that struck thee? And blaspheming, many other things they said against him.

(John xviii, 15-18; xviii, 25-27.) And Simon Peter followed Jesus: and so did another disciple. And that disciple was known to the high priest and went in with Jesus into the court of the high priest. But Peter stood at the door without. The other disciple, therefore, who was known to the high priest, went out and spoke to the portress and brought in Peter. The maid therefore that was portress saith to Peter: Art not thou also one of this man's disciples? He saith: I am not. Now the servants and ministers stood at a fire of coals, because it was cold, and warmed themselves. And with them was Peter also, standing and warming himself.

And Simon Peter was standing and warming himself. They said therefore to him: Art not thou one of his disciples? He denied it and said: I am not. One of the servants of the high priest (a kinsman to him whose ear Peter cut off) saith to him: Did not I see thee in the garden with him? Again therefore Peter denied: and immediately the cock crew.

(*Harmony.*) But they, holding Jesus, led him to Caiphas, the high priest; and the priests and the scribes and the ancients were assembled together. And the chief priests and the whole council sought false witness for evidence against Jesus, that they might put him to death. For though many false witnesses had come in, and bore false witness against him, their evidence did not agree. And last of all there came in two false witnesses. They, rising up, bore false witness against him, saying: We heard him say, I will destroy this temple of God made with hands, and within three days I will build another not made with hands. And their witness did not agree. And the high priest, rising up in the midst, asked Jesus saying: Answerest thou nothing to the things that are laid to thy charge by these men? But Jesus held his peace and answered nothing. Again the high priest asked him and said to him : I adjure thee, by the living God, that thou tell us if you be the Christ, the Son of the blessed God. And Jesus said to him : Thou hast said it, I am. Nevertheless I say to you, hereafter you shall see the Son of man sitting on the right hand of the power of God, and coming in the clouds of heaven. Then the high priest rent his garments, saying : He hath blasphemed ; what further need have we of witnesses ? Behold, now you have heard the blasphemy, what think you ? But they all answering, condemned him, and said : He is guilty of death. But Simon Peter followed Jesus afar off, and so did another disciple to the high priest's palace. And that disciple was known to the high priest, and went in with Jesus into the court of the high priest. But Peter stood at the door without. Then the other disciple who was known to the high priest went out and spoke to the portress and brought in Peter. And when they had kindled a fire of coals in the midst of the hall, because it was cold, and were sitting about it, Peter sat with the servants to see the end, and warmed himself. Now when Peter was in the court below, there cometh one of the maid servants of the high priest, the maid that was portress ; and when she had seen Peter sitting in the light, and warming himself, and had looked on him, she said : Thou also wast with Jesus of Nazareth, the Galilean. This man also was with him. Art not thou also one of this man's disciples ? But he denied him before them all, saying : Woman, I am not. I know him not. I neither know nor understand what thou sayest. And he went forth before the court, out of the gate, and the cock crew. And again another maid servant saw him, and also began to say to the standers by : This is one of them. This man also was with Jesus of Nazareth. Thou also art one of them. And again he denied with an oath : O man, I am not. I do not know the man. And after a little while, about the space of an hour after, they that stood by came again and said to Peter : Surely thou also art one of them, for even thy speech doth discover thee. Thou also art a Galilean. And another man, one of the servants of the high priest, a kinsman to him whose ear Peter cut off, saith to him : Did I not see thee in the garden with him ? Then he began to curse and to swear that he knew not the man, saying : Man, I know not what thou sayest. I know not this man of whom you speak. And immediately while he was yet speaking the cock crew again. And the Lord turning looked on Peter. And Peter remembered the word that the Lord Jesus had said to him : Before the cock crow twice thou shalt deny me thrice. And Peter went out and began to weep, and wept bitterly. And the men that held him began to spit in his face, and mocked him and buffeted him, and they blindfolded him, and covered his face, and smote him in the face, and the servants struck him with the palms of their hands. And they asked him, saying : Prophesy unto us, O Christ, who is he that struck thee? And many other things blaspheming they said against him.

21. THE MORNING TRIAL. Matthew xxvii, 1, 2 ; Mark xv, 1 ; Luke xxii, 66–71 ; xxiii, 1 ; John xviii, 28.

(Matthew xxvii, 1, 2.) And when morning was come, all the chief priests and ancients of the people took counsel against Jesus that they might put him to death. And they brought him bound and delivered him to Pilate the governor.

(Mark xv, 1.) And straightway in the morning the chief priests holding a consultation with the ancients and the scribes and the whole council, binding Jesus, led him away and delivered him to Pilate.

(Luke xxii, 66–71 ; xxiii, 1.) And as soon as it was day, the ancients of the people and the chief priests and scribes came together. And they brought him into their council, saying : If thou be the Christ, tell us. And he saith to them : If I shall tell you, you will not believe me. And if I shall also ask you, you will not answer me, nor let me go. But hereafter the Son of man shall be sitting on the right hand of the power of God. Then said they all : Art thou then the Son of God ? Who said : You say that I am. And they said : What need we any further testimony ? For we ourselves have heard it from his own mouth. And the whole multitude of them, rising up, led him to Pilate.

(John xviii, 28.) Then they led Jesus from Caiphas to the Governor's hall. And it was morning ; and they went not into the hall, that they might not be defiled, but that they might eat the pasch.

(*Harmony*.) And as soon as it was day, straightway all the chief priests and ancients of the people and scribes came together and held a council against Jesus to put him to death. And they brought him into their council, saying : If thou be the Christ, tell us. And he said to them : If I shall tell you, you will not believe me, and if I shall ask you, you will not answer me nor let me go. But hereafter the Son of man shall be sitting on the right hand of the power of God. Then said they all : Art thou then the Son of God ? And he said : You say that I am. Then said they all : What need we any further testimony ? For we ourselves have heard it from his own mouth. And straightway the ancients and the scribes and the whole council, the whole multitude of them rose up, and binding Jesus led him from Caiphas to the Governor's hall, and brought him bound and delivered him to Pilate the Governor. And they went not into the hall, that they might not be defiled, but that they might eat the pasch.

22. THE DESPAIR OF JUDAS. Matthew xxvii, 3-10.

(Matthew xxvii, 3-10.) Then Judas who betrayed him, seeing that he was condemned, repenting himself, brought back the thirty pieces of silver to the chief priests and the ancients, saying: I have sinned in betraying innocent blood. But they said: What is that to us? Look thou to it. And casting down the pieces of silver in the temple he departed, and went and hanged himself with a halter. But the chief priests, having taken the pieces of silver, said: It is unlawful to put them in the corbona, because it is the price of blood. And having consulted together, they bought with them the potter's field, to be a burying place for strangers. For this cause that field was called Haceldama, that is, the field of blood, even to this day. Then was fulfilled that which was spoken by Jeremias the prophet, saying: And they took the thirty pieces of silver, the price of him that was prized, whom they prized of the children of Israel. And they gave them unto the potter's field, as the Lord appointed to me.

23. JESUS BEFORE PILATE. Matthew xxvii, 11-14; Mark xv, 2-5; Luke xxiii, 2-5; John xviii, 29-38.

(Matthew xxvii, 11-14.) And Jesus stood before the Governor, and the governor asked him, saying: Art thou the king of the Jews? Jesus saith to him: Thou sayest it. And when he was accused by the chief priests and ancients he answered nothing. Then Pilate saith to him: Dost thou not hear how great testimonies they allege against thee? And he answered him to never a word, so that the governor wondered exceedingly.

(Mark xv, 2-5.) And Pilate asked him: Art thou the king of the Jews? But he answering saith to him: Thou sayest it. And the chief priests accused him in many things. And Pilate again asked him, saying: Answerest thou nothing? Behold in how many things they accuse thee. But Jesus still answered nothing: so that Pilate wondered.

(Luke xxiii, 2-5.) And they began to accuse him, saying: We have found this man perverting our nation, and forbidding to give tribute to Cæsar, and saying that he is Christ the King. And Pilate asked him, saying: Art thou the king of the Jews? But he answering said: Thou sayest it. And Pilate said to the chief priests and to the multitudes: I find no cause in this man. But they were more earnest, saying: He stirreth up the people, teaching throughout all Judea, beginning from Galilee to this place.

(John xviii, 29-38.) Pilate therefore went out to them and said: What accusation bring you against this man? They answered and said to him. If he were not a malefactor, we would not have delivered him up to thee. Pilate therefore said to them:

Take him you, and judge him according to your law. The Jews therefore said to him : It is not lawful for us to put any man to death. That the word of Jesus might be fulfilled, which he said, signifying what death he should die. Pilate therefore went into the hall again, and called Jesus, and said to him : Art thou the king of the Jews ? Jesus answered : Sayest thou this thing of thyself, or have others told it thee of me ? Pilate answered : Am I a Jew ? Thy own nation and the chief priests have delivered thee up to me. What hast thou done ? Jesus answered : My kingdom is not of this world. If my kingdom were of this world my servants would certainly strive that I should not be delivered to the Jews : but now my kingdom is not from hence. Pilate therefore said to him : Art thou a king then ? Jesus answered : Thou sayest that I am a king. For this was I born, and for this came I into the world, that I should give testimony to the truth. Everyone that is of the truth heareth my voice. Pilate saith to him : What is truth ? And when he said this, he went out again to the Jews, and saith to them : I find no cause in him.

(*Harmony*.) Pilate therefore went out to meet them, and said : What accusation bring you against this man ? They answered and said to him : If he were not a malefactor we would not have delivered him up to thee. Pilate then said to them : Take him you, and judge him according to your law. The Jews therefore said to him : It is not lawful for us to put anyone to death ; that the word of Jesus might be fulfilled, signifying what death he should die. And they began to accuse him, saying : We have found this man perverting our nation, and forbidding to give tribute to Cæsar, and saying that he is Christ the King. And Jesus stood before Pilate the Governor. And Pilate asked him, saying : Art thou the King of the Jews ? And Jesus answered him and said : Thou sayest it. And the chief priests and ancients accused him in many things. And when he was accused he answered nothing. Then Pilate again asked him : Answerest thou nothing ? Behold in how many things they accuse thee. Dost not thou hear how great testimonies they allege against thee ? But Jesus still answered him not to any word, so that the Governor wondered exceedingly. Pilate therefore went into the hall again, and called Jesus and said to him : Art thou the king of the Jews ? Jesus answered : Sayest thou this thing of thyself, or have others told it thee of me ? Pilate answered : Am I a Jew ? Thy nation and the chief priests have delivered thee up to me. What hast thou done ? Jesus answered : My kingdom is not of this world. If my kingdom were of this world, my servants would certainly strive that I should not be delivered to the Jews, but now my kingdom is not from hence. Pilate therefore said to him : Art thou a king then ? Jesus answered : Thou sayest that I am a king. For this was I born, and for this came I into the world, that I should give testimony to the truth. Everyone that is of the truth heareth my voice. Pilate saith to him: What is truth? And when he had said this he went out again to the Jews, and said to them: I find no cause in him. But they were more earnest, saying: He stirreth up the people, teaching throughout Judea, beginning from Galilee to this place.

24. ESUS BEFORE HEROD. Luke xxiii, 6–12.

(Luke xxiii, 6–12.) And Pilate, hearing of Galilee, asked if the man were a Galilean. And when he understood that he belonged to Herod's jurisdiction, he sent him away to Herod, who himself was also at Jerusalem in those days. And Herod, seeing Jesus, was very glad, for he was desirous of a long time to see him, because he had heard many things of him, and he hoped to see some miracle wrought by him. And he questioned him with many words. But he answered him nothing. And the chief priests and scribes stood by earnestly accusing him. And Herod with his soldiers despised him, and mocked him, putting on him a white garment, and sent him back to Pilate. And Herod and Pilate were made friends together that same day, for before they were enemies one to another.

25. THE SECOND TRIAL BEFORE PILATE : BARABBAS. Matthew xxvii, 15–23 ; Mark xv, 6–14 ; Luke xxiii, 13–23 ; John xviii, 39, 40.

(Matthew xxvii, 15–23.) Now upon the solemn day the governor was accustomed to release to the people one prisoner, whom they would. And he had then a notorious prisoner that was called Barabbas. They therefore, having gathered together, Pilate said : Whom will you that I release to you, Barabbas, or Jesus that is called Christ ? For he knew that for envy they had delivered him. And as he was sitting in the place of judgment his wife sent to him, saying : Have thou nothing to do with that just man ; for I have suffered many things this day in a dream because of him. But the chief priests and ancients persuaded the people that they should ask Barabbas and make Jesus away. And the governor answering said to them : Whether will you of the two to be released unto you ? But they said : Barabbas. Pilate saith to them : What shall I do then with Jesus that is called Christ ? They say all : Let him be crucified. The governor saith to them : Why, what evil hath he done ? But they cried out the more, saying : Let him be crucified.

(Mark xv, 6–14.) Now on the festival day he was wont to release unto them one of the prisoners, whomsoever they demanded. And there was one called Barabbas, who was put in prison with some seditious men, who in the sedition had committed murder. And when the multitude was come up, they began to desire that he would do as he had ever done unto them. And Pilate answered them and said : Will you that I release to you the king of the Jews ? For he knew that the chief priests had delivered him out of envy. But the chief priests moved the people that he should release Barabbas to them. And Pilate again answering, saith to them : What will you then that I do to the king of the Jews ? But they again cried out : Crucify him. And Pilate saith to them : Why, what evil hath he done ? But they cried out the more : Crucify him.

(Luke xxiii, 13–23.) And Pilate, calling together the chief priests and the magistrates and the people, said to them : You have presented unto me this man as one that perverteth the people. And behold, I, having examined him before you, find no cause in this man, in those things wherein you accuse him. No, nor Herod neither. For I sent you to him : and behold, nothing worthy of death is done to him. I will chastise him therefore and release him. (Now of necessity he was to release unto them one upon the feast day.) But the whole multitude together cried out, saying : Away with this man, and release unto us Barabbas : who for a sedition made in the city and for a murder, was cast into prison. And Pilate again spoke to them, desiring to release Jesus. But they cried again, saying : Crucify him, crucify him. And he said to them the third time : Why, what evil hath this man done ? I find no cause of death in him. I will chastise him, therefore, and let him go. But they were instant with loud voices, requiring that he might be crucified. And their voices prevailed.

(John xviii, 39–40.) But you have a custom that I should release one unto you at the pasch. Will you therefore that I release unto you the king of the Jews ? Then cried they all again, saying : Not this man, but Barabbas. Now Barabbas was a robber.

(*Harmony*.) Then Pilate, calling together the chief priests and the magistrates, and the people, said to them : You have brought this man to me as one that perverteth the people ; and behold I, having examined him before you, find no cause in this man, touching those things wherein you accuse him. No, nor yet Herod, for I sent you to him, and behold, nothing worthy of death is done to him. I will chastise him therefore and release him. Now upon the solemn festival day the governor was accustomed to release to the people one of the prisoners, whomsoever they demanded. And he had then a notorious prisoner that was called Barabbas, a robber who was put in prison with seditious men, who in the sedition had committed murder. And when the multitude was come up, they began to desire what he always had done to them. And Pilate answered them and said : You have a custom that I should release one unto you at the pasch. Will you, therefore, that I release unto you the king of the Jews? Whom will you that I release to you, Barabbas or Jesus who is called Christ? For he knew that through envy the chief priests had delivered him up. And as he was sitting in the place of judgment, his wife sent to him, saying : Have thou nothing to do with that just man ; for I have suffered many things this day in a dream because of him. But the chief priests and ancients persuaded the people that they should ask Barabbas and make Jesus away. And the governor answering said to them : Which will you have of the two to be released unto you? But the whole multitude cried out at once, saying : Away with this man, and release unto us Barabbas. And Pilate spoke to them again, desiring to release Jesus : What will you, then, that I do with Jesus, that is called Christ, the king of the Jews ? But they all again cried out : Crucify him, crucify him, let him be crucified. And Pilate said to them the third time : Why, what evil hath he done? I find no cause of death in him. I will chastise him, therefore, and let him go. But they were the more instant with loud voices : Crucify him, let him be crucified. And their voices prevailed.

26. THE SENTENCE. 27. THE SCOURGING AND CROWNING. 28. THE SURRENDER OF PILATE. Matthew xxvii, 24–30 ; Mark xv, 15–19 ; Luke xxiii, 24, 25 ; John xix, 1–16.

(Matthew xxvii, 24–30.) And Pilate seeing that he prevailed nothing, but that rather a tumult was made, taking water, washed his hands before the people, saying : I am innocent of the blood of this just man. Look you to it. And the whole people answering, said : His blood be upon us and upon our children. Then he released to them Barabbas : and having scourged Jesus, delivered him unto them to be crucified. Then the soldiers of the governor, taking Jesus into the hall, gathered together unto him the whole band. And stripping him, they put a scarlet cloak about him. And platting a crown of thorns, they put it upon his head, and a reed in his right hand. And bowing the knee before him they mocked him, saying: Hail, King of the Jews. And spitting upon him, they took the reed and struck his head.

(Mark xv, 15–19.) And so Pilate being willing to satisfy the people, released to them Barabbas and delivered up Jesus, when he had scourged him, to be crucified. And the soldiers led him away into the court of the palace : and they call together the whole band. And they clothed him with purple : and platting a crown of thorns, they put it upon him. And they began to salute him : Hail, King of the Jews. And they struck his head with a reed : and they did spit on him. And bowing their knees they adored him.

(Luke xxiii, 24, 25.) And Pilate gave sentence that it should be as they required. And he released unto them him who for murder and sedition had been cast into prison, whom they had desired. But Jesus he delivered up to their will.

(John xix, 1-16.) Then therefore Pilate took Jesus and scourged him. And the soldiers platting a crown of thorns, put it upon his head : and they put on him a purple garment. And they came to him and said : Hail, King of the Jews. And they gave him blows. Pilate therefore went forth again and said to them : Behold I bring him forth unto you, that you may know that I find no cause in him. (Jesus therefore came forth, bearing the crown of thorns and the purple garment.) And he saith to them : Behold the man. When the chief priests therefore and the servants had seen him, they cried out, saying : Crucify him, crucify him. Pilate saith to them : Take him you and crucify him : for I find no cause in him. The Jews answered him : We have a law, and according to the law he ought to die, because he made himself the Son of God. When Pilate therefore had heard this saying, he feared the more. And he entered into the hall again : and he said to Jesus : Whence art thou ? But Jesus gave him no answer. Pilate therefore saith to him : Speakest thou not to me ? Knowest thou not that I have power to crucify thee, and I have power to release thee. Jesus answered : Thou shouldst not have any power against me, unless it were given thee from above. Therefore he that hath delivered me to thee hath the greater sin. And from henceforth Pilate sought to release him. But the Jews cried out, saying : If thou release this man, thou art not Cæsar's friend. For whosoever maketh himself a king speaketh against Cæsar. Now when Pilate had heard these words, he brought Jesus forth, and sat down in the judgment seat, in the place that is called Lithostrotos, and in Hebrew Gabbatha. And it was the parasceve of the pasch, about the sixth hour, and he saith to the Jews : Behold your King. But they cried out : Away with him, away with him, crucify him. Pilate saith to them : Shall I crucify your king ? The chief priests answered : We have no king but Cæsar. Then therefore he delivered him to be crucified.

(*Harmony.*) And Pilate, seeing that he prevailed nothing, but rather that a tumult was made, having taken water, washed his hands before the people, saying : I am innocent of the blood of this just man ; look you to it. And all the people answering, said : His blood be upon us and upon our children. Then Pilate, being willing to satisfy the people, gave sentence that their petition should be granted. And he released unto them Barabbas who for murder and sedition had been cast into prison, whom they had desired, but delivered up to them Jesus, when he had scourged him, to be crucified according to their will. Then the soldiers of the governor, taking Jesus into the court of the palace, gathered together unto him the whole band, and stripping him, they put a scarlet cloak about him. And platting a crown of thorns, they put it upon his head, and a reed in his right hand. And they came to him, and bowing the knee before him, they mocked him, and began to salute him, saying : Hail, King of the Jews ! And they gave him blows and they did spit upon him, and they took the reed and struck his head, and bowing their knees they worshipped him. Pilate therefore went forth again and said to them : Behold, I bring him forth to you, that you may know that I find no cause in him (so Jesus came forth, bearing the crown of thorns and the purple garment). And he saith to them : Behold the man ! When the chief priests, therefore, and the officers had seen him, they cried out, saying : Crucify him ! Crucify him ! Pilate saith to them : Take him you and crucify him, for I find no cause in him. The Jews answered : We have a law, and according to the law he ought to die, because he made himself the Son of God. When Pilate therefore had heard this saying, he feared the more. And he entered into the hall again, and he said to Jesus : Whence art thou ? But Jesus gave him no answer. Pilate therefore saith to him : Speakest thou not to me ? Knowest thou not that I have power to crucify thee and I have power to release thee ? Jesus answered : Thou shouldst not have any power against me, unless it were given thee from above. Therefore he that hath delivered me to thee hath the greater sin. And from thenceforth Pilate sought to release him. But the Jews cried out, saying : If thou release this man thou art not Cæsar's friend, for whosoever maketh himself a king speaketh against Cæsar. Now when Pilate had heard these words, he brought Jesus forth, and sat down in the judgment seat, in the place that is called Lithostrotos, and in Hebrew Gabbatha. And it was the Parasceve of the Pasch, about the sixth hour, and he said to the Jews : Behold your king ! But they cried out : Away with him, away with him, crucify him ! Pilate saith to them : Shall I crucify your king ? The chief priests answered : We have no king but Cæsar. Then, therefore, he delivered him to them to be crucified.

29. THE WAY OF THE CROSS. Matthew xxvii, 31-34 ; Mark xv, 20-23 ; Luke xxiii, 26-33 ; John xix, 16, 17.

(Matthew xxvii, 31-34.) And after they had mocked him, they took off the cloak from him and put on him his own garments, and led him away to crucify him. And going out, they found a man of Cyrene, named Simon : him they forced to take up his cross. And they came to the place that is called Golgotha, which is the place of Calvary. And they gave him wine to drink mingled with gall. And when he had tasted he would not drink.

(Mark xv, 20–23.) And after they had mocked him they took off the purple from him and put his own garments on him : and they led him out to crucify him. And they forced one, Simon a Cyrenian, who passed by coming out of the country, the father of Alexander and of Rufus, to take up his cross. And they bring him into the place called Golgotha, which being interpreted is, the place of Calvary. And they gave him to drink wine mingled with myrrh. But he took it not.

(Luke xxiii, 26–33.) And as they led him away, they laid hold of one Simon of Cyrene, coming from the country. And they laid the cross on him to carry after Jesus. And there followed him a great multitude of people and of women who bewailed and lamented him. But Jesus turning to them said : Daughters of Jerusalem, weep not over me, but weep for yourselves and for your children. For behold the days shall come wherein they will say : Blessed are the barren, and the wombs that have not borne, and the paps that have not given suck. Then shall they begin to say to the mountains : Fall upon us. And to the hills : Cover us. For if in the green wood they do these things, what shall be done in the dry ? And there were also two other malefactors led with him to be put to death.

(John xix, 16, 17.) Then therefore he delivered him to them to be crucified. And they took Jesus and led him forth. And bearing his own cross, he went forth to that place which is called Calvary, but in Hebrew Golgotha.

(*Harmony.*) And after they had mocked him they took off the purple cloak from him, and put on him his own garments, and led him away to crucify him. And bearing his own cross, he went forth to that place which is called Calvary, but in Hebrew Golgotha. And as they led him away, they found a man of Cyrene, named Simon, the father of Alexander and of Rufus, who passed by coming out of the country ; him they forced to take up his cross to carry after Jesus. And there followed him a great multitude of people and of women, who bewailed and lamented him. But Jesus turning to them, said : Daughters of Jerusalem, weep not over me, but weep for yourselves and for your children. For behold the days shall come wherein they will say : Blessed are the barren, and the wombs that have not borne, and the breasts that have not given suck. Then shall they begin to say to the mountains : Fall upon us, and to the hills : Cover us. For if in the green wood they do these things, what shall be done in the dry ? And there were also two other, malefactors, led with him to be put to death. And they gave him to drink wine mingled with myrrh. And when he had tasted he would not drink.

30. The Crucifixion. 31. The First Word. 32. The Second Word. 33. The Third Word. 34. The Fourth Word. 35. The Fifth Word. 36. The Sixth and Seventh Words. Matthew xxvii, 35-56; Mark xv, 24-41; Luke xxiii, 33-49; John xix, 18-27.

(Matthew xxvii, 35-56.) And after they had crucified him, they divided his garments, casting lots; that it might be fulfilled which was spoken by the prophet, saying: They divided my garments among them; and upon my vesture they cast lots. And they sat and watched him. And they put over his head his cause written: This is Jesus, the King of the Jews. Then were crucified with him two thieves: one on the right and one on the left. And they that passed by blasphemed him, wagging their heads, and saying: Vah, thou that destroyest the temple of God, and in three days dost rebuild it: save thy own self. If thou be the Son of God, come down from the cross. In like manner also the chief priests, with the scribes and ancients, mocking, said: He saved others: himself he cannot save. If he be the king of Israel, let him now come down from the cross, and we will believe him. He trusted in God: let him now deliver him if he will have him. For he said: I am the Son of God. And the selfsame thing the thieves also that were crucified with him reproached him with. Now from the sixth hour there was darkness over the whole earth, until the ninth hour. And about the ninth hour, Jesus cried with a loud voice saying: Eli, Eli, lamma sabacthani? That is: My God, my God, why hast thou forsaken me? And some that stood there and heard said: This man calleth Elias. And immediately one of them running took a sponge and filled it with vinegar and put it upon a reed and gave him to drink. And the others said: Let be. Let us see whether Elias will come to deliver him. And Jesus again crying with a loud voice gave up the ghost. And behold the veil of the temple was rent in twain from the top even to the bottom: and the earth quaked and the rocks were rent. And the graves were opened: and many bodies of the saints that had slept arose, and coming out of the tombs after his resurrection appeared to many. Now the centurion, and they that were with him watching Jesus, having seen the earthquake and the things that were done, were sore afraid, saying: Indeed this was the Son of God. And there were many women afar off, who had followed Jesus from Galilee, ministering unto him: among whom was Mary Magdalen, and Mary the mother of James and Joseph, and the mother of the sons of Zebedee.

(Mark xv, 24-41.) And crucifying him, they divided his garments, casting lots upon them, what every man should take. And it was the third hour, and they crucified him. And the

inscription of his cause was written over : The King of the Jews.
And with him they crucified two thieves : the one on his right
hand and the other on his left. And the scripture was fulfilled
which saith : And with the wicked he was reputed. And they
that passed by blasphemed him, wagging their heads and saying :
Vah ! thou that destroyest the temple of God, and in three days
buildest it up again : save thyself, coming down from the cross.
In like manner also the chief priests, mocking, said with the
scribes, one to another : He saved others ; himself he cannot
save. Let Christ the King of Israel come down now from the
cross, that we may see and believe. And they that were crucified
with him reviled him. And when the sixth hour was come,
there was darkness over the whole earth until the ninth hour.
And at the ninth hour Jesus cried out with a loud voice saying :
Eloi, Eloi, lamma sabacthani ? Which is, being interpreted :
My God, my God, why hast thou forsaken me ? And some of the
standers by hearing said : Behold he calleth Elias. And one
running and filling a sponge with vinegar and putting it upon a
reed, gave him to drink, saying : Stay, let us see if Elias come
to take him down. And Jesus having cried out with a loud
voice gave up the ghost. And the veil of the temple was rent in
two from the top to the bottom. And the centurion, who stood
over against him, seeing that crying out in this manner he had
given up the ghost, said : Indeed this man was the Son of God.
And there were also women looking on afar off : among whom
was Mary Magdalen, and Mary the mother of James the less and
of Joseph, and Salome, who also when he was in Galilee followed
him and ministered to him, and many other women that came
up with him to Jerusalem.

(Luke xxiii, 33–49.) And when they were come to the place
which is called Calvary, they crucified him there ; and the
robbers, one on the right hand, and the other on the left. And
Jesus said : Father, forgive them, for they know not what they
do. But they, dividing his garments, cast lots. And the people
stood beholding. And the rulers with them derided him, saying :
If thou be the King of the Jews, save thyself. And there was
also a superscription written over him in letters of Greek and
Latin and Hebrew : This is the King of the Jews. And one of
those robbers who were hanged blasphemed him, saying : If
thou be the Christ, save thyself and us. But the other answering,
rebuked him, saying : Neither dost thou fear God, seeing thou
art under the same condemnation. And we indeed justly : for
we receive the due reward of our deeds. But this man hath
done no evil. And he said to Jesus : Lord, remember me when
thou shalt come into thy kingdom. And Jesus said to him :
Amen I say to thee : This day thou shalt be with me in paradise.
And it was almost the sixth hour : and there was darkness over

all the earth until the ninth hour. And the sun was darkened, and the veil of the temple was rent in the midst. And Jesus crying with a loud voice, said : Father, into thy hands I commend my spirit. And saying this, he gave up the ghost. Now the centurion seeing what was done, glorified God, saying : Indeed this was a just man. And all the multitude that were come together to that sight and saw the things that were done returned striking their breasts. And all his acquaintance and the women that had followed him from Galilee stood afar off, beholding these things.

(John xix, 18-37.) Where they crucified him, and with him two others, one on each side, and Jesus in the midst. And Pilate wrote a title also : and he put it upon the cross. And the writing was : Jesus of Nazareth, the King of the Jews. This title therefore many of the Jews did read : because the place where Jesus was crucified was nigh to the city. And it was written in Hebrew, in Greek and in Latin. Then the chief priests of the Jews said to Pilate : Write not, The King of the Jews ; but that he said : I am the King of the Jews. Pilate answered : What I have written, I have written. The soldiers, therefore, when they had crucified him, took his garments (and they made four parts, to each man a part) and also his coat. Now the coat was without seam, woven from the top throughout. They said then one to another : Let us not cut it, but let us cast lots for it, whose it shall be ; that the scripture might be fulfilled, saying : They have parted my garments among them, and upon my vesture they have cast lots. And the soldiers indeed did these things. Now there stood by the cross of Jesus, his mother, and his mother's sister, Mary of Cleophas, and Mary Magdalen. When Jesus therefore had seen his mother, and the disciple standing whom he loved, he saith to his mother : Woman, behold thy son. After that he saith to the disciple : Behold thy mother. And from that hour, the disciple took her to his own. Afterwards, Jesus knowing that all things were now accomplished, that the scriptures might be fulfilled, said : I thirst. Now there was a vessel set there, full of vinegar. And they, putting a sponge full of vinegar about hyssop, put it to his mouth. Jesus therefore, when he had taken the vinegar, said : It is consummated. And bowing down his head, he gave up the ghost. Then the Jews (because it was the parasceve), that the bodies might not remain upon the cross on the sabbath day, (for that was a great sabbath day), besought Pilate that their legs might be broken and that they might be taken away. The soldiers therefore came and they broke the legs of the first, and of the other that was crucified with him. But after they were come to Jesus, when they saw that he was already dead, they did not break his legs. But one of the soldiers with a spear

opened his side : and immediately there came out blood and
water. And he that saw it hath given testimony ; and his testimony is true. And he knoweth that he saith true : that you also
may believe. For these things were done that the scripture might
be fulfilled : You shall not break a bone of him. And again
another scripture saith : They shall look upon him whom they
pierced.

(*Harmony.*) And when they were come to the place they
crucified him there ; and the robbers, one on the right hand and
the other on the left, and Jesus in the midst. And the scripture
was fulfilled, which saith : And with the wicked he was reputed.
And Pilate wrote a title also, and he put it upon the cross over his
head. And the writing was : This is Jesus of Nazareth, the King
of the Jews. This title, therefore, many of the Jews read, because
the place where Jesus was crucified was near to the city, and it
was written in Hebrew, in Greek, and in Latin. Then the chief
priests said to Pilate : Write not, The King of the Jews ; but
that he said : I am the King of the Jews. Pilate answered :
What I have written, I have written. And Jesus said : Father,
forgive them, for they know not what they do. Then the soldiers,
after they had crucified him, took his garments (and they made
four parts, to every soldier a part, casting lots upon them what
every man should take), and also his coat. Now the coat was
without seam, woven from the top throughout. They said then
to one another : let us not cut it, but let us cast lots upon it,
whose it shall be, that the word might be fulfilled which was
spoken by the Prophet : They have parted my garments among
them, and upon my vesture they have cast lots. And the soldiers
indeed did these things. And it was the third hour, and they
crucified him. And they sat down and watched him ; and the
people stood beholding. And they that passed by blasphemed
him, wagging their heads and saying Vah, thou that destroyest
the temple of God, and in three days buildest it up again, save
thy own self. If thou be the Son of God, come down from the
cross. In like manner the chief priests with the scribes and
ancients, mocking, derided him, saying : He saved others,
himself he cannot save. If he be Christ, the King of Israel, if he
be Christ the Son of God, let him now come down from the cross,
that we may see and believe. He trusted in God, let him now
deliver him, if he will have him, for he said : I am the Son of
God. And the soldiers also mocked him, coming to him and
offering him vinegar and saying : If thou be the King of the Jews,
save thyself. And the selfsame thing the thieves that were
crucified with him reproached him with, and reviled him. And
one of these robbers, who were hanging, blasphemed him,
saying : If thou be the Christ, save thyself and us. But the other
answering, rebuked him, saying : Neither dost thou fear God,

jeeing thou art under the same condemnation. And we, indeed, sustly, for we receive the due reward of our deeds; but this man hath done no evil. And he said to Jesus: Lord, remember me when thou comest into thy kingdom. Then Jesus saith to him: Amen I say to thee, this day thou shalt be with me in Paradise. Now there stood by the cross of Jesus his mother, and his mother's sister, Mary of Cleophas, and Mary Magdalen. When Jesus therefore saw his mother, and the disciple standing whom he loved, he saith to his mother: Woman, behold thy son. After that he saith to the disciple: Behold thy mother. And from that hour the disciple took her to his own. And when the sixth hour was come there was darkness over the whole earth, until the ninth hour. And about the ninth hour Jesus cried out with a loud voice, saying: Eloi, Eloi, lama sabacthani? which is, being interpreted: My God, my God, why hast thou forsaken me? And some of them that stood there and heard, said: Behold, this man calleth for Elias. Afterwards Jesus, knowing that all things were accomplished, that the scripture might be fulfilled, said: I thirst. Now there was a vessel set there full of vinegar. And immediately one of them, running took a sponge and filled it with vinegar and put it on a reed about hyssop, and offered it to his mouth, and gave him to drink. And others said: Stay, let us see whether Elias will come to take him down and deliver him. When Jesus therefore had taken the vinegar, he said: It is consummated. And Jesus again crying with a loud voice, said: Father, into thy hands I commend my spirit. And saying this, bowing down his head, he gave up the ghost. And behold the sun was darkened, and the veil of the temple was rent in two in the midst from the top even to the bottom, and the earth quaked, and the rocks were rent. And the graves opened, and many bodies of the saints that had slept arose, and coming out of the tombs after his resurrection, came into the holy city and appeared to many. Now the centurion, who stood over against him, and they that were with him watching Jesus, seeing that crying out in this manner he had given up the ghost, having seen the earthquake and the things that were done, were sore afraid, and glorified God, saying: Indeed this was a just man. Indeed this man was the Son of God. And all the multitude of them that were come together to that sight, and saw the things that were done, returned striking their breasts. And there were also women, among whom was Mary Magdalen, and Mary the mother of James the Less and of Joseph, and Salome, and the mother of the sons of Zebedee, who also when he was in Galilee followed him and ministered to him, and many other women that came up with him to Jerusalem. And all his acquaintance and the women stood afar off beholding these things. Then the Jews (because it was the Parasceve) that the bodies might not remain upon the cross on the sabbath day (for that was a great Sabbath day), besought Pilate that their legs might be broken, and that they might be taken away. The soldiers therefore came and they broke the legs of the first, and of the other that was crucified with him. But when they came to Jesus, and saw that he was already dead, they did not break his legs, but one of the soldiers opened his side with a spear, and immediately there came out blood and water. And he that saw gave testimony, and his testimony is true. And he knoweth that he saith true, that you also may believe. For these things were done that the scripture might be fulfilled : You shall not break a bone of him. And again another scripture saith : They shall look upon him whom they pierced.

37. THE END. Matthew xxvii, 57-66 ; Mark xv, 42-47 ; Luke xxiii, 50-56 ; John xix, 38-42.

(Matthew xxvii, 57-66.) And when it was evening there came a rich man of Arimathea, named Joseph, who also himself was a disciple of Jesus. He went to Pilate and asked the body of Jesus. Then Pilate commanded that the body should be delivered. And Joseph taking the body wrapped it up in a clean linen cloth and laid it in his own new monument, which he had hewed out in a rock. And he rolled a great stone to the door of the monument and went his way. And there were there Mary Magdalen and the other Mary, sitting over against the sepulchre. And the next day, which followed the day of preparation, the chief priests and the Pharisees came together to Pilate saying : Sir, we have remembered that that seducer said while he was yet alive : After three days I will rise again. Command therefore the sepulchre to be guarded until the third day : lest perhaps his disciples come and steal him away and say to the people : He is risen from the dead. And the last error shall be worse than the first. Pilate saith to them : You have a guard. Go, guard it as you know. And they departing, made the sepulchre sure, sealing the stone and setting guards.

(Mark xv, 42-47.) And when evening was now come (because it was the Parasceve, that is, the day before the sabbath) Joseph of Arimathea, a noble counsellor, who was also himself looking for the kingdom of God, came and went in boldly to Pilate and begged the body of Jesus. But Pilate wondered that he should be already dead. And sending for the centurion, he asked him if he were already dead. And when he had understood it by the centurion, he gave the body to Joseph. And Joseph, buying fine linen, and taking him down, wrapped him up in the fine linen and laid him in a sepulchre which was hewed out of a rock. And he rolled a stone to the door of the sepulchre.

And Mary Magdalen and Mary the mother of Joseph beheld where he was laid.

(Luke xxiii, 50-56.) And behold there was a man named Joseph who was a counsellor, a good and just man (the same had not consented to their counsel and doings) of Arimathea, a city of Judea ; who also himself looked for the kingdom of God. This man went to Pilate and begged the body of Jesus. And taking him down, he wrapped him in fine linen and laid him in a sepulchre that was hewed in stone, wherein never yet any man had been laid. And it was the day of the parasceve : and the sabbath drew on. And the women that were come with him from Galilee, following after, saw the sepulchre and how his body was laid. And returning, they prepared spices and ointments : and on the sabbath day they rested, according to the commandment.

(John xix, 38-42.) And after these things, Joseph of Arimathea (because he was a disciple of Jesus, but secretly, for fear of the Jews) besought Pilate that he might take away the body of Jesus. And Pilate gave leave. He came therefore and took away the body of Jesus. And Nicodemus also came (he who at the first came to Jesus by night), bringing a mixture of myrrh and aloes, about an hundred pound weight. They took therefore the body and bound it in linen cloths, with the spices, as the manner of the Jews is to bury. Now there was in the place where he was crucified a garden : and in the garden a new sepulchre, wherein no man yet had been laid. There, therefore, because it was the parasceve of the Jews, they laid Jesus, because the sepulchre was nigh at hand.

(*Harmony.*) And when evening was come (because it was the parasceve : that is, the day before the sabbath) a certain rich man of Arimathea, a city of Judea, by name Joseph, who was a senator, a noble counsellor, a good and just man, who also himself waited for the kingdom of God, but secretly for fear of the Jews ; this man had not consented to their counsel and doings ; went in boldly to Pilate and besought him that he might take away the body of Jesus. But Pilate wondered that he should be already dead. And sending for the centurion, he asked him if he were already dead. And when he had understood it by the centurion, he commanded that the body of Jesus should be delivered to Joseph. He came therefore and took away the body of Jesus. And Nicodemus also came, who at first came to Jesus by night, bringing a mixture of myrrh and aloes, about a hundred pound weight. They took therefore the body of Jesus, and buying fine linen, wrapped it up in the linen cloths with the spices, as it is the custom with the Jews to bury. And there was in the place where he was crucified a garden, and in the garden a new sepulchre, his own (Joseph's) monument, which he had hewed out in a rock, wherein never yet any man had been laid. There, therefore, by reason of the Parasceve of the Jews, they laid Jesus, because the sepulchre was nigh at hand. And he rolled a great stone to the door of the monument, and went his way. And Mary Magdalen, and Mary the mother of Joseph, and the women that were come with him from Galilee, following after, sitting over against the sepulchre, beheld where his body was laid. And returning they prepared spices and ointments, and on the Sabbath day they rested according to the commandment. And the next day which followed the day of preparation, the chief priests and the Pharisees came together to Pilate, saying: Sir, we have remembered that that seducer said, while he was yet alive: After three days I will rise again. Command, therefore, the sepulchre be guarded until the third day, lest his disciples come, and steal him away, and say to the people: He is risen from the dead; so the last error shall be worse than the first. Pilate said to them: You have a guard; go, guard it as you know. And they, departing, made the sepulchre sure with guards, sealing the stone.

HARMONY OF THE PASSION

		MATTHEW	MARK	LUKE	JOHN
1	The Eve of the Passion				
2	The Council of the Priests	xxvi, 1–5	xiv, 1, 2	xxii, 1, 2	
3	The Compact with Judas	xxvi, 14–16	xiv, 10, 11	xxii, 3–6	
4	The Preparation of the Supper	xxvi, 17–19	xiv, 12–16	xxii, 7–13	
5	The Supper	xxvi, 20	xiv, 17	xxii, 14–18	
6	The Washing of the Feet			xxii, 24–30	xiii, 1–20
7	The Last Warning to Judas	xxvi, 21–25	xiv, 18–21	xxii, 21–23	xiii, 21–35 I. COR.
8	The Holy Eucharist	xxvi, 26–29	xiv, 22–25	xxii, 19, 20	xi, 23–25 JOHN
9	The Coming Failure of the Twelve	xxvi, 31–35	xiv, 27–31	xxii, 31–38	xiii, 36–38
10	Introduction to the Discourse				
11	The Discourse at the Supper				xiv, 1
12	The Promise of the Holy Ghost				xvi, 33
13	Conclusion of the Discourse				
14	The Sacerdotal Prayer				xvii, 1–20
15	The Heart of Jesus at the Supper				
16	The Agony in the Garden	xxvi, 30 xxvi, 36–46	xiv, 26 xiv, 32–42	xxii, 39–46	xviii, 1
17	The Capture of Jesus	xxvi, 47–56	xiv, 43–52	xxii, 47–53	xviii, 2, 11
18	Jesus before Annas				xviii, 12–14 xviii, 19–24
19	Jesus before Caiphas	xxvi, 57–75	xiv, 53–72	xxii, 54–71	xviii, 15–18
20	The Denial of Peter				xviii, 25–27
21	The Morning Trial	xxvii, 1, 2	xv, 1	xxiii, 1	xviii, 28
22	The Despair of Judas	xxvii, 3–10			
23	Jesus before Pilate	xxvii, 11–14	xv, 2–5	xxiii, 2–5	xviii, 29–38
24	Jesus before Herod			xxiii, 6–12	
25	The Second Trial before Pilate. Barabbas	xxvii, 15–23	xv, 6–14	xxiii, 13–23	xviii, 39, 40
26	The Sentence				
27	The Scourging and Crowning	xxvii, 24–30	xv, 15–19	xxiii, 24, 25	xix, 1–16
28	The Surrender of Pilate				
29	The Way of the Cross	xxvii, 31–34	xv, 20–23	xxiii, 26–33	xix, 16, 17
30	The Crucifixion				
31	The First Word				
32	The Second Word				
33	The Third Word	xxvii, 35–56	xv, 24–41	xxiii, 33–49	xix, 18–37
34	The Fourth Word				
35	The Fifth Word				
36	The Sixth and Seventh Words				
37	The End	xxvii, 57–66	xv, 42–47	xxiii, 50–56	xix, 38–42

The Mayflower Press, Plymouth.
William Brendon & Son, Ltd.

The Savior has a title which He cherishes above all others — the Good Shepherd.
Seeking out some poor unfortunate sinner was His most favored work.
Now He turns an anxious eye toward us — will we follow in His footsteps?

Often it will take every ounce of courage and initiative to go out and seek the ones who have strayed. As we look down some darkened alley, the lazy-chair in the corner will stretch out its comforting arms as it never did before; the call of the ninety-nine will fill us with a self-satisfied, but false, feeling of justification — the roaring lion is a clever devil.

Jerry, the first three beads of my Rosary will be set aside as a daily prayer to Mary, asking her to make you a determined and fearless shepherd. Remember me also so that my courage may not be found wanting.

Joe